Lecture Notes in Computer Science 12268

More information about this series at http://www.springer.com/series/7409

Robert Thomson · Halil Bisgin ·
Christopher Dancy · Ayaz Hyder ·
Muhammad Hussain (Eds.)

Social, Cultural, and Behavioral Modeling

13th International Conference, SBP-BRiMS 2020
Washington, DC, USA, October 18–21, 2020
Proceedings

 Springer

Editors
Robert Thomson
United States Military Academy
West Point, NY, USA

Halil Bisgin
University of Michigan-Flint
Flint, MI, USA

Christopher Dancy
Bucknell University
Lewisburg, PA, USA

Ayaz Hyder
The Ohio State University
Columbus, OH, USA

Muhammad Hussain
University of Arkansas at Little Rock
Little Rock, AR, USA

ISSN 0302-9743   ISSN 1611-3349 (electronic)
Lecture Notes in Computer Science
ISBN 978-3-030-61254-2   ISBN 978-3-030-61255-9 (eBook)
https://doi.org/10.1007/978-3-030-61255-9

LNCS Sublibrary: SL3 – Information Systems and Applications, incl. Internet/Web, and HCI

This Springer imprint is published by the registered company Springer Nature Switzerland AG
The registered company address is: Gewerbestrasse 11, 6330 Cham, Switzerland

Preface

Improving the human condition requires understanding, forecasting, and impacting socio-cultural behavior both in the digital and non-digital world. Increasing amounts of digital data, embedded sensors collecting human information, rapidly changing communication media, changes in legislation concerning digital rights and privacy, the spread of 4G technology to third world countries, and so on, are creating a new cyber-mediated world where the very precepts of why, when, and how people interact and make decisions is being called into question. For example, Uber took a deep understanding of human behavior vis-à-vis commuting, developing software to support this behavior, saving human time (and capital), and reducing stress, indirectly created the opportunity for humans with more time and less stress to evolve new behaviors. Scientific and industrial pioneers in this area are relying on both social science and computer science to help make sense of and impact this new frontier. To be successful, a true merger of social science and computer science is needed. Solutions that rely only on the social science or only on the computer science are doomed to failure. For example: Anonymous developed an approach for identifying members of terror groups such as ISIS on the Twitter social media platform using state-of-the-art computational techniques. These accounts were then suspended. This was a purely technical solution. The response of those individuals with suspended accounts was just moved to new platforms and resurfaced on Twitter under new IDs. In this case, failure to understand basic social behavior resulted in an ineffective solution.

The goal of this conference is to build this new community of social cyber scholars by bringing together and fostering interaction between members of the scientific, corporate, government, and military communities interested in understanding, forecasting, and impacting human socio-cultural behavior. It is the charge of this community to build this new science, its theories, methods, and its scientific culture, in a way that does not give priority to either social science or computer science, and to embrace change as the cornerstone of the community. Despite decades of work in this area, this new scientific field is still in its infancy. To meet this charge, to move this science to the next level, this community must meet the following three challenges: deep understanding, socio-cognitive reasoning, and re-usable computational technology. Fortunately, as the papers in this volume illustrate, this community is poised to answer these challenges. But what does meeting these challenges entail?

Deep understanding refers to the ability to make operational decisions and theoretical arguments on the basis of an empirical based deep and broad understanding of the complex socio-cultural phenomena of interest. Today, although more data is available digitally than ever before, we are still plagued by anecdotal based arguments. For example, in social media, despite the wealth of information available, most analysts focus on small samples, which are typically biased and cover only a small time period, and use that to explain all events and make future predictions. The analyst finds the magic tweet or the unusual tweeter and uses that to prove their point. Tools that can help the analyst to reason using more data or less biased data are not widely used, are often more complex than the average analyst wants to use, or take more time than the analyst wants to spend to generate results. Not only are more scalable technologies needed, but so too is a better understanding of the biases in the data and ways to overcome them, and a cultural change to not accept anecdotes as evidence.

Socio-cognitive reasoning refers to the ability of individuals to make sense of the world and to interact with it in terms of groups and not just individuals. Today most social-behavioral models either focus on (1) strong cognitive models of individuals engaged in tasks and so model a small number of agents with high levels of cognitive accuracy but with little, if any, social context, or (2) light cognitive models and strong interaction models and so model massive numbers of agents with high levels of social realisms and little cognitive realism. In both cases, as realism is increased in the other dimension the scalability of the models fail, and their predictive accuracy on one of the two dimensions remains low. In contrast, as agent models are built where the agents are not just cognitive but socially cognitive, we find that the scalability increases and the predictive accuracy increases. Not only are agent models with socio-cognitive reasoning capabilities needed, but so too is a better understanding of how individuals form and use these social-cognitions.

More software solutions that support behavioral representation, modeling, data collection, bias identification, analysis, and visualization support human socio-cultural behavioral modeling and prediction than ever before. However, this software is generally just piling up in giant black holes on the web. Part of the problem is the fallacy of open source; the idea that if you just make code open source, others will use it. In contrast, most of the tools and methods available in Git or R are only used by the developer, if that. Reasons for lack of use include lack of documentation, lack of interfaces, lack of interoperability with other tools, difficulty of linking to data, and increased demands on the analyst's time due to a lack of tool-chain and workflow optimization. Part of the problem is the not-invented here syndrome. For social scientists and computer scientists alike it is just more fun to build a quick and dirty tool for your own use than to study and learn tools built by others. And, part of the problem is the insensitivity of people from one scientific or corporate culture to the reward and demand structures of the other cultures that impact what information can or should be shared and when. A related problem is double standards in sharing where universities are expected to share and companies are not, but increasingly universities are relying on that intellectual property as a source of funding just like other companies. While common standards and representations would help, a cultural shift from a focus on sharing to a focus on re-use is as or more critical for moving this area to the next scientific level.

In this volume, and in all the work presented at the SBP-BRiMS 2020 conference, you will see suggestions of how to address the challenges just described. The SBP-BRiMS 2020 carries on the scholarly tradition of the past conferences out of which it has emerged like a phoenix: the Social Computing, Behavioral-Cultural Modeling, and Prediction (SBP) Conference, and the Behavioral Representation in Modeling and Simulation (BRiMS) Society's conference. A total of 66 papers were submitted as regular track submissions. Of these, 33 were accepted as full papers for an acceptance rate of 50%. Additionally, there were a large number of papers describing emergent ideas and late-breaking results. This is an international group with papers submitted with authors from many countries.

The conference has a strong multidisciplinary heritage. As the papers in this volume show, people, theories, methods, and data from a wide number of disciplines are represented including computer science, psychology, sociology, communication science, public health, bioinformatics, political science, and organizational science. Numerous types of computational methods used include, but are not limited to, machine learning, language technology, social network analysis and visualization, agent-based simulation, and statistics.

This exciting program could not have been put together without the hard work of a number of dedicated and forward-thinking researchers serving as the Organizing Committee, listed on the following pages. Members of the Program Committee, the Scholarship Committee, publication, advertising, and local arrangements chairs worked tirelessly to put together this event. They were supported by the government sponsors, the area chairs, and the reviewers. A special thanks goes to Ms. Sienna Watkins for coordinating and handling the management logistics for the entire event.

This year, the conference, like so many others, was held remotely. Despite that, we are seeing an upsurge in interest in the type of work that this conference and community fosters. We hope you and your families are staying safe in these difficult and trying times.

August 2020

Kathleen M. Carley
Nitin Agarwal

Organization

Conference Co-chairs

Kathleen M. Carley   Carnegie Mellon University, USA
Nitin Agarwal   University of Arkansas at Little Rock, USA

Program Co-chairs

Halil Bisgin   University of Michigan-Flint, USA
Christopher Dancy II   Bucknell University, USA
Muhammad Hussain   University of Arkansas at Little Rock, USA
Ayaz Hyder   The Ohio State University, USA
Robert Thomson   United States Military Academy, USA

Scholarship and Sponsorship Committee

Nitin Agarwal   University of Arkansas at Little Rock, USA
Christopher Dancy II   Bucknell University, USA

Publicity Chair

Donald Adjeroh   West Virginia University, USA

Local Area Coordination

David Broniatowski   The George Washington University, USA

Proceedings Chair

Robert Thomson   United States Military Academy, USA

Agenda Co-chairs

Robert Thomson   United States Military Academy, USA
Kathleen M. Carley   Carnegie Mellon University, USA

Journal Special Issue Chair

Kathleen M. Carley   Carnegie Mellon University, USA

Tutorial Chair

Kathleen M. Carley   Carnegie Mellon University, USA

Graduate Program Chairs

Fred Morstatter   University of Southern California, USA
Kenneth Joseph   University at Buffalo, USA

Challenge Problem Committee

Kathleen M. Carley   Carnegie Mellon University, USA
Ayaz Hyder   The Ohio State University, USA

BRiMS Society Chair

Christopher Dancy II   Bucknell University, USA

Technical Program Committee

Amir Karami
Andre Harrison
Andy Novobilski
Angela Hamilton
Antonio Luca Alfeo
Ariel Greenberg
Aruna Jammalamadaka
Aryn Pyke
Aunshul Rege
Bianica Pires
Binxuan Huang
Brandon Oselio
Brent Auble
Brian Goode
Christopher Dancy
Dan Calacci
Dian Hu
Dmitriy Babichenko
Douglas Flournoy
Emanuel Ben-David
Erika Frydenlund
Eun Kyong Shin
Farshad Salimi Naneh Karan
Gayane Grigoryan
Geoffrey Dobson

Ghita Mezzour
Gian Maria Campedelli
Halil Bisgin
Hamdi Kavak
Hemant Purohit
Huan Liu
Hung Chau
Iain Cruickshank
James Fould
James Kennedy
Jiebo Luo
John Johnson
Jordan Schoenherr
Joshua Irwin
Juan Fernandez-Gracia
Juliette Shedd
Kenneth Joseph
Kiran Kumar Bandeli
Kristen Greene
Larry Lin
Larry Richard Carley
Laurie Fenstermacher
Lu Cheng
Lucas Overbey
Ma Regina Justina E. Estuar

Mansooreh Karami
Mark Finlayson
Martin Smyth
Maryetta Morris
Matthew Babcock
Michelle Vanni
Muhammad Nihal Hussain
Nasrin Akhter
Neil Johnson
Neslihan Bisgin
Pål Sundsøy
Pedram Hosseini
Peng Fang
Peter Chew
Prakruthi Karuna
Rahul Pandey
Reginald Hobbs
Rey Rodrigueza
Ria Baldevia
Rick Galeano
Robert Chew
Robert Thomson

Sahiti Myneni
Salem Othman
Samer Al-Khateeb
Santosh K. C.
Saurabh Mittal
Shahryar Minhas
Shuyuan Mary Ho
Stephen Marcus
Talha Oz
Tazin Afrin
Thomas Magelinski
Tom Briggs
Truong-Huy Nguyen
Tuja Khaund
Usha Lokala
Vito D'Orazio
Wen Dong
Xiaoyan Li
Xinyue Pan
Yi Han Victoria Chua
Yi-Chieh Lee

Contents

Beyond Words: Comparing Structure, Emoji Use, and Consistency Across Social Media Posts

Melanie Swartz[1]([✉]) [ID], Andrew Crooks[2] [ID], and Arie Croitoru[1] [ID]

[1] George Mason University, Fairfax, VA, USA
{mswartz2,acroitor}@gmu.edu
[2] University at Buffalo, Buffalo, NY, USA
atcrooks@buffalo.edu

Abstract. Social media content analysis often focuses on just the words used in documents or by users and often overlooks the structural components of document composition and linguistic style. We propose that document structure and emoji use are also important to consider as they are impacted by individual communication style preferences and social norms associated with user role and intent, topic domain, and dissemination platform. In this paper we introduce and demonstrate a novel methodology to conduct structural content analysis and measure user consistency of document structures and emoji use. Document structure is represented as the order of content types and number of features per document and emoji use is characterized by the attributes, position, order, and repetition of emojis within a document. With these structures we identified user signatures of behavior, clustered users based on consistency of structures utilized, and identified users with similar document structures and emoji use such as those associated with bots, news organizations, and other user types. This research compliments existing text mining and behavior modeling approaches by offering a language agnostic methodology with lower dimensionality than topic modeling, and focuses on three features often overlooked: document structure, emoji use, and consistency of behavior.

Keywords: Data mining · Social media · Emojis · User behavior modeling

1 Introduction

As social media users engage with online conversations and form virtual communities, social media analysis often focuses on the topics discussed [15], user activity patterns [9], and networks arising from interactions of users [10, 16]. Often overlooked is the communication style associated with a user's social media posts. For instance, analysis of the specific words used can provide a fingerprint of the individual posting the content [8] and reveal shared linguistic styles of the online community [5]. Users also adapt their language to address limitations and norms associated with technology [14] (e.g., character limits, availability of emojis). Within this paper, we propose to move beyond just words, as the structural components of a document's composition and the way in which emojis are used within a document, such as a tweet, also provide cues about the individual and social norms for online communication styles and preferences.

© Springer Nature Switzerland AG 2020
R. Thomson et al. (Eds.): SBP-BRiMS 2020, LNCS 12268, pp. 1–11, 2020.
https://doi.org/10.1007/978-3-030-61255-9_1

In this paper we introduce and demonstrate a language-agnostic methodology to characterize structures of content and emoji use within a document, measure consistency of structures across a set of documents, and cluster documents and users with similar patterns and behavior. By comparing these patterns and behaviors across users and user roles such as journalists, bots, and others, we can generate baselines and gain insights into the unique or shared structures of communication styles and emoji use.

Three main contributions of this research are: 1) a novel methodology for structural content analysis; 2) analysis of the structure of emoji use as the attributes, position, order, and repetition of emojis within a document; and 3) user behavior modeling with regards to consistency of structure of document and emoji use. Benefits of our approach include it is language-agnostic, requires less dimensions than traditional topic modeling, and yields additional measures that can be combined with other text and user metrics. Further, this paper addresses a gap of current social media analysis by focusing on the structural components of communication style, enables comparison of emoji use, and models consistency of user behavior based on social media content. In what follows, Sect. 2 provides an overview of current approaches to content analysis and analysis of emoji use, followed by our methodology in Sect. 3. We then present and discuss our results (Sect. 4), and conclude with areas for further work (Sect. 5).

2   Background

2.1   Content Analysis of Social Media

Content analysis of social media has mainly focused on the words contained in posts to identify discussion topics or associate groups of users based on their use of specific terms, hashtags, or group of words identified via topic modeling [15, 16]. Recently, content analysis combined with other metrics for user activity and network connections, has been applied in order to identify or categorize bots [10, 15, 16]. Analysis of the structure of social media is fairly nascent. [9] considered number of words in text in addition to user activity metrics to identify user intent in spreading misinformation. In addition to content length, [17] took into account content type such as presence of urls, and hashtags to describe activity associated with troll accounts. [1] examined the order of lexical properties of a tweet (such as place name, event date and time, event description) in order to improve the effectiveness of messaging during earthquakes. While [7] focused on the order of content within a tweet and impact on communication styles.

2.2   Analysis of Emoji Use

There is still much more to be learned about the way visual content, including emojis, are used in social media [4]. However, most social media research pertaining to emojis has focused on the meaning of emojis or emojis as indicators of sentiment or sarcasm (e.g., [3]). Only recently has the emphasis shifted to the behavior and structure of emoji use. [12] revealed differences in the way emojis are used based on document types such as tweets, user names, and profile descriptions. [11] identified how emojis are used as structural markers based on where they are placed in text.

3   Measuring Document Structure, Emoji Use, and Consistency

In this section, we first describe how to represent structures of a document (3.1). Then we characterize the structure of emoji use as the attributes of emojis used (3.2) plus the position, order, and repetition of emojis within a document (3.3). Next, we explain how to measure consistency of structures across a set of documents (3.4). Finally, we describe how to cluster users based on structures (3.5) and consistency scores (3.6).

3.1   Document Structure, Content Structure, and Emoji Spans

In order to define the structures of a document, first identify the types of content associated with documents in the collection. For the purpose of this paper we use data from Twitter and view a single tweet as a document. For tweets, we identify content types: retweet indicator, text, emoji, punctuation, hashtag, mention, and url. Each document is divided into spans by content type, irrespective of spaces, and assigned a sequential number as span number. Span length is the number of features per span. Document structure is represented as a list with the content type and number of features for each span, in order of occurrence. Similarly, content structure is a list of span content types in order. Representing a document and content structure in this way enables comparison of documents based on the type or order of contents and enables grouping of documents with similar structural format and style.

For documents containing emojis, we identify which emojis are used as a sorted list of unique emojis. We use the emoji spans (i.e., the spans with content type of emoji) and document structure to describe the way that emojis are used in a document, which we refer to as the structure of emoji use. Figure 1 shows a sample tweet represented as document structure, content structure, emoji spans, and unique emojis. In the next two sub-sections, we demonstrate the structure of emoji use as the emoji attributes paired with the analysis of the position, order, and repetition of emojis within a document.

Document contents	♥♥♥@Nationals win 🌎 World Series ⚾🎽 #Champs #Nats https://www.mlb.com							
Content type	Emoji	Mention	Text	Emoji	Text	Emoji	Hashtag	Url
Span number	1	2	3	4	5	6	7	8
Span length	3	1	1	1	2	2	2	1
Document structure	[(emoji,3), (mention,1), (text,1), (emoji,1), (text,2), (emoji,2), (hashtag,2), (url,1)]							
Content structure	[emoji, mention, text, emoji, text, emoji, hashtag, url]							
Emoji spans	[[♥,♥,♥], [🌎], [⚾,🎽]]							
Unique emojis	[🌎, ♥, 🎽, ⚾, ♥, ♥]							

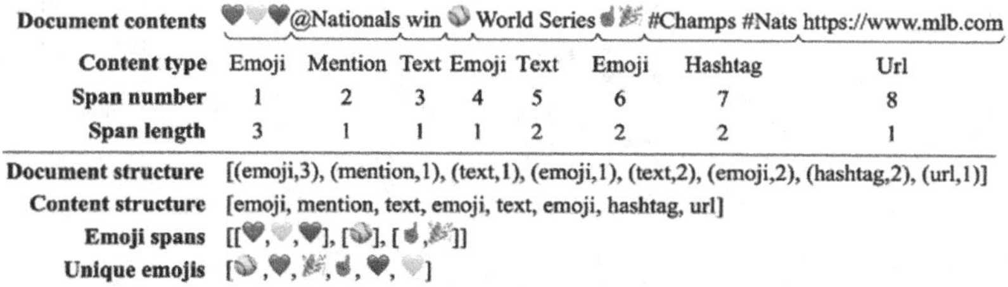

Fig. 1. Structures of a sample tweet.

3.2   Attributes of Emojis in a Document

For each emoji in the emoji spans and in the unique emojis list we describe the emoji along eight attributes noted below. These eight attributes were chosen because each can be used alone or in combination to enable comparison of emojis. Additional attributes could be added such as sentiment or meaning. The first three attributes are from Unicode [2] and were chosen based on previous research showing the value of using emoji group and sub-group for comparison of emoji use [12]. The other attributes are based on heuristics used to sort emojis.

1. **Unicode Group**: Unicode assigns each emoji to one broad category (e.g., Smileys & Emotion, Animals & Nature, Food & Drink, Travel & Places, Objects, Symbols, Flags, and People & Body which also includes Activity).
2. **Unicode Sub-Group**: Unicode assigns emoji to sub-category (e.g., face-smiling).
3. **Unicode Name**: The Unicode emoji name (e.g., "face with tears of joy").
4. **Type**: A label assigned by mapping sub-group to another descriptive property based on a research topic. For this paper, we use shape, anthropomorphic, and other.
5. **Anthro-type**: For anthropomorphic (human like) emojis, we map sub-groups to: face, face-gesture, hand-gesture, body-gesture, body-part, single person, multiple.
6. **Shape**: Indicated by emoji name: triangle, circle, square, star, heart.
7. **Color**: Indicated by emoji name: red, blue, yellow, pink, purple, orange, green, brown, white, black. We also include the five Fitzpatrick skin-tone colors used for emojis: light, light-medium, medium, medium-dark, and dark. We use the name because color appearance may vary across platforms.
8. **Direction**: Based on words in emoji name to indicate: up, down, left, or right.

To demonstrate how the above set of attributes enables descriptive comparison of similarities and differences of individual emojis, consider these two emojis, ▲ and ☝. There are differences in appearance and type with one a red triangle (type of shape) and the other a hand holding up an index finger (anthropomorphic hand-gesture). Yet they are similar in direction of pointing "up". Table 1 summarizes attributes for these emojis.

Table 1. Emoji attributes.

Emoji	Group	Sub-group	Name	Type	Anthro-type	Shape	Color	Direction
▲	Symbol	Geometric	Up-pointing red triangle	Shape	None	Triangle	Red	Up
☝	People & body	Hand-single-finger	Index pointing up: medium skin tone	Anthro	Hand-gesture	None	Medium	Up

3.3 Emoji Position, Order, and Repetition

Position of Emojis in a Document. We describe the general position of emojis in a document based on relative position of emoji as: first, beginning, middle, end, or last. We use document structure to derive relative position based on span number for the emoji content in relation to total number of spans in the document, divided into thirds, (e.g., the first third of spans is the beginning). Content in the very first and last spans are labeled as such. Documents with less than five spans are only first, middle, or last.

Emoji Order. The order of emojis and attributes are noted both within and across emoji spans. We take into account emoji order, as emoji color order within the same emoji span could result in a set of emojis taking on different meanings, based on context of text or user. For example, the set of heart emojis 💙🤍❤️ with color order red, white, blue could represent colors of a sports team (as in Fig. 1) or a country flag (e.g., Netherlands or United States). The order of emojis or attributes can also indicate a pattern. For example, "❤️ text ❤️", represents a pattern we call emoji reversal which occurs when two consecutive emoji spans contain the same emojis or attributes, but the order in the second span is reversed.

Emoji Repetition. We categorize repetition of emojis or emoji attributes as three types: redundant, emphasis, and amplification. Redundant is the repetition of the same emoji or attribute within the same span, sometimes representing magnitude or quantity, (e.g., 😂😂). Emphasis is often used to draw attention and generally occurs when two emoji spans contain the same emojis regardless of order (e.g., "🚨Alert🚨", "🌊Blue-wave🌊"). Amplification is repetition of an attribute across different emojis within the same span or across multiple spans (e.g., color red in: "🔺Vote❤️🟥 all Red ! 🔴").

3.4 Measure of Consistency

With the structures of document contents and emoji use represented, we can then measure consistency of these structures across a set of documents, such as a user's or group's tweets. This measure makes it is possible to highlight differences in behavior based on relative consistency in terms of document content, style, or emoji use.

To measure consistency, for a set of documents, iterate across the unique structures (U) (e.g., document structure, content structure, or emoji use). For each unique structure, divide the number of documents in the set with that structure (d_i) by the number of documents for the structure in the set with the most documents (max (Ud)), then square the results. Calculate the measure of consistency for the set of documents, (C), as 1 divided by the sum of theses squares of normalized proportions of documents per unique structure. The resulting measure of consistency ranges between 0 and 1 with larger values indicating greater consistency and smaller values approaching 0 representing greater variation. The measure of consistency is represented by equation:

$$C = 1 / \sum_{i=1}^{U} \left(\frac{d_i}{\max(Ud)} \right)^2 \tag{1}$$

We chose this approach compared to other measures (e.g., Shannon or Simpson's Index) to enable standardized comparison regardless of collection size and to support a variety of distributions for document counts per unique structures. In addition, we add weight for unique structures that comprise a greater proportion of a user's documents.

3.5 Clustering by Structure, Content, and Emoji Use

Even though the text of individual documents varies greatly, users and documents can be clustered based on similarity of document structure, content style, or emoji use. We also identify common structures used across of users, as well as identifying the users of specific structures via aggregation. These approaches support analysis of communication patterns to identify common or unique structures used, structures associated with specific types of users or groups, as well as identifying documents or users that may be related based on similar style defined by the structures used.

3.6 Clustering Users Based on Consistency

In addition, we cluster users based on their consistency scores for structures of document, content, and emoji use. We use the unsupervised clustering algorithm HDBSCAN [6] as it does not require defining the number of clusters, supports multiple dimension data, finds stable clusters within noisy data, and can handle clusters of varying density, size, and shape. For each cluster, we describe behavior traits as low, medium, or high consistency for each factor based on the greatest percent of users of that cluster falling within interquartile ranges for low (first quartile), medium (second and third quartiles), or high (fourth quartile). The composition of users in a cluster is then summarized based on additional information such as keywords in user profile descriptions or labeled data such as if account has previously been labeled as bot-like. Clustering users based on consistency enables comparison and grouping of users with similar behavior patterns associated with their communication style.

4   Experiment Results and Discussion

4.1 Experimental Setup

We apply our methodology to a corpus of 44 million tweets collected in October and November 2018 related to the 2018 U.S. midterm elections based on keywords, hashtags, and user accounts associated with candidates or political parties. For each of the 3.3 million unique users set of retweets and non-retweets we measure consistency of document structure and content structure. To improve consistency scores and reduce dimensionality, we modified the document structure by removing spans of punctuation and by not including the count of features for text spans. For the 30% of users of emojis in their tweets, we measure consistency of which unique emojis are used and also measure structure of emoji use represented as a vector of attributes, position, order, and repetition of emojis (eVAPOR). Using HDBSCAN we cluster users based on consistency scores for their retweets and non-retweets separately. We then describe the composition of each cluster and measure the percent of accounts labeled as bot-like based on Botometer scores. Next we present the results of our analysis.

4.2 Distributions of Consistency

We compared the distribution of consistency scores for users that sent more than two non-retweets or more than two retweets. Figure 2 shows the range of these scores for tweet text, document structure, content structure, unique emojis, and structure of emoji use. As expected, we found little user consistency in tweet text. In general, users were more consistent in their non-retweets than retweets, especially for content structure and which specific emojis were used. This indicates users tend to use the same order, format, and often the same emojis for their own tweets, whether knowingly or not. Users had less consistency with retweets likely a result of retweeting multiple users. Analysis of user behavior for document structure, content structure, and emojis in tweets reduces dimensionality and yields new information compared to traditional text analysis.

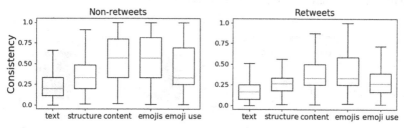

Fig. 2. Distribution of consistency scores for users sending non-retweets (left) and retweets (right) shown with interquartile ranges.

4.3 Analysis of Structures for Document, Content, and Emoji Use

Using the methodology presented in Sect. 3, we identified common structures of non-retweets and retweets used by a large percent of tweets or users. Table 2 shows the most common non-retweet content structures with emojis. Analysis of these structures used by bot accounts led to identification of additional accounts likely to be bots not yet labeled. Tweets of these accounts exhibited identical content structure and structure of emoji use, although the tweets had different text, urls, emojis, and document structures (e.g. same content type order with variation in number of urls, emojis, and mentions). Given the similarity of the user profile descriptions and names for these users, it would not be surprising if these accounts are related. This is just one of many examples we found demonstrating structural content analysis can identify specific styles of communication that may be a signature for an individual or group of users.

Table 2. Most common content structures with emojis for non-retweets.

Content Structure	Percent of tweets	Percent of users
[atmention, text, emoji]	18%	31%
[text, emoji]	6%	15%
[atmention, text, emoji, text]	4%	9%
[text, emoji, url]	2%	5%
[atmention, text, emoji, hashtag]	2%	4%
[atmention, emoji]	1%	4%

4.4 Clustering Users Based on Consistency

We compared consistency scores for user non-retweets and retweets across four dimensions: document structure, content structure, unique emojis used, and emoji use. Clustering users based on consistency scores in two dimensions reveals groups of users in the dataset with similar behaviors for document structure and emoji use, content structure and unique emojis used, Fig. 3. With the t-SNE algorithm we visualize the clusters of users with similar behavior across four dimensions, Fig. 4.

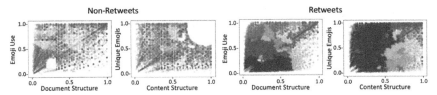

Fig. 3. Clusters of users with similar behavior across two factors in non-retweets (left) and retweets (right) Colors indicate cluster assignments.

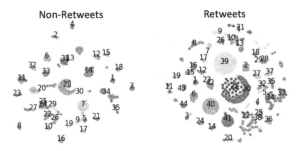

Fig. 4. Clusters of users with similar behavior across four factors for non-retweets (left) and retweets (right). Each cluster is labeled with a number.

4.5 Behavior Traits and Composition of Users in Clusters

For each cluster of users, we describe the behavior traits in terms of low, medium, or high consistency across each of the four dimensions. While most clusters had medium consistency for at least one dimension, 6.5% of non-retweet and 4.8% of retweet users were grouped into clusters that had high consistency across all four dimensions. We then calculated the percent of user accounts for each cluster that were likely bots based on Botometer scores [13]. One of the non-retweet clusters had 45% bots, compared to the average 19% for other clusters. While not all bot-like users had high consistency scores, this particular cluster did for each of the four factors. This could indicate that additional users within this cluster may be related or also bots but not yet identified by existing bot detection algorithms.

Next, we analyzed the composition of user roles per cluster and by behavior. We define users by role based on keywords in their user profile (e.g., journalists and news organizations, marketers, businesses, celebrities, government, activists, veterans, students). Most users were clustered into groups with medium consistency scores across the four factors for non-retweets. However, the user group with verified user accounts and indicating the user is a journalist, reporter, or news organizations (which we label as 'News') had the greatest percent of users with high consistency across all four factors in non-retweets. Many of their tweets appear to be auto-generated using a template as tweets exhibited same structure but changing information such as top news and weather reports throughout the day. Similarly, 'Marketer' also had high percent of users with high consistency and tweets with similar structure and emoji use were indicating weekly or daily sales or specials. While most users had relatively low consistency in retweets, the user group of retired military veterans had the greatest percent of users with high consistency for which emojis were used and the way emojis were used in retweets. This could indicate that tweets with specific emojis and style of emoji use are more likely to be retweeted by this group. Table 3 summarizes the top user roles based on percent of users for categories indicating consistency of behavior associated with document structure and structure of emoji use in non-retweets.

Table 3. Top user roles and percent per consistency category for document structure and structure of emoji use in non-retweets.

		Consistency of structure of emoji use		
		Low	Medium	High
Consistency of document structure	Low	9% Celebrity 8% Activist	11% Bot 10% Activist	5% Coach 4% Government
	Medium	9% Bot 7% Coach	66% Marketer 45% Coach	12% Government 11% Veteran
	High	2% Business 2% Artist	12% Student 10% Celebrity	20% News 16% Marketer

While it is not easy to verify authenticity of a user account or role, we demonstrate how to identify unique and common patterns and traits among a group of users with the same attributes in their user profile description. Overall, our results reveal how new insight can be gained by identifying and analyzing communication style patterns of individuals and groups of users with similar roles or behaviors for consistency across structures or emoji use in their documents.

5 Conclusions and Future Work

This paper introduces and demonstrates a new language-agnostic approach for structural content analysis and user behavior modeling by characterizing the structure and emoji use of a document, and then measuring and clustering by user consistency. With this methodology we described signatures of communication styles and behaviors for individuals, user groups, and clusters of users. We also identified users with document structural properties and user consistency metrics similar to accounts already labeled as bot-like. Limitations of our study are that we focused on only one collection of tweets related to American politics and it is difficult to verify authenticity of user accounts. Areas for further research could compare tweet styles and author consistency for other topics and user roles such as sports, tourism, and health or message effectiveness. Structural content analysis and measuring consistency across documents, as presented in this paper, compliments existing text mining techniques and provides a new perspective for social media analysis by linking document style and user behavior.

References

1. Comunello, F., Mulargia, S., Polidoro, P., Casarotti, E., Lauciani, V.: No misunderstandings during earthquakes: elaborating and testing a standardized tweet structure for automatic earthquake detection information. In: ISCRAM (2015)
2. Davis, M.: Emoji Charts, v13.0. https://unicode.org/emoji/charts/full-emoji-list.html (2020)
3. Felbo, B., Mislove, A., Søgaard, A., Rahwan, I., Lehmann, S.: Using millions of emoji occurrences to learn any-domain representations for detecting sentiment, emotion and sarcasm. In EMNLP, pp. 1615–1625 (2017)
4. Highfield, T., Leaver, T.: Instagrammatics and digital methods: studying visual social media, from selfies and GIFs to memes and emoji. Commun. Res. Pract. **2**(1), 47–62 (2016)
5. Khalid, O., Srinivasan, P.: Style matters! Investigating linguistic style in online communities. In: ICWSM, pp. 360–369 (2020)
6. McInnes, L., Healy, J., Astels, S.: HDBSCAN: hierarchical density-based clustering. J. Open Source Softw. **2**(11), 205 (2017)
7. Pederson, J.A.: It's not what you tweet but how you tweet it: an experiment of orientation, interactivity, and valence in Twitter. Dissertation, Texas A&M Univ. (2016)
8. Pennebaker, J., Mehl, M., Niederhoffer, K.: Psychological aspects of natural language use: our words, our selves. Annu. Rev. Psychol. **54**(1), 547–577 (2003)
9. Rajabi, Z., Shehu, A., Purohit, H.: User behavior modelling for fake information mitigation on social web. In: Thomson, R., Bisgin, H., Dancy, C., Hyder, A. (eds.) SBP-BRiMS 2019. LNCS, vol. 11549, pp. 234–244. Springer, Cham (2019). https://doi.org/10.1007/978-3-030-21741-9_24
10. Schuchard, R., Crooks, A.T., Stefanidis, A., Croitoru, A.: Bot stamina: examining the influence and staying power of bots in online social networks. Appl. Netw. Sci. **4**(1), 55 (2019)
11. Spina, S.: Role of emoticons as structural markers in Twitter interactions. Discourse Process. **56**(4), 345–362 (2019)
12. Swartz, M., Crooks, A.: Comparison of emoji use in names, profiles, and tweets. In: ICSC, pp. 375–380 (2020)
13. Varol, O., Ferrara, E., Davis, C.A., Menczer, F., Flammini, A.: Online human-bot interactions: detection, estimation, and characterization. In: ICWSM, pp. 280–289 (2017)
14. Walther, J.: Interaction through technological lenses: computer-mediated communication and language. J. Lang. Soc. Psychol. **31**(4), 397–414 (2012)
15. Wirth, K., Menchen-Trevino, E., Moore, R.T.: Bots by topic: exploring differences in bot activity by conversation topic. In: Social Media and Society, pp. 77–82 (2019)

16. Yuan, X., Schuchard, R., Crooks, A.: Examining emergent communities and social bots within the polarized online vaccination debate in Twitter. Soc. Media Soc., **5**(3) (2019)
17. Zannettou, S., Caulfield, T., De Cristofaro, E., Sirivianos, M., Stringhini, G., Blackburn, J.: Disinformation warfare: understanding state-sponsored trolls on Twitter and their influence on the Web. In: WWW 2019, pp. 218–226 (2019)

Bot Impacts on Public Sentiment and Community Structures: Comparative Analysis of Three Elections in the Asia-Pacific

Joshua Uyheng$^{(\boxtimes)}$ and Kathleen M. Carley

CASOS Center, Institute for Software Research, Carnegie Mellon University,
Pittsburgh, PA 15213, USA
{juyheng,carley}@cs.cmu.edu

Abstract. Online disinformation has become a ubiquitous concern in elections worldwide. However, while extensively studied in Western contexts, scant work examines its prevalence and impacts in other geopolitical settings like the Asia-Pacific. This paper probes the influence of online bots on Twitter conversations surrounding recent elections in the Philippines, Indonesia, and Taiwan. Using a combination of machine learning, network analysis, and causal inference tools, we determine that the impacts of bots are mixed across contexts. More specifically, we quantify variations in the extent to which bot activities account for shifts in public sentiment and online community structure over time. We contribute to the extensive literature on online disinformation by providing a general and systematic framework for assessing and comparing the impacts of bot operations across unique geopolitical contexts.

Keywords: Bots · Disinformation · Causal inference · Elections · Asia

1 Introduction

Around the globe, the last decade witnessed the unprecedented rise of both social media platforms and large-scale efforts to weaponize them. Utilizing coordinated systems of bots, trolls, and fake news, digital disinformation campaigns took advantage of online social networks to manipulate public opinion, heighten political polarization, and potentially influence real-world outcomes [3,14].

This work is supported in part by Office of Naval Research under grant N000141812106 and N000141812108. Additional support was provided by the Center for Computational Analysis of Social and Organizational Systems (CASOS) and the Institute for Software Research at Carnegie Mellon University. The views and conclusions contained in this document are those of the authors and should not be interpreted as representing the official policies, either expressed or implied, of the Office of Naval Research, or the U.S. Government.

R. Thomson et al. (Eds.): SBP-BRiMS 2020, LNCS 12268, pp. 12–22, 2020.
https://doi.org/10.1007/978-3-030-61255-9_2

Numerous studies discuss the insidious impacts of online disinformation especially in electoral contexts, which notably featured high-stakes participation from state-level actors [10]. Research in this area, however, has tended to concentrate around Western nations like the United States and Western Europe, especially in relation to campaigns orchestrated by Russia to disrupt prevailing the geopolitical order in the North Atlantic [6,11]. Prevailing work may therefore overrepresent issues specific to Western contexts, despite the rich and likewise troubling evidence of online disinformation impacting real-world events in other regions of the world like the Asia-Pacific and the Global South [9,13].

In this work, we analyze the impacts of online disinformation in three elections from the last year which took place in the Asia-Pacific. Implementing an integrated pipeline of machine learning and network analytic tools [2,14], this work employs a social cyber-security lens to measure bot activities and infer their relationship with public sentiment and community structures. In sum, we aim to accomplish three objectives: firstly, to meaningfully characterize bot activities in electoral discourse; secondly, to infer causal influences of bot activities on online conversations; and thirdly, to introduce a systematic and broadly generalizable framework for facilitating comparative analysis of disinformation across diverse geopolitical contexts. Our findings emphasize the importance of not only detecting bot activities, but also precisely quantifying their impacts in a manner that accounts for both nationally specific political conflicts as well as wider geopolitical dynamics [3,4,7].

2   Methods

Social cyber-security posits a multidisciplinary and multimethod view to understand both social and computational dimensions of online disinformation [4]. To operationalize this view, we employed an interoperable pipeline of machine learning and network analytic tools to identify inauthentic bot accounts, characterize their interactions with other participants in the Twitter conversation, measure public sentiment, and assess community structures for their level of echo-chamberness [3,14]. The extracted features were represented as time series to causally infer the impact of bots on public sentiments and community structures in online electoral discourse in the Philippines, Indonesia, and Taiwan.

2.1   Data Collection

The Twitter REST API was used to collect tweets related to: (a) the 2019 Philippine elections (PH; 7 months), (b) the 2019 Indonesian elections (ID; 5 months), and (c) the 2020 Taiwanese elections (TW; 3 months). To facilitate temporal analysis, we divided each dataset into a series of three-day intervals. Table 1 summarizes the key statistics of each dataset, such as the total number of tweets and unique users represented. We note that because Twitter's sampling algorithm is not necessarily uniform and random, our findings as constrained by these data collection parameters [8]. While dataset timelines largely reflect

Table 1. Summary of Twitter datasets related to three Asian elections.

Election	Tweets	Users	Keywords	Candidates	
				Government	Opposition
Philippines	1.2M	280K	#Halalan2019, #PHVote	Sonny Angara, Bong Go, Imee Marcos	Bam Aquino, Chel Diokno, Mar Roxas
Indonesia	2.2M	330K	#Pemilu2019, #Pilpres	Joko Widodo	Prabowo Subianto
Taiwan	240K	76K	#TaiwanVotes, #Taiwan2020	Tsai Ing-Wen	Han Kuo-Yu

differences in the lengths of campaign periods, we are also unable to conclude whether disparities in dataset sizes are primarily explained by uneven periods of data collection or actual differences in Twitter use across countries. We also provide a sample of keywords used for data collection. For parsimony, additional keywords not included in Table 1 include the names of all candidates as well as identified campaign slogans.

We examined specific campaigns for each election by taking subsets of each dataset containing the names or slogans of associated candidates. For the Philippines, which featured a senatorial race, we focused on the three government and opposition candidates who garnered the highest number of votes in each political camp. For Indonesia and Taiwan, which each revolved around contests for the presidency between the incumbent and a popular challenger, we focused on the presidential candidates. It is worth noting that for each of the three elections, none of the opposition candidates won. Noting the significant influence of China in the Asia-Pacific, we also examined all tweets containing mentions of China or its colloquial equivalents. In parallel to Russian operations in the West [11], we sought to determine whether the regional superpower would also feature in electoral discourse in the three nations of interest [7].

2.2   Bot Detection

We identified inauthentic accounts in each election dataset using BotHunter, which is based on a supervised random forest classifier trained on a labeled dataset of Russian accounts [2]. BotHunter has been successfully deployed in past studies of online disinformation with comparable performance to other existing bot detection methods [13,14]. To heighten precision, we used a threshold of 60% to distinguish bot accounts from human users.

2.3   Bot Activities

Using the identified bot accounts, we measured a number of descriptive statistics to characterize their activities over time. We measured the raw number of tweets sent out by bot versus human accounts to assess their level of raw participation in online electoral discourse. In addition, we noted the first appearance of each unique account to measure the cumulative participation of bots and humans in the Twitter conversation. Faster increases in cumulative participation signal whether bots or humans are more specifically engaged in electoral talk, as they indicate whether each set of accounts begins to discuss related topics early on or only close to the election date. We performed similar measurements on interactions, noting the raw number of mentions, replies, and retweets which took place between two users, as well as the first appearance of any such interactions between unique pairs of users. Of particular interest here were the relative dynamics of bot-to-bot, bot-to-human, and human-to-human interactions.

2.4   Network Influence

We used ORA to represent Twitter conversations in terms of social networks [5], denoting users with nodes, and their interactions with directed, weighted edges. Mentions, replies, and retweets were all aggregated for edge weighting. Influence was assessed using measures of closeness, betweenness, and eigenvector centrality [13]. These centrality measures respectively correspond to the degree to which accounts propagate or receive information from other accounts, their ability to broker information transmission between groups, and their connectedness to other influential accounts. We were specifically interested in quantifying the relative influence of bot accounts in contrast to human accounts.

2.5   Sentiment Analysis

The first index we used to measure the impact of bot accounts was public sentiment. We used Netmapper to measure the emotional valence of all tweets on a scale ranging from -1 to $+1$ [14]. We computationally assess sentiment in this work as it has been robustly linked to disinformation tactics aiming to shift public opinion by stoking positive or negative feelings toward electoral candidates [9]. Following known disinformation strategies, such measures allow us to assess whether bots might seek to implement narrative or information maneuvers, seeking to strategically *excite* or *dismay* supporters or critics of various electoral candidates [3].

2.6   Echo-Chamberness

As a second index of disinformation impact, we measured community structure for each campaign in terms of the relative proportion of internal links between users who talked about a certain candidate relative to their external links or interactions with others who did not speak about the same candidate. By taking the percentage difference between internal and external links, we produced an index of how echo-chamberlike a group was over time [5]. Extant debates in online disinformation studies have discussed at length the salience of echo chambers as a pathological group dynamic which develop in online conflicts [14]. Again drawing on known disinformation maneuvers, increases in echo-chamberness might correspond to network maneuvers that *build* or *bridge* groups, whereas decreases in echo-chamberness might indicate maneuvers to *nuke* or *narrow* online communities [3].

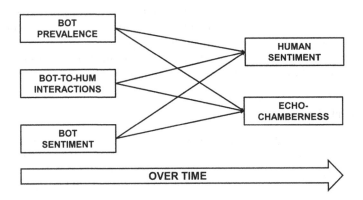

Fig. 1. Causal model of bot activities on public sentiment and community structure.

2.7   Causal Inference

To assess the causal influence of bot activities, we employed vector autoregression models (VARs) which model the relationships between multiple time series [12]. VAR models have been used in related work, for instance, to determine the relative agenda-setting impacts of the Twitter discourse of politicians on the talk of regular accounts and vice versa [1]. Granger causality tests on VAR models quantify the extent to which time series data of the regressors explain variations in a dependent variable beyond its own temporal dynamics. We used the Aikake Information Criterion (AIC) to determine the optimal number of lags to retain in the model. Our overall causal inference model is summarized by Fig. 1, wherein bot prevalence, bot-to-human interactions, and mean bot sentiment was used to predict the sentiments of humans and their level of echo-chamberness over time.

3   Results

3.1   Bot Prevalence

Across all three contexts, bots featured non-negligible prevalence, which we measured in different ways. Figure 2 shows that over time, the percentage of tweets sent out by bots generally lay between 9.29–21.08% in the Philippines, 4.42–9.89% in Indonesia, and 7.15–13.13% in Taiwan. In the Philippines, however, bot activity appeared to be especially pointed as they began to participate in the online electoral discourse much earlier than human users. All throughout the time of data collection, bots recurred in the Philippine data while many humans only appeared close to the elections. For instance, 25% of the unique bots had already begun talking about the elections about a month before a comparable proportion of unique humans. In contrast, for Indonesia and Taiwan, the cumulative participation of bots and humans appears highly synchronized.

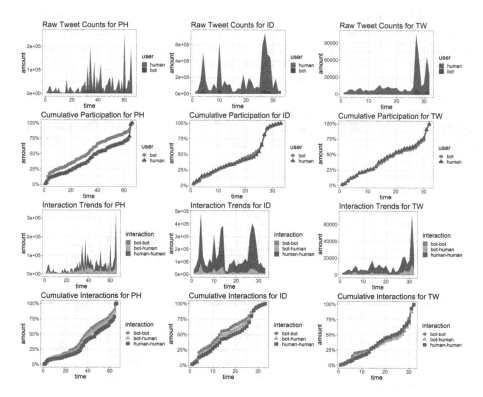

Fig. 2. Raw and cumulative participation of bots and humans over time. **Row 1:** Raw number of tweets over time. **Row 2:** Cumulative percentage of unique bot and human accounts over time. **Row 3:** Raw number of interactions over time. **Row 4:** Cumulative percentage of unique interactions over time. All time units are in three-day intervals.

In terms of interactions, we further note that a majority took place between humans. However, a non-negligible proportion of mentions, replies, and retweets also occurred between bots and humans, at any time ranging between 12.75–48.61% of all interactions in the Philippines, 10.06–18.45% in Indonesia, and 8.86–32.49% in Taiwan. Only a minuscule fraction appear to occur between bots. Interestingly, in both the Philippines and Indonesia, interactions involving bots occurred earlier than human interactions, while in Taiwan again, this earliness was seen only in the first month of data collection. Altogether these findings combine to form a distinct temporal picture of bot activity and interactions, highlighting their common salience across the three contexts, while also show-casing their differences in terms of how early bots appeared in online electoral discourse.

3.2   Bot Influence

In terms of influence, Fig. 3 shows that humans consistently have higher influence across all three centrality measures. This means that despite the notable pres-ence of bots in all datasets, humans are still the primary drivers of information within and across communities. However, we also note that over time, a larger proportion of bots than humans were among the most influential accounts. This may indicate that while not all bots successfully accrue influence in the online conversation (resulting in low overall averages), a small number of bots may nonetheless successfully become influencers. This was most clearly the case early in the Indonesian dataset, but most prominently in the Philippines throughout the observed time period. These measurements amply suggest that bots occupied influential enough positions in the social network to potentially impact public sentiment and community structures.

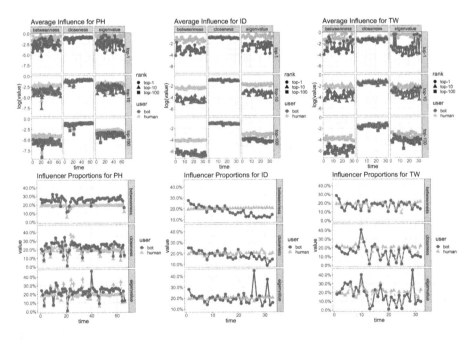

Fig. 3. Influence of bots and humans measured by betweenness, closeness, and eigen-value centrality. **Row 1:** Average centrality scores (log scale) of the top 1, 10, and 100 most influential bots and humans. **Row 2:** Percentage of humans and bots in the top 20% most influential accounts over time. All time units are in three-day intervals.

3.3   Causal Inference on Bot Impacts

Finally, we present causal inference results linking the level of bot activity, bot-to-human interactions, and bot sentiments to public sentiment and echo-chamberness. Figure 4 shows the results of our Granger causality tests, which suggest mixed bot impacts across contexts and storylines. Figure 5 indicates the magnitude and direction of VAR coefficients, highlighting whether bot activities increased or decreased the impact indices of interest. The AIC criterion indicated that a single time lag was optimal for all models, meaning bot activities from the previous three-day window predicted those in the succeeding period.

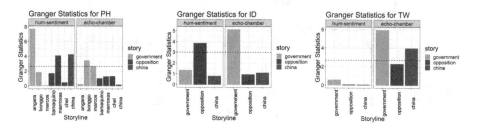

Fig. 4. Granger statistics measuring causal impacts of bots on public sentiment and echo-chamberness. Broken lines represent the threshold for statistical significance at a $\alpha = .05$ threshold.

In the Philippines, bots increased positive sentiment toward administration-supported Sonny Angara and China, while promoting negative sentiment toward opposition contender Mar Roxas. Echo-chamberness was also increased in relation to Bong Go and Imee Marcos, both part of the incumbent government's coalition. Meanwhile, in Indonesia, bots appeared to raise positive sentiment toward opposition bet Prabowo Subianto while increasing the echo-chamberness of communities discussing the incumbent Joko Widodo. However, no effects were detected in relation to China. Finally, in Taiwan, we found no evidence for bot impacts on public sentiment. Bots did, however, seem to increase echo-chamberness in relation to incumbent Tsai Ing-Wen while decreasing echo-chamberness of communities discussing China.

4   Discussion

Our shift to causal analysis from the descriptive approaches more common in prevailing work allowed precise distinctions between the *intent* of bot activities and their actual *impacts*. For instance, while notable levels of bot activity were detected across campaigns, we quantitatively identified in which cases the presence and interactions of bots significantly explained succeeding shifts in public sentiment and echo-chamberness of community structures. Furthermore, by harnessing flexible and generalizable metrics like sentiment and echo-chamberness,

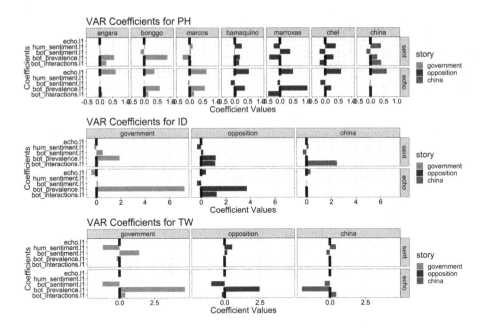

Fig. 5. VAR coefficients for bot impacts. Dashed line at zero indicating no effect.

our tools facilitated comparative analysis of diverse campaigns along meaningful dimensions. From a practical standpoint, frameworks such as those we present here may therefore help pinpoint information operations requiring more urgent attention and potential intervention across unique geopolitical contexts [3,14].

In the Asia-Pacific, such concerns are sharpened by populist and elite capture of democratic institutions as well as local vulnerabilities to regional superpowers [7,10]. In the Philippines, consistent positive effects for China and top adminis-tration candidates, coupled with negative effects for a key opposition bet, suggest the promotion of state interests facilitated by state-sponsored machinery [9,13]. Such impacts are particularly troubling in view of the opposition slate's eventual failure to win any senate seats as well as incumbent president Duterte's pivot to cozy relations with China [7]. That said, we do not claim a one-to-one cor-respondence between online discourse and electoral outcomes. For instance, in Indonesia, despite positive shifts in public sentiment for presidential challenger Subianto, incumbent Widodo nonetheless emerged the winner. Finally, in Tai-wan, bots succeeded in shaping community structure but not sentiment. While consolidating the conversation about incumbent Tsai, bots appeared to sequester online groups discussing China. This suggests that while bots may fail to trigger collective emotional shifts, their effects on information flow (i.e., who talks to whom) may still be significant to explore in-depth. In contrast to the Philip-pines and Indonesia, where primarily positive propaganda might be deployed to promote Chinese interests, it is also possible that bot-driven fragmentation of the China discussion is spurred by competing campaigns, given the salience of debates regarding 'reunification' with the mainland on the election trail.

At this juncture, we revisit caveats on the quality of data collected and our techniques for data enrichment. Improved results would entail not only the refinement of computational tools for analyzing bots, sentiment, and social networks, but also greater transparency on the part of social media platforms in sharing research with the academic community [8]. Moreover, while we explore aggregated claims of disinformation impacts, they do not speak to how such causal pathways manifest in psychologically and culturally specific ways. Thus, pressing causal questions remain open, such as the extent to which the inferred temporal relationships corresponded to actual shifts in public opinion or bot-driven provocations of already existing political views, which may exceed the assumptions of Granger causality. Echoing the multi-view approach advocated by social cybersecurity, understanding the online disinformation landscape requires both social and computational perspectives, for which our findings here might present an informative albeit partial model [3,4].

References

1. Barberá, P., et al.: Who leads? Who follows? Measuring issue attention and agenda setting by legislators and the mass public using social media data. Am. Polit. Sci. Rev. **113**(4), 883–901 (2019)
2. Beskow, D.M., Carley, K.M.: Bot-hunter: a tiered approach to detecting & characterizing automated activity on Twitter. In: SBP-BRiMS: International Conference on Social Computing, Behavioral-Cultural Modeling and Prediction and Behavior Representation in Modeling and Simulation, vol. 8 (2018)
3. Beskow, D.M., Carley, K.M.: Social cybersecurity: an emerging national security requirement. Mil. Rev. **99**(2), 117 (2019)
4. Carley, K.M., Cervone, G., Agarwal, N., Liu, H.: Social cyber-security. In: Thomson, R., Dancy, C., Hyder, A., Bisgin, H. (eds.) SBP-BRiMS 2018. LNCS, vol. 10899, pp. 389–394. Springer, Cham (2018). https://doi.org/10.1007/978-3-319-93372-6_42
5. Carley, K.M., Diesner, J., Reminga, J., Tsvetovat, M.: Toward an interoperable dynamic network analysis toolkit. Decis. Support Syst. **43**(4), 1324–1347 (2007)
6. Ferrara, E., Varol, O., Davis, C., Menczer, F., Flammini, A.: The rise of social bots. Commun. ACM **59**(7), 96–104 (2016)
7. Montiel, C.J., Boller, A.J., Uyheng, J., Espina, E.A.: Narrative congruence between populist president Duterte and the Filipino public: shifting global alliances from the United States to China. J. Commun. Appl. Soc. Psychol. **29**(6), 520–534 (2019)
8. Morstatter, F., Pfeffer, J., Liu, H., Carley, K.M.: Is the sample good enough? Comparing data from Twitter's streaming API with Twitter's firehose. In: Seventh International AAAI Conference on Weblogs and Social Media (2013)
9. Ong, J.C., Cabañes, J.V.A.: When disinformation studies meets production studies: social identities and moral justifications in the political trolling industry. Int. J. Commun. **13**, 20 (2019)
10. Ong, J.C., Tapsell, R., Curato, N.: Tracking digital disinformation in the 2019 Philippine midterm election. New Mandala (2019)

11. Ruck, D.J., Rice, N.M., Borycz, J., Bentley, R.A.: Internet research agency Twitter activity predicted 2016 us election polls. First Monday **24**(7) (2019)
12. Toda, H.Y., Phillips, P.C.: Vector autoregression and causality: a theoretical overview and simulation study. Econom. Rev. **13**(2), 259–285 (1994)
13. Uyheng, J., Carley, K.M.: Characterizing bot networks on Twitter: an empirical analysis of contentious issues in the Asia-Pacific. In: Thomson, R., Bisgin, H., Dancy, C., Hyder, A. (eds.) SBP-BRiMS 2019. LNCS, vol. 11549, pp. 153–162. Springer, Cham (2019). https://doi.org/10.1007/978-3-030-21741-9_16
14. Uyheng, J., Magelinski, T., Villa-Cox, R., Sowa, C., Carley, K.M.: Interoperable pipelines for social cyber-security: assessing Twitter information operations during Nato trident juncture 2018. Comput. Math. Organ. Theory 1–19 (2019)

Understanding Colonial Legacy
and Environmental Issues in Senegal
Through Language Use

Kamwoo Lee[1][✉], Jeanine Braithwaite[1], and Michel Atchikpa[2]

[1] University of Virginia, Charlottesville, USA
{kamwoolee,jeaninebraithwaite}@virginia.edu
[2] Université Cheikh Anta Diop de Dakar, Dakar, Senegal
michelatchikpa@gmail.com

Abstract. Language is a reflection of issues and value systems of a society. This study tries to understand sensitive public issues in Senegal through language use. To this end, we utilize word embeddings, a numerical word representation, to analyze concepts, connotations, and nuances of several words. State-of-the-art machine learning methods can effectively extract the word embeddings from a collection of texts. Since people in different societies possess different mindsets and language uses, comparing semantic differences of words in different corpora is an efficient way to draw cross-cultural insights and implications. In this study, we extract word embeddings from Senegalese newspapers and French Wikipedia and then compare the results to identify different word sentiments in Senegalese cultures to understand the past, present, and future of the country.

Keywords: Senegal · Colonial legacy · Environmental issues · Word embeddings

1 Introduction

Interviews and surveys are often embraced as primary methods for social science studies. However, there is a limitation on collecting truthful data, especially opinions, through questionnaires when the subject matter is inherently sensitive, such as religion, race, and gender. Interviewee or survey participants might not give honest answers or, even if they are willing to, they might not realize their unconscious thoughts and behaviors. When it comes to sentiments of the general public, using language and texts can be an option since language collectively reflects values and concepts within society.

In this paper, we present our analysis of sensitive social issues that have been captured in Senegalese texts. We utilize state-of-the-art machine learning techniques to extract word representations called word embeddings, which map vocabulary to a multi-dimensional semantic vector space. We create two sets of

© Springer Nature Switzerland AG 2020
R. Thomson et al. (Eds.): SBP-BRiMS 2020, LNCS 12268, pp. 23–34, 2020.
https://doi.org/10.1007/978-3-030-61255-9_3

word embeddings from Senegalese newspapers (SnText) and Wikipedia pages in French (FrText), separately. We treat FrText as a reference point as it has more diverse context, larger size, and better text quality than any other French text corpus. We then compare those semantic representations word-by-word between the two sources to expose Senegalese specific viewpoints and perceptions.

Broadly stated, we create conceptual "semantic scales" with word vectors and "measure" the value of each word. Any pair of antonyms can act as a semantic scale. For example, ⟨*haut-bas* (high-low)⟩ scale measures a symbolic height of a word concept. ⟨*bien-mal* (good-evil)⟩ scale measures moral standards associated with a word. On the ⟨*bien-mal* (good-evil)⟩ scale, the word *"Allah"* is inclined to ⟨*bien* (good)⟩ in SnText whereas it is more close to ⟨*mal* (evil)⟩ in FrText. This difference is easily understandable considering that the vast majority of the Senegalese population is Muslim, whereas many European French speaking countries have historically been at odds with Islam as shown through FrText. Similarly, a lot of words such as *pays* (country), *culture* (culture), *résident* (resident), and *norme* (norm) have contrasting conceptual values between SnText and FrText on the ⟨*blanc-noir* (white-black)⟩ scale, which obviously reflects the difference in skin color. We seek to take this approach an additional step further and expose some sensitive issues in Senegal that are hard to quantify otherwise.

2   Background and Related Work

This paper proposes a new text-based approach to study social issues of Senegal. This section summarizes selected findings that comprise the methodological foundation of our study. It also provides an overview and brief history of Senegal.

2.1   Natural Language Processing and Word Embeddings

Natural Language Processing (NLP) is a subfield of information engineering and artificial intelligence, broadly defined as the automatic manipulation of speech and text. NLP applications explore how computers can be used to understand and manipulate natural language for high-level tasks, including semantic analysis, document classification, information retrieval, and machine translation. Transforming text into something a computer algorithm can digest, or in other words, representing text numerically, typically involves feature extraction.

Words can be seen as discrete, categorical data since each word represents a distinct meaning. Feature extraction is a process of mapping from such categorical data to real-valued numbers. Conceptually, it projects a word from a vocabulary size dimension to a lower dimensional space. One of the most recent word feature learning techniques is word embedding, which represents each word as a real-valued vector based on the textual context in which the word is found [19]. It is a powerful tool to extract both semantic and syntactic meanings from a large unlabeled corpus, with the idea being that more similar words are closer to one another in the embedding space.

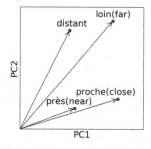
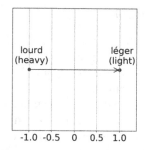

Fig. 1. Several words vectors in FrText displayed in 2-dimension using PCA. Close words have similar angles (left) and a pair of antonyms defines a semantic scale (right)

Since word embedding is a numerical vector, it is possible to measure the similarity between different words. The most widely used measure is the cosine similarity defined by $\cos(w_x, w_y) = \frac{w_x \cdot w_y}{||w_x|| \cdot ||w_y||}$, which ranges from -1 (most distant) to 1 (closest). The reasoning behind the cosine similarity is that similar words have similar semantic vectors, and the angle between the vectors is small. Additionally, by subtracting two vectors of antonyms gives a new set of direction and magnitude, which defines a conceptual semantic scale between the two antonyms (Fig. 1). The cosine similarity between a semantic scale and a word gives a conceptual value of the word on the scale.

2.2 Biases and Stereotypes Captured by Word Embeddings

Bolukbasi et al. suggested that the word embeddings trained on Google News articles exhibit female/male gender stereotypes to a disturbing extent [2]. The word embeddings pinpoint sexism implicit in the text. For instance, given an analogy puzzle, "man is to computer programmer as woman is to x", the embedding vectors find that x = homemaker. Some of the most extreme occupations as projected on the female-male gender direction are homemaker, nurse, receptionist, librarian for woman and maestro, philosopher, captain, architect for man. Caliskan et al. statistically showed that training word embeddings from text data absorbs more diverse semantic biases in the text [4]. They replicated a spectrum of known biases, such as flowers (pleasant) vs. insects (unpleasant) and European-American names (pleasant) vs. African-American names (unpleasant), using word embeddings, demonstrating that this machine learning technique can be a tool for studying historical biases and prejudicial attitudes.

Considering the fact that the word embeddings blatantly reflect the biases and stereotypes of language users, it can be generalized to capture collective minds, and even the intuition, of the language users. Also, since people in different societies have different mindsets, we believe that the word embeddings can be a tool for better understanding the culture, value systems, and contemporary issues of a society through language. Thus, when trained on Senegalese text, the embeddings can reveal varying opinions or viewpoints on social issues expressed throughout the country.

2.3   Senegal

The Republic of Senegal is situated on the westernmost point of the African continent. The official language of Senegal is French, which was inherited from the colonial era dated from the mid-15th century to 1960. Currently, almost all official documents and newspaper articles are in French, but most Senegalese people also use ethnic spoken languages, such as Wolof, native to their particular area or people. Senegal is recognized by its historical past in colonization since it was one of the major sources of slave deportation to other continents [15]. As with many developing countries, Senegal has its own potentials and problems. We believe that NLP and word embedding techniques can contribute to identifying, and even prioritizing, the country's assets and liabilities by taking advantage of unstructured text data.

3   Training Word Embeddings

Training word embeddings involves a lot of different moving parts, from collecting texts from multiple websites to using various NLP techniques to extract relevant information. This section provides explanations for the sequential steps to show how each part contributes to our analysis of public sentiments, expressed in SnText and FrText. Since both are in French, some steps are different from English NLP.

3.1   Text Processing Steps

1) Data Collection

   We collected past and current articles that are accessible through an exhaustive web search during the period of 4/1/2019–4/20/2019 from 15 newspaper websites[1] in Senegal. Although there are spoken languages like Wolof in Senegal, almost all newspapers and websites are in French. For FrText, we collected a database dump of all Wikipedia articles in French through CirrusSearch. The dump is a 4/15/2019 snapshot. We extracted plain text from the dump with Wikiextractor [1].

2) Tokenization and Lemmatization

   Tokenization is the process of breaking down a text into minimal meaningful units, called tokens. This process also splits contractions (e.g., "*l'hôtel*" → "*l*" and "*hôtel*"). Lemmatization performs vocabulary and morphological analysis of the word and converts each word to its original form (e.g., *fais, fait, faisons, faites, font* → *faire*). In many cases, especially in English, derived word forms are preserved in word embeddings for syntactic analysis such as tense and plurality. However, since our focus is semantic analysis and French

---

[1] actusen.sn,   www.dakaractu.com,   www.dakarmatin.com,   www.dakarmidi.net, www.ferloo.com,   homeviewsenegal.com,   www.impact.sn,   www.koldanews.com, www.lequotidien.sn,   www.leral.net,   letemoin.sn,   senego.com,   www.sudonline.sn, teranganews.sn.

has more numerous conjugations for subject, gender, and tense than English, we decided to perform lemmatization to decrease the size of vocabulary and better utilize the limited corpus to learn the semantics of each word.

3) Detecting Phrased Words and Text Cleaning

In English NLP, a single word is usually treated as a token. However, since a lot of words are phrased in French (e.g., *salle de bain* for bathroom), it is necessary to extract phrased words and treat them as a single token for meaningful analysis. We extracted bigram phrases from FrText using the Gensim phrase detection algorithm [16] (min_count = 200, common_terms = all articles and prepositions) and then converted the phrases in FrText and SnText into tokens by concatenating with underscores (e.g., *salle de bain* → *salle_de_bain*). We further removed non-Roman characters such as punctuation and special characters to increase system performance and changed every word to lower case to have consistent capitalization. After the cleaning, there are around 100M tokens 360K unique words in the SnText corpus, and there are 1B tokens and 7M words in the FrText corpus.

4) Training Word Embeddings

We chose the Global Vectors for Word Representation (GloVe) algorithm [14] to train our word embeddings. This algorithm first constructs a co-occurrence matrix that has the information on how frequently a word appears in high-dimensional contexts in a large corpus. Then, the algorithm reduces the dimension while retaining most of the variance in the high-dimension. The lower-dimensional matrix then becomes a set of word embeddings. We trained the word embeddings with 200 dimensions both on SnText and FrText.

3.2   Validation of the Word Embeddings

Since training word embeddings is an unsupervised machine-learning process, there are no right answers to test the result. However, it is still necessary to validate the word embeddings learned from our text collections before using them as the basis of our analysis. We first visually examined word groupings to see if similar and related words are located nearby in the semantic vector space, and spatially close words are similar and related. To visualize positions of words with 200 dimensions, we utilized T-distributed Stochastic Neighbor Embedding (t-SNE), which is a popular machine learning algorithm for visualizing high-dimensional data in two-dimensional space while keeping relative pairwise distance between points [13]. In Fig. 2, words that were far from each other in 200-D space are located far away in 2-D space, and initially close words are also converted to close ones in the lower dimension. Both word embeddings from SnText and FrText show consistent and coherent word groupings.

For more quantitative validation, we evaluated our word vectors on a word similarity task, based on French translation of the MEN dataset, which was developed specifically for computational semantics testing [3]. This dataset contains word pairs with human similarity ratings. We removed word pairs that have the same French translation (e.g., *voiture:voiture* for automobile:car) and some words that have significantly different two or more meanings in French (e.g.,

word groups in SnText   word groups in FrText

Fig. 2. Closest 5 words to *sénégal* (Senegal), *problème* (problem), and *langue* (language) in SnText and FrText. The different words in the same groups, especially in the *sénégal* group, reflect cultural, geographical contexts of the word.

essence for gasoline, essence, and species). We measured the cosine similarities of the embeddings for each pair in the dataset and then calculated the Spearman's rank correlation coefficient (Rho) with the human judgment. The Spearman's Rho is 0.48 for SnText and 0.52 for FrText. We also used the Spearman's Rho to choose parameters of our word embedding model.

4 Social Issue Analysis with Word Embeddings

The essence of word embeddings for our study is being able to measure conceptual values of a word on a chosen semantic scale in the vector space. In order to examine the possibilities of word embeddings as a social issue analysis tool, we try three approaches: 1) comparing the conceptual values of words on the semantic scales, 2) examining orders of conceptual values for a list of words, and 3) inspecting orientations of the semantic scales. We present the three approaches with three different social issues in the following subsections. For notational simplicity, we denote a semantic scale as ⟨A – B⟩ where A has (+) value and B has (−) value on the scale.

4.1 Legacy of French Assimilation

During the colonial period, the French had a policy of assimilation [12]. Influenced by their colonial ideology, the French claimed to "civilize" indigenes and taught their subjects that, by adopting French language and culture, they could eventually become black Frenchmen. The 'Four Communes' (Goree, Saint Louis, Dakar, and Rufisque) in Senegal exemplify this policy [7]. The French colonists gave citizenships to inhabitants of those towns when they were "civilized" enough. As a result, deliberately by the French or inadvertently by the public, the Senegalese society developed unfavorable views for some of its indigenous tradition [17]. We see an aspect of this legacy through the words "*tradition*

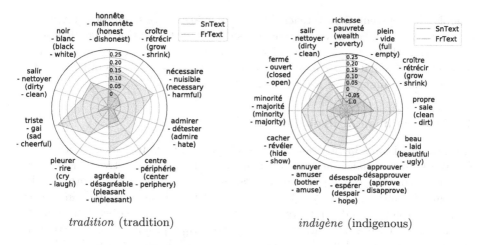

tradition (tradition)   *indigène* (indigenous)

Fig. 3. Measurement of words on semantic scales that give most contrasting values between SnText and FrText. Each spoke represents a semantic scale with positive value outside and negative value inside.

(tradition)" and "*indigène* (indigenous)" that have significantly different conceptual values in Senegalese texts (Fig. 3).

Senegalese texts collectively relate the words "*tradition* (tradition)" and "*indigène* (indigenous)" to negative words such as "*triste* (sad)", "*salir* (get dirty)", "*cacher* (hide)", and "*désepoir* (despair)". Similar words like *traditionnel* (traditional), "*culture* (culure)", and "*coutume* (custom)" have a similar tendency. Although we cannot decisively conclude that these differences originated only from colonialism, it is hard to make these disturbing connections without implicating the colonial legacy. French colonialism still has an impact on the Senegalese society in many arenas, notably in the education system. Our study suggests, for example, that language education most directly affects the perspectives of the people, including the writers of Senegalese newspapers, as captured in the SnText dataset.

The French colonists vigorously and systematically oppressed indigenous African languages, cultural values and local religious beliefs [17]. Through legislation and its administrators, the French authorities tried to maintain a highly centralized system whereby they controlled the language of instruction, the curriculum, and the aims of the education system. Therefore, throughout colonial rule, the French language was imposed, and the indigenous languages were marginalized and stigmatized [6]. After its independence, Senegal chose French as the official language of the country, keeping its high status as the language of administration, media, education, international communication, etc. Despite numerous efforts undertaken, such as recognizing indigenous languages as the national languages, the national languages remain markedly absent from the official domains. French continues to dominate virtually the entire education system, from kindergarten to university. Currently, there are no government or private schools that systematically teach literature, mathematics, physics, finance or computer sciences, or any other school subjects in the national languages [6]. Considering that language is a vehicle of tradition, custom, and culture, it is understandable that Senegalese texts have negative connotations of those words in the French language as used in Senegal.

4.2 Environmental Problems

Another possibility in utilizing the word embeddings is to look at vocabulary for well-known social issues and estimate their perceived relative order. There are many current, pressing issues in Senegal. According to the World Bank's Systemic Country Diagnostic (SCD), the poverty rate is over 40%, indicators continue to lag behind for maternal health, nutrition and education, and the labor market features high inactivity and underemployment rates [20]. We measured the following 14 words on ⟨*difficile-facile* (difficult-easy)⟩ scale to try to compare them:

> *pauvreté* (poverty), *chômage* (unemployment), *crime* (crime), *corruption* (corruption), *maladie* (disease), *illettrisme* (illiteracy), *discrimination* (discrimination), *guerre* (war), *famine* (famine), *sécheresse* (drought), *sanitaire* (sanitation), *malnutrition* (malnutrition), *inégalité* (inequality), *inondation* (flood)

The word *sanitaire* (sanitation) has a significantly high value when compared with other problems in SnText. The value is also twice as high as the same word in FrText (Fig. 4). When looking at the order of the words, we notice that the top difficult problems in SnText are closely related to water. Even the word *eau* (water) is much closer to ⟨*difficile* (difficult)⟩ side while it is almost neutral in FrText.

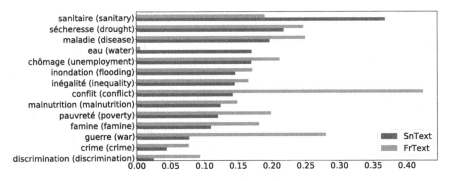

Fig. 4. Measurement of words for typical public problems on ⟨*difficile-facile* (difficult-easy)⟩ scale. The word *eau* (water) is included for further explanation.

Senegal, like all other Sahelian countries, has experienced serious droughts in the past. Today, with the impact of climate change, droughts have more serious consequences for rural and urban populations [18]. Water scarcity first impacts the agriculture sector, and the economic impacts propagate to all sectors of the agriculture-based country, which then exacerbates other major social problems such as unemployment, poverty, and malnutrition [9]. The complication arises in that water is not a solution for the problems. In big cities including Dakar, Senegal's most populated city, sanitation infrastructures, such as sewers, are in bad condition. The sanitary sewers in cities are not deep enough so that they easily overflow when rainfall exceeds their low capacity resulting in larger after-effects such as strong smells and disease spread [5]. Although social problems cannot be measured or prioritized by a single criterion, it is useful to know which issues receive most public attention. In this sense, the word embedding analysis can give a collective summary of social issues.

4.3   Past - Present - Future in Senegal

Since the semantic scales derived from the word embeddings exhibit the perspectives of people who use the language, we could further examine the perspectives by comparing different semantic scales. Specifically, it is possible to look at how orientations of different value scales are aligned. We can check the orientations of two scales by calculating the cosine distance. Normally, many semantic scales are independent. For instance, the ⟨femme-homme (woman-man)⟩ scale usually does not bear a strong relation to the ⟨difficile-facile (difficult-easy)⟩ scale. However, in SnText, we found inéteresting alignments between ⟨passé-présent (past-present)⟩ scale and others, such as ⟨abnormal-normal (abnormal-normal)⟩, ⟨amateur-profesionnel (amateur-professional)⟩, and ⟨haine-amour (hatred-love)⟩. Similar patterns can be found with ⟨passé-futur (past-future)⟩ scale (Fig. 5). When we ran the same analysis in FrText, the cosine similarities of all of these scales are less than 0.05, suggesting that they are independent in general.

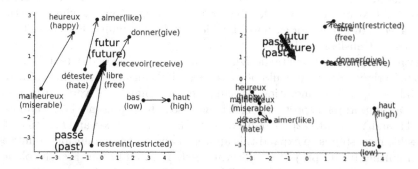

Fig. 5. Semantic scales that are aligned with ⟨passé-futur (past-future)⟩ scale (left) in SnText and in FrText (right), displayed in reduced 2 dimension using PCA.

This result could originate from Senegalese history, current optimism, or prospects for the future. Senegal's economic development trajectory supports this expectation. Senegal has one of the fastest-growing economies in Sub-Saharan Africa. Driven by diversified exports and favorable external conditions, such as the decline of global oil, commodities and food prices, the Senegalese economy has been expanding at more than 6% annually since 2014 [20]. The forecast for the future is hopeful, particularly with oil and gas production expected in 2022. Growth accelerated to over 7% in 2017, and is expected to remain over 6% in 2018 and in the following years [21].

There have been other factors that have contributed to Senegal's optimism. Senegal has been one of the most stable and politically open countries in Africa, with three major peaceful political transitions since independence in 1960 [20]. It has been considered an "exception" in West Africa where many countries have been plagued by military coups, civil wars and ethnic/religious conflicts [8]. An additional illustration is that while Sufi Islam is the dominant religious practice in Senegal, religious minorities including Christianity have long been accepted and given the freedom to practice their religion. Furthermore, Senegal has a long history of fostering global intellectual, diplomatic, and financial connections [8].

It is hard to measure such vague concepts as optimism and hope in a society since a few socio-economic indicators cannot capture the future-oriented attitudes of the population. Quantifying them, however, can help guide public policy and embrace a more holistic approach. Specifically, optimism measurement with word embeddings can supplement existing surveys such as the World Happiness Index by the United Nations.

5   Discussion

This study emphasizes the value of word embeddings in studying social issues in Senegal. Several limitations remain, and many extensions are possible. The case studies that we presented in Sect. 4 are by no means an exhaustive analysis on the issues. Each individual topic deserves a more dedicated, in-depth study. On the methodological side, we tried to find a recurrent tendency of difference between SnText and FrText under a chosen topic rather than showing statistical significance of difference for each word, which can lead to multiple research topics as shown by Caliskan et al. [4].

With a proper experimental design, such as language use of different groups in different periods in time, it could be possible to find causal relationships of why a word takes a specific connotation. Tracing semantic changes of words historically can be an important aspect of social issue research as presented by Hamilton et al. [11] and Yao et al. [22] We only compared Senegalese texts and French texts. A possible next step is to expand this approach and compare multiple countries. One promising future project is collecting texts from all former French colonies and examining their similarities and differences. One can also inspect conceptual values of words in multiple, different languages by utilizing pre-trained word embeddings, such as Word2Vec for 157 languages introduced by Grave et al. [10].

6   Conclusion

This paper demonstrated that training word embeddings from Senegalese texts and analyzing representative words can shed light on social issues in the country. While French is the official language in Senegal, we found different connotations between FrText and SnText on the same words, and we believe these different interpretations reflect the mindsets of Senegalese society. Senegalese texts collectively (1) carry unfavorable views of the country's past, including tradition, (2) voice water-related problems as the most challenging of contemporary issues, and yet (3) also expresses public optimism about the future. We believe that quantifying multi-faceted semantics of words enables researchers and policy makers to utilize textual data, especially when there are not enough structured data, such as survey and census data, to study opinions on public issues.

Acknowledgments. This research was supported by the Global Infectious Disease Institute at the University of Virginia (UVA). We also thank Senegal Research Group members at UVA for their feedback to this research: Grace Wood, Gabrielle Posner, and Jordan Beeker. We also would like to show our deepest gratitude to Fama Gueye, an exchange scholar from Université Cheikh Anta Diop de Dakar for her insights in social issues of Senegal.

References

1. Attardi, G.: WikiExtractor: a tool for extracting plain text from Wikipedia dumps (2009)
2. Bolukbasi, T., Chang, K.W., Zou, J.Y., Saligrama, V., Kalai, A.T.: Man is to computer programmer as woman is to homemaker? Debiasing word embeddings. In: Advances in Neural Information Processing Systems, pp. 4349–4357 (2016)
3. Bruni, E., Tran, N.K., Baroni, M.: Multimodal distributional semantics. J. Artif. Intell. Res. **49**, 1–47 (2014)
4. Caliskan, A., Bryson, J.J., Narayanan, A.: Semantics derived automatically from language corpora contain human-like biases. Science **356**(6334), 183–186 (2017)
5. De La Ville, P.D., Dakar, D.: Republique du senegal (2012)
6. Diallo, I.: 'To understand lessons, think through your own languages'. An analysis of narratives in support of the introduction of indigenous languages in the education system in Senegal. Lang. Matters **42**(2), 207–230 (2011)
7. Diouf, M.: The French colonial policy of assimilation and the civility of the originaires of the four communes (Senegal): a nineteenth century globalization project. Dev. Change **29**(4), 671–696 (1998)
8. Diouf, M.: Tolerance, Democracy, and Sufis in Senegal. Columbia University Press (2013)
9. Garcia, L.: Impact du changement climatique sur les rendements du mil et de l'arachide au Sénégal: Approche par expérimentation virtuelle. Ph.D. thesis, Montpellier SupAgro (2015)
10. Grave, E., Bojanowski, P., Gupta, P., Joulin, A., Mikolov, T.: Learning word vectors for 157 languages. arXiv preprint arXiv:1802.06893 (2018)
11. Hamilton, W.L., Leskovec, J., Jurafsky, D.: Diachronic word embeddings reveal statistical laws of semantic change. arXiv preprint arXiv:1605.09096 (2016)

12. Lewis, M.D.: One hundred million Frenchmen: the "assimilation" theory in French colonial policy. Comp. Stud. Soc. Hist. **4**(2), 129–153 (1962)
13. van der Maaten, L., Hinton, G.: Visualizing data using t-SNE. J. Mach. Learn. Res. **9**(Nov), 2579–2605 (2008)
14. Pennington, J., Socher, R., Manning, C.: Glove: global vectors for word representation. In: Proceedings of the 2014 Conference on Empirical Methods in Natural Language Processing (EMNLP), pp. 1532–1543 (2014)
15. Rawley, J.A., Behrendt, S.D.: The Transatlantic Slave Trade: A History. University of Nebraska Press (2005)
16. Řehůřek, R., Sojka, P.: Software framework for topic modelling with large corpora. In: Proceedings of the LREC 2010 Workshop on New Challenges for NLP Frameworks, pp. 45–50. ELRA, Valletta, Malta, May 2010. http://is.muni.cz/publication/884893/en
17. Salhi, K.: Rethinking francophone culture: Africa and the Caribbean between history and theory. Res. Afr. Lit. **35**(1), 9–29 (2004)
18. Sène, A., Sarr, M.A., Kane, A., Diallo, M.: L'assèchement des lacs littoraux de la grande côte du sénégal: mythe ou réalité? cas des lacs thiourour warouwaye et wouye de la banlieue de dakar. J. Anim. Plant Sci. **35**(2), 5623–5638 (2018)
19. Turian, J., Ratinov, L., Bengio, Y.: Word representations: a simple and general method for semi-supervised learning. In: Proceedings of the 48th Annual Meeting of the Association for Computational Linguistics, pp. 384–394. Association for Computational Linguistics (2010)
20. World Bank Group: Systematic country diagnostic of Senegal. World Bank, Dakar (2018). http://hdl.handle.net/10986/30852
21. World Bank Group: Senegal (2019). https://www.worldbank.org/en/country/senegal/overview. Accessed 6 Oct 2019
22. Yao, Z., Sun, Y., Ding, W., Rao, N., Xiong, H.: Dynamic word embeddings for evolving semantic discovery. In: Proceedings of the Eleventh ACM International Conference on Web Search and Data Mining, pp. 673–681. ACM (2018)

Deploying System Dynamics Models for Disease Surveillance in the Philippines

Joshua Uyheng[1,2]([⊠]) (ID), Christian E. Pulmano[2],
and Ma. Regina Justina Estuar[2] (ID)

[1] Carnegie Mellon University, Pittsburgh, PA 15213, USA
juyheng@cs.cmu.edu
[2] Ateneo de Manila University, Quezon City, Philippines
{cpulmano,restuar}@ateneo.edu

Abstract. Disease surveillance is vital for monitoring outbreaks and designing timely public health interventions. However, especially in developing contexts, disease surveillance efforts are constrained by challenges of data scarcity. In this work, we discuss the deployment of system dynamics simulation models to aid in local disease surveillance programs in the Philippines. More specifically, we propose that (a) available time series records of disease incidence can be used to initialize simulation models with high accuracy and interpretability, and (b) virtual experiments can be used to test various what-if scenarios in designing potential interventions. Experiments with three years of data on dengue fever in the Western Visayas region illustrate our proposed framework as deployed on the FASSSTER platform. We conclude by outlining challenges and potential directions for future work.

Keywords: Disease surveillance · System dynamics · Simulation

1 Introduction

Disease surveillance refers to a variety of methods and systems related to monitoring the spread of outbreaks in a population [2,9]. However, especially in developing nations, disease-modelling efforts can be constrained by challenges of data scarcity [4,6]. Unlike systems in more developed nations, requisite pipelines for data collection and analysis are often under-funded or require technological resources exceeding local capacities [11,12]. These obstacles limit possibilities for

This research is supported by the Philippine Council for Health Research and Development of the Department of Science and Technology (PCHRD-DOST), the Engineering Research and Development for Technology (ERDT) program, the Ateneo Social Computing Science Laboratory, and the Ateneo Center for Computing Competency and Research (ACCCRe). The views in this document are those of the authors and do not represent the official policies of the Department of Science and Technology or the Philippine government.

© Springer Nature Switzerland AG 2020
R. Thomson et al. (Eds.): SBP-BRiMS 2020, LNCS 12268, pp. 35–44, 2020.
https://doi.org/10.1007/978-3-030-61255-9_4

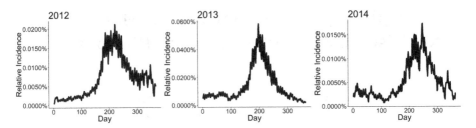

Fig. 1. Time series of annual dengue incidence in Western Visayas from 2012 to 2014.

adequate disease surveillance activities and hence the ability to respond effectively with data-driven solutions.

Leveraging existing data sources on disease incidence, we posit that a simulation framework may address these issues by producing timely and valuable analytic insights for disease surveillance [3,8,15]. We draw upon rich past studies leveraging systems of ordinary differential equations to model epidemic dynamics [1,5]. Here, we refer to such models as system dynamics models. In these models, human populations are subdivided into mutually exclusive classes corresponding to different stages of a disease. For instance, humans may be divided into susceptible sub-populations (i.e., those who may be infected but are currently disease-free) and infected sub-populations (i.e., those who are currently under the effects of the disease). Outbreak dynamics under these models are captured by the transition of human populations between susceptible and infected categories. Model parameters control these dynamics by quantifying crucial aspects of the outbreak, such as the rate at which disease is transmitted, the rate of recovery, and possibly mortality rates [10].

In this paper, we specifically deploy a simulation-based paradigm to demonstrate how: (a) model initializations can provide accurate and interpretable characterizations of local epidemic dynamics, and (b) virtual experiments may facilitate the analysis of what-if scenarios for intervention design. In the first phase of this study, high Pearson correlations and low normalized errors in comparison to historical incidence data suggest highly valid model initializations. By leveraging these validated parameter estimates in phase two, we introduce a flexible and generalizable framework for weighing relative costs and benefits of different intervention strategies. We apply our proposed framework to dengue fever in the Western Visayas region of the Philippines, specifically through its integration in FASSSTER, a local web-based disease surveillance platform.[1] We conclude by outlining challenges and potential directions for extending this work.

2 Methods

2.1 Data Collection

We performed our experiments on historical incidence of dengue fever in the Western Visayas Region of the Philippines. We specifically used three years

---

[1] FASSSTER website accessible at: https://fassster.ehealth.ph/.

Table 1. Parameters for dynamical model of dengue.

Parameter	Description	Interest
a	Transmission Rate (Vector to Human)	Estimated
b	Transmission Rate (Human to Vector)	Estimated
r	Recovery Rate	Estimated
ψ	Disease Fatality Rate	Estimated
λ_H	Human Birth Rate	Computed Directly[a]
μ_H	Human Mortality Rate	Computed Directly[a]
λ_V	Vector Birth Rate	Estimated
μ_V	Vector Mortality Rate	Estimated

[a]Using data from the Philippine Statistics Authority: https://psa.gov.ph.

worth of data obtained from the Philippine Integrated Disease Surveillance and Response database. Figure 1 visualizes the trends of these outbreaks over time. The data consisted of aggregated and anonymized electronic medical records of disease incidence alongside the date of disease onset. In 2012, a total of 11702 unique cases of dengue were recorded, followed by 22563 in 2013, and 8529 in 2014. Following procedures described by prior work [3], we extrapolated cumulative disease incidence and used them to fit our annealed system dynamics models.

2.2 System Dynamics Model of Dengue Fever

For our case study, we utilized a four-variable system dynamics model of dengue fever. As a vector-borne disease, dengue fever is modelled using interactive dynamics between human populations and populations of vectors which spread the disease, in this case *Aedes aegypti* [3,13]. The model we deployed follows the formulation given by prior work in this area [15] as presented in Eqs. 1–4. Table 1 summarizes the parameters of the given system of ODEs alongside whether or not we are specifically interested in estimating them in this work.

$$\frac{dH_S}{dt} = \lambda_H - aV_I H_S + rH_I - \mu_H H_S \tag{1}$$

$$\frac{dH_I}{dt} = aV_I H_S - rH_I - \psi H_I \tag{2}$$

$$\frac{dV_S}{dt} = \lambda_V - bV_S H_I \tag{3}$$

$$\frac{dV_I}{dt} = bV_S H_I - \mu_V V_I \tag{4}$$

Equation 1 models changes in the susceptible human population as positively driven by human birth rates and recovery from infection. Decreases in the susceptible human population are driven by natural mortality and a nonlinear term which combines the transmission rate of the disease from vectors to humans,

the current number of infected vectors, and the current number of susceptible humans. The latter nonlinear term reappears in Eq. 2, thereby increasing the
infected human population, which is in turn reduced by recoveries from infection
as well as fatalities from the disease. Similar nonlinear dynamics are represented
between Eqs. 3 and 4, driven by the transmission rate from humans to vectors, as
well as current populations of infected humans and susceptible vectors. Natural
birth and mortality rates for vectors are also accounted for in these latter two
equations.

2.3   Simulated Annealing for Parameter Estimation

For the first phase of our analysis, we initialized our system dynamics model
using historical disease incidence data. To estimate model parameters, we utilized
a simulated annealing algorithm, a metaheuristic framework for optimizing an
objective function within pre-defined parameter constraints. We carefully note
here that the meaning of 'simulated' in simulated annealing is distinct from the
system dynamics simulations which constitute our framework. We define our
objective function in terms of a normalized mean square error (NRMSE) in Eq. 5
below, where $X = [X_1, X_2, \ldots, X_d]^T \in \mathbb{R}^d$ represents a vector of daily incidence
values over a period of d days, and $\hat{X} = [\hat{X}_1, \hat{X}_2, \ldots, \hat{X}_d]^T \in \mathbb{R}^d$ represents model
estimates over the same time period.

$$f(X, \hat{X}) = \sum_{i=1}^{d} \frac{\left(X_i - \hat{X}_i\right)^2}{X_i} \tag{5}$$

This objective function expresses model errors in terms of the normalized
distance between predicted values and historical values. Normalization by the
true value at each time point controls for outlier quantities or steep differences
in disease incidence which may occur within the year. This mirrors prior work
using genetic algorithms and a similarly normalized absolute difference as an
objective [3,15].

As summarized in Algorithm 1, the simulated annealing procedure iteratively
generates new proposals for parameter estimates S_i using a *neighbor* function,
which in our case simply examines a random set of parameter values close in
Euclidean distance. Given proposed parameter estimates, Runge-Kutta numerical methods RK were used to integrate the system of differential equations
to produce predicted values of daily disease incidence $\hat{X}$ [7]. These daily estimates were used to compute the objective f against known historical values X.
New values were accepted if they produced better scores than the current best
parameters S_{best} with some exponentially defined probability controlled by a
temperature hyperparameter T. Temperature gradually lowers over time as a
function of a *temperature* function, which in our case computes a decreasing
fraction of a maximum temperature (T_{max}) divided by the number of iterations
completed. This behavior allows the algorithm to escape local optima early on
while eventually stabilizing toward a best solution in later iterations. For each

---

Algorithm 1. Simulated annealing algorithm for model initialization.

$S_{now} \leftarrow S_{initial}$
$S_{best} \leftarrow S_{now}$
$\hat{X}_{now} \leftarrow RK(S_{now})$
for i = 1 to maxiter **do**
    $S_i \leftarrow neighbor(S_{now})$
    $T_{now} \leftarrow temperature(i, T_{max})$
    $\hat{X}_i = RK(S_i)$
    if $f\left(X, \hat{X}_i\right) \leq f(X, \hat{X}_{now})$ **then**
        $S_{now} \leftarrow S_i$
        if $f\left(X, \hat{X}_i\right) \leq f(X, \hat{X}_{best})$ **then**
            $S_{best} \leftarrow S_i$
        end if
    else if $\exp\left[\dfrac{f(X, \hat{X}_{now}) - f\left(X, \hat{X}_i\right)}{T_{now}}\right] > rand(0, 1)$ **then**
        $S_{now} \leftarrow S_i$
    end if
end for
return S_{best}

---

instance that we run simulated annealing, we terminated the algorithm after 1000 iterations (*maxiter*). All computations were run on R with packages deSolve and GenSA [14,16].

2.4   Virtual Experiments for Evaluating Interventions

In the second phase of our analysis, we ran a battery of virtual experiments to evaluate the potential impacts of several intervention strategies. We were specifically interested in two types of interventions: **Strategy A** would reduce transmission from vectors to humans (e.g., mosquito nets; decrease a); while **Strategy B** would reduce vector birth rates (e.g., eradication of stagnant water sources; decrease λ_V). For both interventions, we tested six levels of varying intensity: decreasing current levels by 0% (no intervention), 0.01%, 0.05%, 0.1%, 0.5%, and 1%.

The benefits of each intervention were computed in terms of the percentage reduction of total individuals infected throughout the one-year period. Current levels were based on the best parameter estimates for each year. For increased interpretability, impacts of each strategy were further estimated using standard OLS linear regression on simulated results. Regression coefficients corresponded to the average linear effect of every percentage point of reduction in model parameters as a result of each intervention strategy. We note that for both parameter estimation and virtual experiments on intervention strategies, data as well as analysis scripts are deployed on the FASSSTER website.

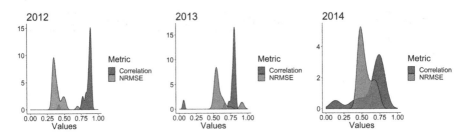

Fig. 2. Summary of annealed model performance in terms of both Pearson correlation (green) and normalized root mean square error (purple). (Color figure online)

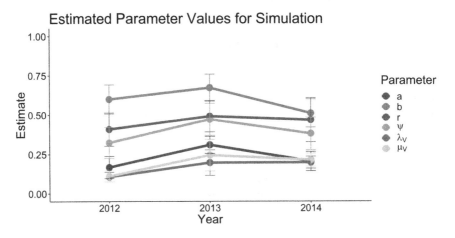

Fig. 3. Estimated parameters for initialization of system dynamics model of dengue fever. Error bars represent 95% confidence intervals.

3   Results

3.1   Model Initialization

As desired, parameter estimates generated by the simulated annealing algorithms achieved low values of the objective function (NRMSE) as well as high values of Pearson correlation (Pearson correlation). This indicates that the model matches point-wise historical data as well as its overall trends. Figure 2 shows that for the three years of disease incidence we examined, the distribution of NRMSE scores was generally right-skewed while the distribution of Pearson correlation scores was generally left-skewed. This indicated that our algorithm successfully obtained local optimum values of the objective function while increasing its overall ability to model historical dengue outbreaks. We are therefore relatively confident that we have obtained valid initializations for our simulation model from a numerical performance standpoint.

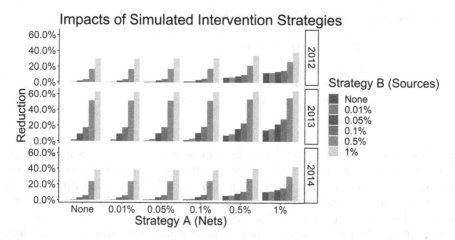

Fig. 4. Estimated reduction in dengue incidence given varying levels of implementation for Strategy A and Strategy B. Higher values indicate more effective strategies.

Figure 3 further summarizes the results of parameter estimation for each year, expressed in terms of their average values across 30 separate runs with 95% confidence intervals. A similar pattern appears to be detected for the transmission rate from vectors to humans (parameter a) and humans to vectors (parameter b), as well as disease mortality (parameter ψ), whereby the three parameters increase in 2013 and fall in 2014. From a face value standpoint, these trends may intuitively correspond to the large number of people infected in 2013 relative to 2012 and 2014. Meanwhile, recovery rates seemed relatively stable, as did parameters related to vector birth and mortality. We would also intuitively not expect significant changes in these values over the relatively short amount of time observed here.

3.2 Simulated Interventions

Figure 4 shows the potential impacts of different intervention strategies on reducing total disease incidence. Across all years, disease reduction would go above 20% at maximum levels of implementation for Strategy A and B. This indicates that even at implementation levels which effectively reduce parameter values by 1%, significant drops in disease incidence may be observed. The largest impacts were observed in our 2013 simulations, reaching over 60% in certain cases. This may be explained by the observation that 2013 historical data had the largest historical incidence of dengue to begin with.

Across constant levels of Strategy A, increased levels of Strategy B resulted in significant impacts in reducing the spread of dengue. We underscore the effect, for instance, of increasing the level of Strategy B from 0.1% to 0.5%. For 2013 data, crossing this threshold pushed disease reduction from around 20–25% to above 40%. Conversely, increasing levels of Strategy A did not result in similarly dramatic reductions in disease incidence, especially at already high levels of Strategy

Table 2. Linear regression results for average intervention impacts.

Coefficient	Estimate (Std. error)	t-value	p-value
Intercept	3.23 (1.30)	2.49	.0144
Strategy A	9.80 (2.41)	4.05	$<1 \times 10^{-5}$
Strategy B	41.83 (2.41)	17.29	$<2 \times 10^{-16}$

B. Modest gains, however, were nonetheless observed when increasing Strategy A at low levels of Strategy B. These interpretations were further borne out by our linear regression results, which explained $R^2 = 74.54\%$ of the variability in our simulations. As summarized in Table 2, Strategy B would have a statistically significant average impact of a 41.83% reduction ($t = 17.29, p < 2 \times 10^{-16}$) in total disease incidence for a full percentage point of reduction in vector birth rate. Strategy A, on the other hand, would also have a statistically significant average impact of a 9.80% reduction ($t = 4.05, p < 1 \times 10^{-5}$) in total disease incidence for a full percentage point of reduction in vector-to-human contact.

In the context of our example, these findings suggest that interventions similar to the eradication of stagnant water sources may be valuable to prioritize for reducing dengue incidence. That said, it may still be effective to implement programs like the distribution of mosquito nets should the former strategy be infeasible to perform at optimum levels.

4   Discussion

We now discuss the implications of our findings based on the performance of our proposed system dynamics framework in estimating model parameters for initializing our simulations and evaluating potential intervention strategies for reducing disease incidence. In general, we found that simulated annealing methods produced interpretable parameter estimates with decent levels of accuracy for modeling disease incidence benchmarked against historical data. This result suggests that even our relatively simple SISI model meaningfully captured the vector-borne dynamics of dengue transmission. This insight is especially valuable in light of the scarcity of rich epidemiological data in regional provinces like Western Visayas in the developing context of the Philippines, as it opens potential opportunities for data-driven investigation even in the absence of direct measurements of vector populations in the area. In this view, we highlight the flexibility of our parameter estimation procedure as an optimization method. Due to its metaheuristic nature, it is not limited by the restrictive assumptions of differentiability and convexity common in other optimization algorithms. It is also highly parallelizable and customizable with various parameter constraints which may enforce domain knowledge. Thus, our framework may readily be adapted for more complex system dynamics models of epidemics as well as possibly agent-based approaches. That said, precisely because of the non-convexity of our specified objective function, the risk of encountering local optima remains

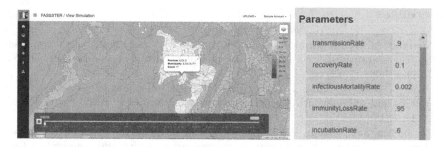

Fig. 5. Dashboard view of disease models and parameter inputs on FASSSTER. Left: Visualization of historical or simulated disease prevalence with customizable system dynamics models for different types of epidemics. Right: Parameter settings for a given disease which may be set to best parameter estimates from simulated annealing or adjusted manually for virtual experiments.

important to consider. We carefully note that model parameters achieving high levels of numerically evaluated performance are not equivalent to direct epidemiological measurements, highlighting the sustained value of human-in-the-loop principles when deploying our framework in practice.

Our proposed framework likewise demonstrated readily interpretable comparisons between different intervention strategies through the use of virtual experiments. On a conceptual level, we illustrated the impacts of targeting different drivers of disease transmission, which may be difficult to parse at face value when considering the system dynamics model on its own. From a practical standpoint, these evaluations provide intuitive value to public health officials who may wish to reason about alternative plans of action in the context of highly constrained resources. That said, we also note that the model we present does not produce exact statistics for disease reduction, as they do not encompass numerous complex factors involved in various interventions, such as the efficiency of local governments or human compliance. Hence, as above, we recommend that usage of simulated estimates be coupled with real-world assessments of feasibility and efficacy not currently encoded in the models studied.

In conclusion, we note that the tools employed in this research are in themselves not new. However, their novel combination in an interoperable fashion for disease surveillance in developing regions exemplifies the practical value such computational methods may have in real-world settings. Through their integration in FASSSTER, a local web-based platform, our proposed framework is currently being deployed in practice. Figure 5 presents a snapshot of the FASSSTER dashboard, through which users might visualize the spread of diseases governed by different system dynamics, conduct parameter estimation, or run virtual experiments. With adequate training, local analysts and policymakers may be empowered to fully take advantage of the functionalities described here in the interest of better understanding as well as mitigating the adverse impacts of infectious diseases in the region.

References

1. Andraud, M., Hens, N., Marais, C., Beutels, P.: Dynamic epidemiological models for dengue transmission: a systematic review of structural approaches. PLoS ONE **7**(11), e49085 (2012)
2. Choi, J., Cho, Y., Shim, E., Woo, H.: Web-based infectious disease surveillance systems and public health perspectives: a systematic review. BMC Public Health **16**(1), 1238 (2016)
3. Co, J., Tan, J.A., Estuar, R.J., Espina, K.: Dengue spread modeling in the absence of sufficient epidemiological parameters: comparison of SARIMA and SVM time series models. In: Proceedings of the RAIS Conference: The Future of Ethics, Education and Research, pp. 232–242. Research Association for Interdisciplinary Studies, Rockville (2017)
4. Coker, R.J., Hunter, B.M., Rudge, J.W., Liverani, M., Hanvoravongchai, P.: Emerging infectious diseases in southeast Asia: regional challenges to control. Lancet **377**(9765), 599–609 (2011)
5. Cooch, E.G., Conn, P.B., Ellner, S.P., Dobson, A.P., Pollock, K.H.: Disease dynamics in wild populations: modeling and estimation: a review. J. Ornithol. **152**(2), 485–509 (2012)
6. DebRoy, S., Prosper, O., Mishoe, A., Mubayi, A.: Challenges in modeling complexity of neglected tropical diseases: a review of dynamics of visceral leishmaniasis in resource limited settings. Emerg. Themes Epidemiol. **14**(1), 10 (2017)
7. Dormand, J.R.: Numerical Methods for Differential Equations: A Computational Approach. CRC Press, Boca Raton (2018)
8. Espina, K., Estuar, M.R.J.E.: Infodemiology for syndromic surveillance of dengue and typhoid fever in the Philippines. Procedia Comput. Sci. **121**, 554–561 (2017)
9. Kilimba, T., Nimako, G., Herbst, K.: Data everywhere: an integrated longitudinal data visualization platform for health and demographic surveillance sites. In: Proceedings of the 6th ACM Conference on Bioinformatics, Computational Biology and Health Informatics, pp. 551–552. ACM (2015)
10. Mandal, S., Sarkar, R.R., Sinha, S.: Mathematical models of malaria-a review. Malaria J. **10**(1), 1–19 (2011)
11. Nsubuga, P., Nwanyanwu, O., Nkengasong, J.N., Mukanga, D., Trostle, M.: Strengthening public health surveillance and response using the health systems strengthening agenda in developing countries. BMC Public Health **10**(1), S5 (2010)
12. Phalkey, R.K., Yamamoto, S., Awate, P., Marx, M.: Challenges with the implementation of an integrated disease surveillance and response (IDSR) system: systematic review of the lessons learned. Health Policy Plan. **30**(1), 131–143 (2013)
13. Shim, E.: Dengue dynamics and vaccine cost-effectiveness analysis in the Philippines. Am. J. Trop. Med. Hyg. **95**(5), 1137–1147 (2016)
14. Soetaert, K.E., Petzoldt, T., Setzer, R.W.: Solving differential equations in R: package desolve. J. Stat. Softw. **33** (2010)
15. Uyheng, J., Rosales, J.C., Espina, K., Estuar, M.R.J.: Estimating parameters for a dynamical dengue model using genetic algorithms. In: Proceedings of the Genetic and Evolutionary Computation Conference Companion, GECCO 2018, pp. 310–311. ACM, New York (2018). https://doi.org/10.1145/3205651.3205716. http://doi.acm.org/10.1145/3205651.3205716
16. Xiang, Y., Gubian, S., Suomela, B., Hoeng, J.: Generalized simulated annealing for global optimization: the Gensa package. R J. **5**(1) (2013)

MDR Cluster-Debias: A Nonlinear Word Embedding Debiasing Pipeline

Yuhao Du$^{(\boxtimes)}$ ⓘ and Kenneth Joseph ⓘ

University at Buffalo, Buffalo, NY 14260, USA
{yuhaodu,kjoseph}@buffalo.edu

Abstract. Existing methods for debiasing word embeddings often do so only superficially, in that words that are stereotypically associated with, e.g., a particular gender in the original embedding space can still be clustered together in the debiased space. However, there has yet to be a study that explores why this residual clustering exists, and how it might be addressed. The present work fills this gap. We identify two potential reasons for which residual bias exists and develop a new pipeline, MDR Cluster-Debias, to mitigate this bias. We explore the strengths and weaknesses of our method, finding that it significantly outperforms other existing debiasing approaches on a variety of upstream bias tests but achieves limited improvement on decreasing gender bias in a downstream task. This indicates that word embeddings encode gender bias in still other ways, not necessarily captured by upstream tests.

Keywords: Word embedding · Social bias · Debias

1 Introduction

A literature has rapidly developed around the question of how to identify, characterize, and remove bias from ("debias") word embeddings. Attempts to do so are critical in ensuring that real-world applications of natural language processing (NLP) do not cause unexpected harm. For example, word embeddings that reflect stereotypical and/or prejudicial social norms might be used as input to other algorithms that, e.g., rank men higher than more qualified women for job searches of particular occupations [2].

However, recent work has raised questions about existing efforts to measure biases in word embeddings, and our ability to debias them. With respect to measurement, Ethayarajh et al. [4] provide both empirical and theoretical evidence that the most common method of measuring bias in word embeddings, the *Word Embedding Association Test* (WEAT), provides unreliable measures of practical and statistical significance. With respect to debiasing, Gonen and Goldberg [5] provide experimental evidence that male-stereotyped words are still easily distinguishable from female-stereotyped words after running two of the most well-known methods for debiasing, the Hard-Debias method of [1] and the Gender Neutral GloVe (GN-Glove) approach [20].

© Springer Nature Switzerland AG 2020
R. Thomson et al. (Eds.): SBP-BRiMS 2020, LNCS 12268, pp. 45–54, 2020.
https://doi.org/10.1007/978-3-030-61255-9_5

These two debiasing methods, like nearly all others, operate under the assumption that social biases in word embeddings can be defined as a specific direction (or in some cases, a subspace) of the embedding space. This direction is characterized by the difference between sets of bias-defining words. For example, the Hard-Debiasing method of Bolukbasi et al. [1] approach works roughly as follows for gender debiasing. First, a "gender direction" is identified by using differences in the embedding space between sets of gender-paired words, e.g. "man" and "woman". This direction is then essentially removed from all other words,[1] with the idea being that gender will no longer be represented by the embeddings of the remaining terms because all gender information, contained on the gender direction, is now gone.

What Gonen and Goldberg show is that while this approach removes some forms of gender information, one can still easily pick up gender stereotypes in word embedding space based on different, but equally valid, definitions of bias metrics. Inspired by their work, we propose a new debiasing procedure which combines a post-processing step, introduced in [7], to unfold manifolds in high word embedding space, followed by a simple linear debiasing approach, Cluster-Debias, that finds a better direction along which to remove bias to address these cluster-based bias measures.

We evaluate our debiasing approach for several "upstream" tasks, including bias tests and word similarity tests. In addition, we ask, what does this means for downstream performance on a standard NLP task? We compare embeddings debiased using our approach with the approaches of [20] and [1] on a coreference resolution task and a sentiment analysis task. Through these efforts, the present work makes the following contributions to the literature:[2]

- We find evidence that debiased embedding clusters are partially due to manifold structure in high dimensional word embedding space.
- We introduce a new pipeline to perform debiasing, and show it can reduce the clustering-based word embedding bias measures introduced by [5].
- However, despite significant upstream improvements, our approach does not significantly decrease bias in the downstream task of coreference resolution.

2   Related Work

2.1   Bias Definition

Critical to debiasing is how bias is actually defined. The vast majority of works use a directional definition. Under this approach, a single direction in the embedding space defines a particular bias that the authors expect to exist, e.g. the "gender direction". Detractors of the directional definition of bias, like Gonen

---

[1] Except for "gender definitional" words like "king and queen".
[2] Code and data to replicate our work are at https://github.com/yuhaodu/MDR-Cluster-Debias.git.

and Goldberg, have argued that it is inappropriate, because a single gender (or race, etc.) dimension may not capture all forms of bias encoded in the data. This issue has led others to define bias in terms of clustering, or word proximity. The idea is that the removal of a single dimension, or subspace [12], is not sufficient to remove bias, in that one can easily identify terms that are close to the opposing seed terms in the original embeddings in the unbiased embeddings as well. Because of this, protected information (e.g. gender) can potentially leak to machine learning algorithms in downstream tasks. The primary contribution of our work is to propose a debiasing pipeline to resolve these *cluster-based biases*.

2.2 Debiasing Word Embeddings

Several methods have been proposed to remove social biases from various kinds of NLP methods; see Sun et al. [17] for a recent review on gender specifically. Bolukbasi et al. [1] proposed two methods for word embeddings specifically, Hard Debiasing and Soft Debiasing. These methods remove gender neutral words' projection over a gender space defined by gender definitional words. Zhao et al. [20] modify the GloVe algorithm to train debiased embeddings directly from a co-occurrence matrix by adding constraints in the training objective of GloVe [14] to force gender neutral words perpendicular to some gender space.

Except these two seminal works, several others have proposed novel methods for debiasing. Most of these have been extensions of the hard-debiasing method. [12] extend the hard debias method to the multi-class setting, [4] improve the way gender-biased words are selected, and [3] propose simpler versions of the algorithm and the use of names as a means of identifying directions in the space that represent social biases. One exception is the work of Kaneko et al. [8], who propose an autoencoder based method which is able to project current word embedding into another space which preserves the word semantic information while removing the gender bias. However, their work still evaluates results using a directional approach. The present work extends current debiasing algorithms in terms of debiasing based on recently identified cluster-based bias definition.

3 Our Debiasing Pipeline

We base our debiasing pipeline on pretrained GloVe embeddings [14]; however, the approach generalizes to any other pretrained embedding. The pipeline contains two parts: the first is a post-processing procedure, which is used to re-embed original word vectors into a new space via a manifold learning algorithm. The second is the application of a direction-based debiasing method to remove gender information in the re-embedded word vectors.

3.1 Post-processing Procedure

As a post-processing procedure, we use Manifold Dimensionality Retention (MDR) from [7]. Hasan et al. [7] are motivated by the observation that word embeddings slightly underestimate the similarity between similar words and overestimate the similarity between distant words. This indicates that word embedding space contains non-linear manifold structure. Thus, they propose the MDR to unfold the manifold structure to improve word representation and results show that re-embedded word embeddings achieve better performance in word similarity tests. Inspired by their observation and Gonen and Goldberg's observation that gendered words are easily separated by a non-linear SVM method, we believe non-linear manifold structure in the word embedding space could potentially prevent linear directional based debias method from mitigating gender bias. Thus, we apply MDR as a post-processing procedure.

In MDR, we start from an original embedding space with vectors ordered by words frequencies. We then carry out the following steps:

1. Select a sample window of vectors that are used to learn the manifold.
2. Fit a manifold learning model to the selected sample using Locally Linear Embedding (LLE) [16].
3. The resulting fitted model is then used to transform all the word vectors in the original space to the new re-embedding space.

In Step 1, a sample window is sliding on the word vectors ordered by word frequencies. The window length L and window start S of the sample window are hyper-parameters. Additional, S will decide the computational complexity on manifold learning. As shown in prior work [6], trained word embeddings are biased toward word frequency. In order to keep learned manifold from skewing towards high frequency or low frequency words, we select S as 5000. For the choice of L, we choose 1000 following the suggestion introduced in the prior work [7]. Selections of these two parameters work well in terms of preserving semantic information in word embeddings which is shown later in Sect. 5.1.

3.2   Cluster-Debias

Gonen and Goldberg show that, after *debiasing*, one can still easily cluster biased words using linear K-means clustering method. We hypothesize that this observation is due to a mismatch between the direction that previous debiasing method removes and that gender bias lies along. Thus, we propose a simple approach that incorporates a cluster-based definition of bias to perform debiasing. The procedure carried out by Cluster-Debias is as follows:

1. Identify, via a particular word pair a and b (e.g. "he" and "she"), the form of bias to be addressed.
2. Identify the bias subspace by $D_{bias} = E_a - E_b$, where E_w represents the word vector of word w.
3. Calculate the bias of word vectors along D_{bias} following the methods in [1]
4. Select the top k most biased words, i.e. the k nearest neighbors to a and b
5. Apply PCA over these $2k$ word vectors and extract the first principle component D_{pc}.
6. Debias all word vectors E_ws by removing D_{pc} from them. This can be expressed as $E'_w = E_w - \langle E_w, D_{pc} \rangle \cdot D_{pc}$.

At a high level, our approach retains much of the logic from Bolukbasi et al. [1]. However, instead of assuming that the gender direction is aligned with the word pairing(s) we identify, we instead assume that this direction can be better identified by incorporating information from the distribution of the word vectors that are proximal to a and b. We therefore assume, based on the observations of Gonen and Goldberg [5], that it is more appropriate to select a direction based on the clustered structure of the embedding space around the words of interest, rather than on those words themselves. Note that it is not guaranteed that the Cluster-Debias approach will overcome the issues with Hard-Debias. Like the Hard-Debias method, we remove only a single dimension from the embedding space. This direction is simply more informed by clustering structure than the prior work. Here, we focus on comparing to prior work, and so consider gender. Thus a and b are "he" and "she", respectively. Additionally, we set $k = 1000$ for all experiments below.

4   Evaluation Methods

There is, of course, a tradeoff between removing gender information and maintaining other forms of semantic information that are useful for downstream tasks. As such, we evaluate embeddings from bias-based evaluation measures and semantic-based evaluation measures. In addition, we are also interested in whether or not upstream evaluation results can be transferred to downstream tasks. As such, our evaluation is carried out along two dimensions – bias-based versus semantic-based and upstream versus downstream.

As an upstream measure of semantics, we focus on semantic similarity-based measures. We compute the cosine similarity between word embeddings and measure Spearman correlation between human similarity rating and cosine similarity for the same semantic relatedness datasets used to evaluate biased embeddings in prior work [18]. For downstream evaluation, we identify two NLP tasks – coreference resolution and sentiment analysis. To build coreference resolution models, we use the coreference resolution system proposed in [10]. We apply the original parameter settings for the model and train each model 100 K iterations and evaluate models with respect to their performance on the standard OntoNote v5 dataset [15]. For sentiment analysis, we train an LSTM with 100 hidden units on the Stanford IMDB movie review dataset [11] and we also leverage the model [9] to train a binary classifier on the MR dataset of short movie reviews [13].

For bias-based evaluation, we use the same six cluster-based bias measures that are proposed by Gonen and Goldberg as our upstream bias-based evaluation tasks. The first one we call *Kmeans Accuracy*. We first select the top 500 nearest neighbors to the terms "he" and "she" in the original embedding space. We then check the accuracy of alignment between gendered words and clusters identified by Kmeans. The second one we call *SVM Accuracy*. We consider the 5000 most biased words (2500 from each gender) in the original embedding space. *After debiasing*, we check the accuracy of a RBF-kernel SVM trained on a random sample of 1000 of these words (500 from each gender) predicting gender bias of the remaining 4000. The third one we call *Correlation Profession*. We extract the list of professions used in [1] and compare the correlation between the percentage of male/female socially biased words among the k nearest neighbors of the professions and their directional bias in the original embedding space. For three metrics listed above, lower scores indicate better debiasing results. The rest three are gender-related association experiments called *WEAT* introduced in [2]. Three experiments evaluate the associations between female/male and family and career words, arts and mathematics words, arts and science words respectively. For these tests, a higher p-value means lower association which indicates better debiasing results.

For downstream evaluation of bias, We again leverage the coreference model that is trained following the procedure introduced above as our model for bias-based tests. The difference between here and there is that we compare performance using the gendered coreference resolution dataset WinoBias developed by Zhao et al. [19]. The testing portion of the WinoBias dataset evaluates the extent to which a coreference resolution model exhibits gender stereotyping by assessing the degree to which it applies gender stereotypical pronouns to individuals described using a set of gender-associated occupations. They create two different datasets–"anti-stereotype", in which gender associations are reversed (e.g. "The secretary ... he"), and "pro-stereotype", in which gender associations are retained (e.g. "The secretary ... she"). Differences in performance between the two datasets are used as an indicator of gender bias in the coreference dataset and gender bias in coreference algorithm.

5   Experiments

We train GloVe [14] on a 2017 dump of English Wikipedia to obtain pre-trained 300-dimensional word embeddings for 362179 words. We then create several baselines and word embeddings debiased by our proposed methods:

GloVe: is the pretrained word embedding introduced above. This baseline denotes a non-debiased version of the word embeddings.

Hard-GloVe: We apply hard-debiasing [1] method by using released code[3] to our pretrained GloVe word embedding and obtain a hard-debiased version of the pretrained GloVE embeddings.

GN-GloVe: We apply the code[4] from original authors of GN-GloVe [20] and train our own version of GN-GloVe.

Cluster-GloVe: We apply Cluster-Debiased method to our pretrained GloVe embeddings to obtain debiased GloVe embeddings.

MDR-GloVe: We apply our Post-Processing Procedure MDR on pretrained GloVe embeddings.

MDR-Cluster: We apply the proposed Post-Processing Procedure on pretrained GloVe embedding and then use Cluster-debias method to debias it.

---

[3] https://github.com/tolga-b/debiaswe.
[4] https://github.com/uclanlp/gn_glove.

Table 1. Results for our upstream bias evaluations. The first three rows are extracted directly from prior work [5]. The last four rows are the debiased word embeddings using our proposed pipeline. Bolded results are the best-performing in each column according to the given metric.

Embedding	Kmeans Acc.	Corr. Prof.	SVM Acc.	Work/Family P-val	Math/Art 1 P-val	Math/Art 2 P-val
Original GloVe	0.999	0.820	.99			
Hard-GloVe	0.925	0.606	.89	<.0001	<.0001	.0467
GN-GloVe	0.856	0.792	.97	<.0001	<.0001	<.0001
Cluster-GloVe	**0.53**	0.74	0.80	<.0001	**0.76**	0.20
MDR-GloVe	1.000	0.88	0.99	<.0001	0.09	0.03
MDR-Cluster	0.556	**0.38**	**0.518**	0.00015	0.43	0.26
MDR-Hard	0.915	**0.38**	0.86	**0.002**	0.42	**0.51**

MDR-Hard: To test whether our Post-Processing Procedure works for other debias methods. We apply proposed Post-Processing Procedure on pretrained GloVe embedding and then use Hard-debias method to debias it.

5.1 Results

Upstream Cluster-Based Bias Test. Table 1 displays results from our upstream bias evaluations, and shows that our new debiasing strategies significantly improve over prior work. Results can be summarized as follows:

1. Cluster-GloVe outperforms GN-Glove and Hard-GloVe on all cluster-bias based tests because of following reasons. First, Post-debias Cluster Accuracy of Cluster-GloVe is 0.53, which means that debiased gendered words are not separable by K-means. Cluster-GloVe is also the most difficult to classify post-hoc using an SVM (it has lowest SVM Classifier Accuracy). And it shows no gender bias on two of the three WEAT tests (p-values of last two columns show no significant results). With respect to deficiencies in the Cluster-GloVe, embeddings still are highly separable by SVM, and as evidenced from the correlational professions experiment and the Work/Family WEAT, retain gender stereotypes for occupations.
2. Our Post-Processing method is able to help not only the Cluster-Debias method but also HardDebias. MDR-Cluster and MDR-Hard outperform Cluster-GloVe and Hard-GloVe respectively.
3. MDR-Cluster achieves the best overall performance and is the only method that prevents SVM from classifying gender stereotyped words, which validates the efficiency of our debias pipeline. But MDR-Cluster still struggles with work/family associations WEAT test.

These results provide two insights into the observations of Gonen and Goldberg. First, Cluster-GloVe, as a directional based debias method, out-performs

Table 2. Performance on co-reference resolution task for models trained using the given embedding. All performance scores are given as F1 scores. Bolded results are the best-performing in each column.

Model	OntoNote	Anti-Stereotype	Pro-Stereotype	WinoBias Mean	WinoBias Diff.
GloVe	72.49	60.995	81.535	71.265	20.54
Hard-Debias	71.87	63.27	77.69	70.48	14.42
GN-GloVe	**72.69**	65.47	81.415	73.4425	15.945
Cluster-debias	71.94	63.685	82.125	72.905	18.44
MDR	71.93	65.715	**83.59**	**74.6525**	17.875
MDR-Hard	71.70	66.18	79.78	72.98	**13.6**
MDR-Cluster	72.01	**66.73**	80.66	72.69	13.93

Hard-GloVe (also a directional based debias method) in terms of removing post-bias clusters identified by K-Means. This observation suggests that there is a mismatch between the direction that gendered words distribute along and the direction that prior debias methods remove. Second, the fact that Cluster-GloVe removes post-debias clusters identified by K-Means, but not non-linear SVM, and that MDR-Cluster removes both, suggests that manifold structure in the word embedding space is able to leak protected gender information to non-linear method (e.g. SVM). That validates our decision on using MDR to unfold manifold structure in the word embedding space as our post-processing step.

Upstream Semantic Similarity and Relatedness. We find that, compared with others, word embeddings debiased by our proposed pipeline achieve as-good or higher performance on most benchmark datasets for our upstream semantic test. The most critical comparison is to the original embeddings, where on average, MDR-Cluster achieves 60.2 Pearson correlation with the ground truth ratings on the five benchmark tasks, while GloVe achieves 56.2. This indicates that, according to the word similarity test metric, our proposed debiased pipeline can keep or amplify the semantic information in the original word embeddings.[5]

Downstream Results - Coreference Resolution. Table 2 shows the performance difference between coreference resolution algorithms based on the different debiased GloVe embeddings. Among the embeddings considered, we find that MDR-Hard and MDR-Cluster show the best performance on the Wino-Bias datasets on WinoBias Difference and the Anti-Stereotype metric. This suggests that in addition to showing improvements on the tasks studied by Gonen and Goldberg, MDR-Hard and MDR-Cluster methods we propose can attenuate more protected gender information in the word embeddings. We further can find that different methods' performances are similar on OntoNote dataset

---

[5] Full result tables are available at https://github.com/yuhaodu/MDR-Cluster-Debias.git.

which indicates that our debias pipeline doesn't deprecate the semantic information that are essential for coreference resolution. However, differences between the various debiasing strategies are limited, compared to their overall difference from the unbiased, original embeddings.

Downstream Results - Sentiment Analysis. Finally, we find that the models trained on MDR-cluster achieve a similar accuracy on sentiment classification on the MR dataset. However, using the MDR-Cluster embeddings, accuracy on IMDB dataset is 68.5% (95 % confidence interval [68.2%, 68.9%]), while using GloVe embeddings, accuracy is 80.9% ([80.5%, 81.3%]). This drop in sentiment analysis performance is indicative that debiasing along certain dimensions of stereotyping (e.g., gender), may have important downstream effects. Although the present work focused on addressing issues raised in [5], this finding on an important downstream task suggests future work is needed on this point.

6   Conclusion

The present work addresses the fact, introduced in prior work [5], that gendered terms remain clustered in the embedding space of debiased word embeddings. We propose a two-step pipeline solution to combat this issue. Our pipeline combines a post-processing step—MDR [7] and a debiasing method—Cluster Debias. It is able to outperform state-of-art debias methods on mitigating bias on the measures proposed by Gonen and Goldberg [5]. The success of our pipeline also validates our proposed reasons behind the observations made by Gonen and Goldberg. First, that there existed a mismatch between the direction that gendered terms distributed along and the direction that debiasing methods remove. And second, that the non-linear classifier (e.g. SVM) is able to separate gendered words from manifold structure in the high dimensional word embedding space.

We also test our pipeline on downstream tasks. We find that our model outperforms existing approaches on the coreference resolution tasks in terms of mitigating gender bias. However, critically, the improvement seen is not nearly as stark as our improvement over prior methods on the upstream bias tasks we consider. This indicates that word embeddings encode gender bias in *still* other ways, not necessarily captured by the cluster-based measures from prior work. As such, in order to avoid a "whack-a-mole" approach for mitigating bias, we encourage a focus on the development of more downstream tasks, relative to further upstream analysis.

References

1. Bolukbasi, T., Chang, K.W., Zou, J., Saligrama, V., Kalai, A.: Man is to computer programmer as woman is to homemaker? Debiasing word embeddings. In: Proceedings of the 30th International Conference on Neural Information Processing Systems (2016)

2. Caliskan, A., Bryson, J.J., Narayanan, A.: Semantics derived automatically from language corpora contain human-like biases. Science **356**(6334), 183–186 (2017)
3. Dev, S., Phillips, J.: Attenuating bias in word vectors (2019)
4. Ethayarajh, K., Duvenaud, D., Hirst, G.: Understanding undesirable word embedding associations. In: Proceedings of the 57th Annual Meeting of the Association for Computational Linguistics (2019)
5. Gonen, H., Goldberg, Y.: Lipstick on a pig: debiasing methods cover up systematic gender biases in word embeddings but do not remove them. In: NAACL-HLT (2019)
6. Gong, C., He, D., Tan, X., Qin, T., Wang, L., Liu, T.Y.: FRAGE: frequency-agnostic word representation. In: Proceedings of the 32th International Conference on Neural Information Processing Systems (2018)
7. Hasan, S., Curry, E.: Word re-embedding via manifold dimensionality retention. In: Proceedings of the 2017 Conference on Empirical Methods in Natural Language Processing (2017)
8. Kaneko, M., Bollegala, D.: Gender-preserving debiasing for pre-trained word embeddings. arXiv:1906.00742 [cs], June 2019
9. Kim, Y.: Convolutional neural networks for sentence classification. In: Proceedings of the 2014 Conference on Empirical Methods in Natural Language Processing (2014)
10. Lee, K., He, L., Zettlemoyer, L.: Higher-order coreference resolution with coarse-to-fine inference. In: Proceedings of the 2018 Conference of the North American Chapter of the Association for Computational Linguistics: Human Language Technologies, Volume 2 (Short Papers) (2018)
11. Maas, A.L., Daly, R.E., Pham, P.T., Huang, D., Ng, A.Y., Potts, C.: Learning word vectors for sentiment analysis. In: Proceedings of the 49th Annual Meeting of the Association for Computational Linguistics: Human Language Technologies (2011)
12. Manzini, T., Lim, Y.C., Black, A.W., Tsvetkov, Y.: Black is to criminal as caucasian is to police: detecting and removing multiclass bias in word embeddings. arXiv abs/1904.04047 (2019)
13. Pang, B., Lee, L.: Seeing stars: exploiting class relationships for sentiment categorization with respect to rating scales. In: Proceedings of the 43rd Annual Meeting of the Association for Computational Linguistics (2005)
14. Pennington, J., Socher, R., Manning, C.D.: Glove: global vectors for word representation. In: Proceedings of the 2014 Conference on Empirical Methods in Natural Language Processing, pp. 1532–1543 (2014)
15. Weischedel, R., et al.: OntoNotes v5 release. https://catalog.ldc.upenn.edu/LDC2013T19. Accessed 22 Aug 2019
16. Roweis, S.T., Saul, L.K.: Nonlinear dimensionality reduction by locally linear embedding. Science (2000)
17. Sun, T., et al.: Mitigating gender bias in natural language processing: literature review. arXiv:1906.08976 [cs], June 2019
18. Zablocki, E., Piwowarski, B., Soulier, L., Gallinari, P.: Learning multi-modal word representation grounded in visual context. In: AAAI (2017)
19. Zhao, J., Wang, T., Yatskar, M., Ordonez, V., Chang, K.W.: Gender bias in coreference resolution: evaluation and debiasing methods. In: NAACL-HTC (2018)
20. Zhao, J., Zhou, Y., Li, Z., Wang, W., Chang, K.W.: Learning gender-neutral word embeddings. In: EMNLP (2018)

Modeling Interventions for Insider Threat

Luke J. Osterritter$^{(\boxtimes)}$ (iD) and Kathleen M. Carley (iD)

Center for Computational Analysis of Complex and Organized Systems, Institute for Software
Research, Carnegie Mellon University, Pittsburgh, PA, USA
losterritter@cmu.edu, kathleen.carley@cs.cmu.edu
http://www.casos.cs.cmu.edu

Abstract. The threat of malicious actions by trusted insiders is a difficult issue
to predict and combat. This paper presents an agent-based model that simulates a
way in which social interventions can curb or eliminate the occurrence of malicious insider attacks, or "insider threats", within an organization. There are several
precursors to an individual taking malicious action against an organization. One
such factor, social isolation from one's peers, may lend itself to proactive remediation techniques. Here we attempt to model the occurrence of malicious insider
attacks for which social isolation is a precursor, then demonstrate the effects of
social interventions on the emergence of such behavior.

Keywords: Insider threat · Agent-based modeling · Cyber security

1 Introduction

When discussing "insider threat", most are referring to the occurrence of malicious
attacks by a trusted organizational insider, though there is some debate regarding who
are regarded to be "insiders" and whether or not such acts are always inherently malicious. The CERT Guide to Insider Threat [2] formalizes the definition of a malicious
insider threat as being "a current or former employee, contractor, or business who has
or had authorized access to an organization's network, system, or data and intentionally
exceeded or misused that access in a manner that negatively affected the confidentiality,
integrity, or availability of the organization's information or information systems". This
is in contrast to a related but distinct type of insider threat that is the result of individuals
not acting maliciously, but nonetheless still causing harm to their organization through
information spillage, or inadvertent leaks, as described by Carley and Morgan [3].

The problem of malicious insider attacks is difficult to study due to low base rates
of occurrence and difficulty of prediction and detection, per Andersen et al. [1]. For
this reason, and for the fact that doing experiments regarding the interplay of people
and organizations on a meaningful scale could prove difficult or impossible, treating the
study of insider threat as a modeling problem is ideal. Further, while other work has
explored the ideas of modeling the occurrence of insider threat and the importance of
both positive and negative incentives in prevention and reaction, the work in this paper
is concerned specifically with the interaction of entities in an organization, how their

© Springer Nature Switzerland AG 2020
R. Thomson et al. (Eds.): SBP-BRiMS 2020, LNCS 12268, pp. 55–64, 2020.
https://doi.org/10.1007/978-3-030-61255-9_6

links with one another can be a precursor to malicious actions and, most importantly, how the effects of social intervention strategies on the occurrence of insider threats can be modeled.

2 Background

Sokolowski et al. [7, 8] chose to apply a model of behavior described in prior literature to inform the actions of agents within an organization. Over time, the employees modeled in the simulation could become disgruntled, which in turn could lead them to becoming an insider threat. The rate at which they become disgruntled is based in some part on the culture of their organization. They sought to answer the question of "how and when an insider develops a disposition towards becoming an insider threat" but did not touch on possible remediation or intervention to the issue. Similarly, Martinez-Moyano et al. [5] employs a system dynamics approach that concerns itself with the acuity of certain types of employees to detect threats, the ability of potential insiders to successfully carry out such attacks, and the efficacy of policy-based remediation to curb such attacks as measured by the amount of profit gain or loss.

Another system dynamics approach by Sticha and Axelrad [9] explores the ways in which employee disgruntlement can increase in the face of organizational factors culminating in insider attacks, while also making use of Bayesian belief networks as a method of predicting related factors. Another compelling hybrid approach proposed by Carley and Morgan [3] uses both an agent-based and dynamic network model approach to simulate information leakage from organization over time with regard to stress on the organization, and the actions of agents placed within a social context. The information leakage described in this research is the result of unintentional actions or negligence, as opposed to the intentional effects of malicious organizational actors (Table 1).

Table 1. Docking table comparing model to Sokolowski and Moore models.

	Sokolowski	Moore	Osterritter
Modeling approach	System dynamics	System dynamics	Agent-based
Organizational factors	Yes	Yes	Yes
Intervention based on perception of support	No	Yes	No
Intervention based on network connectedness	No	No	Yes
Behavioral factors	Yes	Yes	Yes
Includes social network features	No	No	Yes

Moore et al. [6] describes a system dynamics approach that models the occurrence of insider threat within an organization, while also allowing for an analysis of revenue saved or lost by employing interventions that increase employee's perception of organizational support, thereby lessening the occurrence of disgruntlement and counter-productive workplace behaviors. Importantly, they also define three avenues in which an employee and their employer's interests can align to avoid dissatisfaction; job engagement, perceived organizational support, and connectedness at work. The model described in this paper will focus primarily on an employee's connectedness at their job and the affect that preventing this connectedness from severing can affect the occurrence of both disgruntlement and active malicious behavior.

The aforementioned insider threat models attempt to accurately represent a base occurrence of malicious insider attacks, while also considering organizational, psychological, or social factors. Some also attempt to model the efficacy of interventions on some precursor to insider threat or focus on the social network present in organizations and their resulting effects on agents. Each of these approaches has merit, and inspiration has been drawn from each of them to inform the model described in this paper.

Using the positive intervention of ensuring social connectedness has real-world applicability. Consider the case of Chelsea Manning, who was convicted in 2013 of leaking classified and sensitive documents. A New York Magazine article from 2011 [4] reported that Manning described herself as lonely, and further describes the isolation she experienced from family and fellow soldiers. While issues present in this case are varied and complex, and it is impossible to say whether improved social connectedness would have resulted in a different outcome in this instance, we can clearly see that social isolation was a prominent factor.

3 Model Details

The model is an agent-based model built in NetLogo 6.0.4 [10, 11]. The plane itself represents the organization, while each circle represents an employee within the organization. The number of nodes within the organization is configurable, as is the number of links present between all nodes at the start time; the base run and all virtual descriptions described in this paper have the node count set to 100 and the number of links set to 200. Included for awareness of the social network are monitors that display the minimum and maximum degree of any node at the current time step, as well as a graph that displays the current degree distribution of all nodes, with the Y-axis labeled "# of Nodes" and the X-axis labeled "Degree" (Fig. 1).

For all runs, on setup the number of nodes configured by the user are created and the amount of links are distributed randomly amongst the available nodes. Each agent is populated with several variables initialized; a disposition counter is set to 0, a disposition threshold and active threat threshold are set to 30 and 35 respectively, and Boolean variables representing whether the agent is an active threat or an interventionist are set to false. Each agent is placed at random X and Y coordinates, and their default color is green.

A user-configurable setting can be configured controlling the presence of a special type of agent called an "interventionist". These agents are meant to represent an organizational intervention to the problem of social isolation. These agents are blue in color, and at each fourth time step (once per month), they randomly create an additional link with another agent. This setting is configurable as off, low, medium, or high rates of intervention, which translate to the existence of 0, 1, 2, or 3 interventionist agents, respectively. Interventionist agents do not accrue disposition and are not at risk of becoming a malicious insider.

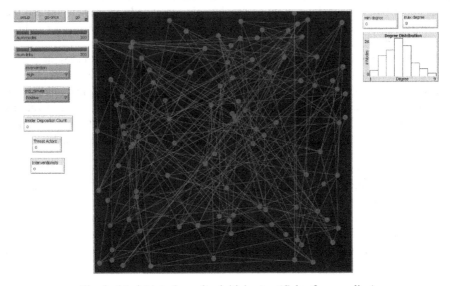

Fig. 1. Model interface after initial setup (Color figure online)

At each time step, 30% of agents with a link count above zero are asked to destroy one link. Similarly, 30% of all agents are asked to create a new link with a random agent. If an agent does not have any links after this process occurs, their disposition counter increases by a factor of 1 times the modifier based on the organizational climate. User-defined levels of organizational climate can be set as positive, neutral, or negative. A positive organizational climate will reduce all agent's accumulation of poor disposition by 10%, while a negative climate will increase the accumulation by 10%. A neutral climate does not have an effect on this rate. Once an agent reaches its disposition threshold, its color becomes white. Agents who then break their threat threshold are shown as red.

The results of the base runs of the model, with the organizational climate set to neutral, the intervention level set to off, and the default of 100 nodes and 200 links are described in Table 2.

Table 2. Base run details

	Time 1040, 1 run	Time 1040, 20 runs
Intervention level	Off	Off
Organizational climate	Neutral	Neutral
Interventionists	0	0
Agents with disposition above threshold	28	22.65 (avg) 4.09 (stdev)
Active malicious insiders	7	8.8 (avg) 2.82 (stdev)

4 Virtual Experiments

4.1 Experimental Design

The three virtual experiments conducted with this version of the model were chosen to highlight the efficacy of social intervention on various levels of organizational climates, while also providing a comparison with the base model run. The results of each experiment after one run and 20 runs are described in the tables below, with a discussion following. The organizational climate and social intervention level are manipulated as independent variables, while the occurrence of active malicious insiders and disgruntled employees are dependent variables.

For the purposes of these experiments all other levels, including the intrinsic agent disposition thresholds for both disgruntlement and active insider behavior, are held constant.

4.2 Virtual Experiment 1

Virtual experiment 1 details an organization with a neutral climate and a low level of intervention. This would be representative of an organization for which employees do not harbor strong positive or negative feeling, and for which the organization has recognized the problem of social isolation and taken basic steps to prevent its occurrence (Table 3 and Fig. 2).

When compared to the base run, we can see that the number of active insider threats has decreased, on average, by about half. This suggests that even organizations that are not explicitly viewed negatively by employees would still benefit by taking steps to maintain social connectedness between their employees.

4.3 Virtual Experiment 2

The second virtual experiment describes an organization that is perceived unfavorably by its employees, and one that is taking only basic steps to prevent the occurrence of social isolation of its employees (Table 4 and Fig. 3).

Table 3. Virtual experiment 1 details – neutral organizational climate with low intervention

	Time 1040, 1 run	Time 1040, 20 runs
Intervention level	Low	Low
Organizational climate	Neutral	Neutral
Interventionists	1	1
Agents with disposition above threshold	6	10.65 (avg) 2.23 (stdev)
Active malicious insiders	2	3.55 (avg) 1.64 (stdev)

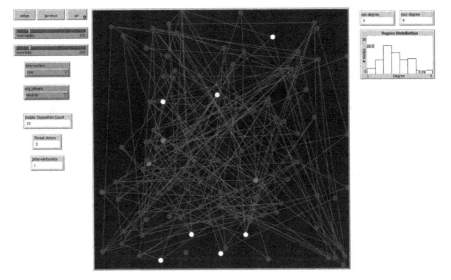

Fig. 2. Results for one run of virtual experiment 1 (Color figure online)

These results suggest that a negative organizational climate has a strong effect on the emergence of disgruntled employees and active insider threats, though taking steps to curb social isolation does have some mitigating effect. Further, it suggests that even if an organization with a negative climate is taking rudimentary steps to improve employee isolation, a greater effort may be necessary to compensate for the poor climate its employees are experiencing.

4.4 Virtual Experiment 3

The final virtual experiment detailed in this paper represents an organization that is not viewed favorably by its employees, but one in which the organization recognizes that fostering social connections between its employees is an important endeavor (Table 5 and Fig 4).

Table 4. Virtual experiment 2 details – negative organizational climate with low intervention

	Time 1040, 1 run	Time 1040, 20 runs
Intervention level	Low	Low
Organizational climate	Negative	Negative
Interventionists	1	1
Agents with disposition above threshold	12	15.6 (avg) 3.73 (stdev)
Active malicious insiders	8	7.5 (avg) 2.31 (stdev)

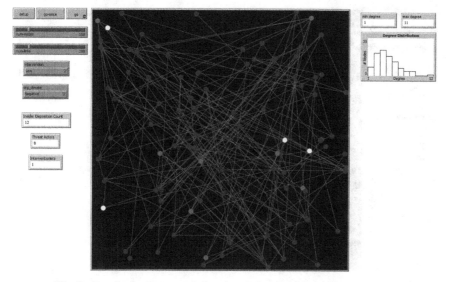

Fig. 3. Results for one run of virtual experiment 2 (Color figure online)

The results of this experiment suggest that for even a negative level of organizational climate, a high level of social intervention on behalf of the organization can drastically mitigate the occurrence of employee disgruntlement and realized acts of malicious insider actions. While this experiment accounts for only one avenue by which insider threat can occur within an organization, it does make a strong case for the importance of positive social intervention for the mitigation of malicious behavior.

Table 5. Virtual experiment 3 details – negative organizational climate with high intervention

	Time 1040, 1 run	Time 1040, 20 runs
Intervention level	High	High
Organizational climate	Negative	Negative
Interventionists	3	3
Agents with disposition above threshold	1	2 (avg) 1.55 (stdev)
Active malicious insiders	0	.85 (avg) .081 (stdev)

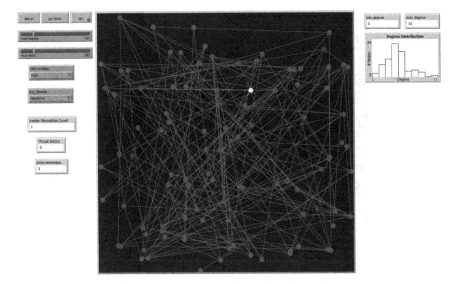

Fig. 4. Results for one run of virtual experiment 3 (Color figure online)

5   Discussion

The virtual experiments described above reveal a scenario in which social interventions can help to reduce or eliminate those instances of insider threat which feature social isolation as a precursor. In a neutral organizational climate, even a low intervention rate can reduce the number of malicious insider occurrences by half, whereas employing a high level of intervention could possibly eliminate instances of insider threat in organizations with a negative climate.

It should be mentioned that a disgruntled employee will not, on some timeline, become an insider threat for certain. Disgruntlement alone is not enough to cause a person to act maliciously against their employer, or else anyone who leaves a job would also act against their former organizations. However, it can be, when coupled with other factors such as, but not limited to, hostile behavior, family life, or organizational changes, be a precursor to becoming an active malicious insider. It is an important precursor that warrants representation in the model.

It is our belief that this first version of the model provides a strong proof-of-concept for realizing the social interplay at work in organizations, the cause and occurrence of malicious insider attacks, and possible intervention strategies. Importantly, it furthers the notion that positive incentives and interventions are a powerful tool to use against insider threat.

However, there is much future work to be done. One area in which the model can be strengthened is in its formation of social networks. The current social network substantiation only depicts links between employees within an organization; link creation and removal is stochastic, though a more realistic approach may be to model a slower ebb and flow of social links with more rules for social affinity.

Creating networks that exhibit a more defined, realistic community structure would strengthen face validity, as would modeling not only social links within the organization, but links of agents to coworkers, family, and outside agents - those who would solicit the actions of an insider for their own benefit. Similarly, modeling of the organization as an agent itself could prove beneficial, as well as modeling other organizations, such as industry competitors or adversarial regimes.

There are ways in which psychological factors can be measures which could help provide validation for models of insider threat. These could be measured through employee surveys, records of managerial complaints, or empirical observation. To what degree such data could be collected would depend on the nature of the organizations themselves (for instance, whether a government entity or a corporation), and which laws, policies, and organizational cultural norms would apply. It would be valuable for future work to identify which data could be measured and to what degree across organizations in different industries.

The next iteration of this model will also account for all three avenues of aligning employee and employer needs described by Moore et al. [6], to include perceived organizational support and job alignment, as well as social connectedness as we have modeled here. We believe it is possible that understanding the social network of people within organizations with regards to more precursors to disgruntlement will lead to new avenues of understanding and further methods of intervention to prevent insider threat.

6   Conclusion

We have introduced an agent-base model to simulate the occurrence of insider threat within an organization based primarily on the presence or absence of socially isolated employees. We conducted a set of three virtual experiments to assess the occurrence of active malicious insider activity in organizations with varying levels of hostility and varying levels of social intervention. This is the first step in work that will explore the power of agent-based models and social network analysis to perceive and understand the problem of insider threat and the role of positive interventions on its occurrence.

References

1. Andersen, D.F., et al.: Preliminary system dynamics maps of the insider cyber-threat problem. In: Proceedings of the 22nd International Conference of the System dynamics Society, pp. 25–29 (2004)
2. Cappelli, D.M., Moore, A.P., Trzeciak, R.F.: The CERT guide to insider threats: how to prevent, detect, and respond to information technology crimes (Theft, Sabotage, Fraud). Addison-Wesley, Boston (2012)
3. Carley, K.M., Morgan, G.P.: Inadvertent leaks: exploration via agent-based dynamic network simulation. Comput. Math. Organ. Theory **22**(3), 288–317 (2016). https://doi.org/10.1007/s10588-016-9215-3
4. Fishman, S.: How bradley manning became one of the most unusual revolutionaries in american history. N. Y. Mag. (2011) https://nymag.com/news/features/bradley-manning-2011-7/
5. Martinez-Moyano, I.J., Rich, E., Conrad, S., Andersen, D.F., Stewart, T.R.: A behavioral theory of insider-threat risks. ACM Trans. Model. Comput. Simul. **18**(2), 1–27 (2008). https://doi.org/10.1145/1346325.1346328
6. Moore, A.P., et al.: The Critical role of positive incentives for reducing insider threats. SEI Tech. Rep., SEI-2016-T, 1–30 (2016) http://www.sei.cmu.edu
7. Sokolowski, J.A., Banks, C.M.: An agent-based approach to modeling insider threat. In: Simulation Series, vol. 47, pp. 36–41 (2015). https://www.scopus.com/inward/record.uri?eid=2-s2.0-84937798371&partnerID=40&md5=b6308a2e815ab9f0c3493e0dbc56b0af
8. Sokolowski, J.A., Banks, C.M., Dover, T.J.: An agent-based approach to modeling insider threat. Comput. Math. Organ. Theory **22**(3), 273–287 (2016). https://doi.org/10.1007/s10588-016-9220-6
9. Sticha, P.J., Axelrad, E.T.: Using dynamic models to support inferences of insider threat risk. Comput. Math. Organ. Theory **22**(3), 350–381 (2016). https://doi.org/10.1007/s10588-016-9209-1
10. Wilensky, U.: NetLogo (1999). http://ccl.northwestern.edu/netlogo/. Center for Connected Learning and Computer-Based Modeling, Northwestern University, Evanston, IL
11. Wilensky, U., Rand, W.: NetLogo Random Network model (2008). http://ccl.northwestern.edu/netlogo/models/RandomNetwork. Center for Connected Learning and Computer-Based Modeling, Northwestern Institute on Complex Systems, Northwestern University, Evanston, IL

Validating Social Media Monitoring: Statistical Pitfalls and Opportunities from Public Opinion

Michael C. Smith[✉][iD], Thomas A. Mazzuchi[iD], and David A. Broniatowski[iD]

The George Washington University, Washington, DC, USA
mikesmith@gwu.edu

Abstract. Social media are a promising new data source for real-world behavioral monitoring. Despite clear advantages, analyses of social media data face some challenges. In this paper, we seek to elucidate some of these challenges and draw relevant lessons from more traditional survey techniques. Beyond standard machine learning approaches, we make the case that studies that conduct statistical analyses of social media data should carefully consider elements of study design, providing behavioral examples throughout. Specifically, we focus on issues surrounding the validity of statistical conclusions that may be drawn from social media data. We discuss common pitfalls and techniques to avoid these pitfalls, so researchers may mitigate potential problems of design.

Keywords: Social media monitoring · Validity · Study design · Public opinion

1 Introduction

Social media are a promising new source of big data for surveillance of public behavior, with myriad applications including disaster response, public health, and political views [e.g. 3,20,28]. Social media possess significant potential to enable large-scale statistical analysis of population trends with their breadth and depth of data, lack of response bias, and access to minority viewpoints [12,15,19,27,29]. However, they also possess disadvantages that should be addressed if we are to leverage their potential. Because of their relative novelty, social media's weaknesses are not yet well-characterized [15]. In contrast, traditional public opinion surveys have well-known and well-studied limitations including cost, limited coverage of minority populations, and non-sampling biases associated with response, measurement, and nonresponse [2,6,17,23,39]. High-quality research takes such threats to validity [11] into account when designing surveys and applying statistical methods when analyzing results. This paper makes the case that studies conducting statistical analyses of social media data should account for similar elements of study design that affect validity.

The outline of this paper is as follows. The next section discusses design elements of social media research that might impact their statistical analysis.

© Springer Nature Switzerland AG 2020
R. Thomson et al. (Eds.): SBP-BRiMS 2020, LNCS 12268, pp. 65–74, 2020.
https://doi.org/10.1007/978-3-030-61255-9_7

Each of four subsections includes corresponding lessons learned from public opinion research using surveys [e.g., 2, 29]. To achieve requisite validity, it is critical that social media studies handle heterogeneity of respondents, control variance from the social media setting, properly estimate effect sizes, and decide representativeness vs nuance; statistical tools may be productively imported. The final section concludes with discussion and implications for research using social media data.

2   Threats to Statistical Conclusion Validity on Social Media

[37] defines four types of research validity relevant to drawing conclusions from data: statistical conclusion validity, construct validity, internal validity, and external validity. Whereas social media data are relatively insensitive to threats to external validity due to their being observed "in the wild", conclusions based on this organic data are especially vulnerable to the other three types [37]. In this paper, we focus on threats to statistical conclusion validity that researchers may encounter when analyzing social media data[1]. Statistical conclusion validity refers to whether an association between variables is observable, reasonable, and trustworthy. In what follows, we provide an organizing taxonomy of broad themes, building upon the statistical and experimental design literatures to enable researchers to address challenges to statistical conclusion validity on social media.[2] Specifically, we incorporate lessons learned from the literature on measuring public opinion using surveys, the gold standard for monitoring constructs like behavior or culture in a population. Major threats include heterogeneity of units, extraneous variance in the experimental setting, and inaccurate estimation of effect sizes such as due to invalid distributional assumptions [37]; one may also import statistical tools and tests. We illustrate these lessons as they relate to the validity of social media research with several examples, including using Twitter to investigate vaccine hesitancy and refusal.

2.1   Threat 1: Heterogeneity of Units

Heterogeneity of units refers to a situation in which instances of one's unit of analysis, e.g., experimental subjects or social media accounts, cannot be assumed to be exchangeable; increased variance related to variables of interest could obscure relationships that social media monitoring wants to observe. One relevant example of heterogeneity of units may be due to variance within demographic categories. For example, [34] found that African Americans as a whole are less likely to report vaccine uptake than Caucasians. However, reported vaccination behavior among African-Americans varied significantly with several within-group factors, including education, trust in government, and perceived

---

[1] See [10] for discussion of the remaining types of validity in a social media context.

[2] See [31] for an extensive list of challenges on social data beyond those discussed here.

risk [33]; this highlighted significant heterogeneity that was initially unexamined [34]. Similar concerns apply to social media users who may vary significantly in unexpected ways. For example, Twitter accounts may represent individual users, news organizations, government agencies, corporate entities, bots, etc., each of which may display different behaviors [42]. If researchers assume these accounts are all one type, their different behaviors could undermine results. This highlights the need to control for important covariates. Just as we control for e.g., personality differences in surveys, existing and future work [e.g., 36,41] can control for differences in sharing and use of social media associated with known and inferable account features. This would increase conclusion validity when monitoring behavioral or cultural factors.

2.2   Threat 2: Extraneous Variance in Experimental Setting

Not all questions can be answered in social media settings, despite their having copious amounts of data. Behavioral and cultural studies should ensure their chosen setting can support their desired analyses. For example, prior qualitative studies may provide insight into whether certain types of content are likely to be present and relevant, such as [21] which documents common tropes underlying anti-vaccine content online.

On the other extreme, extraneous variance may result from undetected, and perhaps undetectable, behaviors that "pollute" samples. For example, [26] illustrated that Google Flu Trends prominently biased its results towards media coverage, instead of actual flu infection. This biased many studies and results using the Trends, until future work such as [9] addressed the problem to achieve better national-level correlations.

As another example, recent work has highlighted that social "bots" (i.e., automated accounts) may artificially alter proportions of online content reflecting public opinion. Although this problem is not fully characterized, leading algorithms such as Botometer [14] aim to assign a score indicating likelihood of an account being a bot. To illustrate the potential impact and reach of social bots, we randomly sampled 10,000 tweets from our vaccine dataset [15], and ran Botometer over the associated 8,604 users. Botometer displays its output in quintiles, which can be roughly interpreted as having increasing likelihoods of being a bot. Figure 1 indicates that the vast majority of accounts are of uncertain provenance, and cannot be classified with high confidence as either human or bot – said another way, the majority of bots are currently undetectable. In addition, Botometer could not score 19% of accounts (reasons for this include accounts that have been terminated, perhaps because of violations of Twitter's terms of service). While segmenting by bot-like behavior may hold promise to identify meaningful social effects [8], this depends on detection algorithms. Recent work has succeeded in progressing this detection [4,24, e.g.], though the cat-and-mouse situation is rapidly evolving. This potentially widespread presence of bots on social media constitutes a source of unknown variance that requires future research to characterize.

In principle, one could control for this by segmenting accounts by bot scores. However, this trades statistical power for generalizability because of the relatively small proportion of accounts with low bot/high human likelihoods. Furthermore, this may introduce sampling bias because human accounts that nevertheless display bot-like behavior would be excluded from the sample. Finally, even if bots are identified, they differ from one another in their behaviors (e.g., social bots may pose as people, or news bots may re-post news stories), and so may contribute different sources of variance in social monitoring.

2.3 Threat 3: Inaccurate Estimation of Effect Sizes

One primary source of inaccuracy when estimating effect sizes in behavioral studies is due to incorrect distributional assumptions [37]. Especially on social media, assumptions like normality may not hold because of network effects, such as those driving shares, likes, or use of hashtags [e.g. 13, 25]. These typically require statistical characterization and transformation prior to analysis. For example, the vast majority of messages on Twitter are never retweeted. This means common techniques to analyze behaviors exhibited in those messages, such as regression, Student's t-test, or Analysis of Variance (ANOVA), may generate inaccurate results. Under these circumstances, one may consider separate analysis of messages that are shared more than some threshold versus those that are not. For instance, one may use a logistic regression to determine the factors increasing the likelihood of at least one share [as in 7]. A secondary analysis may examine those messages that are shared more than some threshold; however, these data are still frequently not normally distributed, violating regression assumptions unless transformed. For example, the distribution of tweets per follower that have been retweeted at least once, after applying a logit transform, respects normality assumptions - the corresponding analysis predicts changes in the log-odds of a given follower retweeting an article as opposed to total number of retweets.

2.4 Threat 4: Incorporate Statistical Controls from Public Opinion

Social media monitoring may import various statistical controls from the literature on surveying public opinion to evaluate assumptions and underscore results. In the case of probability sampling, these tests check representativeness and proper population coverage. In the case of nonprobability sampling, these tests trade representativeness for validity, along with detailing specifics of study design.

Decide Representativeness vs. Nuance. Not all studies require representativeness, but designs should account for necessary differences. Public opinion studies decide between representing a population of interest and understanding nuances of a specific group or idea. If appropriate, social media research need not claim representativeness, instead relying on nonprobability sampling [as suggested in e.g. 35]. For example, if a nonprobability sampling study aims to study a specific construct, selecting information based on that construct may provide another window into the conversation beyond traditional surveys. For instance, [15] restricted their analysis to vaccine-relevant conversation using a pipeline of keyword and machine-learning classifiers. Building upon this data, we segmented tweets into latent topics using Latent Dirichlet Allocation [5] and conducted a Gi-* statistical hotspot analysis [18], to determine geospatial locations where Twitter users were most likely to tweet about these topics. Here, we make no claims about the representativeness of our data – rather, we simply aim to illustrate how vaccine conversations can vary spatially. It is interesting that discussions of the Californian vaccination bill appear in Ohio and the Appalachian area, suggesting a direction for future work; see Fig. 2. Such nonprobability sampling is powerful to understand nuances among ideas and subgroups [1], if appropriately validated.

By making appropriate choices in data, some studies can perform broad population-level surveillance without true representativeness or individual-level statistics. For example, [9], used Twitter data to track incidence of influenza infection in the United States, validating their model against Influenza-Like Illness (ILI) statistics provided by the US Centers for Disease Control and Prevention (CDC). Although Twitter data is notably not representative of the overall US population [16], this approach was able to improve forecast accuracy when compared to best-of-breed influenza prediction models [32].[3]. This approach may have been successful in large part because the influenza virus does not differentiate between human hosts, meaning that representativeness may not be necessary. In contrast, this broad approach may not succeed if heterogeneity in a sample affects the variable of interest. For example, behaviors may depend on subject-level characteristics, such as how vaccination may depend on trust in government, perceptions of risk, and other factors of personality. Some of these factors may also vary with demographic features, meaning that representativeness along these factors and prediction at the individual level may be necessary to make accurate predictions.

When true representativeness is needed on social media monitoring, more research is needed into how to characterize social media users. For example, it is notoriously difficult to infer the demographics of these users; nevertheless, recent advances [e.g. 22,40] may be able to provide enough accuracy to address potential concerns associated with under- or over-represented groups. However, these algorithms still require significant development and testing to establish reliable results. One barrier to progress in this area is the absence of a technique to determine "ground truth". For example, results of state-of-the-art age and gender classifiers applied to vaccine-related tweets indicate a significant over-representation of male users (79%). These results differ dramatically from Pew center survey data indicating a much more balanced gender distribution on Twitter [50%; 12,16]. In part, this is due to unstated assumptions underlying machine learning models. Specifically, the applied algorithm assigns accounts to "male"

---

[3] These population-level correlations, while a limited success, are a far cry from individual-level responses considered gold-standard [1,2].

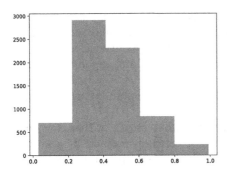

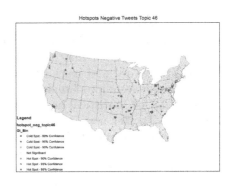

Fig. 1. Histogram of bot scores of 8604 accounts in vaccine tweet dataset. The distribution of bot scores differs significantly from normality as exhibited by an apparent right tail (M = 0.43, SD = 0.17; Med = 0.41; p < 0.001).

Fig. 2. Geographic hotspots of vaccine-negative discussion related to the California government's bill eliminating exemptions from vaccinations in schoolchildren. Higher confidence (more redness) indicates more statistically significant differences from surrounding discussions (Color figure online)

in the event of insufficient evidence – the classifier does not output an "uncertain" category. It is important that machine learning tools make such biases transparent, such that they may be understood and, if necessary, resolved. With reliable, unbiased demographic inference, weighting could address representativeness issues [38]. In sum, designers should consider whether their social media research requires representativeness or nuance, and then leverage appropriate tools to increase validity while recognizing potential associated limitations.

Statistical Tools from Public Opinion. Presuming representativeness is necessary and demographic inference is reliable, several techniques may be adopted wholesale from literature surveying public opinion and applied to social media analyses. Specifically, to ensure probability sampling produces samples that are representative of the population, studies may employ pre- and post-weighting [38]. Weights in these techniques may be informed by the population of interest (for example, demographics might be informed by census information). In addition, survey researchers conduct statistical tests, such as chi-square tests, to ensure samples appropriately cover their respective populations. These techniques may be productively used in social media research that aims for representativeness.

The quality of a given sample that aims to be representative may be evaluated in a straightforward manner and public opinion studies use well-defined statistical tools to evaluate quality of survey results. For example, [43] used t-tests to compare an observed survey error rate with error rates from other surveys. Similarly, high-validity social media research for public opinion evaluates errors at two stages: during and after inference. Inference tools based on machine learning use canonical measures (such as accuracy, precision, recall, and F-score) to evaluate the quality of inference algorithms [e.g., as in a prominent sentiment-evaluation competition; 30]. One must also evaluate data obtained after inference. For example, the means of the F-scores of two demographic inference algorithms may be compared to see if they differ, on average, across a range of holdout sets. Studies could also evaluate convergent validity, as [20] correlated Twitter conversations indicating vaccine intention and receipt with CDC measures of uptake.

3   Conclusion Validity on Social Media: A Checklist

This paper proposes design-related and statistical controls for researchers performing statistical studies of social media data with behavioral examples. Specifically, we focus on possible threats to statistical conclusion validity and propose solutions based on techniques used by survey researchers. As with traditional surveys, researchers should "provide sufficient details about their methods to enable the data user to judge the validity of any claims made" [1]. In particular, social media researchers would do well to consider heterogeneity of their users and accounts; address extraneous variance from the organic setting of social media, such as from bots; properly transform data to estimate effect sizes; and decide representativeness vs nuance, importing appropriate statistical tests to check quality of public opinion surveillance.

We conclude with a checklist aimed at a researcher new to using social media for monitoring to illustrate common threats to validity and techniques to address them.

- Would differences between social media users affect observations of interest? If so, can study measures capture this heterogeneity?
- Have organic sampling frames been investigated?
  - Is the social medium of choice appropriate for the data of interest? Is enough relevant data present?
  - To what degree do social bot accounts influence content and opinion, both in overall data, and among users of interest?
- Have appropriate assumptions been tested (e.g., normality)? Have proper transformations been applied, so that analyses can accurately estimate effect sizes?
- Can statistical techniques be leveraged in study design? Does a study need representativeness or to understand nuance?
  - Can studies employ weighting techniques to check for representativeness?
  - Have study errors been quantified, both during the inference process and when analyzing results from it?

Despite potential challenges to research validity, studies of social media data present a golden opportunity to understand human behavior. By leveraging advances in public opinion research for social media, we "remove the questionnaire from the research process, [and] we are left with the type of natural observation that is valued by many. . . to study behavior without influencing it" [29].

References

1. Baker, R., et al.: Summary report of the AAPOR task force on non-probability sampling. J. Surv. Stat. Methodol. **1**(2), 90–143 (2013)
2. Baker, R., et al.: Evaluating Survey Quality in Today's Complex Environment - AAPOR, May 2016
3. Beauchamp, N.: Predicting and interpolating state-level polls using Twitter textual data. Am. J. Polit. Sci. **61**, 490–503 (2016)
4. Beskow, D.M., Carley, K.M.: Bot conversations are different: leveraging network metrics for bot detection in Twitter. In: 2018 IEEE/ACM International Conference on Advances in Social Networks Analysis and Mining (ASONAM), pp. 825–832. IEEE (2018)
5. Blei, D.M., Ng, A.Y., Jordan, M.I.: Latent Dirichlet allocation. J. Mach. Learn. Res. **3**(Jan), 993–1022 (2003)
6. Bonevski, B., et al.: Reaching the hard-to-reach: a systematic review of strategies for improving health and medical research with socially disadvantaged groups. BMC Med. Res. Methodol. **14**, 42 (2014)
7. Broniatowski, D.A., Hilyard, K.M., Dredze, M.: Effective vaccine communication during the disneyland measles outbreak. Vaccine **34**(28), 3225–3228 (2016)
8. Broniatowski, D.A., et al.: Weaponized health communication: Twitter bots and Russian trolls amplify the vaccine debate. Am. J. Public Health **108**(10), 1378–1384 (2018)
9. Broniatowski, D.A., Paul, M.J., Dredze, M.: National and local influenza surveillance through Twitter: an analysis of the 2012–2013 influenza epidemic. PLoS ONE **8**(12), e83672 (2013)
10. Broniatowski, D.A., Tucker, C.: Assessing causal claims about complex engineered systems with quantitative data: internal, external, and construct validity. Syst. Eng. **20**(6), 483–496 (2017)
11. Campbell, D.T., Stanley, J.C.: Experimental and Quasi-Experimental Designs for Research, 2nd Print edn. Houghton Mifflin Comp, Boston (1967). oCLC: 247359300
12. Culotta, A., Ravi, N., Cutler, J.: Predicting Twitter user demographics using distant supervision from website traffic data. J. Artif. Intell. Res. **55**, 389–408 (2016)
13. Cunha, E., Magno, G., Comarela, G., Almeida, V., Gonçalves, M.A., Benevenuto, F.: Analyzing the dynamic evolution of hashtags on Twitter: a language-based approach. In: Proceedings of the Workshop on Languages in Social Media, pp. 58–65. Association for Computational Linguistics (2011)
14. Davis, C.A., Varol, O., Ferrara, E., Flammini, A., Menczer, F.: BotOrNot: a system to evaluate social bots. arXiv:1602.00975 [cs], pp. 273–274 (2016)
15. Dredze, M., Broniatowski, D.A., Smith, M.C., Hilyard, K.M.: Understanding vaccine refusal: why we need social media now. Am. J. Prev. Med. **50**(4), 550 (2016)
16. Duggan, M., Brenner, J.: The Demographics of Social Media Users – 2012, February 2013
17. Fitzgerald, R., Fuller, L.: I hear you knocking but you can't come in: the effects of reluctant respondents and refusers on sample survey estimates. Sociol. Methods Res. **11**(1), 3–32 (1982)
18. Getis, A., Ord, J.K.: The analysis of spatial association by use of distance statistics. Geograph. Anal. **24**(3), 189–206 (1992)
19. Groves, R.M.: Three eras of survey research. Public Opin. Q. **75**(5), 861–871 (2011)
20. Huang, X., et al.: Examining patterns of influenza vaccination in social media. In: AAAI Joint Workshop on Health Intelligence (W3PHIAI) (2017)

21. Kata, A.: Anti-vaccine activists, web 2.0, and the postmodern paradigm – an overview of tactics and tropes used online by the anti-vaccination movement. Vaccine **30**(25), 3778–3789 (2012)

22. Knowles, R., Carroll, J., Dredze, M.: Demographer: extremely simple name demographics. In: NLP+ CSS 2016, p. 108 (2016)

23. Krumpal, I.: Determinants of social desirability bias in sensitive surveys: a literature review. Qual. Quant. **47**(4), 2025–2047 (2013)

24. Kudugunta, S., Ferrara, E.: Deep neural networks for bot detection. Inf. Sci. **467**, 312–322 (2018)

25. Kwak, H., Lee, C., Park, H., Moon, S.: What is Twitter, a social network or a news media? In: Proceedings of the 19th International Conference on World Wide Web, WWW 2010, pp. 591–600. ACM, New York (2010)

26. Lazer, D., Kennedy, R., King, G., Vespignani, A.: The parable of Google Flu: traps in big data analysis. Science **343**(6176), 1203–1205 (2014)

27. Liao, Q.V., Fu, W.T., Strohmaier, M.: # Snowden: understanding biases introduced by behavioral differences of opinion groups on social media. In: Proceedings of the 2016 CHI Conference on Human Factors in Computing Systems, CHI 2016, pp. 3352–3363. ACM, New York (2016)

28. Lu, Y., Hu, X., Wang, F., Kumar, S., Liu, H., Maciejewski, R.: Visualizing social media sentiment in disaster scenarios. In: Proceedings of the 24th International Conference on World Wide Web, WWW 2015 Companion, pp. 1211–1215. ACM, New York (2015)

29. Murphy, J., et al.: Social Media in Public Opinion Research - AAPOR, May 2014

30. Nakov, P., et al.: Developing a successful SemEval task in sentiment analysis of Twitter and other social media texts. Lang. Resour. Eval. **50**(1), 35–65 (2016)

31. Olteanu, A., Castillo, C., Diaz, F., Kiciman, E.: Social data: biases, methodological pitfalls, and ethical boundaries. SSRN Scholarly Paper ID 2886526, Social Science Research Network, Rochester, December 2016

32. Paul, M.J., Dredze, M., Broniatowski, D.: Twitter improves influenza forecasting. PLoS currents **6** (2014)

33. Quinn, S.C., Jamison, A., An, J., Freimuth, V.S., Hancock, G.R., Musa, D.: Breaking down the monolith: understanding flu vaccine uptake among African Americans. SSM - Popul. Health **4**, 25–36 (2018)

34. Quinn, S.C., Jamison, A., Freimuth, V.S., An, J., Hancock, G.R., Musa, D.: Exploring racial influences on flu vaccine attitudes and behavior: results of a national survey of White and African American adults. Vaccine **35**(8), 1167–1174 (2017)

35. Schober, M.F., Pasek, J., Guggenheim, L., Lampe, C., Conrad, F.G.: Social media analyses for social measurement. Public Opin. Q. **80**(1), 180–211 (2016)

36. Schwartz, H.A., et al.: Toward personality insights from language exploration in social media. In: 2013 AAAI Spring Symposium Series (2013)

37. Shadish, W., Cook, T.D., Campbell, D.T.: Experimental and quasi-experimental designs for generalized causal inference. Wadsworth Cengage learning (2002)

38. Särndal, C., Swensson, B., Wretman, J.: Model Assisted Survey Sampling. Springer, Heidelberg (1992)

39. Tourangeau, R., Rips, L.J., Rasinski, K.: The Psychology of Survey Response. Cambridge University Press, March 2000. Google-Books-ID: bjVYdyXXT3oC

40. Volkova, S., Bachrach, Y.: On predicting sociodemographic traits and emotions from communications in social networks and their implications to online self-disclosure. Cyberpsychol. Behav. Soc. Netw. **18**(12), 726–736 (2015)

41. Wood-Doughty, Z., Mahajan, P., Dredze, M.: Johns Hopkins or Johnny-Hopkins: classifying individuals versus organizations on Twitter. In: Proceedings of the Second Workshop on Computational Modeling of People's Opinions, Personality, and Emotions in Social Media, pp. 56–61 (2018)
42. Wood-Doughty, Z., Smith, M., Broniatowski, D., Dredze, M.: How does twitter user behavior vary across demographic groups? In: Proceedings of the Second Workshop on NLP and Computational Social Science, pp. 83–89 (2017)
43. Yeager, D.S., et al.: Comparing the accuracy of RDD telephone surveys and internet surveys conducted with probability and non-probability samples. Public Opin. Q. **75**(4), 709–747 (2011)

Lying About Lying on Social Media: A Case Study of the 2019 Canadian Elections

Catherine King[✉][iD], Daniele Bellutta[iD], and Kathleen M. Carley[iD]

Carnegie Mellon University, Pittsburgh, PA 15213, USA
{cking2,dbellutt,kathleen.carley}@cs.cmu.edu

Abstract. This paper analyzes a new social media phenomenon in which users are lying about not being bots or about real news being fake news. Twitter data were collected throughout the 2019 Canadian federal election cycle, and we investigated the use of the #FakeNews and #NotABot hashtags. Twitter users connected the #FakeNews hashtag more often to mainstream news sources and reporters rather than actual fake news sites, often as a way to discredit certain reporters or viewpoints. We also found that users of the #NotABot hashtag were no more likely to be human than other users participating in political discourse in our data set. Bots that attempt to pass as human have been reportedly used to amplify misinformation campaigns in the past. This new type of online defensive strategy shows how these campaigns continue to evolve and illustrates how they may be run in the future.

Keywords: Social cybersecurity · Social media analytics · Canada

1 Introduction

Since the 2016 U.S. presidential election, there has been a great deal of international concern that Russia and other countries are trying to increase political division and spread disinformation in Western democratic nations [2]. Several studies over the last few years have characterized these misinformation campaigns and analyzed their potential effects on political discourse [2,10]. Many others have focused on improved detection of bots on social media platforms [3] or improved automatic detection of potentially false or misleading news [9,12]. As detection has improved, we have seen these campaigns continue to evolve. Over the last few years, we have witnessed a new type of phenomenon emerge: lying about lying as a way to provide cover for these campaigns. In this paper, we will characterize the users and targets of the #FakeNews and #NotABot hashtags as they were used during the 2019 Canadian election.

Over the course of the Canadian election cycle, journalists reported on various misinformation campaigns they discovered. In particular, the *National Observer* described the response to the #TrudeauMustGo hashtag with the amplifying

© Springer Nature Switzerland AG 2020
R. Thomson et al. (Eds.): SBP-BRiMS 2020, LNCS 12268, pp. 75–85, 2020.
https://doi.org/10.1007/978-3-030-61255-9_8

#NotABot hashtag. The #NotABot wave was used to boost the #Trudeau-MustGo message and produced a large spike in both hashtags in July 2019. This event raised concerns over a new wave of disinformation, as the journalists feared that the #NotABot hashtag was potentially being used in an inauthentic manner and itself was a form of disinformation [13]. Additionally, as the term "fake news" has caught on in recent years as a way to expose potentially false or misleading news stories, both malicious actors and regular people have started co-opting the term as a way to discredit true news stories and political opponents [15]. Users that are falsely claiming that they are #NotABot or that a real news story is #FakeNews are using these claims as a type of defense, which illustrates a potential playbook for future misinformation campaigns.

2   Related Work

Social cybersecurity is an emerging interdisciplinary field that focuses on how information and network maneuvers on social media can change human behavior and opinions. This field will affect the national security and democratic foundations of our own country as well as of other open societies [5,7,8]. Adversaries use various maneuvers to manipulate social network structure by connecting or breaking up groups. In addition, they manipulate the information on networks by spreading falsehoods and polarizing information or by promoting certain groups and individuals. Bots are used to increase the effectiveness of campaigns' messages in the hope of reaching a larger or more connected audience [8].

Previous research has been conducted in the wake of foreign interference in the 2016 U.S. presidential election to characterize these campaigns and attempt to measure their impacts [2,5,10]. Other studies have focused on improved detection of bots on social media platforms [3] or improved automatic detection of potentially false or misleading news [9,12]. While anecdotally polarization in the US has increased, it is difficult to quantify the precise impact of Russian disinformation campaigns on the 2016 election. Bail et al. found that those most likely to interact with the Russian Internet Research Agency's bot accounts were already highly engaged and polarized users and that it did not significantly change their levels of polarization [2]. Grinberg et al. found that older and more conservative users were more likely to be engaged with fake news but that the overall engagement level is low and highly concentrated [10]. However, it is still unclear how these campaigns impacted voting and other offline behaviors, which is the largest concern for democratic nations.

Consequently, Canada spent the three years since 2016 planning on how to safeguard their 2019 elections [14]. Wang et al. developed a method to identify "polluting groups" in the Canadian election Twitter space, finding that those users they flagged were four times more likely to be suspended over the course of the election cycle [16]. In addition, we have started to see an online reaction to misinformation with users calling out stories or URLs as "fake news". Ribeiro et al., however, found that users were more likely to slap the "fake news" label onto something they disagreed with politically rather than actually calling out false content [15]. Some users during the Canadian election cycle also started falsely claiming that they are #NotABot when amplifying potential misinformation campaigns as a way to provide cover for those campaigns [13]. In this paper, we investigate these new defenses of misinformation.

3 Methods

3.1 Data

We analyzed a Twitter data set collected between 20 July 2019 and 6 November 2019 composed of 16,784,400 tweets written by 1,303,761 accounts using 137,419 hashtags. The data were collected by streaming tweets matching a set of search terms that were supplemented as the political environment developed. The final list of terms is shown in Table 1. This data set is not necessarily representative of all Twitter activity surrounding the 2019 Canadian election.

Table 1. The list of search terms used to gather the Twitter data set on the 2019 Canadian election.

2019 Canadian Election Twitter Search Terms
#TrudeauMustGo, TeamTrudeau, trudeau, #Election2019, #elxn43, #chooseforward, #onpoli, #ItsOurVote, #lpc, #ndp, #cpc, #gpc, #NotAbot, #cdnpoli, #ButtsMustGo, #LavScam, #LiberalsMustGo, BlocQuebecois, #blocqc, cccr2019, #NoTMX, #TMX, #TransMountain, scheer, dougford, fordcutshurt, fordisfailing

Two groups of hashtags were identified for further study. The first group consists of hashtags used to call out supposed misinformation. This group contains all hashtags that included both the words "fake" and "news". The second group consists of hashtags used to allege that an account is not run by a bot. For this group, any hashtag containing both the words "not" and "bot" were considered. Table 2 lists the most popular hashtags in these two groups.

Table 2. The most used hashtags included in the fake-news and not-a-bot groups.

Fake-News Hashtags		Not-A-Bot Hashtags	
Hashtag	Number of Tweets	Hashtag	Number of Tweets
#fakenews	9,741	#notabot	45,605
#fakenewsmedia	3,287	#iamnotabot	921
#fakenewscbc	70	#imnotabot	142
#fakenewsandy	62	#teamnotabot	62
#cbcisfakenews	59	#stillnotabot	53

3.2 Bot Identification

We augmented our Twitter data with additional information on the type of account and on the probability that an account was run by a bot. We made use of the bot probability scores computed on our data by the Tier 1 BotHunter algorithm developed by Beskow and Carley [3]. This system was created by training a random forest regressor on labeled data derived from a forensic analysis of reported bot events, specifically focusing on the known publicized attack on the Atlantic Council Digital Forensic Labs in 2017. The Tier 1 BotHunter algorithm takes into consideration both account and tweet information to determine the probability that a user is a bot. Attributes that the algorithm considers include user attributes (like screen name length and number of tweets), network attributes (including number of friends and followers), the content of a tweet, and general timing of tweets (including account age and the average number of tweets per day). The Tier 2 algorithm also includes the user's timeline data to exploit temporal patterns, while Tier 3 adds the user's friends' timelines to incorporate network patterns. The output of the algorithm is a probability value, not a classification [3].

We used the Tier 1 BotHunter rather than the Tier 2 or Tier 3 models because Tier 1 has been shown to be substantially faster on large data sets than the other tiers without losing much accuracy [4]. We used various probability thresholds throughout our work, ranging from 0.6 to 0.8. A lower threshold would include more accounts, but it might also include some accounts that actually belong to humans. Higher thresholds would have been more conservative but may not capture all the bots in the network.

Many of the accounts predicted by the BotHunter algorithm as likely being bots may be accounts associated with various legitimate organizational accounts, such as those of news sources and government agencies. These accounts often exhibit behavior similar to that of bots, such as sending a high volume of tweets. Therefore, we used Huang and Carley's classification system to remove these kinds of accounts. This algorithm is a hierarchical self-attention neural network for Twitter user role classification, and it outperforms many standard baselines. The algorithm classifies each user into one of seven classes: news media, news reporter, government official, celebrity, company, sports, and normal [11]. Throughout this study, when seeking to detect bots at different BotHunter thresholds, we subsequently disregarded any detected bots that were also not deemed as normal accounts by Huang and Carley's algorithm.

3.3 Detecting Targets of #FakeNews Accusations

Each tweet using a fake-news hashtag needed to be assigned a likely target to evaluate who was being called out as spreading misinformation. For each tweet, the set of targets was assigned as the union of (a) the users mentioned in the tweet who are potential targets, (b) the author of the original tweet if the given tweet is a reply to a tweet made by a potential target, (c) the Web sites linked to in the tweet if the sites belonged to a potential target, and

(d) the specific targets of fake-news hashtags used in the tweet (if any). Links in tweets were associated with targets by un-shortening URLs and manually tying their domains to potential targets. Similarly, some hashtags were associated with potential targets (e.g., the hashtag "#fakenewscbc" was noted as targeting the Canadian Broadcasting Corporation). For this process, a potential target was defined as including political organizations, entities purporting to be news agencies, politicians, and individuals claiming to be reporters.

This method for detecting the likely targets of a tweet using a fake-news hashtag is limited. For example, there are cases in which a Twitter user may reply to a user of the same political inclination and use a fake-news hashtag to call out something that is not directly mentioned in the conversation [15]. Our method is not designed to detect such cases.

4   Results and Analysis

4.1   Network Structure

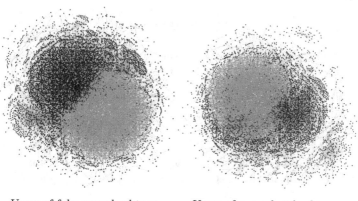

Users of fake-news hashtags.   Users of not-a-bot hashtags.

Fig. 1. The reciprocal communication networks for the users of fake-news hashtags and the users of not-a-bot hashtags. Each has been divided into two groups colored in red and blue using CONCOR. Accounts with a bot score higher than 0.7 that were not filtered out by Huang's algorithm have been colored yellow. (Color figure online)

We analyzed the structure of the reciprocal communication networks for each of the two groups of hashtags we examined. The reciprocal communication network is formed by tying two users together if they both have a communication tie to the other (such as user A mentioning user B and user B retweeting user A). Upon visual inspection, both of the reciprocal communication networks appeared to contain two large groups of users. Figure 1a shows the reciprocal communication network for the users of fake-news hashtags, and Fig. 1b shows the equivalent network for the users of not-a-bot hashtags.

To evaluate the difference between these clusters, we isolated the groups using CONCOR [6], calculated the number of times every hashtag was used in each group, and normalized the count by the total number of hashtag uses in the group. Of particular interest were the usage frequencies for hashtags that demonstrate clear partisan stances, such as "#trudeaumustgo" and "#scheerlies". Table 3 shows the usage frequencies for five liberal-leaning and five conservative-leaning hashtags across the two groups in each of the two networks studied. For each of the hashtags, it is clear that one group uses conservative-leaning hashtags more frequently than the other and that the other group uses liberal-leaning hashtags more frequently than the first group. It therefore seems that both the reciprocal communication networks for fake-news hashtag users and not-a-bot hashtag users are split on a partisan basis.

Table 3. The frequency of use for popular liberal-leaning and conservative-leaning hashtags in the CONCOR groups for the reciprocal communication networks of fake-news hashtag users and not-a-bot hashtag users. Usage frequency was calculated as the number of tweets using a hashtag divided by the total number of hashtag uses in that CONCOR group.

		Usage by #FakeNews Users		Usage by #NotABot Users	
		Red (%)	Blue (%)	Red (%)	Blue (%)
Conservative	#trudeaumustgo	20.93	0.81	21.67	1.52
	#scheer4pm	1.86	0.03	1.93	0.05
	#trudeauworstpm	1.34	0.05	1.34	0.08
	#liberalsmustgo	1.19	0.02	1.25	0.03
	#trudeaumustresign	1.17	0.03	1.19	0.07
Liberal	#istandwithtrudeau	0.08	0.64	0.11	0.65
	#teamtrudeau	0.27	0.61	0.29	0.66
	#scheerlies	0.02	0.45	0.02	0.48
	#scheerdisaster	0.02	0.42	0.02	0.45
	#neverscheer	0.02	0.40	0.03	0.35

4.2   #FakeNews Analysis

For the fake-news hashtags, we were most interested in seeing which types of news agencies or people are targeted the most. We also wanted to find out which types of targets Twitter bots are most interested in calling out as misinformation. Figure 2 shows a bar plot of the number of tweets that were associated with an entity for the ten most-targeted entities. An added bar shows the number of times all other entities were targeted. Each bar also shows the portion of those tweets that came from bots detected using three different thresholds: 0.6, 0.7, and 0.8. Note that, as was mentioned previously, after using BotHunter to detect bots at a given threshold, we disregarded bots that were not deemed as normal by Huang's classification algorithm [11].

As can be seen in Fig. 2, the most targeted entity was the Canadian Broadcasting Corporation (CBC). The second-most targeted entity was Amy McPherson, who *HuffPost* describes as a freelance journalist based in Ontario [1]. The plot shows the most commonly targeted entities to mainly be important Canadian news sources like the CBC, CTV News, the Toronto Star, and Global News as well as prominent Canadian politicians like Andrew Scheer, Justin Trudeau, Catherine McKenna, and Chrystia Freeland.

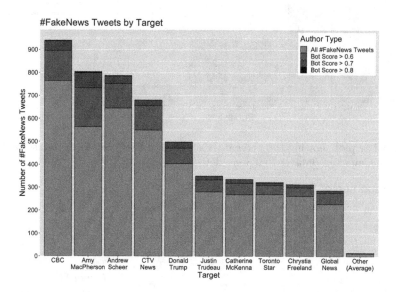

Fig. 2. A plot showing how many times an entity was targeted using a fake-news hashtag by normal users and bots detected with various BotHunter thresholds.

4.3 #NotABot Analysis

We sought to determine whether the proportion of bots using not-a-bot hashtags was different from the proportion of bots in the overall Canadian data. As shown in Figs. 3 and 4, the difference in the percentage of bots is negligible between

Table 4. The percentage of users in the #NotABot group and the rest of the Canadian users that are over the three different bot score thresholds. The p-value is associated with the 2-sample proportion test for equality.

Bot Threshold	All Bots			All Non-Official Bots		
	#NotABot	Canada	P-Value	#NotABot	Canada	P-Value
≥0.60	16.21%	15.97%	0.545	14.38%	9.59%	2.2e−16
≥0.70	5.10%	5.25%	0.540	4.38%	3.00%	1.925e−14
≥0.80	1.47%	1.70%	0.104	1.22%	0.87%	0.00043

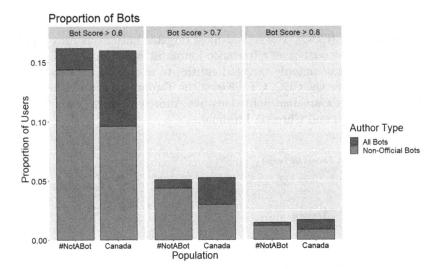

Fig. 3. A bar plot showing the percentage of users in the #NotABot dataset and the rest of the Canadian dataset that were detected as bots at three thresholds.

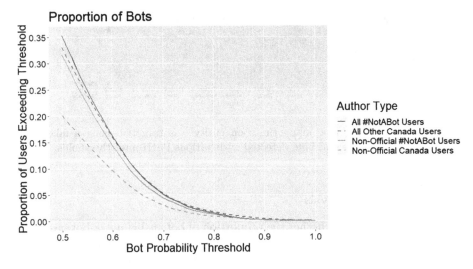

Fig. 4. A plot showing the percentage of users that were detected as bots at all thresholds above 50%.

the population of not-a-bot hashtag users and the rest of the population when looking at just the BotHunter scores. We ran a two-sample proportion test of equality using bot probability thresholds of 0.6, 0.7, and 0.8 (shown in Table 4). None of the tests had statistically significant p-values, indicating that we would not reject the null hypothesis that these two proportions are equal. However, after removing "official" bots using Huang's algorithm [11], we found that the proportion of remaining bots was higher in the #NotABot group than in the general Canadian user group. These differences were statistically significant with p-values near zero.

We additionally ran a Mann-Whitney U test, which is a non-parametric test for the null hypothesis that the distribution of two populations is the same. The test resulted in a highly significant p-value (≈ 0), which indicates that the distribution of bot scores is statistically significantly different between users of not-a-bot hashtags and the rest of the Canadian data. Upon closer inspection, the difference appears small, as the difference in the mean bot score for the two groups is less than 2%. However, these results are in line with the higher percentage of non-official bots found in the #NotABot group overall. Table 5 shows the summary statistics for the bot scores in the #NotABot group and the other data.

Table 5. The summary statistics for the bot scores in the #NotABot group and the rest of the Canadian users.

	Minimum	First Quartile	Median	Mean	Third Quartile	Maximum
#NotABot Users	2.66%	29.20%	42.74%	42.56%	55.01%	99.80%
Canadian Users	1.01%	27.00%	40.99%	41.20%	54.49%	100.00%

5 Discussion

Overall, we found that large and established news agencies are the most associated with fake-news hashtags, indicating that they are frequently targeted with accusations of spreading misinformation. Additionally, we found that using not-a-bot hashtags is not a reliable signal for indicating that one is not, in fact, a bot. After accounting for official bots (government agencies, news reporters, politicians etc.), the proportion of bots is higher in the population using not-a-bot hashtags than in those that do not use those hashtags. Both the network of fake-news hashtag users and the network of not-a-bot hashtag users show a strong partisan divide in their members' usage of other hashtags. In both of these networks, many of these users are attempting to deceive others on what is actually false news and on whether or not they are a bot. It is also clear that accusations calling something fake news come from both liberal-leaning and conservative-leaning groups of users.

6 Conclusion and Future Work

Our work describes some new tactics being used by malicious actors hoping to influence an election. Mainstream news organizations are being labeled as "fake news" at higher rates than news sites that are either fake, satirical, or otherwise not held to high journalistic standards. Additionally, during the Canadian election, a Twitter user claiming not to be a bot was just as likely (if not more likely) to be a bot as anyone else on the platform discussing Canadian politics. Therefore, the #NotABot hashtag is not a good indicator for a user trying to prove that they are a human. These results show that users claiming that they are telling the truth on social media are just as likely to be lying as general users.

Future research will likely build on this initial set of hashtags to investigate how lying about lying on social media may evolve over time and may be used differently in other countries. Malicious actors may continue building on these techniques to discredit anyone who calls out their misinformation campaigns, or these hashtags may be replaced by other hashtags or techniques in the future. Discovering how these hashtags evolve is a challenging problem that itself requires more study.

Additionally, these hashtags have been recently used in a variety of non-political contexts, supposedly as a way to call out false news or to claim that the user themselves is not a bot. Examining how these hashtags are used differently in various contexts could be helpful for understanding these phenomena. Perhaps more importantly, a useful avenue for future research would be to investigate how much of an impact these hashtags are having on human behavior and opinions. It is not clear whether users on these platforms believe someone who makes a claim of not being a bot. While our research shows that people using these hashtags are often lying, the general public may not be aware of this.

Acknowledgements. This work was supported in part by the Office of Naval Research (ONR) Award 00014182106 and the Center for Computational Analysis of Social and Organization Systems (CASOS). The views and conclusions contained in this document are those of the authors and should not be interpreted as representing the official policies, either expressed or implied, of the ONR or the U.S. government. The authors would also like to thank David Beskow for collecting the data used in this study and for running his BotHunter algorithm on the data. We would also like to thank Binxuan Huang for access to his Twitter user classification system.

References

1. Amy MacPherson. https://www.huffingtonpost.ca/author/amy-macpherson/
2. Bail, C.A., et al.: Assessing the Russian Internet Research Agency's impact on the political attitudes and behaviors of American Twitter users in late 2017 (2019)
3. Beskow, D., Carley, K.: Bot-hunter: a tiered approach to detecting & characterizing automated activity on Twitter. In: International Conference on Social Computing, Behavioral-Cultural Modeling and Prediction and Behavior Representation in Modeling and Simulation, July 2018
4. Beskow, D.M., Carley, K.M.: Bot conversations are different: leveraging network metrics for bot detection in Twitter. In: 2018 IEEE/ACM International Conference on Advances in Social Networks Analysis and Mining (ASONAM), pp. 825–832. IEEE, Barcelona, August 2018. https://doi.org/10.1109/ASONAM.2018.8508322. https://ieeexplore.ieee.org/document/8508322/
5. Beskow, D.M., Carley, K.M.: Social cybersecurity: an emerging national security requirement (2019). https://www.armyupress.army.mil/Journals/Military-Review/English-Edition-Archives/Mar-Apr-2019/117-Cybersecurity/

6. Breiger, R.L., Boorman, S.A., Arabie, P.: An algorithm for clustering relational data with applications to social network analysis and comparison with multidimensional scaling. J. Math. Psychol. **12**(3), 328–383 (1975)

7. Carley, K.M., Cervone, G., Agarwal, N., Liu, H.: Social cyber-security. In: Thomson, R., Dancy, C., Hyder, A., Bisgin, H. (eds.) SBP-BRiMS 2018. LNCS, vol. 10899, pp. 389–394. Springer, Cham (2018). https://doi.org/10.1007/978-3-319-93372-6_42

8. Committee on a Decadal Survey of Social and Behavioral Sciences for Applications to National Security, Board on Behavioral, Cognitive, and Sensory Sciences, Division of Behavioral and Social Sciences and Education, National Academies of Sciences, Engineering, and Medicine: A Decadal Survey of the Social and Behavioral Sciences: A Research Agenda for Advancing Intelligence Analysis. National Academies Press (2019)

9. Golbeck, J., et al.: Fake news vs satire: a dataset and analysis. In: WebSci 2018 (2019)

10. Grinberg, N., Joseph, K., Friedland, L., Swire-Thompson, B., Lazer, D.: Fake news on Twitter during the 2016 U.S. presidential election. Science **363**(6425), 374–378 (2019)

11. Huang, B., Carley, K.M.: Discover your social identity from what you tweet: a content based approach. Disinformation, Misinformation, and Fake News in Social Media-Emerging Research Challenges and Opportunities (2020)

12. Levi, O., Hosseini, P., Diab, M., Broniatowski, D.: Identifying nuances in fake news vs. satire: using semantic and linguistic cues. In: Proceedings of the Second Workshop on Natural Language Processing for Internet Freedom: Censorship, Disinformation, and Propaganda, pp. 31–35. Association for Computational Linguistics (2019)

13. Orr, C.: A new wave of disinformation emerges with anti-Trudeau hashtag. https://www.nationalobserver.com/2019/07/25/analysis/new-wave-disinformation-emerges-trudeaumustgo

14. Panetta, A., Scott, M.: Unlike U.S., Canada plans coordinated attack on foreign election interference (2019). https://politi.co/30WXcIa

15. Ribeiro, M.H., Guerra, P.H.C., Meira Jr., W., Almeida, V.A.: "Everything I disagree with is #FakeNews": correlating political polarization and spread of misinformation. In: Data Science + Journalism Workshop, KDD 2017, Halifax, Canada (2017)

16. Wang, J., Levy, S., Wang, R., Kulshrestha, A., Rabbany, R.: SGP: spotting groups polluting the online political discourse (2019)

Breadth Verses Depth: The Impact of Tree Structure on Cultural Influence

Rhodri L. Morris[1,2](✉)(iD), Liam D. Turner[1,2](iD), Roger M. Whitaker[1,2](iD), and Cheryl Giammanco[3]

[1] School of Computer Science and Informatics, Cardiff University, Cardiff, UK
{MorrisRL6,TurnerL9,WhitakerRM}@cardiff.ac.uk
[2] Crime and Security Research Institute, Cardiff University, Cardiff, UK
[3] U.S. Army Combat Capabilities Development Command,
Army Research Laboratory, Aberdeen Proving Ground, MD, USA
cheryl.a.giammanco.civ@mail.mil

Abstract. Cultural spread in social networks and organisations is an important and longstanding issue. In this paper we assess this role of tree structures in facilitating cultural diversity. Cultural features are represented using abstract traits that are held by individual agents, which may transfer when neighbouring agents interact through the network structure. We use an agent-based model that incorporates both the combined social pressure and influence from an agent's neighbours. We perform a multivariate study where the number of features and traits representing culture are varied, alongside the breadth and depth of the tree. The results reveal interesting findings on cultural diversity. Increasing the number of features promotes strong convergence in flatter trees as compared to narrower and deeper trees. At the same time increasing features causes narrower deeper trees to show greater cultural pluralism while flatter trees instead show greater cultural homogenisation. We also find that in contrast to previous work, the polarisation between nodes does not rise steadily as the number of traits increase but under certain conditions may also fall. The results have implications for organisational structures - in particular for hierarchies where depth supports cultural divergence, while breadth promotes greater homogeneity, but with increased coordination overhead on the root nodes. These observations also support subsidiarity in deep organisational structures - it is not just a case of communication length promoting subsidiarity, but local cultural differences are more likely to be sustained within these structures.

Keywords: Agent-based modelling · Organizational structure · Cultural diversity

1 Introduction

Beyond supporting communication, management and decision-making, organisational structures, both formal and informal, play an important role in shaping

© Springer Nature Switzerland AG 2020
R. Thomson et al. (Eds.): SBP-BRiMS 2020, LNCS 12268, pp. 86–95, 2020.
https://doi.org/10.1007/978-3-030-61255-9_9

an organisation's *culture* [24]. Culture can be thought of as the values and norms held by the members of an organisation, or anything over which individuals can influence each other [2], such as beliefs or behaviours. Importantly, culture plays a role in affecting how organisations may function [10] and the organisation's identity [15,23], alongside shaping the individuals that constitute them.

Interpersonal relationships play an important role in mediating cultural influence. One of the most fundamental structures underlying the relationships across an organisation is the *tree* - in other words a minimally connected sub-network that spans all nodes. Line management structures and hierarchies are common examples. Structures featuring tree-like branching are also not uncommon in groups where formal hierarchies are absent [1,11,22].

Longstanding qualitative studies in the fields of business, sociology and psychology recognise the social implications of *tall* verses *wide* organisational structures [4,14], primarily revealing findings concerning decision making from qualitative analysis. More recently, flatter organisational structures and 'holacracies' at companies such as Zappos and Valve have received much attention [3,8,13,26] based on their alternative approaches to hierarchy. From a network perspective, wide tree structures typically offer a reduced path length for communication but can introduce bottlenecks through dependency on hubs. Conversely, deep structures circumvent this, but can introduce the problem of long communication chains that may impede activity when rapid responses are required. However, beyond communication and decision making, organisational structures also impact the culture of an organisation, as they represent how individuals may provide influence upon each other.

In this paper we investigate the specific role of tree structures in cultural propagation across a group, in particular looking at the shape of a tree, in terms of its breadth verses depth, and the resultant cultural diversity. Using an abstract representation of culture, our approach adopts agent-based modelling to understand how culture may become shared based on social influence. The model is composed of features held by agents, that can be shared through discrete traits. The underlying model [19] generalises the approach taken by Axelrod [2], and also incorporates combined influence from an agent's neighbours, based on social impact theory [17]. This allows us to determine the sensitivity of organisational structure to cultural propagation.

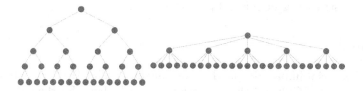

Fig. 1. A taller binary tree, $k = 2, h = 4$ (left), and a flatter tree $k = 5, h = 2$ (right).

1.1 Related Work

Wide ranging literature supports the evolution of culture. From a computational perspective the work of Axelrod [2] provides a fundamental base model which has been extended in many directions. This approach introduces the idea that culture can be represented by a vector of *features*, where each feature takes a value from a set of discrete *traits*. Qualitative work [9] has proposed that in an organisational context, a large number of potential dimensions could be considered (e.g. 20). Axelrod's approach [2] involves agents randomly interacting in pairs over a lattice-based network structure with similarity between agents increasing the chance of a dissimilar feature being copied. This incorporates homophily, where more similar individuals have a greater disposition towards influencing each other [18].

There have been numerous generalisations of Axelrod's work, with two directions standing out in particular: firstly the structure over which cultural influence is performed [16,25], and secondly the combined effect of influence from multiple neighbours [12,19]. In response, Axelrod's model has been examined on different network structures such as Erdős-Rényi random graphs [25], small-world and scale-free networks [16]. Equally compound influence has also been developed and examined, alongside agent-based models of culture represented through simple and complex contagion, often based on the susceptibility, infection and recovery (SIR) model of epidemic propagation [20,28].

Despite these contributions there has been limited consideration of hierarchies, either formal or informal, despite their prevalence in groups and organisations. Stocker et al. [27] examined the effects of flat-vs-tall network structures on an opinion formation model, finding that flatter hierarchies have more fluctuations from consensus than tall. Nekovee et al. [21] compared flat-vs-tall network structures and their effect on the spread of corruption through a network in an epidemic-based model. These models are typically limited in their consideration of culture, since they are limited to a binary representation [27] or variations on SIR-based models [21].

We contribute a new perspective by adopting an agent-based model [19] that considers the combined peer pressure upon the cultural features that an individual holds, while also incorporating the influence of homophily (i.e., similarity) between agents. This more realistically models the spreading of culture based on cumulative popularity of cultural features, and is applied to better understand the role tree structures in cultural propagation.

2 Model

We use the social-impact inspired model introduced in [19], an extension of Axelrod's model of Cultural Dissemination [2], as the basis for the analysis. The model assumes a set of N agents (nodes) that are organised in a connected network structure (see Sect. 3). Each agent is assigned a vector of F features $(\sigma_1, \sigma_2, ..., \sigma_F)$, each with a value from a set T of q possible traits, where $\sigma_k = 1, ..., q$ for feature k. This defines an agent's *culture*, and agents can share some, none, or all traits. Edges between each pair of agents are weighted based on the similarity of their culture, using:

$$sim_{i,j} = \frac{1}{F} \sum_{k=1}^{F} \delta_{\sigma_k(i),\sigma_k(j)}$$

where $\delta_{i,j}$ is Kronecker's delta.

At each iteration, a random agent i is selected and is influenced by multiple neighbours simultaneously. Whether an agent adopts a trait is determined by the number of influencing agents having the trait in question and also the similarity of those influencers to the influenced agent. In this paper, we set the distance measure [19] for influencing neighbours to 1. For each feature k where $k = 1, ..., F$, the selected agent calculates a trait score for each possible trait in T and selects the value of $\alpha' \in T$ that gives the maximal result. The trait score $ts_{\alpha,k,i}$ for node i, trait α and feature k is calculated:

$$ts_{\alpha,k,i} = \sum_{l=1}^{max\ l} \sum_{p^l \in P_i^l} w(p^l)\delta_{k,\alpha}(p^l)$$

where P_i^l as the set of all paths of length l that end at i; $p^l \in P_i^l$; $w(p^l)$ is the product of all edge weights on p^l and $\delta_{k,\alpha}(p^l)$ is a binary variable that is 1 if the source node of the path p^l has α as its kth feature. Thus the target agent i copies the strongest trait α amongst its influencing neighbours.

3   Methods

We place agents in undirected balanced k-ary tree structures of height h and branching factor k and observe differences between wider, flatter trees (low h, higher k) and deeper, narrower trees (low k, higher h). Each tree has a root node at level 0 with k children and h levels of descendents (Fig. 1). The values for h and k were chosen to maintain a similar number of agents across trees (see Table 1).

Table 1. Tree structure configurations as undirected networks

Branching factor (k)	Height (h)	# of Agents	# of (undirected) Edges
2	9	1023	1022
3	6	1093	1092
4	5	1365	1364
6	4	1555	1554
10	3	1111	1110

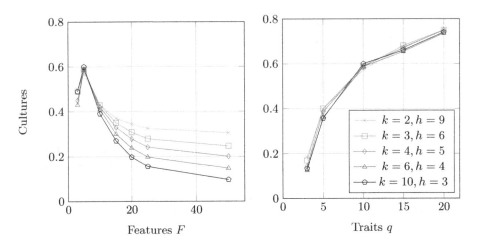

Fig. 2. Left: The number of cultures decreases as the size of the features vector, F, is increased. Deeper trees maintain a higher number of cultures than flatter trees. Note: $q = 10$. Where $q = 5$ and $q = 15$ similar tall vs flat patterns are present. Right: The number of cultures increases as the number of possible traits, q, increases; however there is no discernible difference between different tree structures for $F = 5$.

We vary the number of traits and features across the different tree shapes and observe the effect on cultural spreading behaviour. For each of the tree structures in Table 1 we ran our model for $F = 5, q = 3, 5, 10, 15, 20, 25, 50$ and $q = 10, F = 3, 5, 10, 15, 25, 50$. These parameters were chosen to exemplify the behaviours found in the model, between the states of complete mono-culture and complete polarisation. For each combination of parameters, we ran the simulation 20 times, each with a different random seed and random starting cultures. An additional 100 runs were made on each of $F = 5; q = 10, 11, 12, 13, 14, 15$ to examine the behaviour discussed in Sect. 4.1. For comparison, we also ran Axelrod's model [2] on similar trees and parameter sets as above, as well as a 32×32 square lattice (1024 agents).

Previous works [5,6] based on [2] typically use the number of distinct cultures (i.e. unique trait combinations present at stabilisation) or largest cultural region size (largest area of contiguous identical agents) as metrics for cultural convergence and divergence. However, for our purposes these metrics do not fully illustrate the dynamics taking place because agents often hold traits from multiple cultures simultaneously and therefore cultures counted as distinct may in fact have many traits in common. Similarly, the largest region size may not adequately indicate the amount of fracture in other groups, or the amount of cultural overlap between this largest region and others. A dominant trait may persist across several otherwise different cultures. Consequently, we record the state of edges between nodes. Edges between two nodes with identical traits are considered *homogenised*, edges between two nodes with completely dissimilar traits are labelled *polarised*, and edges between nodes with a mix of common and

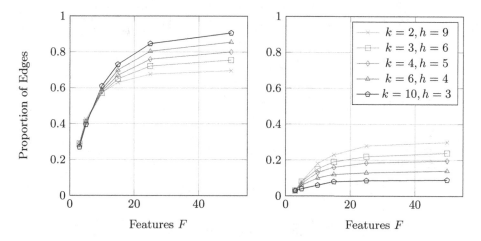

Fig. 3. Left: proportion of homogenised edges. Right: proportion of mixed edges. As the size of the features vector, F, increases, the number of polarised links drops. These links instead become homogenised or mixed. The amount of cultural mixing is greater for deeper trees (right) whereas flatter trees show greater convergence (left).

differing traits are labelled *mixed*. At stabilisation, Axelrod's model will never contain mixed edges; polarised edges may exist along borders of homogenised cultures, whereas in our model mixed edges can occur.

4   Results

As a baseline, we apply Axelrod's model [2] using tree topologies instead of the regular lattice structure. Interestingly the results show consistency with the patterns observed when applied to regular square lattice structures - we are unable to assert correlations between different tree shapes and the number of cultures emerging under the cultural model from [2]. This may serve as another example of how contagion dynamics differ when transmission is *complex* [7] rather than via a simple dyadic interaction. It also motivates the importance of considering combined influences in a cultural context, as presented in Sect. 2. We explore this further below.

4.1   Polarised, Homogenised and Mixed Links in a Model of Social Influence

We find that an increase in the number of features causes the proportion of polarised links to drop as a result of increased convergence. Consequently the proportion of homogenised and mixed links increase. The increase of homogenised links is greater in flatter trees than deep; the latter instead display a greater increase of mixed links (Fig. 3). This is also reflected when counting the number of distinct cultures. While the decrease of cultures due to increased F is

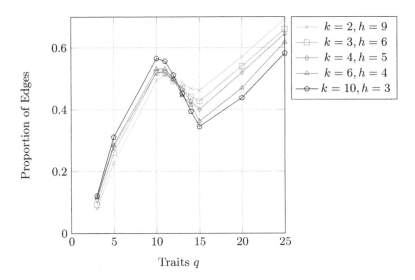

Fig. 4. Proportion of polarised edges when varying traits. As choice increases, an increase in polarisation is expected. However, between $10 \lesssim q \lesssim 15$ polarisation drops, and deeper trees become more polarised that flatter trees.

commonly observed [2,19], the degree to which this decrease occurs is different in flatter trees than taller (Fig. 2). Such a clear trend toward homogeneity in flatter tree structures may seem counter-intuitive if one envisions a typically tall hierarchy as more rigid and autocratic. However, the greater degree of intermediate 'hub' nodes, social reinforcement, and shorter paths of communication may aid convergence. This could have implications for the development of an organisational culture.

When the number of traits is varied, the proportion of homogenised links drops as agents have less chance of similarity. However, how the number of traits affects the proportion of mixed or polarised links is more nuanced (Fig. 4). When the number of traits is small ($q \lesssim 10$), polarisation rises as the number of traits increase. However, between $q \approx 10$ and $q \approx 15$ the proportion of polarised links drops, before rising again at higher trait levels. Furthermore, when $q \lesssim 10$ flatter trees have a greater proportion of polarised links than deeper trees; however when $q \gtrsim 15$ the opposite is true.

In most previous works based on Axelrod's model (e.g. [5,16]) there has existed a positive correlation between the number of traits q and the number of distinct cultures. While the number of cultures also increases in our model, this does not account for the degree to which cultures may overlap. Between $10 \lesssim q \lesssim 15$ the amount of polarisation between existing cultures drops, and cultural mixing increases (Fig. 4). This behaviour is unusual, and has not been observed either in Axelrod's base model or when our model is run on lattice structures. The increase in otherwise different cultures sharing common traits also affects taller trees to a greater extent than it does flatter trees. The inversion

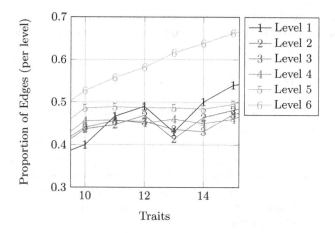

Fig. 5. Polarised edges at different levels of a $k = 3, h = 6$ tree. The higher in the tree an edge, the less likely it is to be polarised between $10 \lesssim q \lesssim 15$.

between $10 \lesssim q \lesssim 15$ suggests that whether a flatter tree structure exhibits more cultural mixing than tall depends on the amount of choices available per cultural feature.

4.2 Polarisation at Different Tree Levels

To examine the dip in polarisation at $10 \lesssim q \lesssim 15$ we also record the proportion of polarised and mixed edges at each level in the tree, where edges at level n are the edges between nodes at level n and their parents. At the lowest level of the tree polarisation continues to climb between $10 \lesssim q \lesssim 15$. As we move up through the levels of the tree the rise in polarisation between $10 \lesssim q \lesssim 15$ is arrested, and at higher levels often reversed (Fig. 5). As trees get flatter, this inversion of polarisation occurs at relatively lower levels and with a steeper decline.

To explain this further, we note that the nodes in the lowest level of these trees each only have a single connection - to their parent. The copying dynamics therefore dictate that they may only stabilise at a state either identical or dissimilar to their parent. As q is increased, polarised links at this level always increase. Despite broader trees having a greater proportion of their nodes in this polarised lowest level, they show the greatest drop in polarisation between $10 \lesssim q \lesssim 15$. That the drop in polarisation occurs largely in the upper levels of the tree may be examined further by experiments on different network structures, such as scale-free or others with differing distributions of node degrees and centralities.

5 Conclusion

In this paper we have applied a model of compound social influence, developed to capture the notion of peer pressure, to tree network structures of differing depth and breadth. We find that whether a tree is narrow and tall, or broad and flat, has a tangible effect on the amount of cultural convergence. In particular, as the number of features is increased flatter trees display greater cultural homogeneity than taller trees, which instead show greater cultural pluralism. When increasing the number of traits we also identify a point at which polarisation between nodes falls rather than rises, and taller trees become more polarised than flatter. Furthermore, some of these behaviours are particular to our model using compound influence as a copying dynamic, rather than dyadic interactions. This reinforces previous findings where complex contagions have resulted in different dissemination behaviours to simple contagions (e.g. [7]). The dynamics observed in these experiments have potential implications for the development of organisational cultures and how traits can propagate. Whether either subsidiarity or centralisation are sought, the shape of a hierarchy can have a notable effect on the spread of behaviours within.

Acknowledgement. This research was sponsored by the U.S. Army Research Laboratory and the U.K. Ministry of Defence under Agreement Number W911NF-16-3-0001. The views and conclusions contained in this document are those of the authors and should not be interpreted as representing the official policies, either expressed or implied, of the U.S. Army Research Laboratory, the U.S. Government, the U.K. Ministry of Defence or the U.K. Government. The U.S. and U.K. Governments are authorized to reproduce and distribute reprints for Government purposes notwithstanding any copyright notation hereon.

References

1. Arazy, O., Nov, O., Ortega, F.: The [wikipedia] world is not flat: on the organizational structure of online production communities. In: 22nd European Conference on Information Systems, ECIS 2014. Association for Information Systems (2014)
2. Axelrod, R.: The dissemination of culture: a model with local convergence and global polarization. J. Conflict Resolut. **41**(2), 203–226 (1997)
3. Bernstein, E., Bunch, J., Canner, N., Lee, M.: Beyond the holacracy hype. Harvard Bus. Rev. **94**(7), 13 (2016)
4. Carzo Jr., R., Yanouzas, J.N.: Effects of flat and tall organization structure. Adm. Sci. Q. 178–191 (1969)
5. Castellano, C., Marsili, M., Vespignani, A.: Nonequilibrium phase transition in a model for social influence. Phys. Rev. Lett. **85**(16), 3536 (2000)
6. Centola, D., Gonzalez-Avella, J.C., Eguiluz, V.M., San Miguel, M.: Homophily, cultural drift, and the co-evolution of cultural groups. J. Conflict Resolut. **51**(6), 905–929 (2007)
7. Centola, D., Macy, M.: Complex contagions and the weakness of long ties. Am. J. Sociol. **113**(3), 702–734 (2007)
8. Clegg, A.: Boss-less business is no workers' paradise. Financial Times, September 2019. https://www.ft.com/content/34a86220-d639-11e9-8d46-8def889b4137
9. Delobbe, N., Haccoun, R.R., Vandenberghe, C.: Measuring core dimensions of organizational culture: a review of research and development of a new instrument. Unpublished manuscript, Universite catholique de Louvain, Belgium (2002)

10. Denison, D.R.: Corporate Culture and Organizational Effectiveness. Wiley, Hoboken (1990)
11. Diefenbach, T., Sillince, J.A.: Formal and informal hierarchy in different types of organization. Organ. Stud. **32**(11), 1515–1537 (2011)
12. Flache, A., Macy, M.W.: Local convergence and global diversity: from interpersonal to social influence. J. Conflict Resolut. **55**(6), 970–995 (2011)
13. Foss, N.J., Dobrajska, M.: Valve's way: wayward, visionary, or voguish? J. Organ. Des. **4**(2), 12–15 (2015)
14. Hankinson, P.: An empirical study which compares the organisational structures of companies managing the world's top 100 brands with those managing outsider brands. J. Prod. Brand Manag. (1999)
15. Hatch, M.J., Schultz, M.: Relations between organizational culture, identity and image. Eur. J. Mark. **31**(5–6), 356–365 (1997)
16. Klemm, K., Eguíluz, V.M., Toral, R., San Miguel, M.: Nonequilibrium transitions in complex networks: a model of social interaction. Phys. Rev. E **67**(2), 026120 (2003)
17. Latané, B.: The psychology of social impact. Am. Psychol. **36**(4), 343 (1981)
18. McPherson, M., Smith-Lovin, L., Cook, J.M.: Birds of a feather: homophily in social networks. Ann. Rev. Sociol. **27**(1), 415–444 (2001)
19. Morris, R., Turner, L., Whitaker, R., Giammanco, C.: The impact of peer pressure: extending Axelrod's model on cultural polarisation. In: 2019 IEEE International Conference on Cognitive Computing (ICCC), pp. 114–121. IEEE (2019)
20. Nekovee, M., Moreno, Y., Bianconi, G., Marsili, M.: Theory of rumour spreading in complex social networks. Physica A **374**(1), 457–470 (2007)
21. Nekovee, M., Pinto, J.: Modeling the impact of organization structure and whistleblowers on intra-organizational corruption contagion. Physica A **522**, 339–349 (2019)
22. Oedzes, J.J., Van der Vegt, G.S., Rink, F.A., Walter, F.: On the origins of informal hierarchy: the interactive role of formal leadership and task complexity. J. Organ. Behav. **40**(3), 311–324 (2019)
23. Parker, M.: Organizational Culture and Identity: Unity and Division at Work. Sage (2000)
24. Schein, E.H.: Organizational Culture, vol. 45. American Psychological Association (1990)
25. Singh, P., Sreenivasan, S., Szymanski, B.K., Korniss, G.: Accelerating consensus on coevolving networks: the effect of committed individuals. Phys. Rev. E **85**(4), 046104 (2012)
26. Spicer, A.: No bosses, no managers: the truth behind the 'flat hierarchy' facade. The Guardian, July 2018
27. Stocker, R., Cornforth, D., Bossomaier, T.R.: Network structures and agreement in social network simulations. J. Artif. Soc. Soc. Simul. **5**(4) (2002)
28. Zhou, J., Liu, Z., Li, B.: Influence of network structure on rumor propagation. Phys. Lett. A **368**(6), 458–463 (2007)

Optimizing Attention-Aware Opinion Seeding Strategies

Charles E. Martin[✉], Dana Warmsley, and Samuel D. Johnson

HRL Laboratories, Malibu, CA 90265, USA
{cemartin,dmwarmsley,sdjohnson}@hrl.com

Abstract. In this work we introduce a new type of Independent Cascade Model (ICM) that goes beyond current ICMs by incorporating the effects of information *salience* and *exposure* that we call ICM-SE. ICMs are a well-studied class of models designed to capture information spreading on networks where the standard objective is to identify a set of nodes to seed with information such that some measure of information spread is maximized. To our knowledge, we are the first to incorporate the effects of salience and exposure within the ICM framework, which brings additional realism to our ICM, but also introduces additional challenges in identifying good strategies for information seeding. Therefore, our second contribution is to introduce and demonstrate the effectiveness of a powerful class of search algorithms called Estimation of Distribution Algorithms (EDA) for this type of problem. We show that our EDA approach outperforms the typical greedy search approach on graphs drawn from various popular network classes. We also identify and investigate quantitative and qualitative differences between the strategies from EDA versus those from greedy search.

1 Introduction

The influence maximization problem is at the heart of many applications involving person-to-person sharing of information, products, and opinions and is a component in modern social media advertising, political campaigning, and online activism. The crux of the influence maximization problem is a combinatorial question:

> What is the most "important" set of individuals in a social system that, if they endorse a particular product/politician/cause, will exert the most collective influence on the rest of the social network and ultimately lead to the widest adoption of said product/politician/cause?

First posed as an explicit optimization problem independently by Domingos and Richardson [2] and Kempe et al. [4], the influence maximization problem has since received considerable attention by researchers posing the problem in the contexts of different information dynamics (c.f. the survey [5]). Subsequent work on the ICM itself has explored various heuristics for speeding up the computation

© Springer Nature Switzerland AG 2020
R. Thomson et al. (Eds.): SBP-BRiMS 2020, LNCS 12268, pp. 96–106, 2020.
https://doi.org/10.1007/978-3-030-61255-9_10

of (approximately optimal) seeding strategies; see [3, Section 1.5] for a short survey of such work.

In this work we take up the influence maximization problem in the context of a dynamic that is inspired by that originally analyzed by Kempe *et al.* – the independent cascade model – which incorporates some novel extensions that take into account information *saliency* and *(over-)exposure* in an effort to model the attention span of individuals. These extensions are inspired by past analyses of real world online networks (for example, [9,10]). We develop a seeding approach using ideas from a class of algorithms called *estimation of distribution algorithms (EDAs)* and demonstrate its performance through numerical simulations.

We developed and applied an Estimation of Distribution Algorithm (EDA) for identifying effective seeding strategies in our extension to the independent cascade model. Estimation of Distribution Algorithms [1] are a class of search algorithms that fall under the umbrella of Evolutionary Computation. They are particularly well-suited for optimization in discrete domains and are scalable to combinatorial search-spaces. In general, an EDA learns a probability distribution over the space of potential solutions to a problem such that samples drawn from this distribution are likely to represent good solutions (i.e., they have high fitness). Here, we use the term "fitness" to refer to a user-defined measure of solution quality. This measure is typically specified by a non-negative real-valued function f called the "fitness-function". The particular fitness function used in this work is described in Sect. 4.

We find that, on average, our EDA method identifies higher-performing strategies compared to a baseline greedy approach in randomly sampled graphs using multiple random graph models. An analysis of the individual and group-level properties of seed nodes selected by each strategy over a number of simulations reveal that our EDA algorithm is able to spread nodes more evenly across the network, contributing to its enhanced performance over the baseline method. Given this, and the fact that EDA is no more computationally expensive to run than greedy search, we see EDA as a straight-forward, but effective alternative to greedy search for identifying strategies in Independent Cascade Models.

2   Model

In this section we describe our model of information spread. Our model is based on the independent cascade model (ICM) [3,4], extending it to incorporate a notion of information salience as well as a notion of information (over-)exposure.

Let $G = (N, E)$ be a directed graph where the node set $N = \{1, \ldots, n\}$ represents a society of individuals (or groups) and a directed edge $(i, j) \in E$ indicates the flow of information from i to j.

Recall that the independent cascade model is a model of information propagation through a social network. In its original form, this model considers an initial set $A_0 \subset N$ of *active* nodes at time $t = 0$ and proceeds in discrete time steps $t = 1, 2, \ldots$. When a node i first becomes active at time t, it makes a single attempt to activate each of it's inactive neighbors j independently with probability p (a system parameter). The dynamics end when no further activations take place.

In our extension of the ICM, we focus on multiple information contagions (or information tokens), with each token behaving like the single "contagion" in the standard ICM but having subtle effects on each other's propagation behavior. In our setup, at each time step, new seed activations take place. The seed activations at time t involve the information token τ_t. When an individual $i \in N$ receives τ_t they are "activated" with respect to τ_t. Individuals can be simultaneously activated by multiple τ_t's (e.g., τ_0, τ_3, etc.). Like the independent cascade model, when an individual gets activated by τ_t at time $t' \geq t$, they get a single opportunity to τ_t-activate their τ_t-inactive neighbor j at time $t' + 1$. However, in addition to the system parameter p, the probability that i successfully τ_t-activates j now also depends on both how "old" the information τ_t is and how many other $\tau_{t'}$s j has been activated by up to this current time step. That is, the probability that j is activated by i's transmission of τ_t at time $t' > t$ is

$$p \cdot f(t' + 1 - t) \cdot g(k_j(t')), \tag{1}$$

where $f : \mathbb{N} \mapsto [0, 1]$ is a function that represents the salience of information as a function of its age, $g : \mathbb{N} \mapsto [0, 1]$ is a function that captures how the number of activations from other information tokens effects the activation of additional ones, and $k_j(t')$ is simply the number of activations that j has incurred up to time t'.

3   Methods

In this Section, we describe our Estimation of Distribution Algorithm (EDA) for identifying effective seeding strategies for maximizing information exposure. Figure 1 shows a diagram that explains at a high-level the process implemented by our EDA. We initialize the probability distribution of the EDA to a uniform distribution, which provides good coverage of the strategy-space. Next, a set of strategies is sampled from the distribution and the fitness of each strategy is evaluated using a simulator that implements our ICM-SE. The fittest strategies are selected and used to update the distribution (explained below). Lastly, based on a termination criterion, such as convergence of the evolutionary process, either a new batch of strategies are sampled from the updated distribution or the fittest strategy is returned.

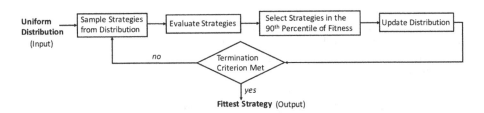

Fig. 1. Diagram illustrating the process underlying our EDA method for evolving effective strategies.

Our EDA learns a distribution P over the discrete strategy-space S. Let $\aleph = \{1, ..., n\}$ be the set of node indexes in ICM-SE and $\tau \in [1, 2, ..., t]$ index the time-steps at which information is injected into the network. Initially, P is a uniform distribution over S, which expresses our lack of prior knowledge about the characteristics of strategies with high fitness. However, if such prior knowledge exists, it is straight-forward to incorporate. We implemented P using the probabilistic generative model described by Algorithm 1.

Algorithm 1: Generative model for strategies

Result: sampled strategy
1 strategy $\leftarrow$ empty 2D array;
2 **for** τ *from 1 to t* **do**
3 $\quad$ $\aleph \leftarrow \{1, ..., n\}$;
4 $\quad$ **for** i *from 1 to m* **do**
5 $\quad\quad$ $index \sim P(\aleph|\tau)$;
6 $\quad\quad$ strategy$[\tau, i] \leftarrow index$;
7 $\quad\quad$ $\aleph \leftarrow \aleph - \{index\}$;
8 $\quad$ **end**
9 **end**

The result of the algorithm is a sampled strategy represented as a 2D array of natural numbers that indicate the indices of the selected seed nodes for each value of τ. There are $m \leq n$ seed nodes for each τ. In line 5 of the algorithm, a node index is sampled from a conditional probability distribution that is evolved by our EDA. We chose to decompose the full joint distribution P into t conditional distributions to reduce the dimensionality of the problem. In line 7, the sampled index is removed from the set of available seed nodes, thus preventing its reuse for the current τ.

During the evolutionary process, the conditional distributions are repeatedly updated using the best performing strategies. Specifically, for each τ, our EDA maintains a vector $v_\tau \in \mathbb{R}^n$, where $P(\aleph|\tau) \equiv v_\tau / \|v_\tau\|_1$. Initially, $v_\tau = \mathbf{1}$, for all τ (i.e., a uniform distribution). Given a strategy $\mathbf{s} \in \mathbb{N}^{t x m}$, the entry $\mathbf{s}[\tau, i]$ in v_τ is updated according to

$$v_\tau[\mathbf{s}[\tau, i]] \leftarrow cv_\tau[\mathbf{s}[\tau, i]]. \tag{2}$$

Here, the constant $c > 1$ is a "concentration" factor that controls the exploration vs. exploitation trade-off inherent to combinatorial search processes. A larger value for c accelerates the rate of convergence of the EDA, potentially at the cost of finding lower quality strategies. We found that $1.05 \leq c \leq 1.1$ works well (see Fig. 3).

4   Results

We ran a series of experiments to test the effectiveness of our EDA method and uncover the characteristics of the strategies that it evolves for our ICM-SE.

We investigated networks from three well-known classes: Barabasi-Albert (B-A) [8], Power Law Cluster (PLC) [6], and Relaxed Caveman (RC) [7]. All networks had $n = 100$ nodes and information was injected into the network during the first $t = 5$ time-steps. For each $\tau \in [1, 2, ..., t]$, $m = 5$ nodes were seeded with information. A simulation run terminated once information could no longer be passed between nodes, at which point the fitness function f was computed as the fraction of nodes that received information injected at all t time-steps. Our objective in defining f this way was to investigate the ability to maximize the *diversity* of information exposure, as opposed to just the overall rate of exposure to any information.

To test the effectiveness of our approach, we compared the performance of the best performing strategies evolved by EDA to strategies determined by a greedy search algorithm. We chose greedy search because it is the most common method for identifying strategies in Independent Cascade Models. We also included the performance of purely random strategies as a baseline. For each graph class (RC, PLC, and B-A) and for each strategy optimization method (EDA, greedy search, and random), we ran 50 trials. In each trial, a graph from one of the three classes was randomly generated and a strategy was identified by one of the three methods. Due to the stochastic nature of our ICM-SE, every strategy was run 10 times on a given graph and the fitness of the strategy was the average fitness across all 10 runs.

Figure 2 illustrates our results. For each graph class, it shows a comparison of the average performance of strategies from each method. We can see that for each graph class the average fitness of strategies from EDA is higher than those from greedy search and purely random strategies. Furthermore, the computational expense of running the EDA search process is no greater than that of greedy search and in some cases it is less.

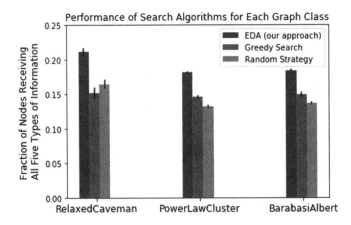

Fig. 2. Comparison of the average fitness of strategies from different methods on graphs from each class. On average, EDA finds better performing strategies than those from greedy search and random strategies for each graph class. The error bars are 90% confidence intervals.

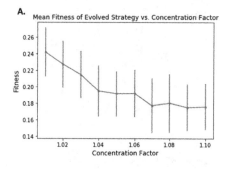

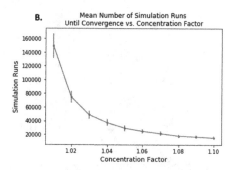

Fig. 3. Sensitivity Analysis: Figure A shows the desired dependence of mean strategy performance (fitness) on the concentration factor from our EDA method. We can see that performance increases as the concentration factor is decreased due to increasing exploration. However, as show in Figure B, the computational expense of the search process grows roughly exponentially as the concentration factor is decreased. In general, it is advisable to make the concentration factor as small as computational resources permit.

To better understand why our EDA method outperformed the greedy approach, we evaluated both individual and group-level properties of the chosen seed nodes to uncover common characteristics of each strategy. At the level of the individual seed node, we analyzed node centrality, participation in long-range links (links connecting different clusters) and cluster membership. In particular, for each simulation and each strategy, we calculated the fraction of chosen seed nodes with higher than average centrality measures for degree, closeness, betweenness, Information and Current Flow centralities. Since most real-world networks exhibit clustering, we further analyzed the extent to which seed nodes were dispersed across different clusters and whether or not they connected one cluster to another. At the group level, we investigated the *group* degree, closeness and betweenness centralities of the collection of seed nodes in each simulation. We also calculated the average of the shortest path lengths between all pairs of seed nodes and the diameter of the seed node-induced subgraph to further investigate the spread of the seed nodes in the graph.

In order to compare the two strategies, we identified the fraction of simulations for which 1) EDA chose seed nodes with a given attribute at a higher rate than the other, 2) The greedy search chose seed nodes with a given attribute at a higher rate and 3) EDA and greedy featured similar seed node selections. A strategy was identified as choosing more seed nodes with a given attribute in a simulation if the attribute values differed by at least 10%. As shown in Fig. 4, the greedy search is prone to selecting seed nodes with higher node and group centrality measures. EDA's strategy chooses seed nodes that are more evenly scattered throughout the network, as evidenced by higher average pairwise shortest path lengths and higher seed node-induced subgraph diameters. An analysis of cluster membership (after performing spectral clustering on each graph) supports this finding; EDA showed at least 10% improvement over the

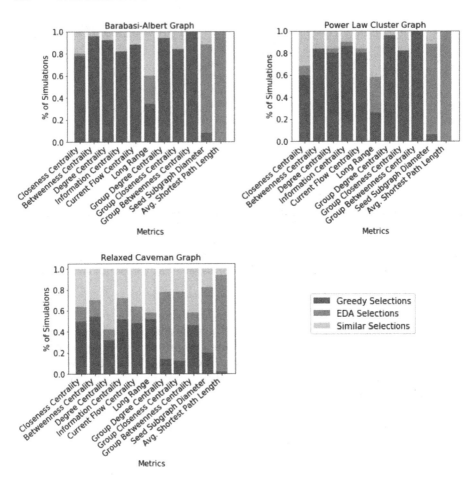

Fig. 4. Comparison of EDA and greedy search for each graph type for varying seed node properties. On average, greedy search selects seed nodes with high centrality, while EDA selects seed nodes that are more spread out in the graph.

Table 1. Percent of simulations with all clusters seeded

	Greedy	EDA
Barabasi-Albert	68%	78%
Power Law Cluster	54%	68%
Relaxed Caveman	16%	60%

greedy search in ensuring that each cluster contained at least one seed node (see Table 1). Further, the greedy search fails to seed all clusters in a graph at $\geq$1.4 times the rate of EDA.

Strategy characteristics differ when applied to the RC graph, which exhibits a much higher level of clustering than the others (.75 clustering coefficient as compared to .15 and .19 for the B-A and PLC graphs, respectively). Furthermore, the RC graph generally consists of a number of tightly clustered subgraphs with few long-range links between them. This structure makes it difficult for information to diffuse from one cluster to another, so it serves as an interesting case to test the effectiveness of the EDA and greedy strategies. While greedy search still chooses nodes with higher centrality at a greater rate than EDA, this effect is dampened for the RC graph. Instead, greedy search appears to focus more on selecting nodes with long-range links that connect the tightly-knit clusters. As before, EDA chooses seed nodes that are better spread throughout the graph. In this more clustered environment, we see (in Table 1) that EDA offers a much greater improvement (44%) over the greedy search in successfully seeding all clusters than for the other graphs (10% and 14%). EDA also seeds a larger number of clusters than the greedy search for 60% of simulations. Finally, greedy search left at least one cluster unseeded at 2.1 times the rate of EDA for the RC graph, as compared to 1.4 and 1.5 times the rate of EDA for the PLC and B-A graphs, respectively. EDA's ability to distribute seeds amongst the clusters in the RC graph contributes to the large increase in the group degree and group closeness centrality measures exhibited in Fig. 4c.

EDA's improvement over greedy search is explained by its ability to balance the selection of long-range links with the dispersion of seed nodes throughout the graphs. In the B-A and PLC graphs, the EDA and greedy strategies performed similarly in choosing seed nodes belonging to long-range links, while EDA did better in choosing seed nodes that could reach the periphery of the network. While this is not true for the RC graph, its ability to more evenly seed the clusters results in a group of seed nodes that are 1) more widely reachable from all nodes and 2) allows for information to propagate within the clusters even if it is difficult for information to exit clusters. Figure 5 offers an illustration of these points. The graph comparisons for Barabasi-Albert (1a, 1b) and Power Law Cluster (2a, 2b) illustrate that the greedy search chooses seed nodes that are compactly placed in the most connected portion of the network, while EDA also chooses seed nodes on the periphery of the network. In the RC graph (3a, 3b), EDA chooses nodes that are both on the periphery of the network and more evenly distributed through the clusters.

EDA's performance holds under varying conditions, including comparison to multiple types of greedy searches (temporal-first and spatial-first) and the incorporation of heterogenous populations (each individual was given randomly chosen information salience decay (linear, exponential or constant decay) and exposure (concave, sigmoid or constant) functions).

5   Discussion

In contrast to greedy search, which identifies a strategy by *sequentially* picking the seed nodes that most increase the fitness, our EDA method *concurrently*

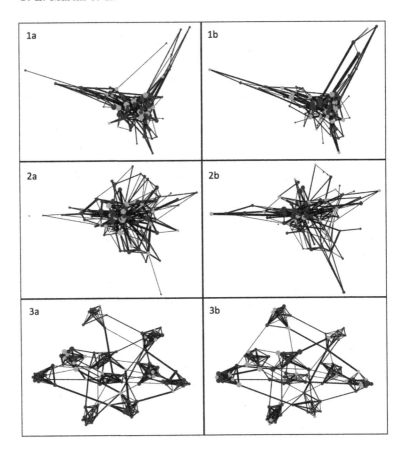

Fig. 5. Graph visualization of greedy search and EDA strategies. Figures 1a, 2a and 3a represent simulations of greedy search on the Barabasi-Albert, Power Law Cluster and Relaxed Caveman graphs, respectively. Figures 1b, 2b, 3b are the corresponding simulations of EDA. Seed nodes are red, node size represents diversity of information received, edge thickness indicates the amount of information passed via an edge.

searches over all seed node possibilities. Depending on the problem, this means that EDA has the potential to discover high-performing strategies that greedy search cannot. Based on our analysis, it appears that the concavity of the exposure function is one of the primary drivers behind EDA outperforming greedy search. Specifically, the concavity implies that when a node first starts to receive information it becomes *more* likely to transmit information in the future. However, after it has received enough information to pass the inflection point of the exposure function, any additional information reduces its future likelihood of transmitting information. This behavior of the system is problematic for greedy search because once it has selected a group of seed nodes that form a portion of a strategy it cannot go back and change its selection in response to unfavorable (e.g., blocking) conditions in the system that occur in response to newly selected seed nodes. This is especially evidenced in how the exposure function hinders the greedy search's strategy of selecting nodes of high centrality that tend to be clustered together. With the continuous selection of central seed nodes in the more highly connected portions of the graph, greedy search causes the nodes of those subgraphs to become saturated with information fairly quickly. Due to overexposure, they will then fail to spread information to the more peripheral nodes. EDA's ability to choose seed nodes that are spread across a graph allow for both central and peripheral nodes to share and receive information without experiencing the same blocking issue that the greedy search does.

6   Conclusions and Future Work

We found that on average our EDA method identifies higher-performing strategies compared to greedy search for graphs from each of the classes that we tested (RC, PLC, and B-A). Through the analysis of the individual and group-level properties of seed nodes chosen by each strategy over a number of simulations, we found that EDA's ability to spread nodes more evenly across the network largely contributes to its enhanced performance over the greedy search. Given this, and the fact that EDA is no more computationally expensive to run than greedy search, we see EDA as a straight-forward, but effective alternative to greedy search for identifying strategies in Independent Cascade Models. In future work, we plan to investigate the effectiveness of our EDA approach in ICMs that incorporate additional layers of realism, such as the ability of nodes to transmit previously seen information after a suitable "refractory" period. Such enhancements make the strategy-space more complex, thus requiring new efficient search methods.

References

1. Larrañga, P., Lozano, J.A.: Estimation of Distribution Algorithms: A New Tool for Evolutionary Computation, vol. 2. Springer, Heidelberg (2001). https://doi.org/10.1007/978-1-4615-1539-5
2. Domingos, P., Richardson, M.: Mining the network value of customers. In: Proceedings of the Seventh ACM SIGKDD International Conference on Knowledge Discovery and Data Mining, KDD 2001, pp. 57–66. ACM, New York (2001)
3. Kempe, D., Kleinberg, J., Tardos, É.: Maximizing the spread of influence through a social network. Theory Comput. 11(4), 105–147 (2015)
4. Kempe, D., Kleinberg, J., Tardos, É.: Maximizing the spread of influence through a social network. In: Proceedings of the Ninth ACM SIGKDD International Conference on Knowledge Discovery and Data Mining, KDD 2003, pp. 137–146. ACM, New York (2003)
5. Li, Y., Fan, J., Wang, Y., Tan, K.-L.: Influence maximization on social graphs: a survey. IEEE Trans. Knowl. Data Eng. 30(10), 1852–1872 (2018)
6. Holme, P., Kim, B.J.: Growing scale-free networks with tunable clustering. Phys. Rev. E 65(2), 026107 (2002)
7. Fortunato, S.: Community detection in graphs. Phys. Rep. 486(3-5), 75–174 (2010)

8. Barabási, A.-L., Albert, R.: Emergence of scaling in random networks. Science **286**(5439), 509–512 (1999)

9. Romero, D.M., Meeder, B., Kleinberg, J.: Differences in the mechanics of information diffusion across topics: idioms, political hashtags, and complex contagion on Twitter. In: Proceedings of the 20th International Conference on World Wide Web, WWW 2011, pp. 695–704 (2011)

10. Lerman, K., Ghosh, R., Surachawala, T.: Social contagion: an empirical study of information spread on Digg and Twitter follower graphs. arXiv preprint, arXiv:1202.3162 (2012)

Polarizing Tweets on Climate Change

Aman Tyagi[1]([✉])[iD], Matthew Babcock[2][iD], Kathleen M. Carley[1,2][iD],
and Douglas C. Sicker[1,2][iD]

[1] Engineering and Public Policy, Carnegie Mellon University,
Pittsburgh, PA 15213, USA
{amantyagi,sicker}@cmu.edu, kathleen.carley@cs.cmu.edu
[2] Institute for Software Research, Carnegie Mellon University,
Pittsburgh, PA 15213, USA
mbabcock@andrew.cmu.edu

Abstract. We introduce a framework to analyzes the conversation between two competing groups of Twitter users, one who believe in the anthropogenic causes of climate change (Believers) and a second who are skeptical (Disbelievers). As a case study, we use Climate Change related tweets during the United Nation's (UN) Climate Change Conference – COP24 (2018), Katowice, Poland. We find that both Disbelievers and Believers talk within their group more than with the other group; this is more so the case for Disbelievers than for Believers. The Disbeliever messages focused more on attacking those personalities that believe in the anthropogenic causes of climate change. On the other hand, Believer messages focused on calls to combat climate change. We find that in both Disbelievers and Believers bot-like accounts were equally active and that unlike Believers, Disbelievers get their news from a concentrated number of news sources.

Keywords: Climate change · Polarization · Twitter conversations · UN's COP24 · Hashtags · Label propagation

1 Introduction

Social media platforms such as Twitter have become an important medium for debating and organizing around complex social issues [22]. One such complex issue with significant socio-economic and political implications is climate change. Debates over climate change involve different groups with different inherent motivations and beliefs. For instance, among the people who are skeptical of climate science findings are people who outright reject the data that climate change is occurring, and others who argue that climate change is occurring due to non-anthropogenic causes. Similarly, there is significant difference in beliefs among

The authors would like to acknowledge the support of Department of Engineering and Public Policy, Carnegie Mellon University and Center for Computational Analysis of Social and Organizational Systems (CASOS), Carnegie Mellon University.

R. Thomson et al. (Eds.): SBP-BRiMS 2020, LNCS 12268, pp. 107–117, 2020.
https://doi.org/10.1007/978-3-030-61255-9_11

people who believe in anthropogenic causes of climate change. Work by [18] argue that there are groups who believe that impact of climate change is exaggerated (so-called "luke-warmers"), others who argue that we need an across-the-board technological change in energy production [23] or even end of capitalism [4,17]. Furthermore, some groups argue that it is already too late to avoid climate catastrophe [21]. In this paper, we analyze conversations between two broad competing groups of Twitter users, one who believes in anthropogenic causes of climate change (Believers) and a second who are skeptical or outright deny climate change is occurring (Disbelievers). To this end, we classify users into Disbelievers and Believers in Twitter conversations.

In this paper, we present a case study by analyzing conversations- Believers and Disbelievers, during United Nation's (UN) Climate Change Conference – COP24 (2018), Katowice, Poland. Previous studies about climate change discussions on social media, such as [25] and [13], lacked the context of a significant event. They also didn't take into account the behavior of bots during such an event. We examine what role, if any, that bots play within Disbeliever and Believer competing groups. By restricting the study to a particular event, we were able to manually inspect large fractions of stories in the competing groups. This case study should be helpful to inform future studies regarding climate change conversations on social media that cover longer time span. Our research questions are as follows:

1. What are the conversational subtopics within the Believer and Disbeliever groups, and what does common word use by these competing groups highlight? Do individuals of one group interact with individuals of the other group? What are the popular sources of information within these groups?
2. Are bots more active in one particular group over another?

We analyze these research questions using Twitter conversations on climate change during COP24. We describe our data collection method in Sect. 2.1. We use hashtag based method to classify users into Disbelievers and Believers described in Sect. 2.2. In Sect. 3 and Sect. 4 we present our results and their implications. Through this research study we provide a framework to analyze polarizing networks and the implications for climate change discussion.

2   Data Collection and Method

Twitter has been an important social media platform to study conversations about natural disasters, medical decisions, race relations and numerous other important issues [14]. We look at four main types of communication on Twitter in this paper: 1) Tweeting, 2) Retweeting, 3) Replying, and 4) Mentioning. We call the sum of the four types of communication as "all communication". In this paper, we look at these communications as networks and find network measures to compare and contrast communication from and between Disbelievers and Believers.

2.1 Data Collection

UN Framework Convention on Climate Change's (UNFCCC) Conference of Parties (COP) is an annual meeting of different states represented at the UN and acts as a venue to discuss the progress and establish obligations with regards to responding to climate change [1]. This event provided an opportunity to look at the Disbeliever and Believer climate change messaging on Twitter in context of a significant event.

We collected tweets with hashtags and certain keywords from November 27th to December 20th, 2018 using Twitter's API. We decided on collection hashtags based on hashtags related to #climatechange found on best-hashtags.com. We added more keywords based on these hashtags and news articles found after searching for keyword "COP24" on Google[1]. The combined data set contains a total of 1,379,584 distinct tweets (including retweets).

2.2 Method

We identified competing groups of Believers and Disbelievers by hashtags used by these groups. Hashtags have been shown to be a realistic substitute to identify stances among different groups on social media [15]. For example, previous studies suggest that climate Disbelievers use terms such as hoax and scam [20]. We analyzed common hashtags used in our dataset and found that "ClimateHoax" and "ClimateChangeIsReal" hashtags are used mostly by Disbelievers and Believers respectively. There are 528 distinct tweets with keyword "#ClimateHoax" and 9,008 tweets with keyword "#ClimateChangeIsReal" in our data set. We manually checked all tweets with hashtag "ClimateHoax" and randomly sampled 1,000 tweets from data subset with hashtag "ClimateChangeIsReal". We identified 96% of tweets with "#ClimateHoax" as climate change Disbeliever tweets. For "#ClimateChangeIsReal" out of the 1,000 randomly selected tweets, we identified about 99% as climate Believer tweets. We therefore conclude that hashtag "ClimateHoax" and hashtag "ClimateChangeIsReal" can be used as proxies for tweets broadcasted by Disbelievers and Believers respectively in our data set.

To identify more hashtags used by Believers and Disbelievers, we use the method described in [24]. We choose hashtags which are most used with hashtag "ClimateHoax" and hashtag "ClimateChangeIsReal" and are associated with conspiracy in case of Disbelievers or have similar meaning to "ClimateChangeIsReal" in case of Believers[2]. We give an initial weight of -1 to Disbeliever hashtags and $+1$ to Believer hashtags. We use these labels in a weighted hashtag x hashtag co-occurrence network, to find an average label from -1 to 1 for other

---

[1] Hashtags and keywords used for collection:#COP24, #ClimateChange, #ClimateHoax, #ParisAgreement,#IPCC, #InsideCOP24,#Climate, #ClimateChangeisReal, #ClimateAction, #GlobalWarming, COP24, Climate Change, Paris Agreement, Climate Hoax, IPCC, Climate, Global Warming.

[2] Disbeliever hashtags: ClimateHoax, YellowVests and Qanon. Believer hashtags: ClimateChangeIsReal,ClimateActionNow, FactsMatter, ScienceMatters, ScienceIsReal.

hashtags. The method used for propagating labels to other hashtags is reported in Algorithm 1. We aggregate hashtags used by each user and found a weighted average of all hashtags used by a particular user. We label a user as Disbeliever, Believer or unclassified if the weighted average was negative, positive or zero respectively. We assume that within our collection period Disbelievers or Believers do not change their stance and hence unlike in [24] we only look at aggregate polarized hashtags over entire dataset. Overall, we found a set of 8,413 tweets from 2,170 Disbelievers and 120,497 tweets from 15,640 Believers. We randomly sampled 100 users from both groups of users and manually checked their timeline to find approximately 91% of Disbelievers as showing activity akin to a Disbeliever and about 96% of Believers showing activity akin to a Believer.

Algorithm 1: Label Propagation Algorithm

Input: Graph G; Nodes $= n$; Edges $= e$; Edge Weight $= e_{ij}$, $i \in n$ and $j \in n$
initialize $\gamma = 100$ and $i=0$;
for *each n* **do**
    define $l = \text{integer}(i/\gamma)$; $i+=1$;
    for *each n* **do**
        if *n not labeled* **then**
            compute $t = $ neighbors of n;
            compute $t_l = $ labeled neighbors of n;
            if $|t_l| + l \geq t$ **then**
                initialize *score, c*
                for *each $t_i \in t$* **do**
                    score += label $t_i * e_{nt_i}$
                    c += e_{nt_i}
                end
                update label $n = score/c$
            end
        end
    end
end

BOT Detection: To find bots accounts in our data set, we used CMU's Bot-Hunter [6,7]. The output of Bot-Hunter is a probability measure of bot-like behavior assigned to each account. Unless otherwise stated, we report our analysis for a probability threshold of 0.5, as done in various machine learning classification methods [19]. In other words, we classified an account as bot-like if output probability from Bot-Hunter was greater than 0.5. At 0.5 threshold level we found 596,282 bot-like accounts out of total 1,035,416 users in our data set.

Account Type: We used a classification model trained on the users' tweets and personal descriptions to find news agency accounts associated with our list of user accounts. The model is similar to the state-of-the-art model used in [9]. The paper describes the model as a long-short term memory neural network [16] with an attention mechanism [5]. In total, we find 2.2% of Believer tweets as classified to be from news agencies and 6.2% of Disbeliever tweets as classified to be from news agencies.

3   Results

We begin by discussing topics of discussion within Believers and Disbelievers. Then we look at inter-group and intra-group interaction. Lastly, we look at the popular news agencies and contrast bot-like account's behavior in these two groups.

3.1   Topics of Discussion

To understand the conversations of both the groups we found the most frequent words used by these competing groups. The results are presented below:[3]

Believers: climate, change, world, us, need, action, un, global, leaders, future
Disbelievers: climate, change, global, private, us, un, sanders, world, end, warming

We find that Believers use words such as "need", "action", "leaders" and "future" more often, potentially indicating tweets calling for action to combat climate change. On the other hand, Disbelievers use words such as "private" (referencing "private jet"), "sanders", "end" and "warming", potentially indicating attacks on pro-climate change personalities and their messaging.

To further our understanding of the conversations and to find topics of opinions within these group, we performed topic modelling of tweets by Believers and Disbelievers using Latent Dirichlet Allocation (LDA) [10]. We ran our model to find top ten topics on the unigrams of tweets generated after removing common stop words. Among the top ten topics we report the top 3 list of words we were able to infer topics about in Table 1. In the first topic Disbelievers use words such as "scam" and "fakenews" with words associated with "climate change", potentially calling out climate change as scam or fake. In the second topic Disbelievers are calling out personalities believing in human caused climate change. In the third topic Disbelievers are talking about yellowvests movement which relates to the French movement against raising fuel taxes based on climate policy [12]. On the other hand, for the first topic Believers use words related to using renewables and giving up fossil fuel. This can be inferred from the use of word "keepitintheground", as the word is used on social media to ban any new use of fossil fuel [2]. The second topic for Believers is about the climate change politics in Australia with words such as "auspol" (short for Australian politics) and "stopadani". Specifically, "stopadani" is used in social media to protest against Adani group of companies digging Carmichael coal mine in Queensland, Australia [26]. Lastly, the third topic for Believers relates to COP24 with word "takeyourseat" used in COP24 to signify the People's seat initiative launched by the UN [1].

---

[3] Note that in the construction of unigrams, we exclude common stop words.

Table 1. Table of top 10 words (excluding hashtags) used by Disbelievers and Believers.

Disbelievers			Believers		
climate	climate	yellowvests	science	climatechangeisreal	cop
scam	bernie	maga	climate	climatechange	climateaction
change	sanders	trump	year	auspol	climate
nuclear	travel	carbontax	keepitintheground	climatestrike	katowice
industry	potus	france	climateemergency	climateactionnow	world
fakenews	month	macron	record	greennewdeal	takeyourseat
crisis	change	policy	renewableenergy	climate	leader
record	planet	french	bcpoli	cdnpoli	solar
global	great	people	end	stopadani	change
agw	face	hoax	fact	globalwarming	poland

3.2 User Accounts and Conversations

We first look at different Twitter networks formed from various communications to contrast Believers and Disbeliever. In Fig. 1, we report figures for all four networks. In the retweet network, we can see a clear distinction between Believers and Disbelievers; Disbelievers retweet other Disbelievers more than they retweet Believers, and vice versa for Believers. The mentions network of Disbelievers and Believers shows more links between these groups meaning that Believers and Disbelievers do mention users from other groups on tweets. The reciprocal network has less activity between the groups than the mentions network, suggesting that although users from one group mention people from other group, they tend to have reciprocal relationships with their own group. The reply network has a much lower number of nodes compared to other networks which suggests that users in both groups prefer mentioning or retweeting rather than replying to tweets. The stark contrast in mentions and reciprocal activity confirms that users from one group do not engage in conversations with users from another group. After establishing differences in different type of behavior on Twitter, next we look at the combined communication of these groups to check how much these groups talk within themselves, i.e. how much "echo-chambery" these groups are.

To compare echo-chamber effects in these two groups, we combine all the above networks to make a network of all communications to find echo-chamberness(e)[4] for each group with and without unclassified accounts. We find that for Disbelievers $e = 0.007$ and for Disbelievers with unclassified accounts $e = 0.003$. On the other hand, for Believers $e = 0.006$ and for Believers with unclassified accounts $e = 0.003$. The values of e is small compared to a denser symmetric graph because the communications network does not represent the actual follower's network of the users. The e of both groups decreases on adding

---

[4] For a unimodal network G, the e of G is $(r * d)^{(1/3)}$, where r is the reciprocity of graph G, that is the fraction of edges in the graph that are reciprocal (a symmetric graph has $r = 1$), and d is the density of graph G.

unclassified accounts, which indicates that each group is talking more to themselves, this is marginally truer for Disbelievers compared to Believers.

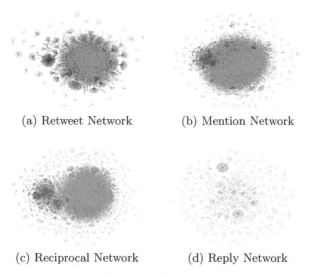

(a) Retweet Network   (b) Mention Network

(c) Reciprocal Network   (d) Reply Network

Fig. 1. Communication networks between Twitter accounts classified as Disbelievers (red) and Believers (green). The graphs were made using ORA-PRO [3,11]. (Color figure online)

The e metric results suggests that more communication is happening within these groups compared to outside these groups. Next, we look at the difference in fraction of most crucial and influential spreaders of information in both the networks. This helps us determine whether or not these groups are influenced by multiple influencers or via a central actor. ORA-PRO twitter report labels users as "super spreader" as the most influential users in spreading information and "super friends" as most crucial users in bi-directional communication on twitter [3,11]. Super spreaders in ORA-PRO are defined as user accounts in sum of mentioned-by and retweeted-by network which are in top 3 of following measures: 1) Often mentioned/retweeted by others, 2) Iteratively mentioned/retweeted by others, and 3) Often mentioned/retweeted by groups of others. To compare the two groups, we look at the fraction of user accounts labelled as super spreaders and super friends. We find that Disbelievers (0.48%) have fractionally higher percentage of super spreaders than Believers (0.37%). Disbelievers also have higher fraction of users classified as super friends than compared to Believers (0.38% vs 0.28%). We conclude that Disbelievers have higher fraction of influential users in the network compared to Believers.

We look at the popular news sources within our different groups. In Fig. 2, we present a word cloud of the names of accounts classified as news agency (Sect. 2.2) by the number of tweets in the competing groups. "Patriot News" dominates Disbelievers' tweets (including retweets), but for Believers there is no one account which dominates.

Fig. 2. Word cloud of tweets by news agencies classified as Disbeliever (left) and Believer (right).

Next, we compare bot-like activity in the two groups of Believers and Disbelievers. In Fig. 3, we report the bot-like account's activity at different probability thresholds for an account to be classified to be bot-like for the Believers and Disbelievers. We find that the fraction of tweets and user accounts classified as bots are similar for both the groups at all threshold levels. This indicates that bots are similarly active in both the groups.

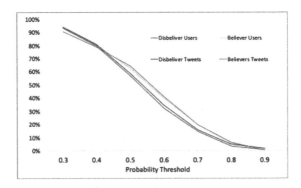

Fig. 3. Percentage of bots and tweets at different probability threshold for an account to be classified to be bot-like as predicted by Bot-Hunter [6] for climate Disbelievers and Believers group.

4   Discussion

We classify users into two competing communities to compare and contrast the hashtags, bot percentage and messaging in the communities. We use climate change as case study to find groups with opposite views. An important finding of this paper is that different communities in climate change discussion primarily use different sets of hashtags. We find that Disbelievers words usage focus more on attacking personalities believing in anthropogenic origin of climate change and their messaging; on the other hand, Believers words usage focuses on callings to combat climate change. Our results indicate that unlike conversations on personalities in opposing groups, messages about social movements are dominated by discussion on movements aligned towards group's beliefs rather than calling out movements driven by contrasting beliefs.

We looked at the network structure of Believers and Disbelievers for these twitter interactions. We found greater homophily in retweet, reply and reciprocal networks compared to the mention network. This is consistent with the fact that typically users retweet, equivalent to resharing, if they endorse that message and are hence more likely to endorse a message from users aligned to their own perspective. On the other hand, mentioning activity could be a way to call out or malign members of other community. For all the types of networks, we found that both Disbelievers and Believers talk within their group more than with the other group; this is more so the case for Disbelievers than for Believers. Our results confirm findings from [25], which concluded that there are segregated communities in climate change conversations on Twitter. Moreover, Disbelievers communication activity is influenced by higher fraction of users in their group compared to Believers. This coupled with the fact that Disbelievers are more "echo-chambery" suggests that higher fraction of conversations within Disbelievers happen with the influencers compared to Believers' network. We conclude that Disbelievers are more organized around certain influencers in their network compared to Believers.

We found that unlike Believers, Disbelievers get their news from a concentrated number of news sources and hence may be more vulnerable to manipulation. We also found that in both Disbelievers and Believers bot-like accounts were equally active. This is in similar vein with previous findings that bot-like accounts tend to stir conversations in differently politically aligned groups rather than concentrating on conversations in one group [8]. We conclude that bot activity is further creating and nourishing the divide between Believers and Disbelievers.

References

1. Conference of the parties (COP). https://unfccc.int/process/bodies/supreme-bodies/conference-of-the-parties-cop/
2. What does 'keep it in the ground' really mean? Read this, December 2017. https://www.uschamber.com/series/above-the-fold/what-does-keep-it-the-ground-really-mean-read
3. Altman, N., Carley, K.M., Reminga, J.: Ora user's guide 2018. Carnegie-Mellon University. Pittsburgh PA Institute of Software Research International, Technical Report (2018)
4. Angus, I.: Facing the Anthropocene: Fossil Capitalism and the Crisis of the Earth System. NYU Press, New York (2016)

5. Bahdanau, D., Cho, K., Bengio, Y.: Neural machine translation by jointly learning to align and translate. arXiv preprint arXiv:1409.0473 (2014)
6. Beskow, D., Carley, K.M., Bisgin, H., Hyder, A., Dancy, C., Thomson, R.: Introducing Bothunter: a tiered approach to detection and characterizing automated activity on Twitter. In: International Conference on Social Computing, Behavioral-Cultural Modeling and Prediction and Behavior Representation in Modeling and Simulation. Springer (2018)
7. Beskow, D.M., Carley, K.M.: You are known by your friends: leveraging network metrics for bot detection in Twitter. In: Tayebi, M.A., Glässer, U., Skillicorn, D.B. (eds.) Open Source Intelligence and Cyber Crime. LNSN, pp. 53–88. Springer, Cham (2020). https://doi.org/10.1007/978-3-030-41251-7_3
8. Bessi, A., Ferrara, E.: Social bots distort the 2016 US presidential election online discussion. First Monday **21**(11-7) (2016)
9. Binxuan Huang, K.M.C.: Discover your social identity from what you tweet: a content based approach. Disinformation, Misinformation, and Fake News in Social Media - Emerging Research Challenges and Opportunities (2020)
10. Blei, D.M., Ng, A.Y., Jordan, M.I.: Latent Dirichlet allocation. J. Mach. Learn. Res. **3**, 993–1022 (2003)
11. Carley, K.M.: Ora: a toolkit for dynamic network analysis and visualization (2017)
12. Cigainero, J.: Who are France's yellow vest protesters, and what do they want?, December 2018 . https://www.npr.org/2018/12/03/672862353/who-are-frances-yellow-vest-protesters-and-what-do-they-want
13. Cody, E.M., Reagan, A.J., Mitchell, L., Dodds, P.S., Danforth, C.M.: Climate change sentiment on Twitter: an unsolicited public opinion poll. PloS One **10**(8), e0136092 (2015)
14. Dredze, M., Wood-Doughty, Z., Quinn, S.C., Broniatowski, D.A.: Vaccine opponents' use of Twitter during the 2016 US presidential election: implications for practice and policy. Vaccine **35**(36), 4670–4672 (2017)
15. Evans, A.: Stance and identity in Twitter hashtags. Language@ internet 13(1) (2016)
16. Hochreiter, S., Schmidhuber, J.: Long short-term memory. Neural Comput. **9**(8), 1735–1780 (1997)
17. Klein, N.: This Changes Everything: Capitalism vs. the Climate. Simon and Schuster, New York (2015)
18. Matthews, P.: Why are people skeptical about climate change? Some insights from blog comments. Environ. Commun. **9**(2), 153–168 (2015). https://doi.org/10.1080/17524032.2014.999694
19. Pedregosa, F., et al.: Scikit-learn: machine learning in python. J. Mach. Learn. Res. **12**, 2825–2830 (2011)
20. Runciman, D.: A climate of conspiracy, September 2015. https://www.opendemocracy.net/en/climate-of-conspiracy/
21. Scranton, R.: Learning to Die in the Anthropocene: Reflections on the End of a Civilization. City Lights Publishers, San Francisco (2015)
22. Segerberg, A., Bennett, W.L.: Social media and the organization of collective action: using Twitter to explore the ecologies of two climate change protests. Commun. Rev. **14**(3), 197–215 (2011). https://doi.org/10.1080/10714421.2011.597250
23. Shellenberger, M., Nordhaus, T.: The death of environmentalism: global warming politics in a post-environmental world. Verlag nicht ermittelbar (2004)
24. Tyagi, A., Field, A., Lathwal, P., Tsvetkov, Y., Carley, K.M.: A computational analysis of polarization on Indian and Pakistani social media (2020)

25. Williams, H.T., McMurray, J.R., Kurz, T., Lambert, F.H.: Network analysis reveals open forums and echo chambers in social media discussions of climate change. Global Environ. Change **32**, 126–138 (2015). https://doi.org/10.1016/j.gloenvcha.2015.03.006

26. Zajac, M., Foundation, A.C.: Stop Adani: how a grassroots environmental movement is ticking SDG boxes in Australia, February 2018. https://impakter.com/stop-adani-grassroots-environmental-movement-ticking-sdg-boxes-australia/

Characterizing Sociolinguistic Variation in the Competing Vaccination Communities

Shahan Ali Memon[1(✉)] , Aman Tyagi[2] , David R. Mortensen[1] ,
and Kathleen M. Carley[1,2]

[1] School of Computer Science, Carnegie Mellon University,
Pittsburgh, PA 15213, USA
{samemon,dmortens,kathleen.carley}@cs.cmu.edu
[2] Engineering and Public Policy, Carnegie Mellon University,
Pittsburgh, PA 15213, USA
amantyagi@cmu.edu

Abstract. Public health practitioners and policy makers grapple with the challenge of devising effective message-based interventions for debunking public health misinformation in cyber communities. *Framing* and *personalization* of the message is one of the key features for devising a persuasive messaging strategy. For an effective health communication, it is imperative to focus on *preference-based framing* where the preferences of the target sub-community are taken into consideration. To achieve that, it is important to understand and hence characterize the target sub-communities in terms of their social interactions. In the context of health-related misinformation, vaccination remains to be the most prevalent topic of discord. Hence, in this paper, we conduct a sociolinguistic analysis of the two competing vaccination communities on Twitter: *pro-vaxxers* or individuals who believe in the effectiveness of vaccinations, and *anti-vaxxers* or individuals who are opposed to vaccinations. Our data analysis show significant linguistic variation between the two communities in terms of their usage of linguistic intensifiers, pronouns, and uncertainty words. Our network-level analysis show significant differences between the two communities in terms of their network density, echo-chamberness, and the EI index. We hypothesize that these sociolinguistic differences can be used as proxies to characterize and understand these communities to devise better message interventions.

Keywords: Vaccination · Sociolinguistic analysis · Social network analysis

1 Introduction

Health-related misinformation has detrimental effects on the public health. According to researchers, many preventable diseases have re-emerged as a consequence of the drop in immunization rates due to declining trust in vaccines

© Springer Nature Switzerland AG 2020
R. Thomson et al. (Eds.): SBP-BRiMS 2020, LNCS 12268, pp. 118–129, 2020.
https://doi.org/10.1007/978-3-030-61255-9_12

caused by the misinformation on the web [18]. Moreover, distrust in vaccines and health expertise is only expected to increase in the next decade [15].

Debunking public health misinformation requires an effective health communication such as a *message-based intervention*. For an effective message-based intervention, it is imperative to focus on *preference-based framing* where the preferences of the target sub-community are taken into consideration. These preferences can be defined over three main aspects: (i) choice of the messenger, (ii) medium of information dissemination, and (iii) content of the message. A message intervention is effective if the message is delivered by a *trusted* source using an optimal medium of dissemination. In online communities, this translates to identifying the *influencers* or nodes with high *degree centrality* in the social network such as shown in [20]. Choosing the content of the message, on the other hand, requires a thorough understanding of how the target community members interact with each other, what *language choices* they make, and how those language choices reflect their *non-negotiable social identities*.

Vaccination related misinformation is arguably the most prevalent form of misinformation online. Therefore, for the purposes of this study, we chose to tap into vaccination discourse on Twitter. We study the conversations between two competing groups of Twitter users: (i) those who believe in the effectiveness of vaccinations *(pro-vaxxers)*, and (ii) those who are skeptical *(anti-vaxxers)*. The goal of our study is to characterize the two competing vaccination communities in terms of their sociolinguistic variation. We hypothesize that understanding the interactions of the members of these communities can help devise a better messaging strategy.

Prior work includes the sociolinguistic analysis of Twitter in multilingual societies [16], predicting community membership using word frequencies [7], identifying effective vaccine communication using fuzzy trace theory [4], understanding the evolution of competing views around vaccination at the system level [15], and sociolinguistic study of online echo-chambers [10].

We extend the work by Duseja and Jhamtani in [10] to study vaccination-based communities on Twitter by understanding their differences in usage of linguistic intensifiers, pronouns, and uncertainty words. We also conduct a network-level analysis by computing the network density, EI index, and echo-chamberness for the two target communities.

2   Dataset

To construct our dataset, we employ a three-stage process: (i) we first collect data using a set of hashtags via the Twitter search and the Twitter streaming API; (ii) we use this data to identify the two communities; and (iii) finally, to mitigate survivorship bias [6] and collect more data per individual, we collect timelines of the identified pro- and anti-vaxxers. We describe this process in detail in the following subsections. In the Sect. 2.4, we present the statistics for the final set of data we use to conduct our analyses.

2.1   Data Collection

We first collect a set of known pro-vaccination and anti-vaccination hashtags from our domain knowledge as well as from the background literature [9]. List of these hashtags can be found in Table 1. We use these hashtags to collect Twitter data through the Twitter Streaming API, and augment it with data collected from Twitter Search API. The data consists of Tweets from 29th October 2019 to 12th November 2019. Based on [5], we filter out all tweets that do not include the lemmas "vacc" or "vax" (case insensitive) as part of their tweet text. This is to remove any possible noise in the data.

Table 1. This table shows the hashtags used for the task of data collection. We use camel-casing for better readability.

Stance	Hashtags
Pro-vaccination	*VaccinesSaveLives, VaccinesWork, WorldImmunizationWeek, VaxWithMe, HealthForAll, WiW, ThankYouLaura*
Anti-vaccination	*LearnTheRisk, VaccineInjury, VaccineDeath, VaccineDamage, VaccinesCauseAutism, CDCFraud, CDCWhistleBlower, CDCTruth, WakeUpAmerica, HearUs, HealthFreedom*
Unidentified	*Vaccine, Vaccines, Vaccinate, VaccinateUS*

2.2   Community Detection

Label Propagation. To be able to conduct any analysis, it is imperative to identify the competing groups. Assigning a stance to a tweet or a twitter user is a non-trivial problem. Therefore, we use a similar method as described in [22,23] to find anti-vaxxers and pro-vaxxer groups based on the weighted combination of the *valence* of their hashtags. In this study, we assume that retweets indicate endorsement.

In the previous studies such as [11], hashtags have been shown to work as realistic proxies for identifying stances among different groups on social media sites. In [22], hashtags are used to identify twitter users who believe in anthropogenic causes of climate change and those who do not. Similarly, in [23], hashtags could also be used to identify polarization in political discourse and how the polarization can change with time.

We use community detection method based on the work done in [23]. We first choose 2 seed hashtags for each of the polarized groups: *#VaccinesSaveLives* and *#VaccinesWork* for pro-vaccination and *#VaccineInjury* and *#LearnTheRisk* for anti-vaccination. We assign pro-vaccination seeds a valence of $+1$, and anti-vaccination seeds a valence of -1.[1] We then create a hashtag co-occurrence graph

---

[1] We randomly sample 100 tweets for each of these hashtags. For pro-vaccination hashtags, 98% of tweets with hashtag *#VaccinesSaveLives* and 97% of tweets with hashtag *#VaccinesWork* were related to pro-vaccination. For anti-vaccination hashtags, 88% of tweets with hashtag *#LearnTheRisk* and 93% of tweets with hashtag *#VaccineInjury* were related to anti-vaccination.

to identify most co-occurring hashtags with the chosen seeds, and choose those that are semantically similar, as well as the ones that are known to be pro-vax and anti-vax hashtags from the background literature [4,5,9] to manually assign a hard valence of $+1$ and -1. We then use a variant of label propagation algorithm [25] described as Algorithm 1 below to assign valence to each of the remaining hashtags. Similar to [23] the input to the algorithm is a hashtag-to-hashtag co-occurrence graph where hashtags represent nodes, and nodes are connected if they co-occur. The edges are weighted by the frequency of co-occurrence.

Algorithm 1: Label Propagation Algorithm

Input: Nodes $= n$; Edges $= e$; Edge Weight $= e_{ij}$, $i \in n$ and $j \in n$
initialize $\gamma = 50$ and i;
for *each n* **do**
  define $l = integer(i/\gamma)$; $i{+}{=}1$;
  for *each n* **do**
    if n *not labeled* **then**
      compute $t =$ neighbors of n;
      compute $t_l =$ labeled neighbors of n;
      if $|t_l| + l \geq t$ **then**
        initialize *score, c*
        for *each $t_i \in t$* **do**
          score $+=$ label $t_i * e_{nt_i}$
          c $+= e_{nt_i}$
        end
        update label $n = score/c$
      end
    end
  end
end

Stance Identification. Once we have identified the valence of a set of hashtags, we aggregate hashtags used by each user and find a weighted average of the valence of all hashtags used by a particular user. We label a user as pro-vaxxer, or anti-vaxxer if the weighted average was positive, or negative respectively.

Using the algorithm, 3295 users are identified as pro-vaxxers, 2967 as anti-vaxxers. We randomly sample 100 users that were classified as pro-vaxxers and 100 users that were classified as anti-vaxxers to evaluate the quality of assignment. We find 96% of the labeled pro-vaxxers as pro-vaxxers, and 80% of the labeled anti-vaxxers as anti-vaxxers.

2.3   Timeline Extraction

Both Twitter streaming API and the Twitter search API do not allow the collection of data beyond a certain time period to be able to extract historical tweets. As a consequence, we collect our initial set of tweets within a fixed time window of 15 days. Because our goal was to study how the non-negotiable social identities of users correlated to their linguistic choices on Twitter, windowing the data by time period of 15 days could lead to high survivorship bias where users with higher activity within the chosen days could introduce bias in our analyses by having a higher influence. This is why, we decided to augment our data with timelines of identified individual users. This may not remove the survivorship bias completely, but may help mitigate it.

At the end of timeline extraction, we only retain one copy of each of the tweets. More concretely, to avoid over-inflating the effect of certain tweets that are more viral than the other, we use only unique tweet texts. This is an important preprocessing step to conduct a sociolinguistic frequency-based analysis.

2.4   Data Statistics

At the end, our sociolinguistic analysis is conducted on an overall 6262 Twitter users with an aggregate of 588,110 tweets. This included 3295 pro-vaxxers with 310461 pro-vaccination tweets, and 2967 anti-vaxxers with 277649 anti-vaccination tweets, making it an average of about 94 tweets per user for both pro- and anti-vaxxers.

3   Methodology

We conduct two types of analyses to characterize the two competing groups: *linguistic analysis* and *network analysis*.

3.1   Linguistic Analysis

We test three linguistic variables which are described as follows.

Linguistic Intensification. We first study the differences in the usage of linguistic intensifiers. Intensifiers are words, or phrases that strengthen the meaning of other expressions and show emphasis. Examples include amplifiers (e.g. "really", "very"), usage of swear words, general interjections (e.g. "wow", "omg"), and exclamations. Intensifiers are commonly used to bolster argumentation to persuade the target audience. We hypothesize that users that are pro-vaxxers use more intensifiers. This is because pro-vaxxers have been found to frequently debunk anti-vaxxers' claims with scientific evidence [2]. Therefore, they would seem to take the corrective approach intended to persuade anti-vaxxers, hence using more intensifiers.

Pronominal Usage. Pronouns play a key role in models of narrative and discourse processing [12]. Because most of the vaccine-related misinformation is based on personal anecdotes, we would expect pronominal usage to be high amongst anti-vaxxers. To test this, we identify various different categories of pronouns (e.g. "subject pronouns", "object pronouns", "third-person pronouns"), a complete list of which can be found in Table 2.

Use of Uncertainty Words. Previous research [10] has found the use of uncertainty words (e.g. "might", "likely") as a negative linguistic correlate of echo-chamberness. This is based on the hypothesis that because users not in echo-chambers are exposed to alternate views, they may be less certain of their ideas. We adopted the list of uncertainty words from [10] to test if that is true i.e. if there is a significant difference in the use of uncertainty words across the two vaccination communities.

Table 2. This table shows the lexical categories we use for the sociolinguistic analysis along with the chosen list of words for each category (lexicon).

Lexical category	Lexicon (vocabulary)
Intensifiers	
Amplifiers	*amazingly, -ass, astoundingly, awful, bare, bloody, crazy, dead, dreadfully, colossally, especially, exceptionally, excessively, extremely, extraordinary, fantastically, frightfully, fucking, fully, hella, holy, incredibly, insanely, mad, mightily, moderately, most, outrageously, phenomenally, precious, quite, radically, rather, real, really, remarkably, ridiculously, right, sick, so, somewhat, strikingly, super,supremely, surpassingly, terribly, terrifically, too, totally, uncommonly, unusually, veritable, very, wicked*
Swear words	*fu*****, etc.* A complete list of words can be found on Wikipedia's English swear words page [].
General interjections	*wow, hooray, ouch, uh oh, ew, aw, omg*
Exclamation	*!**
Uncertainty words	*may, might, perhaps, maybe/may-be, potentially, possibly, likely, probably, probable, possible, think, seem, believe, presume, would be, could be*
Pronouns	
Demonstrative	*this, that, these, those*
Possessive	*ours, mine, yours, theirs, his, hers*
Quantifier	*few, several, some, all, much, one, fewer, many, more, most, plenty, less, little, enough*
Reflexive	*myself, herself, ourselves, themselves, yourself, himself, itself, yourselves*
First-Person	*I, we, us, me, myself, my, mine, our, ours*
Second-Person	*you, yours, you're, your*
Third-Person	*he, she, theirs, themselves, them, her, him, his, himself, hers, herself, it, its, itself, they*
Gendered third-person	*he, she, her, him, his, himself, hers, herself*
Subject	*I, she, he, they, we, you, it*
Object	*me, us, them, him, you, her, it*
IT	*it, it's, its, itself*

3.2 Network Analysis

We also compute three network-level measures to characterize the network structure of the two target communities. We describe each of these measures in detail in their respective sections below.

Network Density. Network density is defined as the ratio of actual connections and potential connections [13]. Dense networks tend to "groupthink" [21] where conformity of ideas is highly valued and difference of opinions is discouraged.

EI Index. The EI (External-Internal) index was developed by Krackhardt and Stern in [17] as a measure of dominance of external over internal ties. More concretely, assuming two groups based on some attribute, one group defined as internal and the other as external, the EI index is computed as follows:

$$EI = \frac{EL - IL}{EL + IL} \tag{1}$$

where EL represents the number of external links and IL represents the number of internal links. EI index is a useful proxy for identifying echo-chamberness.

Echo-Chamberness. To compare the echo-chamber effect in the two vaccination groups, we also directly compute the echo-chamberness of the two communities. We use the following definition of echo-chamberness: For a given network G, the echo-chamberness (EC) is defined as:

$$EC = (r * d)^{1/3} \tag{2}$$

where r is the reciprocity [24] of graph G or the ratio of bi-directional edges and the total number of edges in G, and d is the density of graph G.

3.3 Evaluation

Test Statistics. For each sub-category of the linguistic features in Table 2, we use two test statistics to compute the difference between the two groups. These are as follows:

1. The overall proportion of tweets that contain any of the words for a given lexical category (T_1)
2. The mean of the proportions of tweets of individual users containing any of the words for a given lexical category (T_2)

We use these test statistics to compute (i) the difference of proportions between the two groups, and (ii) the difference of means of proportions between the two groups.

The first test statistic regards each tweet independently. We use the second test statistic to account for differences in the linguistic choices of individual users.

Statistical Significance: For the first statistic, we use a two-sample z-test for the difference of proportions (Z_1). For the second statistic, we use an independent z-test for the difference in means (Z_2). For all the tests, our $\alpha = 0.05$.

4   Results and Discussion

4.1   Linguistic Analysis

The summary of our linguistic analysis across all the lexical categories can be found in Table 3.

Table 3. This table shows the summary of our analyses across all the linguistic categories. The first column shows the lexical category. The second and third columns show the first test statistic as a percentage for pro-vaxxers and anti-vaxxers respectively. The fourth and fifth column display the z-score and p-value for the z-test for the difference of proportions. The sixth and seventh columns show the second test statistic as a mean percentage for pro-vaxxers and anti-vaxxers respectively. The eighth and ninth columns display the z-score and p-value for the independent z-test for the difference in means

Lexical category	T_1 (Pro)	T_1 (Anti)	z-score (Z_1)	p-value (Z_1)	T_2 (Pro)	T_2 (Anti)	z-score (Z_2)	p-value (Z_2)
Intensifiers	45.90%	50.60%	−36.25	<.001	11.63%	14.96%	−6.59	<.001
Amplifiers	31.40%	37.10%	−45.32	<.001	10.91%	13.66%	−5.66	<.001
Swear words	4.0%	5.60%	−27.40	<.001	.57%	1.04%	−3.26	<.001
General interjections	17.50%	16.70%	7.89	<.001	.43%	.58%	−1.37	.17
Exclamation	1.10%	2.20%	−34.17	<.001	–	–	–	–
Uncertainty words	5.7%	7.0%	−20.84	<.001	4.12%	5.07%	−3.23	.001
Pronouns	55.80%	62.20%	−49.68	<.001	55.94%	61.83%	−7.38	<.001
Demonstrative	17.63%	20.91%	−31.84	<.001	18.61%	21.73%	−5.20	<.001
Possessive	1.30%	1.60%	−9.39	<.001	1.49%	1.67%	−.92	.36
Quantifier	15.3%	16.0%	−6.70	<.001	15.20%	16.83%	−3.06	.002
Reflexive	.80%	.86%	−2.26	.02	1.49%	.92%	3.43	<.001
First-Person	21.20%	23.44%	−20.67	<.001	20.96%	22.54%	−2.45	.01
Second-Person	16.40%	18.5%	−20.69	<.001	15.22%	16.47%	−2.23	.03
Third-Person	14.8%	20.9%	−60.51	<.001	14.29%	20.84%	−11.74	<.001
Gendered third-person	3.60%	5.60%	−36.84	<.001	3.15%	4.92%	−5.96	<.001
Subject	28.90%	37.50%	−69.53	<.001	27.64%	35.55%	−10.89	<.001
Object	21.64%	26.90%	−46.77	<.001	19.66%	24.51%	−7.91	<.001
IT	8.30%	10.29%	−26.16	<.001	8.21%	9.44%	−3.07	.002

Linguistic Intensification. We observe that our initial hypothesis that pro-vaxxers use more intensifiers is false. What we find is that anti-vaxxers employ significantly more linguistic intensifiers than pro-vaxxers. This holds true across all the sub-categories of intensifiers with the exception of the use of general interjections where the difference is marginal and not significant. While intensifiers are used as a persuasion technique, the observed results can possibly be explained by an old theory in speech communication that correlates the use of intensifiers with perceived powerlessness [3,14]. Intensifiers and hedges are used more generally by people with low social power [3]. Because anti-vaxxers are a minority group, it is a possible argument one could make as perceived minority leads to perceived low social power which could lead to high linguistic intensification.

Pronominal Usage. From our analyses, we find that with the exception of reflexive and possessive pronouns, anti-vaxxers show a significantly high pronominal usage across all the categories. This difference is prominent specifically for third-person, gendered third-person, subject, and object pronouns. In sociolinguistic literature, pronouns are predominantly linked with narrative discourse structure. For example object pronouns such as "him" or "his" and gendered third-person pronouns "he" or "she" have a referential property, where their semantic interpretation is dependent on what they are referring to. Anaphoric references define objects already defined in the discourse [26] which creates a better narrative viewpoint. Like intensifiers, pronouns are also found to be used heavily by people with lower levels of perceived power [19].

Use of Uncertainty Words. In terms of the use of uncertainty words, while we do find a significant difference between the two communities, we do not observe the same effect observed in the background literature [10]. In fact, we find a counter-intuitive result i.e. that the anti-vaccination community with higher echo-chamberness (as observed in Sect. 4.2) tends to use more uncertain words than pro-vaccination community. This is an evidence that not all echo-chamber communities show certainty in their tweets as observed in [10].

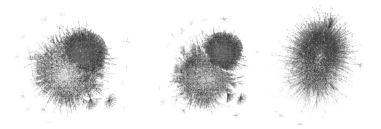

Fig. 1. Mention (left), retweet (middle), and reply (right) networks of pro (in green) and anti (in red) vaccination communities created using ORA-PRO [1,8] (Color figure online)

4.2   Network Analysis

Along with the linguistic analysis, we also compute various network level measures on the communication networks of the two target groups. These measures include the *network density*, *EI index*, and *echo-chamberness*. We also visualize the three communication networks as shown in Fig. 1. All the network-based measures, and graphs were computed using ORA-PRO [1,8].

We observe that anti-vaccination communities tend to have higher network density, negative EI indices with higher absolute values, and higher echo-chamberness across all the communication networks. On the other hand, the EI index for the pro-vaccination communities is positive for mention and retweet networks displaying dominance of external ties. A summary of network-level measures can be found in Table 4. Interestingly from the network graphs we can observe that on some level the two competing groups are almost detached. This is specifically visible in the retweet network graph in Fig. 1.

Table 4. This table shows the network-level measures for the three types of networks: mention network, retweet network, and reply network

Measure	Mention network	Retweet network	Reply network
Network density	1.7e−5	1.1e−5	3.1e−6
Network density (Pro)	1.5e−5	1.0e−5	2.2e−6
Network density (Anti)	4.1e−5	3.2e−5	6.3e−6
EI Index (Pro)	0.025	0.023	−0.167
EI Index (Anti)	−0.276	−0.432	−0.572
Echo-chamberness (Pro)	0.0064334823	0.005364444	0.0043579605
Echo-chamberness (Anti)	0.009268834	0.007850341	0.005905038

5 Limitations and Future Work

One minor limitation of our study is that in the data collection phase, the number of collected hashtags for the two communities was unbalanced. This could potentially have introduced some bias in our downstream tasks such as label propagation. A possible limitation pertaining to the network analysis is that we do not normalize our EI indices to avoid losing precision. This, however gives us stronger results as while the nodes in the anti-vaccination network are lower than the pro-vaccination network, the EI index for anti-vaxxers is more negative than pro-vaxxers. Finally, all our analyses are correlational in nature, and do not depict causation. This remains to be one of the important future directions to test whether a certain network characteristic causes linguistic changes in the network or vice-versa.

6 Conclusion

In this paper, we have carried out a comparison between two online competing vaccination communities: *pro-vaxxers* and *anti-vaxxers*. We have studied these communities in relation to their linguistic and social interactions. We conduct two kinds of analyses: (i) linguistic, and (ii) network-level. We observe anti-vaxxers to display more frequent usage of linguistic intensification, pronouns, and uncertainty words. We also observe significant differences in the network structures of the two communities with *anti-vaxxers* displaying higher echo-chamberness. These results suggest that anti-vaxxers form a tighter community prone to the presentations of anecdotes, and so may be more resistant to factual knowledge from outside the group.

Acknowledgement. This work was partially supported by a fellowship from Carnegie Mellon University's Center for Machine Learning and Health to Shahan Ali Memon. We also acknowledge Lori Levin (LTI,CMU), Bhiksha Raj (LTI,CMU), Rita Singh (LTI,CMU), Matthew Babcock (ISR,CMU), Ingmar Weber (QCRI, HBKU), and members of CMU's Center for Computational Analysis of Social and Organizational Systems (CASOS) for insightful comments and discussions.

References

1. Altman, N., Carley, K.M., Reminga, J.: Ora user's guide 2018. Carnegie-Mellon University. Pittsburgh PA Institute of Software Research International, Technical Report (2018)
2. Boser, B.L.: Mothers' anti-vax to pro-vax conversions. Recovering Argument, p. 21 (2018)
3. Bradac, J.J., Mulac, A., Thompson, S.A.: Men's and women's use of intensifiers and hedges in problem-solving interaction: molar and molecular analyses. Res. Lang. Soc. Interact. **28**(2), 93–116 (1995)
4. Broniatowski, D.A., Hilyard, K.M., Dredze, M.: Effective vaccine communication during the Disneyland measles outbreak. Vaccine **34**(28), 3225–3228 (2016)
5. Broniatowski, D.A., et al.: Weaponized health communication: Twitter bots and Russian trolls amplify the vaccine debate. Am. J. Public Health **108**(10), 1378–1384 (2018)
6. Brown, S.J., Goetzmann, W., Ibbotson, R.G., Ross, S.A.: Survivorship bias in performance studies. Rev. Financ. Stud. **5**(4), 553–580 (1992)
7. Bryden, J., Funk, S., Jansen, V.A.: Word usage mirrors community structure in the online social network twitter. EPJ Data Sci. **2**(1), 3 (2013). https://doi.org/10.1140/epjds15
8. Carley, K.M.: Ora: a toolkit for dynamic network analysis and visualization (2017)
9. Dredze, M., Wood-Doughty, Z., Quinn, S.C., Broniatowski, D.A.: Vaccine opponents' use of Twitter during the 2016 US presidential election: implications for practice and policy. Vaccine **35**(36), 4670–4672 (2017)
10. Duseja, N., Jhamtani, H.: A sociolinguistic study of online echo chambers on Twitter. In: Proceedings of the Third Workshop on Natural Language Processing and Computational Social Science, pp. 78–83 (2019)
11. Evans, A.: Stance and identity in twitter hashtags. Language@ internet **13**(1) (2016)
12. Gibbons, A., Macrae, A. (eds.): Pronouns in Literature. Palgrave Macmillan UK, London (2018). https://doi.org/10.1057/978-1-349-95317-2
13. Giuffre, K.: Cultural production in networks (2015)

14. Hosman, L.A.: The evaluative consequences of hedges, hesitations, and intensifies: powerful and powerless speech styles. Human Commun. Res. **15**(3), 383–406 (1989)
15. Johnson, N.F., et al.: The online competition between pro-and anti-vaccination views. Nature **582**(1–4), 230–233 (2020)
16. Kim, S., Weber, I., Wei, L., Oh, A.: Sociolinguistic analysis of Twitter in multilingual societies. In: Proceedings of the 25th ACM Conference on Hypertext and Social Media, pp. 243–248 (2014)
17. Krackhardt, D., Stern, R.N.: Informal networks and organizational crises: an experimental simulation. Soc. Psychol. Q. **51**, 123–140 (1988)
18. Levy, G.: Public confidence in vaccines sags, new report finds. https://www.usnews.com/news/health-care-news/articles/2018-05-21/public-confidence-in-vaccines-sags-new-report-finds
19. Nerbonne, J.: The secret life of pronouns what our words say about US. Lit. Linguis. Comput. **29**(1), 139–142 (2014)
20. Sanawi, J.B., Samani, M.C., Taibi, M.: # vaccination: identifying influencers in the vaccination discussion on twitter through social network visualisation. Int. J. Bus. Soc. **18**(S4), 718–726 (2017)
21. Smelser, N.J., Baltes, P.B., et al.: International Encyclopedia of the Social & Behavioral Sciences, vol. 11. Elsevier, Amsterdam (2001)
22. Tyagi, A., Babcock, M., Carley, K.M., Sicker, D.C.: Polarizing tweets on climate change. In: To appear in International Conference SBP-BRiMS (2020)
23. Tyagi, A., Field, A., Lathwal, P., Tsvetkov, Y., Carley, K.M.: A computational analysis of polarization on Indian and Pakistani social media (2020)
24. Wasserman, S., Faust, K., et al.: Social Network Analysis: Methods and Applications, vol. 8. Cambridge University Press, Cambridge (1994)
25. Xiaojin, Z., Zoubin, G.: Learning from labeled and unlabeled data with label propagation. Technical report, Technical Report CMU-CALD-02-107, Carnegie Mellon University (2002)
26. Young, L., Harrison, C.: Systemic Functional Linguistics and Critical Discourse Analysis: Studies in Social Change. A&C Black, London (2004)

On Countering Disinformation with Caution: Effective Inoculation Strategies and Others that Backfire into Community Hyper-Polarization

Amirarsalan Rajabi[iD], Chathika Gunaratne[iD], Alexander V. Mantzaris[iD], and Ivan Garibay[(✉)][iD]

Complex Adaptive Systems Laboratory, University of Central Florida, Orlando, FL, USA
igaribay@ucf.edu

Abstract. The increasing adoption of social media platforms as a means of communication has made them into one of the main targets for disinformation and misinformation campaigns due, in part, to the speed increase and cost decrease of communication provided by these platforms. Given that facts and opinions are proposed, discussed and adopted by users of these platforms, countering this threat needs a better understanding of the dynamics by which false and misleading information spreads and gets adopted by users. This work develops an agent-based model that simulates an organized disinformation campaign performed by a group of users referred to as *conspirators*, which are opposed by a parallel organization acting as a barrier to the spread of disinformation, the *inoculators*. The exploration of the simulation results shows how different macroscopic states in respect to a disinformation infection and the stages for a macroscopic consensus exist. The control of the simulation based upon the model parameters allows the progression of the complete network to converge and separate over time. This provides insight into a plausible feature of social networks where the macrostate of the system depends upon the parameter values and can be modified. The relationship between these values is explored and provides intuition into aspects of a community which are necessary to withstand disinformation campaigns. The results also provide an important cautionary note that after a certain degree of conspiracy counter measures a network may become hyper-polarized.

Keywords: Disinformation · Polarization · Inoculation · Agent-based modeling · Social media · Misinformation

1 Introduction

The spread of disinformation within social networks is a problem of major concern. With ever-increasing adoption of social media platforms by a larger portion

© Springer Nature Switzerland AG 2020
R. Thomson et al. (Eds.): SBP-BRiMS 2020, LNCS 12268, pp. 130–139, 2020.
https://doi.org/10.1007/978-3-030-61255-9_13

of society, and increasing diversity and complexity of online social networks, the problem of disinformation spread in the context of social media platforms poses a broader threat to human society. Social network ties are shown to have influence upon users' choices and preferences [13]. In the way in which the positive nature of connection growth through homophily can induce polarization indirectly, the ability for users (and promotional user accounts) to influence others can induce a range of negative effect; namely *disinformation* and the promotion of *conspiracy theories*. The growth of the networks and the time dedicated to them by users allows disinformation to 'contaminate' a larger portion of the population. Conspiracy theories, promoted by *conspirators*, promote 'misinformation' and 'disinformation' in others without they themselves necessarily being convinced of the validity of their messages.

The work in [3] found evidence of organized social media campaigns being performed in 70 countries. These 'campaigns' were promoting disinformation based upon the designed criteria and therefore can be considered *disinformation campaigns*. The work of [14] proposes an analysis of disinformation propagation topic modeling. By disinformation campaign, it is meant the organized (or semi-organized) and deliberate dissemination of false information by a set of malicious actors within a social network. These malicious actors are deployed by cyber troops, governments, or political parties, where the creation and spread of disinformation and manipulated media is the most common strategy among them [3]. The term *disinformation* and *conspiracy theories* can almost be used interchangeably in this context depending upon whether the actors are knowingly participating in the originating campaign spreading disinformation.

Quantitative approaches towards understanding collective behavior of human crowds has recently received a considerable amount of attention by the research community and a lot of that effort comes from the field of social physics. Models of *opinion dynamics* which stem from statistical physics, aims at capturing the process of opinion formation in human populations [18]. Various models of opinion dynamics have been developed, representing opinions mathematically in various ways, including discrete and continuous variables [5].

In this work, an agent-based model of continuous opinion dynamics is proposed which describes the activity of users called *conspirators*, with actions pertaining to *disinformation* promotion, and that of the *inoculators*, aimed at inhibiting the promotion of disinformation. Both of these groups of users act on a set of users which are not directly engaged with the content regulation. Those actors which do not actively regulate the content absorbed or that emitted are referred to as *susceptibles*. The efforts for the group of conspirators and inoculators, to diffuse their (dis)information throughout a network of *susceptible* agents is considered to be constant. The idea of introducing agents with fixed opinions and investigating their effect on the dynamics of opinion formation and alteration among the population has been discussed in literature (see [11] for example). We expand on this work in multiple ways as described below.

The introduction of inoculator agents is based upon inoculation theory in social psychology. Originally developed by McGuire [12], inoculation theory aims at protecting beliefs and opinions against external influence and manipulation and has been deployed in disinformation studies [7,16]. The theory has been extended to not only prevent opinions from manipulations, but as a means to change a manipulated opinion and protect it from future manipulation efforts [6].

The model for the simulation is based upon the constant interaction and opinion sharing among agents (discussed in Sect. 2). The simulations explore the dynamics of opinion state of agents as a collective. This allows a view of how the disinformation spreads based upon various conditions. The results (discussed in Sect. 3) show that if there is an absence of domination by either side, the opinion states of the susceptible agents have an increased variance. The simulations also show that a by product of applying greater defenses against disinformation may polarize the community of susceptible users. The work of [8] explains the effects of polarization in a social network and exhibits how influencers maintain and increase their dominance within a polarized discussion. This provides cautionary recommendations on inoculation strategies used in future practice.

2   Model Description

Our proposed model of opinion dynamics is aimed to capture the persistent effort of a group of agents to affect the whole population's opinion. The interaction rules of our model is inspired by the work of [1]. A population of N agents are connected via an underlying network topology which is generated using Barabasi-Albert algorithm [2]. These are called *susceptible* agents that might then be subject to the activity of disinformation, or inoculation, or both. The second type of agents in the model are *conspirator* agents that infect susceptibles with disinformation, and the third type of agents are called *inoculator* agents that inoculate susceptibles with correct information. Conspirators and inoculators, will be added to the network right after the network of susceptible is formed. The model parameters, which will be explained in Subsect. 2.1, determines the number of susceptible, conspirator, and inoculator agents.

A conceptual underlying state of the world Θ exists and we assume that the true value of this variable is 1. This represents the reality that is being discussed between agents, and each susceptible agent has an opinion on it. Conspirators try to manipulate susceptibles' opinion about Θ, and inoculators try to counter their effort. $x_i^s(t)$, $x_i^c(t)$, and $x_i^i(t)$ represent the opinion of susceptible agent i at time t about the true value of the underlying state Θ, that of a conspirator agent, and that of an inoculator agent, respectively. Each agent has an initial opinion $x_i(0)$ on the true value of Θ. This opinion is a randomly generated float number from the interval between 0 and 2 for susceptible agents, it's 0 for conspirators, and is 1 for inoculators. N denotes total number of susceptible agents in the model. Also, the average of the initial opinion of susceptible agents is 1, meaning that initially, there is a consensus among susceptible agents regarding the true value of Θ:

$$x_i^s(0) \in [0,2] \qquad x_i^c(0) = 0 \qquad x_i^i(0) = 1 \qquad \frac{1}{N}\sum_i x_i^s(0) \approx 1 \qquad (1)$$

2.1   Model Parameters

Model parameters control the number of all types of agents. Upon the formation of network of agents, $\beta \in [0, 1]$ (*ratio-targeted*), sets the fraction of susceptible agents that will be the targeted by conspirators and inoculators, and $\alpha \in [0, 1]$ sets the ratio of total number of inoculators to total number of targeted susceptibles.

$$\text{N(targeted susceptibles)} = \text{N(conspirators)} + \text{N(inoculators)} \qquad (2)$$

$$\alpha = \frac{\text{N(inoculators)}}{\text{N(targeted susceptibles)}} \qquad \beta = \frac{\text{N(targeted susceptibles)}}{N} \qquad (3)$$

The number of conspirators and inoculators is thus determined by:

$$\text{no. of conpirators} = N \cdot \beta \cdot (1 - \alpha)$$
$$\text{no. of inoculators} = N \cdot \beta \cdot \alpha \qquad (4)$$

In the model, ρ and $\rho' \in [0, 1]$ are called conspiracy-target-log-rank and inoculation-target-log-rank, respectively. These variables determine how conspirators and inoculators, choose their target susceptible nodes. To understand this parameter, target selection process should be demonstrated first. Considering the fact that in a network, nodes with higher centrality are more influential in the process of information diffusion [10,15,17], node centrality of susceptible agents was set forth as the basis for being selected by conspirators and inoculators. Between various centrality measures, eigenvector centrality was considered in this model, with respect to its broader range of distribution in the scale-free network. To select a target, the model first sorts the susceptible agents based on their eigenvector centrality. The value of ρ then determines which susceptible node gets selected as target. The higher the value of ρ, the higher centrality rank the targeted susceptible agent will have, and this results in a more effective disinformation effort by the conspirator agent. Due to symmetry in the model, the same holds for the value of ρ' and the effectiveness of an inoculator's effort.

Finally, as will be discussed in Sect. 2.2, $p \in [0, 1]$ controls the probability of opinion sharing, following an interaction between two agents. A bigger p value means that following an interaction between two connected agents, there is a higher chance of opinion sharing between them.

2.2   Rules of Interaction

After formation of the network of susceptible agents, creation of the conspirators and inoculators, and connecting them to their susceptible targets, all agents start interacting and opinion sharing. The agent-based model is designed such that at every timestep, each agent communicates with its peers (the set of agents to which she is connected), and following their interaction, there is a potential opinion sharing between them which is controlled by parameter p. Let i and j be the pair of interacting agents at time t, with opinions $x_i(t)$ and $x_j(t)$. The following rules govern their interaction:

If i and j are both susceptibles:

$$\begin{cases} x_i(t+1) = x_j(t+1) = \frac{1}{2}[x_i(t) + x_j(t)] & \text{with probability p} \\ x_i(t+1) = x_i(t) \ \& \ x_j(t+1) = x_j(t) & \text{with probability } 1-p \end{cases}$$

If i is susceptible and j is conspirator:

$$\begin{cases} x_i(t+1) = \frac{x_i(t)+0}{2} & \text{with probability p} \\ x_i(t+1) = x_i(t) & \text{with probability } 1-p \\ x_j(t+1) = x_j(t) = 0 & \text{with probability 1} \end{cases}$$

If i is susceptible and j is inoculator:

$$\begin{cases} x_i(t+1) = \frac{x_i(t)+1}{2} & \text{with probability p} \\ x_i(t+1) = x_i(t) & \text{with probability } 1-p \\ x_j(t+1) = x_j(t) = 1 & \text{with probability 1} \end{cases}$$

3   Experiments and Results

3.1   Collective-Thought

We are interested in observing and analyzing the progression that opinion of the susceptible population experiences in the experiment as a collective. This phenomenon is captured by a property of the model that is called **collective-thought**. Collective-thought is the set of opinions of all susceptible agents: $\Phi = \{x_i^s\}$. To quantitatively analyze collective-thought, three different quantities are measured:

- $\overline{\Phi}$: collective-thought-mean
- $\widetilde{\Phi}$: collective-thought-median
- $var(\Phi)$: collective-thought-variance

Upon starting the model, agents start interacting and opinion sharing. If enough time is given, the opinion of each agent gets to a stationary state. At this state, while the amplitude of timeseries of opinion of each agent is still relatively large, the amplitude of collective-thought properties mentioned above gets very small. We call this state the state of convergence. All the measurements in the experiments are done after the model reaches the convergence state.

3.2   Opinion Profile

In order to clearly display the impact of conspirators and inoculators on the susceptible population, Fig. 1 shows the opinion profile of susceptible agents in two model runs with the same random seed number (same network structure of susceptible agents). There is a column of 100 points at each timestep, which get closer to each other as time goes on. The parameters $N = 100$ and $\beta = 0.1$ are fixed in both runs. In the first run (Fig. 1a), $\alpha = 0$, which means only conspirators are present and inoculators are not present. In the second run (Fig. 1b), both conspirators and inoculators are present ($\alpha = 0.5$, $\rho = 0.07$, $\rho' = 0.2$). The first run (Fig. 1a) shows that under the influence of conspirators, the population moves towards the opinion of 0 and almost converges after 50000 timesteps (clusters of agents are notable due to scale free property of network and presence of hubs and the positioning of conspirators). In the second run (Fig. 1b) on the other hand, the majority of susceptible population split to the two extremes (polarization), and a minority cluster forms in the vicinity of opinion of 0.4.

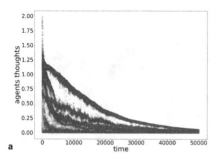 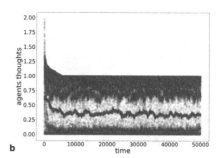

Fig. 1. Opinion profile of all susceptible agents in the course of time. a) only conspirators are present, b) both conspirators and inoculators are present

3.3   Experiment 1: Effect of α and β on Φ

In the first experiment, the influence of β (ratio-targeted) and α (ratio of number of inoculators to targeted susceptibles) on collective-thought is investigated. Probability of interaction was increased between $[0.1,1]$ by intervals of 0.1, number of susceptible agents between 50 and 200 by intervals of 50, α was increased between $[0,0.95]$ by intervals of 0.05, and β was increased between $[0.05,1]$ by intervals of 0.05. ρ and ρ' remain fixed at 1. The model was run 32000 times and Fig. 2 shows the results.

Figure 2a show that as the ratio of inoculators to conspirators increases, collective-thought converges to a value closer to 1, indicating the ability of inoculators in suppressing disinformation effort of conspirators is increasing. As β increases, the collective-thought curve shifts from a logit to a sigmoid shape, indicating that as disinformation campaign gets larger in scale, it gets harder for inoculators with smaller numbers comparing to the number of conspirators (small α), to move the collective-thought towards 1.

Figure 2b displays two properties of the model. First, with higher values of β, collective-thought variance increases, which exposes the fact that as the targeted fraction of susceptibles gets larger, opinion disparity increases in the society and there is more uncertainty in predicting the collective-thought. Another interesting fact that Fig. 2b reveals, is that near α values of 0, 0.5, and 1, there is less variance (uncertainty) and more convergence of opinions for different values of β. This phenomenon reveals the fact that when one of the two campaigns (conspirators or inoculators), has a decisive domination over the opponent in terms of number of agents (α values of 0 or 1), or in the situation where the two campaigns have equal number of agents, it leads to less variance in collective thought, meaning that the convergence state will be of more stable and predictable nature. In contrast, in a situation where no side has a decisive dominance over the opponent, but only a mild dominance in terms of number of agents, it leads to a situation with considerably bigger variance in collective-thought, indicating highly unpredictable and unstable nature.

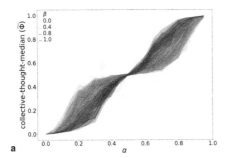 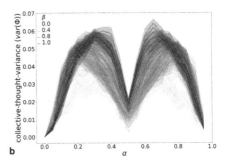

Fig. 2. Experiment 1: effect of varying β and α on collective-thought. a) collective-thought-median increases as the ratio of inoculators (α) increases. b) collective-thought-variance minimizes as there is either a total domination ($\alpha = 0$ or 1), or no domination by one side at all ($\alpha = 0.5$)

3.4   Experiment 2: Effect of ρ on Φ

In second experiment, the effect of centrality of targeted susceptible, on collective-thought measurements is investigated. Number of susceptibles N was fixed at 100. β was fixed at 0.02 and α was fixed at 0.5 (therefore there are 1 conspirator and 1 inoculator in the model). ρ was fixed at 1, but ρ' was increased between [0,1] by intervals of 0.05 . The probability of interaction was also increased between [0.1,1] by intervals of 0.1. The model was run 20000 times and Fig. 3 shows the results.

Figure 3a displays collective-thought mean against normalized eigenvector centrality of the sole inoculator agent in the model, Fig. 3b shows median of collective-thought against normalized eigenvictor centrality, and finally Fig. 3c displays variance of collective-thought against normalized eigenvector centrality. Collective-thought-mean shows a general and consistent move towards 1. Increasing ρ results in targeting susceptibles with higher centrality values. A susceptible agent whose opinion gets affected by an inoculator, will then communicate with a larger and broader set of susceptibles, thus diffusing the opinion of inouclators more effectively.

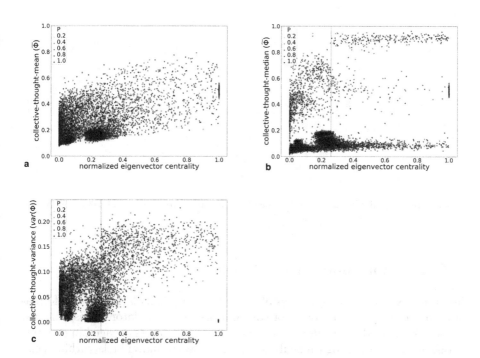

Fig. 3. Experiment 2: effect of varying normalized eigenvector centrality of targeted susceptible, on collective-thought: a) collective-thought-mean, b) collective-thought-median, and c) collective-thought-variance

Looking at Fig. 3b, there seems to be a shift past a normalized eigenvector of 0.3, and median opinion tends to oscillate between extremes. Figure 3c also shows a sudden increase in collective-thought-variance after normalized eigenvector of 0.3. There is little change in collective-thought-mean, and there is a typically high variance. Based on these observations, after point 0.3, skewness of opinion distribution increases and this skew oscillates between extremes. This observation signals an unstable opinion distribution which is hard to predict and tends to polarize. Figure 4 displays the risk of polarization more clearly. Random seed number and all parameters excluding ρ' are fixed. ρ' has taken the values of 0.1, 0.81, and 1 (with corresponding eigenvector centrality values of 0.006, 0.11, and 0.23 for the inoculator after attaching to its target susceptible). With $\rho' = 0.1$ (yellow), It can be observed that after convergence, a majority of susceptible agents end up having an opinion close to zero, while the few others are dispersed elsewhere. With $\rho' = 0.8$ (red), the population gets highly polarized. Basically, ρ' value is high, but not high enough to target the same node that the conspirator agent has targeted, and polarization is the indirect negative consequence of the effort of inoculators. And with $\rho' = 1$ (green), it is observed that the effort of inoculators has not led to polarization.

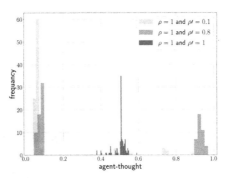

Fig. 4. Impact of varying ρ' on target selection and the subsequent polarization. (Color figure online)

4   Conclusions and Future Work

This study examines the dynamics of the spread and inoculation of disinformation under the competing forces of conspirators and inoculators. It is assumed that actors engaged in disinformation campaigns and actors engaged in countering disinformation through inoculation target specific individuals within social networks.

When the most influential users are targeted by the two competing forces, a domination of one side, or an equal amount of effort in terms of number of inoculators and conspirators leads to less uncertainties in the final opinion state of the collective. The comparison to when there is a relative domination of one side was seen from the simulation and produces changes in the variance. If the domination is not complete the increase in the variance will likely produce friction between users that were previously surrounded by like minded social connections. This may be a negative by product if the counter forces are still active and the reduction in the variance is not obtained. The results also show that there exists a threshold of centrality of target, a critical mass point, beyond which the system enters a state of confusion with shifting opinions and experiences a phase shift. This macroscopic state change can be measured in the network given enough visibility. Unless the two sides target the same susceptibles, quelling the disinformation campaign results in a highly polarized susceptible population. It must be emphasized that countering conspirators is almost always at the expense of further polarizing the susceptible population. Future work will focus on the cognitive heuristics of susceptible agents that are currently following a simplistic model, and also differing the functioning of conspirators and inoculators, more profoundly than the value of the message they are disseminating. Besides, the model should be implemented and tested on other network generation algorithms. We intend to address these challenges in a future study.

References

1. Acemoglu, D., Ozdaglar, A., ParandehGheibi, A.: Spread of (MIS) information in social networks. Games Econ. Behav. **70**(2), 194–227 (2010)
2. Barabási, A., Albert, R.: Emergence of scaling in random networks. Science **286**(5439), 509–512 (1999)
3. Bradshaw, S., Howard, P.: The global disinformation disorder: 2019 global inventory of organised social media manipulation (2019)
4. Castellano, C., Muñoz, M.A., Pastor-Satorras, R.: Nonlinear q-voter model. Phys. Rev. E **80**(4), 041129 (2009)
5. Castellano, C., Fortunato, S., Loreto, V.: Statistical physics of social dynamics. Rev. Modern Phys. **81**(2), 591 (2009)
6. Compton, J.: Prophylactic versus therapeutic inoculation treatments for resistance to influence. Commun. Theory **30**(3), 330–343 (2019)
7. Cook, J., Lewandowsky, S., Ecker, U.K.H.: Neutralizing misinformation through inoculation: exposing misleading argumentation techniques reduces their influence. PloS One **12**(5), e0175799 (2017)
8. Garibay, I., Mantzaris, A.V., Rajabi, A., Taylor, C.E.: Polarization in social media assists influencers to become more influential: analysis and two inoculation strategies. Sci. Rep. **9**(1), 1–9 (2019)
9. Hernon, P.: Disinformation and misinformation through the internet: findings of an exploratory study. Gov. Inf. Q. **12**(2), 133–139 (1995)
10. Kandhway, K., Kuri, J.: Using node centrality and optimal control to maximize information diffusion in social networks. IEEE Trans. Syst. Man Cybern. Syst. **47**(7), 1099–1110 (2016)
11. Klamser, P.P., Wiedermann, M., Donges, J.F., Donner, R.V.: Zealotry effects on opinion dynamics in the adaptive voter model. Phys. Rev. E **96**(5), 052315 (2017)
12. McGuire, W.J.: The effectiveness of supportive and refutational defenses in immunizing and restoring beliefs against persuasion. Sociometry **24**(2), 184–197 (1961)
13. Mutlu, E.Ç., Garibay, I.: Effects of assortativity on consensus formation with heterogeneous agents. arXiv preprint arXiv:2004.13131 (2020)
14. Oghaz, T.A., Mutlu, E.C., Jasser, J., Yousefi, N., Garibay, I.: Probabilistic model of narratives over topical trends in social media: a discrete time model. arXiv preprint arXiv:2004.06793 (2020)
15. Rajabi, A., Talebzadehhosseini, S., Garibay, I.: Resistance of communities against disinformation. arXiv preprint arXiv:2004.00379 (2020)
16. Roozenbeek, J., van der Linden, S.: The fake news game: actively inoculating against the risk of misinformation. J. Risk Res. **22**(5), 570–580 (2019)
17. Saito, K., Kimura, M., Ohara, K., Motoda, H.: Super mediator-a new centrality measure of node importance for information diffusion over social network. Inf. Sci. **329**, 985–1000 (2016)
18. Sîrbu, A., Loreto, V., Servedio, V.D.P., Tria, F.: Opinion dynamics: models, extensions and external effects. In: Loreto, V., et al. (eds.) Participatory Sensing, Opinions and Collective Awareness. UCS, pp. 363–401. Springer, Cham (2017). https://doi.org/10.1007/978-3-319-25658-0_17

Homicidal Event Forecasting and Interpretable Analysis Using Hierarchical Attention Model

Angeela Acharya[1(✉)], Jitin Krishnan[1], Desmond Arias[2], and Huzefa Rangwala[1]

[1] George Mason University, Fairfax, VA, USA
{aachary,jkrishn2,rangwala}@gmu.edu
[2] Bernard M. Baruch College, City University of New York, New York, USA
desmond.arias@baruch.cuny.edu

Abstract. Crime and violence have always imposed significant societal threats across the world. Understanding the underlying causes behind them and making early predictions can help mitigate such occurrences to some extent. We propose a hierarchical attention-based mechanism that utilizes the temporal nature of event incidents obtained from news articles to extract information indicative of future events and make predictions accordingly. Our approach serves two important purposes: a) It models sequential information within the news articles and the sentences that comprise them to learn contextual information using Recurrent Neural Networks. b) The use of attention mechanism ensures that informative sentences and articles are selected for predicting future events and provides an analysis of precursors of the events. Through quantitative and qualitative evaluation, we show that our model can successfully make predictions while also being interpretable, which in turn can help make more informed decisions for social analysis.

Keywords: Homicidal event forecasting · Hierarchical attention · Interpretability · Text mining

1 Introduction

Social violence has a big impact on a country and its people. Therefore, it is imperative to take any steps possible to pacify it. Several prior research [1,12,13] that studied event detection have found that there are some smaller events that occur before the occurrence of any big event (precursors). For instance, activities such as *kidnapping*, *murder*, *protests*, or *strikes* may indicate possible violent crimes in the near future. Motivated by these findings, we use trusted online sources to get news articles from the past few days to capture hidden information about such smaller events and use them to make predictions about a future event. Online news articles succinctly describe the general social events happening within an area in a more formal language which makes them easy to process compared to streaming data from Twitter and Facebook.

© Springer Nature Switzerland AG 2020
R. Thomson et al. (Eds.): SBP-BRiMS 2020, LNCS 12268, pp. 140–150, 2020.
https://doi.org/10.1007/978-3-030-61255-9_14

In particular, we predict the homicidal violence occurrences and provide an interpretative analysis of precursors of those events. We use open-source articles from Colombia as input to our model and police records from the same region as the ground truth. Latin America is one of the most violent regions in the world: it accounts for 33% of the total number of homicides across the world. Colombia is among the four countries in Latin America that have one-quarter of all global homicides [6].

Using the idea of hierarchical attention network [19], we develop a novel approach for homicidal event forecasting and interpretable analysis that models news articles in terms of a sequence of sentences and articles. We use sentence vector representations along with sentence-level attention weights to represent article vectors. Then, the article vectors are combined based on article-level attention weights to get the final output vector representation.

2   Literature Review

Forecasting societal events using online sources has been a popular area of research. Different methods—from traditional machine learning models to complex Deep learning architectures—have been used to address the problem. Traditional machine learning approaches like linear regression model [17], ARIMA model [3] make use of a limited number of input features that cannot capture the complex relationships within the data.

Hossny et al. [9] proposed a method to detect events using streaming data from Twitter. They used a keyword-based approach to identify a set of words that are associated with the events of interests such as protests. Zhao et al. [20] proposed a Multitask learning approach to forecasting events across multiple locations simultaneously. They used two sets of features: shared common features and area-specific features as their input. Nasrin et al. [1] used the same concept to forecast gang-related homicides using common violence-related words and area-specific list of gangs. These models suffer from important limitations. First, they cannot model the sequential information within documents; they do not consider the effect of the relative positioning of different sentences and how they combine to represent an article and thus, cannot model long term dependencies. Secondly, they cannot identify the precursors to the events.

Research has also been done to predict different events using numerical and categorical features instead of textual features. Ertugrul et al. [7,8] proposed methods to forecast opioid overdose from crime incidents using census data and public safety data. Besides just predicting events, different research has been done to model information about or from the events. Kang et al. [10] proposed a method to find cause and effect relationships from textual data connecting those to form an explanation about different events. However, this approach doesn't incorporate aspects such as time and location of events which can have a significant impact on the occurrence of events.

Ning et al. [13] developed a method called *STAPLE* which takes into account spatial and temporal correlations to learn the precursors for events.

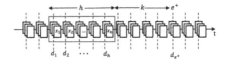

Fig. 1. Figure depicts a sample **positive** training data; d = day, h = history window, k = lead time, x_i = set of articles $\{x_{i1}, x_{i2}, ...x_{in}\}$ on i^{th} day in the history window, e^+ = positive event, and d_{e^+} = day with high homicidal intensity. Our hypothesis is that a homicide event (e^+) happening k days after d_h can be forecasted based on the events happened during the history window h.

Wang et al. [18] proposed a method for event detection which also identities key information representing those events using a multiple instance learning framework [2]. Deng et al. [5] introduced a novel graph convolution network for predicting future events like civil unrest movements. Although the above researches have produced interesting results, they work directly on event datasets, that are filtered versions of news articles rather than working on raw unclassified news articles. For instance, in our dataset, we have articles that do not only mention about societal events but also about sports, movie stars, and other general happenings which makes it a more challenging problem. Similarly, most of the above-mentioned approaches are for events of a more general form. Additionally, the dataset that we use in our experiment is in Spanish, which adds even more complexity: processing Spanish texts using generic tools is not trivial.

3   Problem Statement

The input to our model is a set of news articles $\{\{x_{11}, x_{12}, ...x_{1n}\}$, $\{x_{21}, x_{22}, ...x_{2n}\}$,...$\{x_{h1}, x_{h2}, ...x_{hn}\}\}$ from a geographical region. Here, x_{hn} is the nth news article corresponding to the hth day. So, there can be multiple news articles in a single day and the collection of those over h days (history days) form a single data point $(\{x_1, x_2, x_3, ..x_M\}$, where M is the total number of articles). The corresponding ground truth for that data point is the homicidal violence intensity at a future day d_e as shown in Fig. 1. From the homicide counts obtained from the ground truth, the homicidal violence intensity is calculated by taking the average homicide count over any given window period (w) and comparing it with the median homicide over the entire data. If the average homicide count over the period exceeds the median homicide, we label it as 1 else it is labeled as 0.

$$y_d = \begin{cases} 1 & \text{if } d \text{ has high homicide intensity} \\ 0 & \text{if } d \text{ has low homicide intensity} \end{cases}$$

where, y_d is the homicide intensity corresponding to a day d.
We address the following problems in our approach:

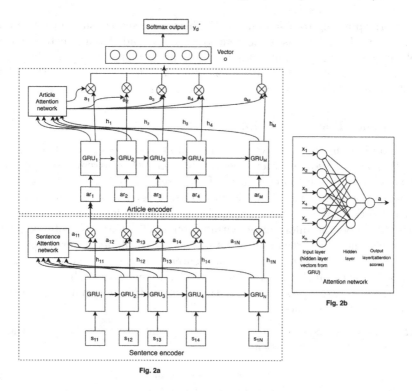

Fig. 2. Fig. 2a demonstrates how sentence vectors combine to form article vectors and how article vectors combine to represent the final output; Fig. 2b is a simple MLP that represents the working of sentence and article attention networks

a) **Generation of meaningful data:** Processing the raw unfiltered contents to get meaningful information was not a trivial problem for us. Additionally, the ground truth data does not have distinct classes in itself; we created them based on the condition described above.

b) **Prediction of homicidal intensity:** We take past h days (history days) of news articles to predict the event k days (lead time) after a given date. The values for h and k are not randomly determined; different combinations of these values are tried to see which one gives the best performance.

c) **Modeling the precursors:** Using the attention weight vectors obtained from the Hierarchical attention network, we analyze which sentences and articles are more important and have a significant effect on predictions.

4   Model Architecture

4.1   Word-to-Sentence Embedding

As shown in Fig. 2, the inputs to sentence encoder are the vector representations of sentences within each article. They are obtained by multiplying the word vectors corresponding to a sentence with their tf-idf scores, summing them up, and averaging them. The use of sentence vectors instead of word vectors reduces model complexity while maintaining the same performance and providing a better interpretation of events. We use pre-trained Glove embedding [14,16] for Spanish words that represent words in a 300-dimensional vector space.

4.2 Sentence Encoder Module

After obtaining the sentence vector representations, the vectors belonging to each article are passed to sentence-level GRU (Gated recurrent unit) [4] layers which create new vector representations for the sentences and capture contextual relationships between them. GRU is an improved version of standard recurrent neural networks [11] that makes use of two gates: update and reset gates to capture the sequential information within inputs. There are "N" total sentences in an article and "M" articles in a data point. Each hidden layer output from the GRU layers is further passed to the sentence attention network which is a Multilayer Perceptron (MLP) [15] with a single hidden layer as shown in Fig. 2b. The attention network produces an output representing how much attention to give to each of the sentences.

Input: $s_{i1}, s_{i2}, s_{i3}, ...s_{iN}$ where, s_{in} is the nth sentence (n ε [1, N]) of the ith article (i ε [1, M]). Mathematically,

$$h_{in} = GRU(s_{in}) \tag{1}$$

$$u_{in} = tanh(h_{in}W_s + b_s) \tag{2}$$

$$a_{in} = \frac{exp(u_{in}u_s)}{\sum_n exp(u_{in}u_s)} \tag{3}$$

$$ar_i = \sum_n h_{in}a_{in} \tag{4}$$

Here, h_{in} is the hidden state representation of a sentence s_{in} given by GRU. u_{in} is the output from the attention network, W_s, and b_s are the weights and biases of the multilayer perceptron and are learnable parameters. We use tanh as our hidden layer activation for the attention network such that the output is between -1 and 1. u_s is the sentence context which is also learnable and helps to determine which sentences have more importance in the given context. a_{in} is the output of the softmax function that calculates the relative importance of a particular sentence as compared to all the other sentences in an article (attention weight). Once we obtain the attention weight and corresponding hidden vector representation for all sentences within an article, we multiply them and sum them over N to obtain the article vector. So, while creating an article vector ar_i, the sentences that are more meaningful to the prediction are given more priority.

4.3 Article Encoder Module

Once the article vectors $\{ar_1, ar_2, ar_3, ..ar_M\}$ for all articles $\{x_1, x_2, x_3, ..x_M\}$ corresponding to a data point are obtained, a similar operation is performed to obtain the article level hidden layer representation using GRU layers and article level attention weights. The GRU network is used to capture a chain of relevant and related articles that might be useful for studying the event and the attention network gives more importance to those articles that have more impact on the output. Mathematically,

$$h_i = GRU(ar_i) \tag{5}$$
$$u_i = tanh(h_i W_{ar} + b_{ar}) \tag{6}$$
$$a_i = \frac{exp(u_i u_{ar})}{\sum_i exp(u_i u_{ar})} \tag{7}$$
$$o = \sum_i h_i a_i \tag{8}$$

Here, o is the output vector that represents all the articles in a data point. Finally,

$$y_d{}^* = softmax(o)$$

where, $y_d{}^*$ is the probability of homicidal event at a day "d" given by the softmax function. We define a threshold of 0.5 on this softmax value to get either a value of 1 or 0 representing the homicide intensity (y_d).

5   Experimental Evaluation

5.1   Dataset Description

We use local news articles from the capital city of Colombia (Bogota), as our input. Bogota has a very high homicide rate, as validated by our ground truth data. The news articles are collected from sources like El Espectador, El Tiempo, El Periodico, and HSB Noticias. We consider data from the years 2015 to 2018. Table 1 shows the data statistics. We filter area level articles from the entire pool of articles by using their geolocation information, whenever provided. For the sources that do not have geolocation information, we use a keyword search approach to filter the articles by area name. 80% of the data is used for training and the remaining 20% is split into validation and test sets.

Table 1. Data statistics: Distribution of articles, sentences, and words within our data. All statistics except total are calculated per day, per article, and per sentence for articles, sentences, and words respectively.

Category	Total	Average	Minimum	Maximum	Std. deviation
Articles	40934	44	4	220	22.9
Sentences	352177	9	1	313	7.19
Words	156551	30	4	2548	25.2

5.2   Feature Engineering and Data Pre-processing

We usually have hundreds of collective articles from the past days. However, we select a fixed number of articles for every data point as input to the GRU units. Upon plotting a histogram of the distribution of articles, we found out that most of the data points have their article-length within the third quartile (Q3) range. Thus, we consider the Q3 value as our maximum article length. Zero-padding is performed for the data points having a lower number of articles. A similar approach is used to select a fixed number of sentences within each article.

Similarly, the general pre-processing methods like removal of punctuation, multiple spaces, stop words are applied for all the experimented models. Additionally, since our data is imbalanced and has a high number of data representing low homicide intensity (0), we use a Random Under Sampler to reduce the number of data points in the majority class.

5.3   Comparative Models

We test and compare our approach with two different types of models: Traditional models and the more recent neural network-based models.

a) **Traditional models:** i) Simple Thresholding: We take an extensive list of violence-related keywords, names of gang members and gangs in Colombia as our features; earlier research [1] has shown an association of gangs with homicidal violence. We then sum up all the articles corresponding to each data point and count the total occurrences of these keywords in the articles. We then define a threshold to classify the articles based on the keyword frequency. ii) Logistic Regression and Random Forest: We use these models to classify our articles based on static violence-related keywords and dynamic keywords that we obtain from a Tf-idf vectorizer. For both of these approaches, the hyperparameters were determined using grid search and the models were validated using 5-fold cross-validation.
b) **Neural network-based models:** i) Multilayer Perceptron (MLP): The MLP model takes its input from a Tf-idf vectorizer and uses two hidden layers. ii) Plain GRU: This model is similar to our proposed model, the only difference being the absence of attention layers. Thus, this model does not provide any interpretation. All of these models were optimized using Binary cross-entropy loss with L2 regularization.

6   Results and Discussion

We evaluate our models in terms of five different performance metrics as shown in Table 2. As we can see, our proposed approach (GRU with attention) has the most stable performance in terms of the metrics considered, giving the highest AUC and accuracy scores. The plain GRU model did not perform as well, which implies that the attention mechanism also has a benefit of improved performance. The traditional methods: Random Forest, Logistic Regression, and

Table 2. Performance of different models on our dataset

Type	Model	Accuracy	AUC	F1 score	Recall	Precision
Traditional	Simple thresholding	0.54	0.53	**0.59**	0.66	**0.52**
	Logistic regression	0.53	0.54	0.52	0.63	0.44
	Random forest	0.58	0.57	0.52	0.52	**0.52**
NN-based	MLP	0.55	0.56	0.57	**0.68**	0.49
	Plain GRU	0.55	0.53	0.44	0.42	0.47
	GRU with attention	**0.61**	**0.63**	0.54	0.61	0.50

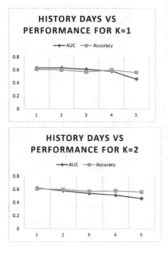

Fig. 3. History days vs. performance plot for different values of leadtime (k)

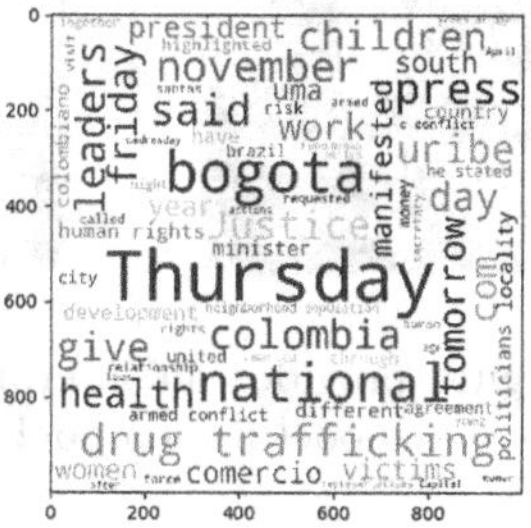

Fig. 4. Word cloud of features selected by Logistic Regression

Simple Thresholding have a decent forecasting performance. However, they are very simple models and cannot perform complex tasks like analysis of precursors.

We also analyze the effect of lead time (k) and history days (h) on the model performance. We experiment with values of h from 1 to 5 and k from 1 to 2. As shown in Fig. 3, we got the best performance (accuracy: 61%, AUC: 63%) when both h and k were set equal to 1: when we used previous day's articles to predict the next day's homicide intensity. The performance seems to be decreasing as we use higher values of h, albeit in a slower rate. This possibly means that more recent news contains more information useful for predicting future events.

Similarly, Fig. 5 shows examples of sentences our model gives the most attention to. Three random articles having high attention weights were selected from a data point based on their article attention weights. Within those articles, the sentences having the highest attention weights were selected based on sentence attention weights. The sentences were converted from Spanish to English using

Google Translate for demonstration. As we can see, the selected sentences are mostly those mentioning about crime, violence, killings, and even though they are from different articles, our model captured a sequence of related events out of all the information that was present. With this analysis, we get a qualitative validation that there is some link between the mentions of such events with the homicidal activities that happen at a future date.

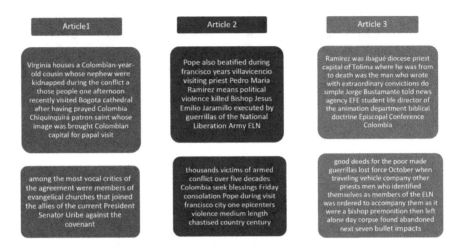

Fig. 5. Figure provides an interpretative analysis of the most important sentences selected by our model from a pool of articles corresponding to a positive event (e^+)

The other models that we experimented with, provide very limited or no interpretability. For instance, if we consider the Logistic regression model, in terms of interpretability, we can only tell which words were given the most weights for prediction, as shown in Fig. 4. Looking at this figure, it is difficult to infer anything about the relationship between the information mentioned in the articles and the outcomes. Our proposed model, however, can explain what kind of events may lead to violence in the future.

One of the major challenges that we faced in our research was finding a sufficient amount of data that would match the complexity of our network. As a part of our future work, we plan to be able to achieve a better performance by either using larger data sets that would justify the complexity of our architecture or by using some simpler models that would not need as much data.

7   Conclusion

In this paper, we proposed and implemented a mechanism based on hierarchical attention to predict and interpret homicidal violence events using news articles. Prior research on homicidal violence prediction ignore the sequential structure of articles while making predictions. Additionally, they lack interpretability: they cannot provide analysis of precursors of the events. We address these limitations by using a two-leveled hierarchical structure that uses Gated Recurrent Neural Networks to capture sequential information within the sentences and articles and attention mechanism to select the most informative contents within them. Our experiments show that the proposed model achieves a promising forecasting performance while also providing a good analytical representation of the events.

References

1. Akhter, N., Zhao, L., Arias, D., Rangwala, H., Ramakrishnan, N.: Forecasting gang homicides with multi-level multi-task learning. In: Thomson, R., Dancy, C., Hyder, A., Bisgin, H. (eds.) SBP-BRiMS 2018. LNCS, vol. 10899, pp. 28–37. Springer, Cham (2018). https://doi.org/10.1007/978-3-319-93372-6_3
2. Carbonneau, M., Cheplygina, V., Granger, E., Gagnon, G.: Multiple instance learning: a survey of problem characteristics and applications. CoRR (2016)
3. Chen, P., Yuan, H., Shu, X.: Forecasting crime using the Arima model. In: Proceedings - 5th International Conference on Fuzzy Systems and Knowledge Discovery, FSKD 2008 (2008)
4. Chung, J., Gülçehre, Ç., Cho, K., Bengio, Y.: Empirical evaluation of gated recurrent neural networks on sequence modeling. CoRR (2014)
5. Deng, S., Rangwala, H., Ning, Y.: Learning dynamic context graphs for predicting social events. In: Proceedings of 25th ACM SIGKDD (2019)
6. Erickson, A.: The washington post (2018). https://www.washingtonpost.com/news/worldviews/wp/2018/04/25/latin-america-is-the-worlds-most-violent-region-a-new-report-investigates-why/
7. Ertugrul, A.M., Lin, Y.R., Mair, C., Taskaya Temizel, T.: Forecasting heroin overdose occurrences from crime incidents. In: SBP-BRiMS (2018)
8. Ertugrul, A.M., Lin, Y.-R., Taskaya-Temizel, T.: CASTNet: community-attentive spatio-temporal networks for opioid overdose forecasting. In: Brefeld, U., Fromont, E., Hotho, A., Knobbe, A., Maathuis, M., Robardet, C. (eds.) ECML PKDD 2019. LNCS (LNAI), vol. 11908, pp. 432–448. Springer, Cham (2020). https://doi.org/10.1007/978-3-030-46133-1_26
9. Hossny, A.H., Mitchell, L.: Event detection in Twitter: a keyword volume approach. CoRR (2018)
10. Kang, D., Gangal, V., Lu, A., Chen, Z., Hovy, E.H.: Detecting and explaining causes from text for a time series event. CoRR (2017)
11. Lipton, Z.C.: A critical review of recurrent neural networks for sequence learning. CoRR (2015)
12. Ning, Y., Muthiah, S., Rangwala, H., Ramakrishnan, N.: Modeling precursors for event forecasting via nested multi-instance learning. In: Proceedings of the 22Nd ACM SIGKDD (2016)
13. Ning, Y., Zhao, L., Chen, F., Lu, C.T., Rangwala, H.: Spatio-temporal event forecasting and precursor identification. In: Proceedings of 25th ACM SIGKDD (2019)
14. Pennington, J., Socher, R., Manning, C.D.: Glove: global vectors for word representation. In: EMNLP (2014)
15. Popescu, M.C., Balas, V.E., Perescu-Popescu, L., Mastorakis, N.: Multilayer perceptron and neural networks (2009). World Scientific and Engineering Academy and Society (WSEAS)

16. Pérez, J.: Spanish word embeddings. https://github.com/dccuchile/spanish-word-embeddings
17. Shingleton, J.S.: Crime trend prediction using regression models for Salinas, California (2012). https://calhoun.nps.edu/handle/10945/7416
18. Wang, W., Ning, Y., Rangwala, H., Ramakrishnan, N.: A multiple instance learning framework for identifying key sentences and detecting events. In: Proceedings of 25th ACM International on Conference on Information and Knowledge Management (2016)
19. Yang, Z., Yang, D., Dyer, C., He, X., Smola, A., Hovy, E.: Hierarchical attention networks for document classification. In: Proceedings of the 2016 Conference of the North American Chapter of the Association for Computational Linguistics (2016)
20. Zhao, L., Sun, Q., Ye, J., Chen, F., Lu, C.T., Ramakrishnan, N.: Multi-task learning for spatio-temporal event forecasting. In: Proceedings of the 21th ACM SIGKDD (2015)

Development of a Hybrid Machine Learning Agent Based Model for Optimization and Interpretability

Paul Cummings$^{(\boxtimes)}$ ⓘ and Andrew Crooks$^{(\boxtimes)}$ ⓘ

George Mason University, 4400 University Dr, Fairfax, VA 22030, USA
{pcummin2,acrooks2}@gmu.edu

Abstract. The use of agent-based models (ABMs) has become more widespread over the last two decades allowing resear chers to explore complex systems composed of heterogeneous and locally interacting entities. However, there are several challenges that the agent-based modeling community face. These relate to developing accurate measurements, minimizing a large complex parameter space and developing parsimonious yet accurate models. Machine Learning (ML), specifically deep reinforcement learning has the potential to generate new ways to explore complex models, which can enhance traditional computational paradigms such as agent-based modeling. Recently, ML algorithms have proved an important contribution to the determination of semi-optimal agent behavior strategies in complex environments. What is less clear is how these advances can be used to enhance existing ABMs. This paper presents Learning-based Actor-Interpreter State Representation (LAISR), a research effort that is designed to bridge ML agents with more traditional ABMs in order to generate semi-optimal multi-agent learning strategies. The resultant model, explored within a tactical game scenario, lies at the intersection of human and automated model design. The model can be decomposed into a format that automates aspects of the agent creation process, producing a resultant agent that creates its own optimal strategy and is interpretable to the designer. Our paper, therefore, acts as a bridge between traditional agent-based modeling and machine learning practices, designed purposefully to enhance the inclusion of ML-based agents in the agent-based modeling community.

Keywords: Agent-based modeling · Machine Learning · Explainable artificial intelligence

1 Introduction

Agent-based models (ABMs) have grown in their application over the last two decades partly because such a style of the model can represent complex systems with minimal knowledge of parameter values or without fully knowing the optimal parameter states to describe the real-world environment (Li et al. 2013). Not only do ABMs allow us to study complex systems, they also provide an intuitive and realistic description of behavior of such systems. Agent-based modeling and simulation platforms offer architectures

© Springer Nature Switzerland AG 2020
R. Thomson et al. (Eds.): SBP-BRiMS 2020, LNCS 12268, pp. 151–160, 2020.
https://doi.org/10.1007/978-3-030-61255-9_15

of varying complexity for the agents, where reactive agents are very simplistic, reacting to environmental stimuli often without any long-term reasoning; finite-state machines require the scripting all of the possible states of the agents and the corresponding behaviors; cognitive agents offer a more flexible description of behaviors in terms of goals and plans.

A generally new area of research is the incorporation or linkage of Machine Learning (ML) into the design of ABMs. ML, as a subset of the general term artificial intelligence (AI), provides automated methods that can detect patterns in data and use them to achieve some tasks. Within ML, deep reinforcement learning (DRL) methods have been regarded as an approach that can: a) generate automated solutions, while b) constraining complexity within the model (François-Lavet et al. 2018). In comparison to ABMs which are designed by model developers with specific attributes and behaviors, DRL models are not told which actions to take. Instead they must discover which actions generate the highest rewards by trying out actions within the environment (Sutton and Barto 1998). Using the experiences gathered, the artificial agent should be able to optimize some objectives given in the form of cumulative rewards, or a as van der Hoog (2017) states "computationally tractable means to address parameter sensitivity analysis, robustness analysis, and could also be used for empirical validation and estimation."

Although linkages between ABMs and ML agents have been researched (e.g., Wolpert et al. 1999; Lee 2017), there are several constraints that limit the use of both. For example, large-scale ABMs can be computationally intensive (Dawid et al. 2012). Often large complex systems can also suffer from unpredictability due to dependencies between parameters (Alahi et al. 2016). In practical terms, integrating a large number of details into a model will make generating ABMs difficult to evaluate; in fact, even small models can be complicated to replicate and analyze simply due to the number of parameters and variations within those parameters (Li et al. 2013). In order to obtain a broad behavior space to determine whether the model is consistent and unchanging, thousands or hundreds of thousands of runs will need to take place to confirm results (van der Hoog 2017). In many cases, this process can be highly manual, which can create high complexity, which is neither efficient or nor feasible (Resnick 1997). Additionally, parameter-heavy systems also suffer from the unpredictability of the results due to unexpected potential dependencies between parameters (Fehérvári 2010).

ML has its own limitations as it relates to developing ABMs; first, despite the efficiency and versatility of neural-network based ML, their internal representation of self-learning machines makes them generally unintelligible (Lee 2019), reducing their value as a research behavior evaluation tool. These models are essentially black boxes (e.g., Castelvecchi 2016), in which one cannot inspect how the algorithm is accomplishing what it is accomplishing. Even for a network with only a single layer, it is generally very difficult to understand how specific patterns arise, due to the complexity of the network. The mechanisms that solve RL models are hidden within an interconnected network of input, hidden, and output layers. Given the collective benefits and constraints between ABMs and ML agents, this paper introduces the concept of a Learning-driven Actor-Interpreter State Representation (LAISR). LAISR attempts to: a) generate an optimal decision-making strategy through its training process, including a more constrained parameter space, and b) describe its behaviors in a human-readable and interpretable approach. This paper therefore presents a model that attempts to solve the integration between traditional agent-based modeling and the incorporation of new ML attributes. In Sect. 2, we will explain the design of the hybrid ABM/ML Model called the Actor-Interpreter Agent. In Sect. 3, we provide a demonstrative example implementation and discuss results in Sect. 4. Finally, in Sect. 5, we provide a summary of the paper and discuss areas of further work (Fig. 1).

2 Learning-Driven Actor-Interpreter State Representation Model (LAISR)

The LASIR model uses a hybrid approach where the initial component, the Actor, uses ML based techniques to derive its behaviors. While the second component, the Interpreter, decomposes behaviors into a model that can be expressed as an ABM. The *Actor* model provides a general way of using deep reinforcement learning to minimize the potential for large parameter spaces by focusing on discrete goals for the agent and assumes a reward value for achieving its policy π_a. In the model, the actor derives a policy for each state and action pair and determines its own optimal policy rather than be provided a set of rules and parameters by a modeler. The *Actor's* machine learning attributes are derived from a Reinforcement Learning (RL) process, where the agent learns by interacting with other agents, the environment, and ultimately receive rewards for performing actions (Neto et al. 2005). The RL system uses neural networks to adjust the input parameters of reinforcement learning systems, so as to reinforce and optimize the learning action and ability. Secondly, it uses a quality Q-value to adjust and improve the neural networks (NN) weights in order to improve the RL algorithm function approximation (Tang et al. 2007). An agent exists within an environment E and responds over multiple iterations of time t (Sutton and Barto 2018). At each time step, the agent enters a state s_t and chooses its action according to its policy π where

$$\pi(a|s) = P[A_t = a|S_t = s] \tag{1}$$

a is the current action given state s. The agent enters the next state $s_t + 1$ and obtains a reward r_t. This process will continue until a terminal state is reached and total reward for that state R_s is given as:

$$R_s = \sum_{k=0}^{\infty} \gamma^k r_{t+k} + 1 \tag{2}$$

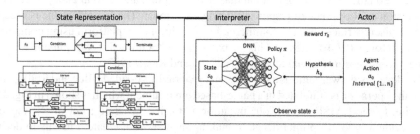

Fig. 1. LAISR model

where R_s is the total accumulated rewards state s with discount factor $\gamma \in [0, 1]$. The agent will maximize the expected return from cumulative s_t states. Q-Learning is designed to explore rather than respond to a fixed set of rules designed by modelers. Instead of directly parameterizing a policy, Q-value learning methods estimate the Q-function which states Q is the maximum future reward for this state and action is the immediate reward plus maximum future rewards for the next state.

In essence, every state-action pair can use the immediate reward to update the value estimate of the initial state-action pair. A similar enhanced approach is the actor-critic (A3C) model, which uses an advantage value $A = Q(s, a) - V(s)$ to create discounted results from previous iterations of the model (Mnih et al. 2016). Where DQN models use a single agent and single neural network in a single environment, A3C can use multiples of each to learn more efficiently (Juliani 2018). The neural network then produces a loss function and determines quality actions. Unlike traditional DQN models, Q values are not determined directly, instead of discounted returns ($R = \gamma(r)$) are estimates of Q(s, a), the advantage function (Mnih et al. 2016).

The *Interpreter* attempts to mimic the state of the Actor ML model and then predicts its behavior in the form of a finite state machine (FSM) representation. In order to do this, the Interpreter examines the Actor state and makes a general prediction about what it believes the next state (or states) will be. It then translates the results of its observations into parameters within a state machine that it develops during the training process. Over time FSM parameters are refined, which explain the Actor agent behavior but are human-readable, state machine format. The Interpreter agents can then compare policies with other Interpreter agents or share the workload of developing the FSM. One can consider the finite state machine as a triple $M = (S, R, t)$, where S is a finite set of states., R is a finite set of symbols called the alphabet., $t : S \times A \rightarrow S$ is the transition function. The inputs to this function are the current state and the last input symbol. While the function value $v(s, x)$ is the state the automaton goes to from state s after reading symbol x. Then the resultant FSM is used as the basis for an agent model that is purely FSM based, which should mimic behaviors of its ML counterpart. We shall now present an example of the Actor-Interpreter model in a game/simulation example.

3   Tactical Air and Ground Warfare Experiment

Tactical air and ground warfare is complex; it involves many dimensions, complicated processes, high costs, and significant hazards, and its doctrine is a set of specialized knowledge on the execution of combat maneuvers (Yining and Yuxian 2003). It governs the decision on the choice of responses during air combat. The same doctrine is used to generate discrete rules within a commercial-grade simulation platform using computer-generated force (CGF) agents. This is based on a traditional 1-v-1 pursuit-evasion problem in three-dimensional airspace (Ardema and Rajan 1987).

We developed a wargame as a simulation-supported, two-sided (Blue and Red) game, where the operation is simulated in a game-based environment which is shown in Fig. 2A. Referring to the LAISR model, our intention is to first generate a set of RL models that provide a type of optimal decision making, and second, create a means to derive descriptive behavior representations in readable formats. Within the simulation there are three layers; a) a *Game/Simulation Layer* (see Sect. 3.1), that represents the simulation content and structure of the overall simulation design, b) a *ML Actor Layer* where agents generate rewards for achieving mission goals, and c) the *Interpretation Layer* (see Sect. 3.2) demonstrates the decomposition process of the agent's policy into a set of finite state based models for evaluation.

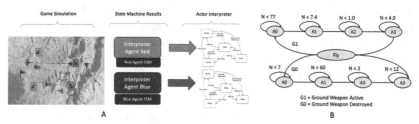

Fig. 2. LAISR tactical experiment diagram (A). Actor finite state machine (B). (Color figure online)

3.1 Game Simulation Layer

The simulation provides the fundamental characteristics of tactical air warfare operations. This also includes the software representation of the models and the platform selected for this effort. The model is designed based on a set of general criteria necessary to begin the wargaming experiment. We first established a common understanding of the objective of the wargaming experiments, including the reason for running the scenario, learning objectives, and external conditions and limitations. A simulated area of 10 km × 10 km area within the game environment was developed to be observable from both a top down (command and control) and a 3D man-in-the-loop (MITL) perspective. Within our model, there are 20 LASIR Agents - ten red and ten blue force agents - in the simulated three-dimensional environment. All agents are tasked to outmaneuver each other so as to enter into a favorable position to eliminate each other using missiles. General game parameters are defined as follows:

- Agents compete to survive in an environment while destroying as many enemy agents as possible.
- One ground weapon exists and fires at enemy fighters.
- Ground weapons should be destroyed first to minimize risk to a fighter squadron.

The objective of the model is that we wish the opposing agents to learn intrinsically that each red/blue agent must first destroy the ground weapon, and second, once ground targets are destroyed, engage air targets, while not being shot down. The winning team has the most agents in the air at the end of the episode. We developed the game layer within the Unity3D framework and used the ML extension library (Juliana 2016) to develop both the *Actor* and the *Interpreter*. Unity3D is a free game platform and toolkit which has been designed to research agent models using several reinforcement learning methods. Within the platform, multi-agent interaction, and agents can be trained using Google's Tensorflow and Keras packages (Pathak 2017).

3.2   Actor/Interpreter Layer

For the Actor model, a reward system as shown in Table 1 was developed within a 3-tuple: case $= (P, A, R)$ where: P is the description of the action, containing all relevant information of the agent state (*a state* $s \in S$); A is an action (or a sequence of actions) that must be performed to solve the problem and; R is the expected reward for performing the action (Ros et al. 2009). Each of the Red and Blue force agents, in this case the stealth tactical fighters, will be given reward signals for completing a number of actions with no specific tactic for how to do so. Reward signals (see Table 1: Q-Learning (P, A, R) Definitions) are used within the A3C model to train the agent's optimal policy. For this simulation 10 agents contribute to the same continuous action space.

Table 1. Q-Learning (P, A, R) definitions and rewards

P	A	R	Normalized
A.0	Destroy ground targets	1	0.88038
A.1	Destroy air targets	.5	0.44019
A.2	Observe ground target current state	.2	0.17608
A.3	Observe locations of hostile	.01	0.0088
A.4	Shot down	-1	0.0088

We created a Curiosity Driven Exploration Model (CDEM) as a reward signal (Pathak 2017). Curiosity or *Intrinsic* reward signals represent the error in an agent's ability to predict its own action consequences in a visual feature space learned by a self-supervised inverse dynamics model (Pathak 2017). CDEM is composed of two models: the Inverse Dynamics Model (IDM), which is used to learn the feature representation of state and next state, and the Forward Dynamics Model (FDM), which generates the predicted features of the next state. The model contains two attributes, an inverse and forward RL model. The IDM (g), which aims at predicting an action $\hat{a}(t)$, which creates internal feature representation of the state $\Phi(s(t))$ and next state $\Phi(s(t + 1))$, respectively. The forward model takes as input Φ(s(t)) and at and predicted feature representation Φ(s(t + 1)) of s(t + 1). Each frame will produce a value which is the difference between FDM $hat\_\Phi(s(t + 1))$ minus IDM.

The Interpreter agent was then employed to retrieve the behavior attributes of the Actor in an interpretable representation (in this case, a finite state machine) representation of these behaviors. Each fighter was assigned an Interpreter agent and provides a hypothesis to what the Actor is trying to accomplish. For each Hypothesis/Strategy, a Moore FSM representation was created using a FSM representation in the C# language. The Interpreter selects two states, for example, $S_0 = A.0$ (Destroy ground targets) and $S_1 = A.1$ (Destroy Air Targets), and evaluates the relationship between the two states. The hypothesis state-transition pair is added to the existing FSM tree as a node in the state diagram. Once included within the state diagram tree, we examine its dominance (Santorini 2018), where new node N has state a that dominates b, b dominates a, or no dominance exists. State dominance is defined as how closely the hypothesis tested with node N matches the state of the observed agent.

4 Results

Experiments were conducted by generating the conditions for developing Actor agents that used an intrinsic curiosity model as a means to delineate two primary behaviors; one, target and destroy ground weapons, and two, engage enemy fighters. During simulations, Actor agents explore the space of possible behaviors and inform which behaviors are rewarded to support incentives from Table 1. The Actor agents were trained over 500,000 episodes within the Unity ML-Agents environment using the CDEM model. The results were evaluated using the Tensorflow analytics website Tensorboard which demonstrates the speed and accuracy of model training. We were able to achieve stable rewards, taking approximately 12 h on an NVIDIA GeForce RTX 2060 6 GB. The Actor was trained over 500,000 episodes and Table 2 reveals the cumulative reward for the agent training increased over the episodes as well as minimum and maximum rewards over the 500,000 episodes.

Table 2. Actor agent results: Cumulative reward

Reward type	Value
Result reward	86.3387494
Min reward	−21.9573917
Max reward	176.8109988
Count (episodes)	500000

Once the Actor agents were trained, 500 skirmishes were run between the red and blue teams. A heat map was created that showed locations of red and blue fighters. Figure 3 presents data for both red and blue Actor agents. Column (A) presents locations before the ground weapon is destroyed. We find that in this column, opposing agents converge on the general artillery location. In Column (B), we observe agent behavior *after* the artillery is destroyed. The heat maps are obtained by averaging over the last 1000 iterations, red regions demonstrate significant occupation of agents. Light Blue regions denote some occupation of agents where full blue is indicated by no concentration. A white cross denotes location of the ground weapon before it is destroyed. The results of the skirmishes showed ML Actor agents converge towards enemy ground weapons until they are destroyed, then they engage in air-to-air combat. The Interpreter agent was run over 500,000 episodes and evaluated based on the frequency of strategies that were used to obtain the closest outcome to the Actor.

The Interpreter derives results of the FSM in the following way:

1. At State S, the Interpreter I_i selects an agent A_i to follow.

	Column A	Column B
	Ground Weapon Attack	Air to Air Combat

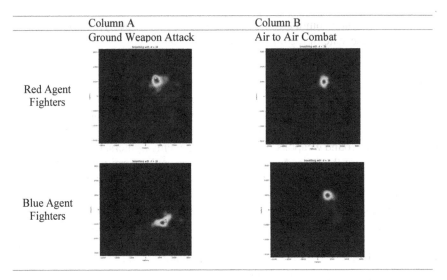

Red Agent Fighters

Blue Agent Fighters

Fig. 3. Heat map representations of actor agents (Color figure online)

2. I_i creates a hypothesis h, which is an estimate, based on the agent's existing state, how it will transition, and what its next state may be.
3. I_i then selects a rule that it believes are being followed by the A_i agent.
4. I_i tests a hypothesis relative to observed states and generates an FSM node. If the hypothesis state-transition pair produces a result whose result is met with higher accuracy than the existing results, a positive reward is given,
5. If a similar node does not exist in the tree, new node is added to the FSM tree as a node in the state diagram tree.
6. Otherwise, the node is pruned, and the process begins again.

Table 3 provides shows the results of how the Actor prioritized its strategies, and how the Interpreter believed the strategies were being optimized. We observe that both the Actor and Interpreter demonstrated an initial strategy for destroying the ground weapon; once the ground weapon was destroyed, agents changed their dominant strategy to air-to-air combat. These calculations could then be used to develop a FSM with probabilities of entering each of these states. Figure 2B (Actor finite state machine) is a visual representation of the FSM developed using the steps above. The plane stays in a fly state when the ground weapon is active (G1). While in G1, each sub state is iterated through; dominant states are given more time and therefore are more likely to be activated by the FSM. Moving into the ground weapon destroyed state (G0) will produce a second set of dominant states with differing levels of priority.

5   Discussion and Future Work

In this paper, we introduced a method that demonstrates how machine learning can be used to model decisions made by agent models. The decomposition of neural networks

Table 3. Actor-interpreter dominant use of strategy

Strategies		Actor		Interpreter	
		Pre-ground Weapon	Post-ground Weapon	Pre-ground Weapon	Post-ground Weapon
A.0	Destroy ground targets	77.10%	7.00%	56.30%	4.21%
A.1	Destroy air targets	7.40%	60.00%	2.45%	60.00%
A.2	Observe ground target current state	1.00%	2.00%	0.03%	3.00%
A.3	Observe locations of hostile	4.00%	12.00%	14.00%	4.60%

for mission planners, instructional designers, and agent modelers, amongst others, can provide an important way to find optimal solutions to complex scenarios. Our approach also provides the basis for how this type of decomposition can be used to develop ML-based models to refine our ability to solve and manage agent behaviors. Initial results of the Interpreter model demonstrate promise. The ML model has provided some novel advantages as a mechanism to derive strategies.

Our approach attempts to address that (1) ML agents do not generally contain a cognitive model or structure that is understandable; this is referred to as the 'black box' problem, and (2) self-learning agents can, at least in part, be deconstructed to examine their strategies. This work also provides additional advantages, including operational planning and learning domain strategies. Using these models to provide results to problem-solving, and reasoning can help learners transfer and apply their knowledge to novel problems and situations (Rudd 2010). These models can solutions also provide methods to generalize across operating environments, adversary, and even game/simulation tools.

Several additional Actor-Interpreter agents are currently being developed. The first is a traffic flow model that demonstrates how an agent can provide optimal examples of streetlight timing, number of cars, and other traffic parameters using ML characteristics. While the second, a Wolf/Sheep predation model highlights Epstein's (2006) note that "agent populations are heterogeneous; individuals may differ in myriad ways—genetically, culturally, by the social network". Furthermore, we are examining how heterogeneous agents optimize their respective states (for example, health/aliveness) and create equilibrium states. In such cases we can then use the Interpreter to better understand the decisions each agent makes to develop its survival strategy.

References

Ardema, M., Rajan, N.: An approach to three-dimensional aircraft pursuit-evasion. Comput. Math. Appl. **13**(1–3), 97–110 (1987)

Castelvecchi, D.: Can we open the black box of AI? Nature News **538**(7623), 20 (2016)

Dawid, H., Gemkow, S., Harting, P., van der Hoog, S., Neugart, M.: The Eurace@Unibi Model: An Agent-Based Macroeconomic Model for Economic Policy Analysis, 1 October 2012. Bielefeld Working Papers in Economics and Management No. 05-2012 (2012)

Epstein, J.: Generative Social Science: Studies in Agent-Based Computational Modeling. Princeton University Press, Princeton (2006)

François-Lavet, V., Henderson, P., Islam, R., Bellemare, M., Pineau, J.: An Introduction to deep reinforcement learning, foundations and trends in machine learning **11**(3–4) (2018)

Juliani, A., et al.: Unity: a general platform for intelligent agents. arXiv preprint arXiv:1809.02627 (2018)

Lee, K., Rucker, M., Scherer, W., Beling, P., Gerber, M., Kang. H.: Agent-based model construction using inverse reinforcement learning. In: Proceedings of the 2017 Winter Simulation Conference (WSC 2017). IEEE Press, pp. 1–12 (2017). Article 95

Li, X., Engelbrecht, A., Epitropakis, M.G.: Benchmark functions for CEC 2013 special session and competition on niching methods for multimodal function optimization. RMIT University, Evolutionary Computation, and Machine Learning Group, Australia, Technical Report, pp. 1–10 (2013)

Mnih, V., et al.: Asynchronous methods for deep reinforcement learning. In: Proceedings of the 33rd International Conference on International Conference on Machine Learning (ICML 2016), vol. 48, pp. 1928–1937. JMLR.org. (2016)

Neto, G., Lima, P.: Minimax value iteration applied to robotic soccer. In: IEEE ICRA 2005 Workshop on Cooperative Robotics, pp. 1–4 (2005)

Resnick, M.: Turtles, Termites, and Traffic Jams: Explorations in Massively Parallel Microworlds (Complex Adaptive Systems). The MIT Press, Cambridge (1997)

Ros, R., Lluis Arcos, J., Lopez, R., Veloso, M.: A case-based approach for coordinated action selection in robot soccer. Artif. Intell. **173**(9–10), 1014–1039 (2009)

Rudd, D.M.: The Effects of Heuristic Problem-Solving Strategies on Seventh Grade Students' Self-Efficacy and Level of Achievement in Mathematics. The College at Brockport (2010)

Sherwood, T., Calder, B.: Automated design of finite state machine predictors for customized processors. In: Proceedings of the 28th Annual International Symposium on Computer Architecture (ISCA 2001). Association for Computing Machinery, New York, pp. 86–97 (2001)

Sutton, R.S., Barto, A.G.: Reinforcement Learning: An Introduction. MIT Press, Cambridge (1998)

Tampuu, A., et al.: Multi-agent cooperation and competition with deep reinforcement learning. PloS One **12**(4), e0172395 (2017)

Tang, L.G., An, B., Cheng, D.J.: An Agent Reinforcement Learning Model Based on Neural Networks. In: Li, K., Fei, M., Irwin, G.W., Ma, S. (eds.) LSMS 2007. LNCS, vol. 4688, pp. 117–127. Springer, Heidelberg (2007). https://doi.org/10.1007/978-3-540-74769-7_14

Van der Hoog, S.: Deep Learning in Discrete-Heuristic Models: A Prospectus (2016)

Wolpert, D.H., Wheeler, K.R., et al.: General Principles of Learning-Based Multi-Agent Systems. In: Autonomous Agents, Seattle, WA. ACM (1999)

Wong, K.-C.: Evolutionary multimodal optimization: a short survey. arXiv preprint arXiv:1508.00457 (2015)

Yining, W., Yuxian, J.: An intelligent differential game on air combat decision. Flight Dyn. **21**, 66–70 (2003)

Canadian Federal Election and Hashtags that Do Not Belong

Thomas Magelinski$^{(\boxtimes)}$, Mihovil Bartulovic, and Kathleen M. Carley

Carnegie Mellon University, Pittsburgh, PA 15213, USA
{tmagelin,mbartulo,carley}@andrew.cmu.edu

Abstract. Topic modeling plays a central roll for understanding discussion on social media platforms such as Twitter. One simple, yet powerful, method of topic analysis on Twitter is performing community detection on the network of hashtags. While this approach is simple and scalable, its interpretability has room for improvement. From a community-detection perspective, some hashtags obscure topics more than they help define them. In this work, we introduce a method of filtering hashtags from topic groups to create more interpretable topics. This modularity-based approach is highly scalable, which we demonstrate through analysis of three networks with approximately one million nodes. These networks were collected the week before, during, and after the Canadian federal election of 2019. Our hashtag filtering method is demonstrated to improve the resulting topics, allowing for easier interpretation. From the resulting topics, it is shown that both liberals and conservatives led effective hashtag campaigns, and that discussion quickly moved away from specific parties and toward issues like climate change in the week following the election.

Keywords: Node filtering · Social cybersecurity · Topic analysis · Twitter · Canadian federal elections

1 Introduction

In the age of disinformation and information operations, analysis of social media discussions is more important than ever. Much of this analysis is done on Twitter, due to its massive user base and generous API. Given this huge amount of information, it would be informative if we could rapidly identify interpretable clusters issues being discussed.

This work was supported in part by the Office of Naval Research (ONR) Award N000141512797 Minerva award for Dynamic Statistical Network Informatics, and the Center for Computational Analysis of Social and Organization Systems (CASOS). Thomas Magelinski was also supported by an ARCS Foundation scholarship. The views and conclusions contained in this document are those of the authors and should not be interpreted as representing the official policies, either expressed or implied, of the ONR.

© Springer Nature Switzerland AG 2020
R. Thomson et al. (Eds.): SBP-BRiMS 2020, LNCS 12268, pp. 161–170, 2020.
https://doi.org/10.1007/978-3-030-61255-9_16

A common approach to dealing with the massive amounts of text contained in social media streams is topic modeling. Topic modeling generally tries to simplify large amounts of text by grouping words into a small number of topics which can be more easily analyzed by humans. Most topic modeling approaches fit probabilistic models to a corpus with word-document relations. Words are then associated with a topic, and it is up to the analyst to interpret what the collection of words means.

Twitter has one feature that makes analysis considerably easier: hashtags. Hashtags allow users to manually tag their post according to topic or theme. Since hashtags are specifically designed to categorize the accompanying text, groups of hashtags are much easier to understand than groups of words. An alternative approach to word-based topic modeling, then, is hashtag-based topic modeling. Groups of hashtags can be found very efficiently in a network science framework, where the problem can be defined as community detection. Community detection of hashtag networks to uncover topics has several advantages over traditional topic models, and has been previously studied.

In this work, we propose a method of filtering out hashtags such that the resulting hashtag-communities have higher modularity. We demonstrate that this filtering leads to topics which are more specific and easier to understand. The filtering technique is demonstrated on three week-long time segments of the Twitter conversation centered around the Canadian federal elections in 2019. The refined topics were then used to show that the political discourse surrounding the elections was divided; hashtags that were for and against the incumbent party were central within the election topic. After the election, analysis shows discussion moving away from specific parties, and towards pressing issues like climate change.

2 Background and Motivation

As social media takes a larger and larger roll in our lives, tools to analyze social media data become more critical. Analysis of Twitter has lead to better understanding of a variety of areas, including political discussion, disinformation, and even ISIS recruiting methods [1,2,11,15]. In this work, we focus on political implications of Twitter.

While artificial behavior is a problem throughout social media, it has become clear that adversarial actors are especially interested in altering political discourse on social media in hopes of changing the outcomes of elections. Understanding and eventually combating these operations is primarily done through the use of inter-operable analysis pipelines [17]. While analysis pipelines have many modules, topic modeling often plays an important roll.

Topic models seek to simplify a large corpus of text by grouping words into "topics," which analysts can then interpret. The most commonly used topic model is Latent Dirichlet Allocation, or LDA [3]. LDA, is a generative statistical model that assumes documents are made up of some topics, and topics are made up of words. Though widely used, the number of topics must be hand-selected, and the interpretation of topics is subjective [9].

While LDA works on any corpus with documents and words, Twitter has an added element of structure: hashtags. Hashtags allow users to self-label their tweet. Researchers have seen that analysis of hashtags, and particularly political hashtags, gives valuable insights to social media conversations and the communities of users within them [15,18]. Based on this, hashtag-based topics should be far more interpretable than word-based topics. In a network science framework, hashtags can be clustered into topics using a community detection algorithm, such as Louvain [4]. Unlike LDA, Louvain leverages the network structure to determine both the number of topics and which hashtags belong to them. This eliminates the subjective judgement required to tune the number of topics when using LDA. Further, many community detection algorithms are highly scalable, meaning they can be applied to much larger social media datasets than LDA can, and results can be obtained faster.

Gerlach, Peixoto, and Altmann formalized and generalized this framework, by reformulating traditional topic modeling as a bi-clustering problem of document-word networks [10]. Feng et al. used similar reasoning to analyze clusters of hashtags in space and time to understand events [9]. Both of these works yield powerful models. However, classical community detection has one problem when it comes to the application of topic models: every word or hashtag *must* be placed in a topic.

In complex networks, some nodes add to group structure by connecting nodes within their group, and other nodes obscure group structure by connecting nodes from other groups [14]. These nodes are called community-hubs and community bridges, respectively, and can be measured with modularity-impact [13]. While both have their role, the "community-bridges" make groups more difficult to interpret, since they are not strongly embedded within their own group. From this lens, some hashtags will be connecting many topics, while not being well-embedded in their own topic.

For example, #morningthoughts is a popular hashtag used to discuss anything users are thinking about in the morning. As a result, it is tied to many hashtag communities, and not particularly strongly tied to any. By forcing the assignment of hashtags like this to a topic, the meaning of that topic is harder to understand. This begs the question: does the filtering of community-bridges lead to higher-quality topics?

Node filtering is closely related to the field of network robustness, which seeks to understand how networks respond to the removal of nodes or edges. Under Holme's framework, we perform a recomputed attack, where centralities are recomputed after each node is filtered [12]. Attacks using community structure have been demonstrated to be extremely effective, and modularity-impact attacks maintain this effectiveness while remaining highly scalable [6,7,13].

Given that algorithms like Louvain seek to maximize modularity, modularity can be thought of as a measure of topic quality [4,14]. It is known that the removal of community-bridges increases modularity [13]. This work explores whether the improvement in modularity, or topic-quality, from node filtering translates to more interpretable topics, bridging us to our primary research question: **RQ1: can modularity-based node filtering increase the intepretability of topics on social media?**

To answer this question, we have collected a large Twitter dataset on three weeks surrounding the Canadian federal election. Topics with and without filtering of community bridges are presented in Sect. 5. We then use the filtered topics to answer a secondary research question: **RQ2: what does topic analysis of the Canadian election discussion tell us?**

3   Canadian Election Twitter Data

Twitter's keyword search on their API allows researchers to collect large amount of data on a topic by providing a number of keywords or hashtags that are likely of importance. We began by performing such a search using a number of keywords relevant to Canadian politics during the election. This list included general keywords such as "cdnpoli" and "election2019" along with more specific keywords about politicians, like "trudeau" and "scheer." This preliminary search identified over 467,153 Twitter users which were actively talking about Canadian politics during the month of the election.

From there, we collected the timeline data on each user. Timeline collections result in user's 3,000 most recent tweets. This is extremely useful in that it is not biased to include search terms, like the keyword approach. Due to account deletions and suspensions, we were able to obtain timeline data from 312,217 accounts. Data outside of the three-week election window was discarded, resulting in a total of 178,394,620 tweets. After the data was collected, it was broken up into three week-long time periods: before the election, during the election, and after the election. The election was held on October 21st of 2019 so, period 1 was October 11–17, period 2 was October 18–24, and period 3 was 25–31.

For each time period a hashtag to hashtag network was created. For each pair of hashtags, the link weight was set to the number of tweets that they both appeared in. Given the size constraints of tweets, this is a strong sense of association. Finally, the largest component of the network was taken. Other network construction or processing methods are an interesting avenue for future work [8]. The summary statistics for these networks are given in Table 1.

Table 1. Summary statistics of hashtag networks

	Number of nodes	Number of edges	Density	Average degree	Degree Std. Dev.
Week before	923,277	8,843,213	$2.0748 * 10^{-5}$	107.5	2,812.6
Week of	1,033,952	10,189,696	$1.9063 * 10^{-5}$	114.3	2,873.2
Week after	953,715	9,197,377	$2.0224 * 10^{-5}$	103.2	2,587.8

4   Methodology

A number of community detection methods are available to group hashtags into topics [4,5,16]. Many of the popular methods rely on modularity maximization. Modularity, Q, is defined as the proportion of edges falling within groups minus the proportion expected to fall within groups from chance:

$$Q = \frac{1}{2m} \sum_{i,j} \left[A_{i,j} - \frac{1}{2m} k_i k_j \right] \delta(c_i, c_j), \qquad (1)$$

where m is the total number of edges in the graph, A is the adjacency matrix, k_i is the degree of node i, c_i is the community of node i, and δ is the Kronecker delta function. Given this definition, modularity can be thought of as a measure of the quality of a partition. This modularity was originally proposed in [14] and it is the most commonly used modularity in Network Science.

Until recently, the Louvain method of modularity maximization was the most popular due to its high-quality partitions and its scalability [4]. However, Traag, Waltman, and Eck demonstrated a fundamental flaw in the Louvain method while introducing the Leiden Method [16]. The flaw is that Louvain grouping may lead to groups that are internally disconnected. Leiden grouping ensures well-connected communities while grouping large networks faster, and often with higher modularity than Louvain. Based on these improvements, we used the Leiden grouping algorithm to group hashtags into topics.

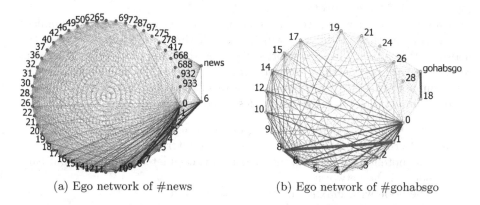

(a) Ego network of #news   (b) Ego network of #gohabsgo

Fig. 1. Comparison hashtag-topic networks. 1a shows the topic connections of #news, including the connection to its own topic, topic 6. 1b shows the same for #gohabsgo, though its topic is topic 18. Link weight is shown as the width.

When it comes to interpreting topics, one must look at the hashtags placed in each group and draw a conclusion about their commonalities. As previously discussed, this process has a number of issues, including the large number of hashtags to check, and the hashtags that are popular but uninformative for topics. Uninformative hashtags will naturally have two properties: they will not be strongly tied to a single community, and the total number of communities they are weakly tied to is large. In other words, hashtags that are too general to be helpful for topic analysis.

To illustrate informative and uninformative hashtags, two hashtag-topic networks are shown in Fig. 1. In 1a, we see that #news is uninformative hashtag. It does not have a strong connection to its own topic, topic 6, and it is connected to many others. On the other hand, #gohabsgo is very informative, showing the opposite properties. We propose filtering hashtags like #news and retaining hashtags like #gohabsgo through a modularity-maximization attack.

Since we can interpret modularity as the quality of topics, it is natural to construct a filter that will increase modularity as much as possible. The node which maximally increases modularity when removed can be calculated extremely efficienetly using modularity-impact [13]. In this work, it was shown that nodes with the highest positive impact satisfy the two properties that we expect from uninformative hashtags.

Removing nodes from a network is highly related to work on network robustness, which looks at how networks respond to targeted removal of nodes [12]. In this space, there are two broad types of attack: initial and recomputed. In the initial case, a centrality measure is calculated for all nodes once, and nodes are deleted in order of that centrality. This is efficient, but is sub-optimal in the presence of network redundancies. The recomputed case solves this by recomputing the centrality measure after each node deletion. Recomputing can make a considerable difference in network impact, but may be prohibitively expensive especially with large networks.

Under this framework, we attack nodes based on their modularity-impact or the amount that modularity will increase if the node is removed from the network. While the hashtag networks are large, the modularity-impact measure scales well with size, so the *recomputed method* was used to filter nodes, and the total number of nodes to filter was set to 5% of the total.

In summary, our workflow can be described as follows:

1. Hashtag to hashtag networks were grouped using Leiden grouping
2. Node filtering was carried out to create more interpretable topics.
   - The potential increase in modularity was calculated for filtering out each node in the network
   - The node with maximum impact was selected
3. Return to step 2 until the 5% of nodes have been filtered.

5   Results and Discussion

The effect of node filtering on modularity can be seen in Fig. 2. We see that initially, modularity changes rapidly as nodes are filtered out. This process has diminishing returns, however, and filtering past our threshold of 5% would

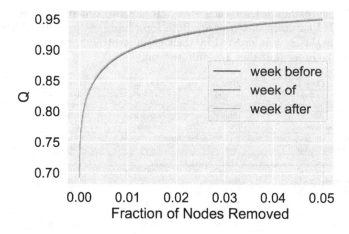

Fig. 2. Modularity for each network as hashtags are filtered.

have only limited further impact. Modularity was roughly the same across networks throughout the filtering process. Each network's modularity increased 35.3–37.3%.

The networks have very similar initial modularities, with values of 0.698, 0.703, and 0.694. Additionally, the hashtags removed in the filtering process are extremely similar across weeks. Across the three networks, 667 of the first 1000 hashtags removed were the same. Because the initial modularities and filtered hashtags are very similar across weeks, the modularity plots in Fig. 2 are nearly identical. This suggests that while the popularity of hashtags may be changing week to week, the way in which hashtags relate to one another does not change as quickly.

Leiden grouping resulted in over 1300 topics for each week. To identify topics relating to Canada, the total number of Canadian-related hashtags was counted for each group. These hashtags include the political hashtags previously discussed like #cdnpoli, as well as any hashtag containing "trudeau," "sheer," and "canada." Each week, we study the 3 topics containing the most of these hashtags. Then, topics are most easily interpreted by looking at high-centrality nodes within them. Not only does modularity-impact give a method of filtering hashtags, it is also a centrality measure [13]. Since hashtags with positive modularity-impact are considered to be "noise" in our topics, hashtags with negative modularity-impact are central to the topic. In fact, this is exactly how the hashtags for Fig. 1 were selected. #news had highest modularity-impact, while #gohabsgo had the lowest. Thus, Table 2 shows the top-5 hashtags in terms of modularity-impact for the top-3 topics in each week. To understand the effect of filtering, the top filtered hashtags are shown as well. The filtered hashtags are shown in the order that they were filtered.

Based on Table 2, the short answer to RQ1 is yes. Across topics, we see that filtering improves interpretability. Filtered hashtags are often very generic

Table 2. Topic summaries for each week. Topics are ordered by the number of Canadian-related hashtags they contain. Both topic hashtags and filtered hashtags are shown. Topic hashtags were ordered by their group centrality, while filtered hashtags are shown in the order that they were filtered out.

		Tag 1	Tag 2	Tag 3	Tag 4	Tag 5
Topic 1	Kept	elxn43	cdnpoli	trudeaumustgo	chooseforward	defundcbc
	Removed	canada	liberals	vote	elections2019	toronto
Topic 2	Kept	80s	funk	capucine	disco	funko
	Removed	love	rt	women	travel	music
Topic 3	Kept	minnesotatrumprally	minnesotafortrump	wearempls	smallfrey	dobbs
	Removed	trump	usa	maga	democrats	thursdaythoughts
Topic 1	Kept	elxn43	cdnpoli	trudeaumustgo	chooseforward	ableg
	Removed	canada	toronto	vote	elections2019	conservative
Topic 2	Kept	babyrepublican	toddlerinchief	paintourcountryred	ks02	yangbeatstrump
	Removed	trump	usa	maga	democrats	election2020
Topic 3	Kept	retrogaming	indiegame	80s	disco	funk
	Removed	rt	travel	women	blog	nature
Topic 1	Kept	cdnpoli	ableg	abpoli	onpoli	actonclimate
	Removed	politics	canada	blog	government	climatechange
Topic 2	Kept	etsy	funk	contemporaryart	disco	アート
	Removed	love	art	animals	music	travel
Topic 3	Kept	ai	iot	machinelearning	bigdata	datascience
	Removed	news	health	tech	healthcare	breakingnews

hashtags like #rt, #women, and #news. When filtered hashtags are a bit more specific, the filtering still results in a much more well defined topic. In week 1 topic two, generic hashtags #trump, #usa, #maga, #democrats, and #thursdaythoughts are filtered out in favor of much more specific hashtags like #minnesotatrumprally and #minnesotafortrump. Another very clear example is the Topic 3 of the post-election week, which represents technology. The filtered hashtags are generic, like #news and #tech while those left over are very specific, like #ai, #iot, and #machinelearning.

The initially ambiguous topics benefit even more from filtering. Topics 2, 3, and 2 in the respective weeks are very similar based on their hashtags. Without filtering, the most common hashtags would be #love, #travel, and #rt, which seem like hashtags that would be used by many blogging communities. After filtering, however, we see that this topic fits the "indie" crowd, those interested in retro video games, independent crafts (from Etsy), and '80s music.

These refined topics allow us to answer RQ2. As expected, each week has a topic specifically dedicated for Canadian politics, Topic 1 for each week. This could be easily identified with or without filtering, but the modularity-based ordering allows us to see which hashtags are most central within the topic. As expected, #elxn43 and #cdnpoli are consistently central.

More interesting, though, is the central position of #trudeaumustgo, #chooseforward, and #actonclimate. These hashtags are direct competitors; "Choose Forward" is the slogan of Justin Trudeau's liberal party, while the second hashtag calls for voting him out of office. This is to suggest that the discussion of the election was contentious, which mirrored the election itself, since the Liberal party barely won and formed a minority government. Following the election, the election-based hashtags are no longer present, while #actonclimate appears. Based on this, it seems that after the election Twitter users have moved on to a discussion about what the new government should take action on.

Outside of the main political hashtags, Canadian hashtags also appear in American political topics. Filtering on these topics show that they are specifically targeted around a Trump rally in Minnesota, and hashtags in opposition of Trump and the republican party. Minnesota's geographic proximity to Canada helps explain the first week's connection to Canadian politics. But the fact that this topic persists through election week suggests that Twitter users are interested in both elections.

6 Conclusion

In this work, we addressed the problem of topic analysis in Twitter. Using a simple but powerful network-based approach results in topics as a collection of hashtags. However, not all hashtags will be useful for understanding the meaning of topics. Therefore we asked two research questions: "Can modularity-based node filtering increase the intepretability of topics on social media?" and "What does topic analysis of the Canadian election discussion tell us?"

First, it was demonstrated that the proposed method of topic detection and modularity-based hashtag filtering is highly scalable, handling networks with over 1 million nodes. This was shown on the hashtag usage networks the week before, of, and after the Canadian federal election. Our method of hashtag filtering substantially improved the interpretability of the resulting topics by removing nodes that bridged topics unnecessarily. General hashtags like #canada were removed in favor of specific hashtags about the election, like #exln43.

These understandable topics, then, allowed for easier characterization of the political discussion around the Canadian federal election. It was seen that the discussion was divided, with central hashtags both for and against the incumbent leader, Justin Trudeau. After the election, the discussion moved passed parties and onto issues, namely climate change. Additionally, discussion of Canadian politics was also intertwined with ongoing campaigns for the American presidential election in 2020.

For this work, the number of hashtags filtered was set to 5% of the total hashtags in the network. While this cutoff struck a reasonable balance between maximizing modularity and filtering few nodes, an automated threshold would be preferred. Given that modularity is monotonically increasing and bounded, a derivative-based method could automatically stop filtering when increases in modularity become small. This would still require a choice of cutoff for the derivative, and would need to be tested on more than just twitter networks, so is left for future work. Additionally, rigorous qualitative studies are to be made, which will better indicate the magnitude of improvement from hashtag filtering.

We believe our method of topic detection and node filtering can play a valuable roll in inter-operable pipelines for social cybersecurity given that it scales to million-node networks, creates topics that are more separated, and, as a result of that separation, creates topics that are more interpretable.

References

1. Babcock, M., Beskow, D.M., Carley, K.M.: Beaten up on Twitter? Exploring fake news and satirical responses during the *Black Panther* movie event. In: Thomson, R., Dancy, C., Hyder, A., Bisgin, H. (eds.) SBP-BRiMS 2018. LNCS, vol. 10899, pp. 97–103. Springer, Cham (2018). https://doi.org/10.1007/978-3-319-93372-6_12
2. Benigni, M.C., Joseph, K., Carley, K.M.: Online extremism and the communities that sustain it: detecting the ISIS supporting community on Twitter. PloS One **12**(12), e0181405 (2017)
3. Blei, D.M., Ng, A.Y., Jordan, M.I.: Latent Dirichlet allocation. J. Mach. Learn. Res. **3**, 993–1022 (2003)
4. Blondel, V.D., Guillaume, J.-L., Lambiotte, R., Lefebvre, E.: Fast unfolding of communities in large networks. J. Stat. Mech. Theory Exp. **2008**(10), P10008 (2008)
5. Clauset, A., Newman, M.E., Moore, C.: Finding community structure in very large networks. Phys. Rev. E **70**(6), 066111 (2004)
6. da Cunha, B.R., González-Avella, J.C., Gonçalves, S.: Fast fragmentation of networks using module-based attacks. PloS One **10**(11), e0142824 (2015)
7. da Cunha, B.R., Gonçalves, S.: Performance of attack strategies on modular networks. J. Complex Netw. **5**(6), 913–923 (2017)
8. Dianati, N.: Unwinding the hairball graph: pruning algorithms for weighted complex networks. Phys. Rev. E **93**, 012304 (2016)
9. Feng, W., et al.: STREAMCUBE: hierarchical spatio-temporal hashtag clustering for event exploration over the Twitter stream. In: IEEE 31st International Conference on Data Engineering, pp. 1561–1572. IEEE (2015)
10. Gerlach, M., Peixoto, T.P., Altmann, E.G.: A network approach to topic models. Sci. Adv. **4**(7), eaaq1360 (2018)
11. Grinberg, N., Joseph, K., Friedland, L., Swire-Thompson, B., Lazer, D.: Fake news on Twitter during the 2016 US presidential election. Science **363**(6425), 374–378 (2019)
12. Holme, P., Kim, B.J., Yoon, C.N., Han, S.K.: Attack vulnerability of complex networks. Physical Review E **65**(5), 056109 (2002)
13. Magelinski, T., Bartulovic, M., Carley, K.M.: Modularity-impact: a signed group centrality measure for complex networks (2020)
14. Newman, M.E.: Modularity and community structure in networks. Proc. Natl. Acad. Sci. **103**(23), 8577–8582 (2006)
15. Small, T.A.: What the hashtag? A content analysis of Canadian politics on Twitter. Inf. Commun. Soc. **14**(6), 872–895 (2011)
16. Traag, V.A., Waltman, L., van Eck, N.J.: From Louvain to Leiden: guaranteeing well-connected communities. Sci. Rep. **9**(1), 1–12 (2019)
17. Uyheng, J., Magelinski, T., Villa-Cox, R., Sowa, C., Carley, K.M.: Interoperable pipelines for social cyber-security: assessing Twitter information operations during NATO trident juncture 2018. Computat. Math. Organ. Theory 1–19 (2019). https://doi.org/10.1007/s10588-019-09298-1
18. Yang, L., Sun, T., Zhang, M., Mei, Q.: We know what@ you# tag: does the dual role affect hashtag adoption?. In: Proceedings of the 21st International Conference on World Wide Web, pp. 261–270 (2012)

Group Formation Theory
at Multiple Scales

Casey Doyle[(✉)], Asmeret Naugle, Michael Bernard, Kiran Lakkaraju,
Robert Kittinger, Matthew Sweitzer, and Fred Rothganger

Sandia National Laboratories, Albuquerque, NM 87185, USA
cldoyle@sandia.gov

Abstract. There is a wealth of psychological theory regarding the drive
for individuals to congregate and form social groups, positing that people
may organize out of fear, social pressure, or even to manage their self-
esteem. We evaluate three such theories for multi-scale validity by studying them not only at the individual scale for which they were originally
developed, but also for applicability to group interactions and behavior.
We implement this multi-scale analysis using a dataset of communications and group membership derived from a long-running online game,
matching the intent behind the theories to quantitative measures that
describe players' behavior. Once we establish that the theories hold for
the dataset, we increase the scope to test the theories at the higher scale
of group interactions. Despite being formulated to describe individual
cognition and motivation, we show that some group dynamics theories
hold at the higher level of group cognition and can effectively describe
the behavior of joint decision making and higher-level interactions.

Keywords: Group dynamics · Social networks · Collective action ·
Communication patterns · Multi-scale dynamics · Organizational
theory · Group behavior

1 Introduction

Emergent organization is a key characteristic of complex social systems, and as
such, social science researchers have done significant work to understand how
people organize themselves into groups [1,8,12]. However, the majority of this
research has focused on the individual-scale, studying how and why people form
and join groups with little attention paid to the dynamics at higher scales [22].

Sandia National Laboratories is a multimission laboratory managed and operated by
National Technology & Engineering Solutions of Sandia, LLC, a wholly owned sub-
sidiary of Honeywell International Inc., for the U.S. Department of Energy's National
Nuclear Security Administration under contract DE-NA0003525. This paper describes
objective technical results and analysis. Any subjective views or opinions that might be
expressed in the paper do not necessarily represent the views of the U.S. Department
of Energy or the United States Government.

ⓒ Springer Nature Switzerland AG 2020
R. Thomson et al. (Eds.): SBP-BRiMS 2020, LNCS 12268, pp. 171–181, 2020.
https://doi.org/10.1007/978-3-030-61255-9_17

This individual focus, however, has left group-level interactions largely unexplained. A better understanding of how scalable various theories are provides information on the social dynamics and causal foundations behind group behavior, with broad applicability including terrorist group emergence, international alliances, protesting behavior, and scientific research communities.

This article addresses this problem by evaluating the hypothesis that cross-scale emergence of groups and recursive interactions have similarities at different scales. Emergent organization is fundamental to social system dynamics [10], where individuals with heterogeneous traits and behaviors organize themselves into groups with their own distinct characteristics and behaviors. These groups can exist at any scale, from a few individuals to collections of countries, and individuals can associate with many groups. Groups can influence individuals, interact with each other, and form groups of groups. The complexities of group dynamics influence group emergence, recursive interactions, and the multi-scale nature of these systems makes understanding them difficult, but by testing the hypothesis that different scales of group dynamics have similar tendencies, we can begin to evaluate whether the substantial social science research that has been done at the individual scale might also apply at higher scales, facilitating new investigation into these complex dynamics.

To this end, we study the data from a massively multiplayer online game (MMOG) that we will refer to as *Game X* [18], in which players can interact and join explicit groups called guilds. Using online gaming datasets to study social group dynamics is not uncommon for this type of research, with well documented benefits and drawbacks for social science research [6]. Examinations of online games have spanned from interviews with players to data-driven studies that build models to mimic the behavior observed in the game [13,24]. Such studies have even extended to epidemiology and, most relevant to this work, the analysis of social ties between players [2,7]. These studies leverage many of the benefits of using MMOGs as interesting social science test beds [14], allowing for the detailed observation of in-game behaviors that would be largely unobtainable from real-world social interactions. *Game X* is particularly useful for investigating the multi-scale potential of group formation theory because in addition to players interacting to form casual groups, the guild construct allows players to declare explicit groups that provide rich temporal data for study.

To investigate the multi-scale nature of group formation theory, we tested a set of existing theories, all of which were initially developed to explain group formation at the individual scale, on the dataset at both the individual and group levels. This analysis helps us to understand whether the data supports the selected theories in general, as well as whether the data suggests that the theories hold at higher scales. This analysis is an initial step in understanding whether multi-scale group dynamics theory is likely to exist, whether individual-level theory on group formation holds at the higher scale, and whether there are parts of the theory that hold better than others. Using this framework to guide our investigation, we show that some existing individual-level theory does hold at multiple scales, thus demonstrating that there is potential for multi-scale theory on group formation.

2   Testing Existing Theory at Multiple Scales

2.1   Dataset Description

The theories discussed in this work were chosen based on both their potential for applicability at multiple scales and their relevance to the game dataset, and then interpreted based on available data. We then tested these theories at both the individual level, looking at individuals joining groups, and the group level, looking at groups merging together into larger groups or decaying as they lose subgroups of their membership. All data on social interactions were derived from the *Game X* dataset, a game where players move in a 2-D world gathering resources, interacting with other players, and building infrastructure such as factories, market centers and cities. *Game X* is open-ended with no specified win conditions, and has been online for more than a decade with hundreds of players.

A key characteristic of this study is the ability of *Game X* players to organize themselves into guilds as player-led groups that have a private communication mechanism. In the game, players are not required to join guilds, and guild membership is entirely voluntary, although it does hold benefits. Guilds are a major part of the game and effectively function as quasi-states that control territory. Guilds can range in size from just 2 players to more than hundreds. Combat often erupts between guilds as they fight over access to resources, territory, differences in culture, or as retribution to actual or perceived slights. Additionally, trade is a central part of the game in order to build more advanced structures and vehicles, including multi-step supply chains involving numerous players that are often managed by guilds. This work uses a dataset encompassing a real-world time period of over 2 years, and contains information about player trade, combat, and communications.

Guild level events of particular interest in this paper include lifecycle events where the guild as a whole undergoes a significant change in its membership. These events fall into multiple categories that are mentioned throughout the paper: birth, death, growth, loss, and merge events. Birth and death events are simply defined as the moments the guild is officially created and disbanded within the game. Guilds always have contiguous lifespans and at least one member; if a guild collapses down to no members and the players wish to reform later, they must form a new independent guild via a new guild birth event. Additionally, players are free to join and leave guilds at any point, and a guild can die simply from all of its members joining other guilds or choosing to be independent. In contrast, growth and loss events are interpreted based on periods of time with abnormal change in membership for guilds. For this work, we analyze two week long time windows, defining an abnormal period as gross gain or loss of members greater than two standard deviations from the mean value for all possible guilds over all possible time windows. Abnormal periods are then filtered such that no growth or loss events overlap with each other. Finally, merge events are a subset of growth and loss events where at least on quarter of players involved in the event all join or originate from the same guild within the two week period following/preceding the event. For example, if twelve players leave Guild A at once (qualifying as a loss event) and four of those players all join Guild B within two weeks, then it would also be categorized as a merge event. Likewise if twelve players join Guild B and four of them come from Guild A then it also qualifies as a merge event.

2.2   Group Cohesiveness

Group cohesiveness theory says that people in highly cohesive groups are motivated to stay in those groups, and to contribute to and advance the group as a whole [5]. This in turn contributes to the group's potency and vitality, leading to healthier groups and greater longevity. Further, it has been theorized that as groups survive longer they become more cohesive, manifesting an increasing density and shrinking average distance over time between members [19]. We considered cohesiveness in the *Game X* dataset to be based on the social network defined by communication frequency between players. We developed this network using a 7-day window of messaging between players; for a given time record x, two nodes u and v have an edge between them of weight w, where w is the raw number of communications between nodes u and v in the time window $t = [x - 7, x]$. To define distance between nodes, we used the normalized inverse weight, $d_{u,v} = w_{avg}/w_{u,v}$, such that the distance between nodes reflects the closeness of the relationship relative to all other relationships in the network.

Using this representation, we determined cohesiveness of social networks by calculating the normalized harmonic closeness centrality, a measure of how close each node is to every other node in the network. The normalized harmonic centrality is calculated for a node u as

$$H(u) = \frac{1}{N - 1} \sum_{u \neq v} \frac{1}{d_{u,v}} \tag{1}$$

where N is the total number of nodes in the network [20,21]. We used this value as a measure for how deeply ingrained individuals are within their social networks, and the average normalized centrality to measure of how dense the network is at critical points.

The theory of group cohesiveness suggests that healthier guilds have higher average centralities, and that individuals with higher centrality within their respective guilds are more socially ingrained and thus less likely to leave. We began testing this theory by comparing the average centrality of individuals in guilds that are undergoing no guild changes (our control group) to those in the week before they leave their guild (either to remain independent or to join another guild). Indeed, Table 1 shows that guild members about to leave their guilds have lower average centrality than those who are stable in their guilds, supporting the theory of group cohesiveness at the individual scale. Interestingly, guilds undergoing loss events show similar drops in average centrality across the guild. This average centrality is calculated guild wide, including players that remain in the guild after the event. When narrowed to merge events the average centrality drops even further. This suggests that not only are the individuals leaving guilds less connected to their neighbors than those in stable guild membership situations, but guilds as a whole become less centralized as they near periods of instability. The above results intuitively confirms group cohesiveness theory as an indicator of guild stability on the individual level, leading to further investigation into the multiscale validity of the theory. To this end, we study a higher level in-game social network where the nodes are groups, and ties between them are messages sent by any member of one group to any member of another. This guild-to-guild network represents the positions of guilds within the overall context of the game. Messaging rates between guilds are chosen over other guild-level connections for consistency with the individual level analysis above to facilitate the comparison. In this formulation, a guild leaving the network is analogous to a guild dying out entirely, while large-scale loss events represent guilds that are able to survive sudden drops in membership. Using these events as our focus times, we found that the average guild to guild centrality across all guilds in the network holds fairly steady across timesteps at $H_{avg} = 0.44$, while the centrality of guilds preceding a death event reaches $H_{death} = 0.32$ at its minimum and $H_{death} = 0.39$ in the final time step before the event. Guilds undergoing loss events that don't lead to their deaths, however, actually show a spike in guild to guild centrality up to a maximum of $H_{loss} = 0.66$ in the final timestep before the event. This is partially explained by players leaving during these loss events messaging other guilds to find new groups to join; however, looking at longer time horizons reveals further nuance. Figure 1 demonstrates that while guilds do see a drop in centrality before death and a growth in centrality before loss events, this is part of an overall trend where dying guilds have lower stable centrality than average, while those that survive their loss events have a higher stable average centrality. This phenomenon fits well with group cohesiveness theory, in that guilds that are more central to the *Game X* social network are a part of a healthier subsystem and are thus more resilient to sudden losses of players, while those that are less central find themselves leaving the system entirely when facing a large exodus of players.

Table 1. Centrality values for guilds undergoing different life cycle events and how they differ from a stable guild.

	Average centrality	Difference from healthy guild
Stable guild	0.70	N/A
Guild change	0.55	21%
Loss event	0.57	19%
Merge event	0.51	28%

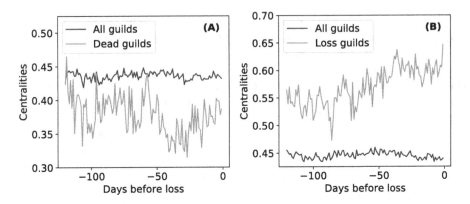

Fig. 1. Average centrality of guilds 120 days before they undergo (a) death and (b) loss events compared to the average centralities across all guilds at the same times.

2.3   Sociometer Theory

Sociometer theory relates the self-esteem of individuals and their social connectedness, measuring social health within a group using social inclusion and risk of rejection [17]. The theory asserts that the self-esteem, or lack thereof, that people feel in relation to a group is a measure of their perceived social exclusion and perceived potential for rejection from that group. Further, sociometer theory relates feelings of belonging to their evaluation of relationships between themselves and others, with negative relational evaluations negatively impacting an individual's perceived social position [16]. Since the theory asserts that an individual's self-esteem can be measured based on the perceived likelihood that the individual will be accepted and included in a social setting [15], we relate the likelihood of changing social settings to individuals' confidence that they will be accepted. For the purposes of this paper we measure this based on messaging rates prior to joining a new guild, assuming that individuals and groups with higher relative self-esteem will need less engagement with their new group as reassurance before making the decision to officially join.

For this analysis, we considered the individual scale by looking at communication rates during the week in which a person joined a group or changed groups, and compared those to communication rates at all other times. We also considered with whom individuals were communicating, specifically evaluating communication with people in guilds the individual was preparing to join compared to communication rates with others. For all of these analyses, we consider the directionality of the messages to identify any reciprocity disparities. Using this data, we compare baseline communication activity to the communications leading up to the individual joining a new social group, identifying patterns that suggest social inclusiveness prior to an individual joining or changing guilds. As shown in Table 2, we found a strong relationship between volume of messages and group dynamics, but no strong relationship regarding reciprocity. In particular, individuals that have never joined a guild before exhibit very high messaging activity towards the group they plan to join; four times the messaging rate to individuals in other guilds or no guilds. This fits with sociometer theory's assertion that group and personal relationships are driven by self-esteem of the individuals, indicating that new players need the most assurance that they will fit in and not be rejected by a new guild before joining. These are the players that would be expected to have the lowest self-esteem, thus needing strong relational evaluations before feeling confident in their fit with a group. The trend also holds for players changing guilds, but it is muted at around a fifty percent increase, further fitting with the hypothesis that players with more experience in guild and social dynamics require less communication before committing to a new guild. To expand this analysis to the group scale, we considered messaging within and between the guilds in *Game X* during times of merge events. We considered mean messages per person in the sub-group of individuals that moved from one guild to another for the month surrounding a merge event. This messages-per-person metric was chosen to control for the size of the sub-group, and we considered a one-month period to capture communication dynamics both before and after the period of player movement. The results, contained in Table 3, show a large amount of communication between the individuals leaving a guild and other individuals inside that guild, mostly involving other leaving members. There is, however, only a small number of messages sent and received by the new guild that the players are moving to, indicating that guild merge events do not have the same consideration period noted for individual player movements. Movement of players within these subgroups does not appear to require establishment of a relationship with the new social group; instead we see a strengthening of bonds and increased communication within the sub-group itself. This suggests that the sociometric effect on self-esteem is not a factor driving guild merge events (or at least in the choice of receiving guild). Instead, the data indicates that the sub-group players have positive group self-esteem through their sense of belonging within the sub-group, and are thus unafraid of rejection in the new larger guild they join together. As a result, using this behavior as a sociometric evaluation for the likelihood of movement at the group-level fails, despite its high correlation at the individual level.

Table 2. Number of messages sent by individuals in the week before changes in their guild membership.

| | With player in | | | | | |
| | Accepting guild | | Other guild | | No guild | |
	In	Out	In	Out	In	Out
Joining new guild	2.2	2.2	0.5	0.6	0.6	0.7
Changing guilds	1.6	1.6	1.1	1.2	0.2	0.3
No guild change	0.9	0.9	0.6	0.6	0.1	0.1

Table 3. Messages sent by players within the sub-group of individuals leaving one guild for another compared to the overall rates of the sending and receiving guilds.

	Messages prior to merge	
	In	Out
Sub group	1.67	1.67
Loss guild	2.43	2.35
Receiving guild	0.24	0.23

2.4   Terror Management Theory and Mortality Salience

Terror management theory [9,23] posits that anxiety over death, caused by the conflict between a person's self-preservation instinct and their knowledge of the inevitability of death, causes humans to seek cultural identity in a variety of ways, one of which is group membership [11]. According to the related mortality salience hypothesis [4], being reminded of one's own mortality enhances these behaviors. We test these theories on individual-level group dynamics in the *Game X* dataset by studying the death rate of players in the days before they chose to join a new guild compared to baseline death rates. Game death in *Game X* consists of a player's character "dying", leading the character to lose skills (temporarily) and equipment (permanently) in the game. We assert that due to the emotional investment, salient experiences, and high degree of social value and support that players derive from role playing games [3,25], game death increases mortality salience by serving as a reminder of death and loss and thus allows us to test the impact of terror management theory within the game. The time windows before players joined guilds were chosen to be those with the highest rate of deaths per day over the window, yielding windows of 2 days before merge events for guilds and 1 day before guild changes for individuals. The resulting pre-event death rates are shown in Fig. 2(a), where in the day before a player joins a new guild, the average number of deaths per day was 0.1005 while over all other times the average number of deaths per day was 0.0069, revealing a pre-event death rate 14.6 times higher than the baseline that indicates a high level of correlation between individual player death and the decision to join a new guild.

At the group level, we used a similar analysis to evaluate the number of deaths per day in a guild before that guild underwent a merge out event (where a group of players simultaneously left one guild for another). As shown in Fig. 2(b), on the day before such a merge event, the average number of deaths per day was 1.914, while over all other times this value was only 0.518. Thus, at the group level deaths were 3.7 times higher than the baseline. This relationship did not hold for the receiving guild, where there was no increase in the deaths per day in the days leading up to receiving the influx of players, indicating that death is only a driving factor in leaving and joining guilds, not guilds recruiting new players from others. Despite the relative rarity of group-level events and the generally more slowly moving dynamics, this result shows a high level of time-separated correlation between deaths and group dynamics, and indicates that the mortality that drives many individuals to join groups in the first place can also push a group as a whole to find other groups with which to combine.

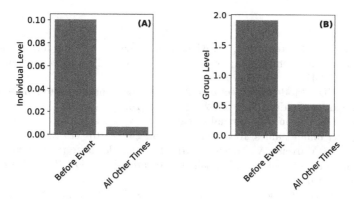

Fig. 2. Deaths per day at the (a) individual and (b) group levels before guild change or merge out events as opposed to all other times.

3   Conclusions

Increasing online social interaction has presented new opportunities to study how people behave in natural settings, providing large-scale datasets with troves of valuable information. By using data from *Game X* to test and expand social theory about what drives individuals into groups, we investigate the potential for theories of individual behavior to hold at higher scales in which groups interact with each other as their own entities. Throughout our analysis we find that, in most cases, groups as a whole do behave similarly to the individuals that make them up. This is most directly evident for terror management theory, where the data had simple and direct approximations of death, but also holds for the theory of group cohesiveness where we show that both groups and individuals on the fringes of their respective networks are at greater risk for leaving the network entirely. In contrast, while we show that while sociometric pressures influence behavior at the individual level, they do not manifest in the same way at the group level.

These results provide evidence that some social theories, despite being formulated with individual cognition and behavior in mind, will hold at multiple scales and describe the behavior of both individuals and groups. Not all theories have this scalability, as some key in on inherently individual aspects of cognition such as self-esteem, but these exceptions simply provide further incentive to continue testing social and psychological theory at multiple scales. In doing so we can not only learn how well the given theory holds, but also gain insight into how groups think, behave, and come to collective decisions. For this reason, future work should consider not only other theories on group behavior, but also how scaled actions for collections of people come about, how group sizes affect the decision-making ability of a group, and how far the scalability holds in the presence of multi-hierarchical group dynamics.

References

1. Backstrom, L., Huttenlocher, D., Kleinberg, J., Lan, X.: Group formation in large social networks: membership, growth, and evolution. In: Proceedings of the 12th ACM SIGKDD, pp. 44–54 (2006)
2. Balicer, R.D.: Modeling infectious diseases dissemination through online role-playing games. Epidemiology **18**(2), 260–261 (2007)
3. Barnett, J., Coulson, M.: Virtually real: a psychological perspective on massively multiplayer online games. Rev. Gen. Psychol. **14**(2), 167–179 (2010)
4. Burke, B.L., Martens, A., Faucher, E.H.: Two decades of terror management theory: a meta-analysis of mortality salience research. Pers. Soc. Psychol. Rev. **14**(2), 155–195 (2010)
5. Cartwright, D., Zander, A.: Group Dynamics, 3rd edn., p. 580. Harper+Row, Oxford (1968)
6. Ducheneaut, N.: Massively multiplayer online games as living laboratories: opportunities and pitfalls. In: Bainbridge, W. (ed.) Online Worlds: Convergence of the Real and the Virtual. Human-Computer Interaction Series. Springer, London (2010). https://doi.org/10.1007/978-1-84882-825-4_11
7. Ducheneaut, N., Yee, N., Nickell, E., Moore, R.: The life and death of online gaming communities: a look at guilds in world of warcraft. In: SIGCHI, pp. 839–848 (2007)
8. Forsyth, D.R.: Group Dynamics. Cengage Learning, Belmont (2018)
9. Greenberg, J., Pyszczynski, T., Solomon, S.: The causes and consequences of a need for self-esteem: a terror management theory. In: Baumeister, R.F. (ed.) Public Self and Private Self. Springer Series in Social Psychology. Springer, New York (1986). https://doi.org/10.1007/978-1-4613-9564-5_10
10. Helbing, D., Yu, W., Rauhut, H.: Self-organization and emergence in social systems: modeling the coevolution of social environments and cooperative behavior. J. Math. Sociol. **35**(1–3), 177–208 (2011)
11. Hogg, M.A., Hohman, Z.P., Rivera, J.E.: Why do people join groups? Three motivational accounts from social psychology. Soc. Pers. Psychol. Compass **2**(3), 1269–1280 (2008)
12. Hogg, M.A., Turner, J.C.: Interpersonal attraction, social identification and psychological group formation. Eur. J. Soc. Psychol. **15**(1), 51–66 (1985)
13. Johnson, N.F., et al.: Human group formation in online guilds and offline gangs driven by a common team dynamic. Phys. Rev. E **79**(6), 066117 (2009)
14. Lakkaraju, K., Epifanovskaya, L.W.E., Stites, M.C., Letchford, J., Reinhardt, J.C., Whetzel, J.: Online Games for Studying Human Behavior. Technical report, Sandia National Lab. (SNL-NM), Albuquerque, NM (United States); Sandia ... (2018)
15. Leary, M.R.: Sociometer theory and the pursuit of relational value: getting to the root of self-esteem. Eur. Rev. Soc. Psychol. **16**(1), 75–111 (2005)
16. Leary, M.R., Baumeister, R.F.: The nature and function of self-esteem: sociometer theory. In: Advances in Experimental Social Psychology, vol. 32, pp. 1–62. Academic Press, January 2000

17. Leary, M.R., Downs, D.L.: Interpersonal functions of the self-esteem motive. In: Kernis, M.H. (ed.) Efficacy, Agency, and Self-Esteem. The Springer Series in Social Clinical Psychology, pp. 123–144. Springer, Boston (1995). https://doi.org/10.1007/978-1-4899-1280-0_7

18. Lee, J., Lakkaraju, K.: Predicting social ties in massively multiplayer online games. In: Kennedy, W.G., Agarwal, N., Yang, S.J. (eds.) SBP 2014. Lecture Notes in Computer Science, vol. 8393. Springer, Cham (2014). https://doi.org/10.1007/978-3-319-05579-4_12

19. Leskovec, J., Kleinberg, J., Faloutsos, C.: Graphs over time: densification laws, shrinking diameters and possible explanations. In: ACM SIGKDD, KDD 2005, Chicago, Illinois, USA, pp. 177–187. Association for Computing Machinery, August 2005

20. Marchiori, M., Latora, V.: Harmony in the small-world. Physica A **285**(3), 539–546 (2000)

21. Rochat, Y.: Closeness centrality extended to unconnected graphs: the harmonic centrality index. Institute of Applied Mathematics, University of Lausanne, Technical report (2009)

22. Smaldino, P., Pickett, C., Sherman, J., Schank, J.: An agent-based model of social identity dynamics. JASSS **15**(4), 7 (2012)

23. Solomon, S., Greenberg, J., Pyszczynski, T.: The Worm at the Core: On the role of Death in Life. Random House, New York (2015)

24. Williams, D., Ducheneaut, N., Xiong, L., Zhang, Y., Yee, N., Nickell, E.: From tree house to barracks. Games Cult. **1**(4), 338–361 (2006)

25. Yee, N.: The psychology of massively multi-user online role-playing games: motivations, emotional investment, relationships and problematic usage. In: Schroeder, R., Axelsson, A.S. (eds.) Avatars at Work and Play. Computer Supported Cooperative Work, vol. 34. Springer, Dordrecht (2006). https://doi.org/10.1007/1-4020-3898-4_9

Towards Agent Validation of a Military Cyber Team Performance Simulation

Geoffrey B. Dobson$^{(\boxtimes)}$ and Kathleen M. Carley

Carnegie Mellon University, Pittsburgh, PA 15213, USA
gdobson@andrew.cmu.edu

Abstract. This paper discusses the design consideration for an agent-based model empirical validation. Agent behaviors are designed in order to create outcome measures clearly aligned with performance. A simulation of a military cyber team engaged in a conflict with an adversarial force is run in order to analyze output data and determine considerations for future validations.

Keywords: Agent-based modelling · Simulation · Validation · Cyber · Military

1 Introduction

The frequency of cyber attacks continue to rise all over the world. According to a 2019 Accenture report [1], cyber attacks have increased 11% since 2018 and 67% since 2014. Militaries are confronting more sophisticated adversaries and continue to evolve their cyberspace operational forces. The purpose of a cyber team is to ensure the access and availability of cyber terrain. Cyber attacks are usually designed to happen fast, causing damage to machines, infecting other machines, and extracting data, before covering tracks and moving on. The U.S. Army is well aware of how fast cyber defenders must recognize and remediate attacks in order to be effective. The Army has a saying, "the golden hour", referring to how long medical troops have to get wounded soldiers attention that will increase the chances of survival. In a recent interview [2], Lieutenant General Stephen Fogarty, chief of Army Cyber Command contrasted that with cyber troop response requirements: "It's probably the golden five minutes, or that golden 20 to 30 min, to recognize what the adversary is putting out there and respond."

The simulation of cyber force deployment is difficult for several key reasons. First, the complexity of terrains and troops is hard to model. Cyber terrain is made up of thousands of different configurations of network devices, routing tables, end-user machines, operating systems, software, and security settings to name a few that would need to be considered. Modeling cyber personnel is also complex. Cyber troops can have different levels of experience, knowledge, skills, and training. When simulating a team, complexity increases due to issues of teamwork, collaboration, communication, and procedures. The Cyber-FIT simulation framework addresses this issue by defining the basic agents and interactions required to simulate effects of concern to military planners. In this paper, the framework will be used to simulate one cyber team deployment and design an agent validation of the simulation results.

R. Thomson et al. (Eds.): SBP-BRiMS 2020, LNCS 12268, pp. 182–191, 2020.
https://doi.org/10.1007/978-3-030-61255-9_18

2 Background

One of the main purposes of an agent-based model is to simulate a phenomenon of interest and then predict a likely range of outcomes under a range of controlled conditions. This leads to a natural tension [3] between transparency and veridicality as the model is developed. That is, as a model becomes more complex, the need for veridicality increases, whereas simpler models need transparency. This paper will discuss the aspects of validation where simplicity will be more important and other aspects where veridicality will be favored from an agent validation perspective. When attempting to empirically validate an agent-based model, early design considerations must be considered. Bert, et al. recommend [4] binning validation efforts into either "conceptual" or "empirical" viewpoints. Conceptual validation is a micro view, where individual processes within the system are analyzed for functionality. Once the main underlying mechanisms of the simulation have been conceptually validated, then empirical validation at the macro-view level can commence. The model presented in this paper was built in this manner, with a spiral development methodology, beginning with basic agent functions and slowly adding more complex behaviors and environment interactions. Windrum et al. [5] described four dimensions to consider when designing an empirical validation for an agent-based model. One dimension includes the type of sensitivity analysis, which will be the majority of discussion for this paper. An across run variability analysis will be conducted in order to analyzed control parameters and independent variables within virtual experiments.

3 Model Overview

The Cyber-FIT simulation framework [6] is an agent-based model that allows for virtual experimentation [7], what-if analysis, and theory development. This version of the framework was developed using the Recursive Porous Agent Simulation (Repast) Toolkit, a java based open source agent-based development environment. This version was improved by adding more complex agent behaviors and outcome data collection. The model contains two main classes of agents: forces and terrain. Each class is further subdivided. Force agents are either defender, attacker, or friendly, and terrain agents are networking, serving, or client. Force agents represent the personnel involved in military operations. Terrain agents represent the cyberspace assets necessary to support kinetic military operations. Table 1 defines each agent subclass.

The current design of Cyber-FIT allows for a simulation to be initialized with two files called Campaign_Setup and Cyber_Forces. The Campaign_Setup file defines the campaign variables needed to setup the conflict. This includes the number and type of kinetic missions, number of friendly forces, and number and type of computer systems per mission. The Cyber_Forces file defines the cyber defender and cyber attacker teams. The cyber defenders have a skill level, job type and team while the cyber attackers have a skill level.

With respect to agent validation, the output variables for each agent will take special consideration. In this paper, the following three agent classes will be discussed: defender, attacker, and terrain. In an actual conflict, defending forces and attacking forces will have

Table 1. Cyber-FIT agent definitions

Force agents	
Defender	Military personnel tasked with defending cyberspace assets
Attacker	Military personnel tasked with attacking cyberspace assets
Friendly	Military personnel tasked with kinetic and non-cyber operations
Terrain agents	
Network	Computer systems meant for networking information such as routers, hubs and switches
Server	Computer systems meant for managing access to resources such as web servers, application servers, mail servers and proxy servers
Client	Computer systems meant for end use such as laptops and tablets

exactly opposite goals with respect to contested terrain. All computer systems within a military conflict, when viewed from either perspective of offensive or defensive, has the same basic states of compromised and not compromised. If a computer system has been successfully attacked, it is considered compromised, regardless of type being a networking, server, or client system. Therefore at an abstract level it is most easy to conceptualize the results of a simulation through the lens of defender, attacker, and terrain.

3.1 Agent Behaviors

Defender agents represent the individual members of defensive cyber forces. Their behavior is based on the normal operations and procedures of cyberspace operators. Each defender agent has a skill level, team assignment, squad assignment, and two vector objects representing their cyber situation awareness. At any given time defender agents will take one of the following four actions: restoral operations, interact with force, interact with terrain, or nothing. Table 2 describes each of these behaviors in more detail and how they can be further broken down.

Attacker agents represent the individual members of offensive cyber forces. Their behavior is based on the actions that must take place [8] in order to traverse the cyber kill chain. Attacker agents have a tier level [9] and three vector objects representing their cyber situation awareness. At any given time attacker agents will take one of the following actions: planning, recon, weaponization, delivery, exploitation, command and control, and actions. Table 3 describes each of these behaviors in more detail and how they can be further broken down.

Terrain agents represent all of the cyberspace hardware assets present in the simulated conflict. Terrain agents have a type, status, list of vulnerabilities, list of payloads, and list of missions supported. At any given time terrain agents might add a vulnerability, remove a vulnerability, receive payload, change status, and create connections with other terrain agents. Table 4 describes each of these behaviors in more detail.

Table 2. Defender agent simulated behaviors

Action	Description
Restoral operations	Agent is aware that there is compromised terrain so focuses all efforts there, sends message to team lead. Agent attempts to restore terrain continuously until successful. Restoral Operations are divided into the following categories: type of compromise, type of terrain, total time to restore, number of successful and unsuccessful restoral operations
Interact with force	Agent is operating under normal circumstances and decides to interact with another defender force agent on its team, or is aware of a compromise and sends message to team lead. Interactions with forces are divided into the following categories: vulnerability update to team lead, vulnerability update to squad mate, compromise message to team lead, status update to team lead, status update to squad mate, resource request to team lead, and miscellaneous message
Interact with terrain	Agent is operating under normal circumstances and decides to interact with one or several terrain agents. Interactions with terrain are divided in the following categories: information read, information write, survey, secure, and restore
Nothing	Agent is not sure what to do so does nothing

Table 3. Attacker agent simulated behaviors

Action	Description
Planning	Agent is planning attack and adds a random number of attacks to its computer system to try to use against contested cyber terrain
Recon	Agent is conducting reconnaissance operations by scanning cyber terrain and finding vulnerabilities. Tier six attacker agents can develop zero day attacks at this time
Weaponization	Agent is developing cyber attack payload using its own machine based on information found during recon actions
Delivery	Agent attempts to deliver cyber attack payload to cyber terrain that is thought to be vulnerable
Exploitation	Agent does nothing while waiting for delivered payload to compromise terrain
Command and Control	Agent receives message that cyber attack was successful and now can interact with compromised terrain
Actions	Agent takes actions associated with cyber attack type that was successful

Table 4. Terrain agent simulated behaviors

Action	Description
Add vulnerability	Agent gets random number and if below configurable threshold, (controlling vulnerability growth rate) adds random number between 1 and 99 to list of vulnerabilities
Remove vulnerability	Agent is interacting with defender agent and removes some number of vulnerabilities from list
Receive payload	Agent is interacting with attacker agent and receives payload for cyber attack that agent may or may not be vulnerable to
Change status	Agent has been compromised by cyber attack or defender agent restores agent to operational
Interact with terrain	Agent creates connection for some number of ticks to another terrain agent due to normal operations or malicious activity

3.2 Agent Output Data

The following three tables show all agent output data collected after each run of the simulation from the current version of Cyber-FIT (Tables 5, 6 and 7).

Table 5. Defender agent output data

Data	Description
Survey_Op_Attempts	Number of times the agent has attempted a survey type defensive cyberspace operation
Survey_Op_Successes	Number of times the agent has successfully executed a survey type defensive cyberspace operation
Secure_Op_Attempts	Number of times the agent has attempted a secure type defensive cyberspace operation
Secure_Op_Successes	Number of times the agent has successfully executed a survey type defensive cyberspace operation
Restoral_Op_Attempts	Number of times the agent has attempted to restore compromised terrain
Restoral_Op_Successes	Number of times the agent has successfully restored compromised terrain
Cyber_SA_Terrain_Status	An array listing all terrain agents that the agent believes to be compromised
Cyber_SA_Terrain_Vulns	A hash table showing all terrain agents that the agent has surveyed and the list of vulnerabilities believed to be present

Table 6. Attacker agent output data

Data	Description
Attack_Attempts	Number of times the agent has attempted a cyber attack
Attack_Successes	Number of times the agent has successfully executed a cyber attack
Data_Exfiltrated	Total number of bytes exfiltrated from compromised terrain agents
Systems_Compromised	Total number of terrain agents compromised
Systems_Downtime	Total number of minutes terrain agents are compromised

Table 7. Terrain agent output data

Data	Description
Vulnerabilities_Total	Total number of vulnerabilities present on agent at any given time
Vulnerability_Severity	Total severity level of vulnerabilities present on agent at any given time
Payloads_Total	Total number of malicious payload software present on agent at any given time
Compromise_Total	Total number of times agent has been compromised
Compromise_Time	Total time agent has been compromised

4 Simulation Setup and Results

For the purpose of empirical validation design, the Cyber-FIT software will be used to conduct a virtual experiment that will alter military cyber team skill in a simulated conflict with a near peer adversary. The current software allows for three skill levels for each defender agent: 1 - beginner, 2 - intermediate, and 3 - advanced. The simulation is emulating two characteristics of cyber troops: efficiency and effectiveness. The skill level of the defender agent determines how efficient they are by altering which actions taken, and in what order. The defender agent skill level also alters effectiveness by changing action success likelihood. In this simulation, a base infrastructure of 10 networking systems, 20 server systems, and 30 client systems are deployed. Next, three kinetic missions are added to the simulation that include 120 friendly forces, 6 networking systems, 18 server systems, and 120 client systems. A cyber protection team (defender agents) is loaded that includes 10 team members: 1 team lead, 5 network operators, and 4 host operators. Each team member will receive the same skill level (1–3) depending on which experiment trial is being run. Last, a tier four adversary (attacker agents) team of 4 operators is added to the simulation. The simulation runs for 14,400 ticks (simulated minutes) which represents a ten day cyber engagement. The following table and figures describe the virtual experiment and results (Table 8).

As expected, the outcome measures improve (from a defensive perspective) as the defender agent skill level increases. Figure 1 shows the force agent performance measure

Table 8. Virtual experiment design

Independent variables		
IV	Variants	Values
Defender agent team size	1	10
Defender agent skill	3	[1–3]
Dependent variables		
DV	Type	
Defender agent restoral success rate	Continuous	
Attacker agent success rate	Continuous	
Terrain agent total compromises	Integer	
Terrain agent total vulnerabilities	Integer	
Terrain agent compromise time	Integer	
This will be a 3 × 10 runs = 30 replications		

Fig. 1. Force agent results

results. With defender agent skill set to one, attacker agents realize an average success rate of 0.57. This means that over half of all cyber attacks the attacker agents attempted resulted in compromised systems. Also, at skill level set to one, defender agent average restoral rate is 0.001. With defender agent skill set to three (advanced), the attacker agents have a much more difficult time. The attacker agent average success rate drops to 0.11. Interestingly, under those circumstances, and underlying agent rulesets, defender agents have a very similar success rate of 0.10. According to this simulation, a team of highly skilled cyber troops will be equally successful in operational results as a tier four adversary. Agent-based simulation can also be very useful for finding trends in the expected outcomes. In this simulation, defender agent outcomes follow a linear trend while attacker agents follow an exponential trend. As shown in Figure 2, terrain agent results show an improving trend as defender agent skill increases. With defender agent skill set to one, average terrain agents compromised is 829.4. This number decreases to 189.4 with defender agent skill set to three. Average terrain agent vulnerabilities decreases from 13,222.6 to 1,742.8 as defender agent skill increases from one to three.

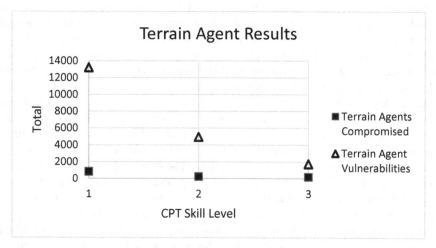

Fig. 2. Terrain agent results

5 Model Output Validation Design Considerations

Ideally, an agent validation would confirm the results of the simulation with respect to key attributes. In this simulation, the skill level of the cyber team was increased to observe projected differences in performance. This specific type of simulation is meant to help decision makers determine how many resources should be spent training cyber troops. Clearly, a better trained force will perform better, but in which ways? This simulation assigned three levels of skill, where in reality there are many more levels and differences in troop skill, experience, certification, and knowledge. In any event, an empirical agent validation could be designed.

5.1 Cyber Force Agent Validation Design Considerations

In this simulation cyber force agents are made of either defending or attacking. For defender agents, the simulated actions were one of four types: restoral operations, inter-actions with forces, interactions with terrain, and nothing. In the simulation that was run, restoral operations were tracked by successful and unsuccessful. Empirical validation of these simulated restoral operations could come from force on force cyber competitions. In these competitions, a trusted team of controllers usually has access to everything that all teams are planning and executing. The best data would come from observers that log all activities of defender teams. Demographic data such as experience level would allow researchers to assign the competitors to different skill level categories. While this data would prove to be the most useful it would be the most resource intensive to obtain. A less expensive data source would be incident response application log files obtained from real world operations. These applications are used by cyber teams to respond to and track cyber attacks. Researchers would be able to see how many operations and the nature of those operations were necessary before incidents were closed. This data would be nearly free to obtain, if available. However, the data would lack the amount of details live observation could provide. Also, there is risk of users not providing all incident detail which would lead to a skewed view of what actually happened. Attacking agent validation would also be best, but most expensive through live observation. Similar to defending agents, some level of attacker agent actions could be ascertained through application log files. Packet captures of cyber attack traffic would provide details of how many attacks were attempted, and at what frequency. Along with packet capture, enterprise and host based security software alerts could validate the success or failure of attack attempts. The most difficult aspect of cyber force agent validation of the data captured in this simulation would be attacker agent actions. The simulated attacker agents follow a methodical cyber kill chain [8] where each step proceeds in order. In the simulation, the attacker agent must complete steps one to four, before proceeding to step five, for example. In actual operations, attacker agent behaviors are likely much more complex. That is, in a live competition an actual attacking competitor may be moving around the cyber kill chain with different attacks and different systems. Careful attention must be paid in how to log specific attack attempts.

5.2 Terrain Agent Validation Design Considerations

In this simulation, terrain agent outcome data included total compromises, total compromise time, and total vulnerabilities. Unlike cyber force agent actions, nearly all terrain actions can be computationally determined through log files. An ideal avenue for terrain agent validation would also be cyber competitions. Many competitions take place on virtual cyber ranges with specialized software that reports the health and activities of virtual machines. The range would be instrumented to log each time a virtual machine received adversary traffic, payload, and ultimately if it were compromised and controlled by attacking competitors. Aggregating the virtual machine activities could yield data nearly identical to the terrain agent outcome data collected in this simulation. Terrain agent validation would be much more complete than the actions of human-based agents.

6 Conclusion

The Cyber-FIT simulation framework was improved to log agent actions and outcome measures associated with team performance. A virtual experiment was conducted showing that cyber defender skill level will significantly impact the projected team performance. The agent outcome variables were designed so that an empirical agent validation would be possible using data accessible from either cyber force on force competitions or open source exercise data.

References

1. Accenture: The Cost of Cybercrime (2019)
2. Freedberg Jr., S.J.: 'The Golden 5 Minutes' The Need for Speed in Information Warfare. Breaking Defense, p. 2019, 21 October 2019
3. Carley, K.M.: Simulating Society: The Tension Between Transparency and Veridicality. In: Agents, Chicago, IL (2002)
4. Bert, F.E., Rovere, S.L., Macal, C.M., North, M.J., Podesta, G.P.: Lessons from a comprehensive validation of an agent based-model: the experience of the pampas model of argentinean agricultural systems. Ecol. Model. **273**, 284–298 (2014)
5. Windrum, P., Fagiolo, G., Moneta, A.: Empirical validation of agent-based models: alternatives and prospects. J. Artif. Soc. Soc. Simul. **10**(2), 8 (2007)
6. Dobson, G.B., Carley, K.M.: Cyber-FIT: an agent-based modelling approach to simulating cyber warfare. In: Lee, D., Lin, Y.-R., Osgood, N., Thomson, R. (eds.) SBP-BRiMS 2017. LNCS, vol. 10354, pp. 139–148. Springer, Cham (2017). https://doi.org/10.1007/978-3-319-60240-0_18
7. Dobson, G.B., Rege, A., Carley, K.M.: Informing active cyber defence with realistic adversarial behaviour. J. Inf. Warfare **17**(2), 16–31 (2018)
8. Cloppert, M.: Security intelligence: attacking the cyber kill chain. 14 October 2009. https://www.sans.org/blog/security-intelligence-attacking-the-cyber-kill-chain/. Accessed 20 Feb 2020
9. U.S. Department of Defense Defense Science Board. Resilient Military Systems and the Advanced Cyber Threat (2013)

Developing Graph Theoretic Techniques to Identify Amplification and Coordination Activities of Influential Sets of Users

Mustafa Alassad[(✉)], Muhammad Nihal Hussain, and Nitin Agarwal

University of Arkansas, Little Rock, AR, USA
{mmalassad,mnhussain,nxagarwal}@ualr.edu

Abstract. Social media, with its accessibility and anonymity, has helped malicious actors to thrive and coordinate several campaigns. Such users successfully utilize social media to coordinate different kinds of movements that could influence political aspects, damage the crucial infrastructure and affect the economy of several countries around the world. Malicious users could coordinate to cripple the transportation system by closing the main highways and bridges in big cities or spreading false security information that causes panic and hysteria in large societies. Since the traditional community detection methods fall short in finding these users, our research proposes an integrated model to find, analyze, and suspend these coordinated malicious sets of users in online complex networks. The Focal Structures Analysis model is a two-level analysis to study individual-level features using closeness centrality and group-level features by implementing the spectral modularity method. The model decomposes the interactions between both individual-level and group-level to find key sets of users that are responsible for propagating behavior through online social media platforms. The proposed model is applied to a fake news YouTube co-commenter network. The outcomes were validated via modularity methods and depth-first search to measure each set's influence at individual-level and at the entire network-level.

Keywords: Focal structures analysis · Closeness centrality · Modularity · Misinformation · Disinformation · Depth-first search method

1 Introduction

Social media, with its power to bring people together, has found its use for both democratic and anti-democratic purposes. While some have used it to spread crucial information during natural disasters that can help coordinate search and rescue operations, others have used it to spread fake news and disinformation as well as to coordinate deviant campaigns. It is important to study these online campaigns to identify the perpetrators and influencers that are effectively able to spread misinformation or mobilize crowds.

Researchers have conducted various studies to identify influential users in complex networks and successfully found the authoritative users based on their centrality values [1, 3]. However, in complex networks, a central user with significant influence cannot

© Springer Nature Switzerland AG 2020
R. Thomson et al. (Eds.): SBP-BRiMS 2020, LNCS 12268, pp. 192–201, 2020.
https://doi.org/10.1007/978-3-030-61255-9_19

mobilize, influence, and encourage thousands of users alone and cannot influence other users in different parts of the network [2]. Therefore, it is important to not only identify influential users but also groups of users that have higher influence or ability to influence the complete network when working together.

Extensive research conducted on identifying the communities in social networks and algorithms such as modularity method [3] succeeded to cluster networks into smaller communities. These community detection methods suffer from resolution limits such as clustering big communities but ignoring active small groups hidden in the network. Moreover, these algorithms focus only on finding groups or communities and do not take the influence of these groups into consideration [2].

Identifying these influential sets of individuals can help governments and intelligence agencies to track such malicious movement. Moreover, in a complex network where it is impossible to track all malicious users' activities and links, or when it is impossible to shut down the entire network, shutting down just the influential sets could disrupt the entire deviant campaign.

Considering the huge need to identify influential sets of users and to overcome the resolution limits and the computation complexities in traditional clustering methods, this paper proposes a comprehensive integrated model between the well-known spectral modularity method [4, 5] and the closeness centrality method [1] to identify influential sets of users in a complex social network. The contributions are categorized into a decomposition model interacting between the traditional spectral modularity method and the well-known closeness centrality method. Also, this research utilizes the Girvan-Newman modularity method and the depth-first search method to validate the outcomes. We finally apply complexity analysis to measure the model's performance utilizing different centrality methods.

The rest of the paper is organized as follows. Section 2 reviews the related works. Section 3 describes the model's methodology. Section 4 explains the experimental results. Section 5 contains conclusion and suggests future research directions.

2 Literature Review

In this section, we provide a brief review of various community detection algorithms, methods to identify focal structures, and studies on misinformation, disinformation, or online fake news.

Central users who have more influence than other users in the network have been extensively studied by many researchers over many years [7–17]. While several of these studies [7–15] focus only on the individual users' (nodes') aspects and neglect the community's part to measure node's influence, others, including [16, 17], measure influence based on users' (nodes') ability to spread, hold and pass information to other in the network and neglect the individuals' aspects [18–20]. Methods such as spectral modularity [1, 3, 21–23] have been applied to investigate complex networks efficiently. Other researchers worked hard to maximize the complex network's modularity values utilizing various optimization methods such as mixed-integer linear programming methods [24], and branch-and-price framework to linearize the NP-hard modularity method [25–29].

Many researchers have worked to provide computational ways to separate and classify all kind of fake news, misinformation, disinformation campaigns in social networks

[30]. Others extended these efforts by building fact-checker tools such as Factmata.com, Hoax-slayer.com, PolitiFact.com, and Snopes.com [31, 32]. However, these efforts also realized that it is a difficult task to prevent such malicious campaigns and suggested to minimize the fake news, misinformation and disinformation by removing suspicious online users [33]. In this regard, Focal Structure Analysis proposed by Şen et al. [2] to identify malicious sets of online users in a Facebook network using a greedy algorithm identified seed sets of users that should be removed or suspended to disrupt the disinformation campaign. But the model by Şen et al. [2] suffered from major drawbacks such as assigning each user to only one focal structure set, ignoring the influential users' capabilities and resources. Also, the model identified none social chain sets. However, our model [34, 35] was able to cluster the same focal structure and overcome those drawbacks. The model was able to the find smallest possible sets of users hidden inside the network, including influential users acting in different sets of groups at the same time.

Due to space limitation, Appendix I, shows the results from both models for Karate club network [6], one of the well-known social networks.

3   Proposed Methodology

The proposed model uses a bi-level mutual reinforcement approach that uses the closeness centrality method in the first level and the spectral modularity method is the second level to identify focal structures.

3.1   Local Analysis-User Level

Closeness centrality measures how close a user is to all other users in the network [3], it is a measure of a user's abilities to spread information efficiently. The measure computes the distances for user to all other users in the network to compute a closeness centrality value for each user. Users with high closeness centrality values have high reachability and can influence others efficiently. Equation (1) is used to measure the closeness centrality value for each user.

$$C_{v_i} = \frac{m}{\sum_j d\left(v_j, v_i\right)} \qquad \forall i \qquad (1)$$

where C_{v_i} is the closeness centrality value of user v_i, measuring the d distance to all users v_j, and m represents the number of users in the network.

Next, the model measures the clustering coefficient for each user as shown in Eq. (2). The clustering coefficient method computes each user's neighbors' friendship. This step helps find active influential users connected to active neighbors, where $\psi(v_i)$ is the clustering coefficient value for every user's neighbors, providing highly dense sets of users that can coordinate with each other.

$$\psi(v_i) = \frac{(\# \ of \ Triangles) \times 3}{\# \ of \ Connected \ Triples \ of \ users} \qquad 0 \leq \psi(v_i) \leq 1 \qquad (2)$$

3.2 Sets of Users Analysis- Network Level

In this level, the model measures every set of users' influence on the entire network and analyses their impact when they join the network. To measure the influence of sets of users identified from the user level analysis, we utilize spectral modularity method proposed by [6] and the change in the network's modularity values when each set is added to the network. A vector parameter $\overline{\overline{c\delta_i}}_{m \times k}$ is assigned to transfer sets between

$$k \leq m$$

user level and network level

$$\varrho_{jx} = \frac{1}{2m} Tr\left(\xi_{jx} B \xi_{jx}^T\right) \qquad\qquad \forall j, x \qquad\qquad (3)$$

$$\xi_{jx} = \{\overline{\overline{c\delta_i}}_{m \times k} \cup \delta_{jx} | \overline{\overline{c\delta_i}}_{m \times k}, \neq \delta_{jx}\} \quad \forall j, x \qquad (4)$$
$$\qquad\quad k \leq m \qquad\quad k \leq m$$

$$\overline{\mu_{jx}^Q} = \max\{\varrho_{1x}, \varrho_{2x}, \dots, \varrho_{jx}\} \qquad\qquad \forall j, x \qquad\qquad (5)$$

$$\mathbb{C}\varrho_{jx} = \delta_{jx}\left(\overline{\mu_{jx}^Q}\right) \qquad\qquad\qquad \forall j, x \qquad\qquad (6)$$

The objective in the network-level is to identify sets of users that maximize the spectral modularity value ϱ_{jx} in each x iteration as shown in Eq. (3), where the model would search for the active set of users that will join the parameter $\overline{\overline{c\delta_i}}_{m \times k}$ and

$$k \leq m$$

maximize the network's sparsity as indicated in Eq. (4), and B is the modularity matrix. In constraint (4), $\xi_{jx} \in R^{m \times k}$ is the union between the sets of users imported from the user-level via $\overline{\overline{c\delta_i}}_{m \times k}$ and the candidate sets of users δ_{jx} that presumably will

$$k \leq m$$

maximize the network's sparsity. Constraint (5) is used to get the maximum modularity value $\overline{\mu_{jx}^Q}$. In constraint (6), $C\varrho_{jx}$ will export the set users $\delta_{jx}\left(\overline{\mu_{jx}^Q}\right)$ from network-level to user-level as a non-dominated solution or the active set that maximized the network's modularity. $C\varrho_{jx}^M$ is the set of users that maximized the modularity values when they joined the network and a vector parameter to interact with the user-level and transfer sets from network-level to user-level. The selected $C\varrho_{jx}^M$ is a focal structure candidate that meets all the criteria from both levels at iteration x.

Figure 1 shows the integrated model between both levels explained in this section. At the user level, the traditional closeness centrality method identifies sets of users connected to active neighbors (users with ability to communicate and coordinate to spread information) and, at the network level, the traditional spectral modularity method searches for the best set of users that jointly maximize the network's modularity values. The model iterates until sets of users that maximize both user level and network level features are identified. Once the model terminates after x iterations, the final set of focal structures sets F is obtained and validated as explained in the next section.

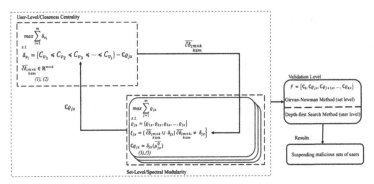

Fig. 1. Focal structure analysis model's overall structure.

3.3 Influential Sets of Users Validation Level

The model integrates two traditional community detection methods to find influential sets of users in complex social networks. For this purpose, the model also uses two methods to validate the identified focal structures quantitatively and calculates the amount of influence they can generate at the user and network levels as shown in Fig. 1.

In the beginning, the model uses the modularity method proposed by [29] to measure the sets' impact at the network level, where the model will suspend every focal structure set separately and measure the changes to the network and its modularity value as explained in Sect. 4. Sets are considered highly influential sets if they maximize the modularity value.

In the second step, the model measures each set's influence at the user level utilizing the depth-first search method proposed by Tarjan [36]. The model will remove one focal structure set from the network at a time and measure the network's changes with respect to the number of weakly connected users as shown in Fig. 1.

4 Experimental Results

The model was applied to the co-commenter network obtained from [2]. The YouTube fake news dataset consists of 16,493 comments on 4,145 videos by 9,661 users. The commenter network was constructed by linking two commenters if they posted on the same video as shown in Fig. 2. The proposed model detected 32 focal structures or sets of influential users. As observed, the model identified sets including users occupying important spots to make them highly influential than other regular users. These sets include users that have high closeness centrality values as presented in Fig. 3. In the second part, the model considered the relationship between every set's users too, where every set should include active coordinating users as shown in Fig. 4.

The validation process as explained in Sect. 3.3 requires two steps to measure the influence every focal structure set has on the users and the entire network. Girvan-Neman modularity method is considered to measure the changes in the whole network's sparsity. This method helps us quantify the impact of each focal structure by measuring

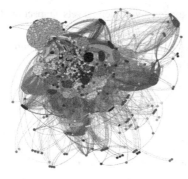

Fig. 2. Fake news co-commenter YouTube channel.

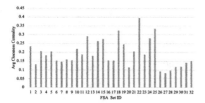

Fig. 3. Set's avg. closeness centrality values.

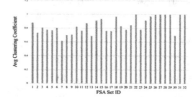

Fig. 4. Set's clustering coefficient values.

the changes in the network i.e., number of new groups generated if the focal structure set is suspended from the network.

The second step in the validation process measures the focal structure sets' influence on the individuals from different parts of the network. The depth-first search method finds the number of disconnected or weakly connected users when a focal structure is suspended from the network.

Table 1 shows the top twenty influential focal structure sets with respect to every set's count of users, impact on modularity value, influence on the individual users, and their active spots in the network. Table 1 lists the impact of each focal structure set. In this complex network, FSA#9, which only includes 45 users, was able to maximize the modularity value from 0.2778 to 0.6827. This spike in the network's sparsity raised the number of the communities from 4 to 750 indicating this set can influence 730 users in the entire network.

The model's performances was also tested with respect to other centrality methods such as betweenness, degree, and eigenvector centrality (as shown in Fig. 5). Investigating results from different centrality measures helps to observe differences in model's performance and identifying the optimum centrality method.

From Fig. 5, the model shows an interesting behavior where the betweenness and eigenvector centrality methods have similar results at all levels of analysis. However, closeness centrality method dominated all others with small differences with respect to the size of the network. Using closeness centrality, the model found higher number of influential sets of users. The other centrality methods showed similar results even though they would use different strategies in the network.

Table 1. The top twenty influential sets' impact on the network.

FSA ID	# of users	# of Weakly conn. users	# of comm.	Max modularity value
FSA#9	45	0.6827	750	730
FSA#8	46	0.6318	670	640
FSA#29	36	0.5591	470	450
FSA#10	12	0.5498	510	470
FSA#2	22	0.5333	590	560
FSA#14	19	0.4964	410	390
FSA#13	75	0.4726	570	560
FSA#3	30	0.4659	690	670
FSA#30	36	0.4647	410	390
FSA#31	30	0.4642	440	390
FSA#23	18	0.4608	430	400
FSA#7	14	0.4596	390	360
FSA#18	9	0.4400	420	390
FSA#4	10	0.4017	340	310
FSA#17	11	0.4007	440	400
FSA#28	14	0.3973	280	240
FSA#11	11	0.3935	340	310
FSA#15	6	0.3906	350	320
FSA#6	10	0.3764	240	190
FSA#16	19	0.3717	480	460

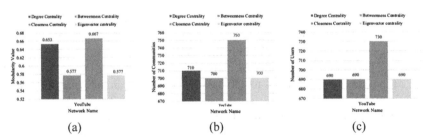

(a)   (b)   (c)

Fig. 5. The model's performance using different centrality methods, (a) comparing the modularity values, (b) analyze the network's sparsity using different centrality methods, (c) analyzing the network's changes on the individual user level.

5 Conclusion and Discussion

This research combined traditional social network analysis measures to analyze a complex YouTube co-commenter network. A two-level model of analysis was conducted to identify key sets of users responsible for spreading fake news on posted videos. This paper extends the research [34] by utilizing closeness centrality method. to identify hidden influential sets of users considering both local and global features. The model quantified the users' influence using the clustering coefficient method, to find active commenters connected to coordinating neighbors, and the spectral modularity method, to measure their influence in the entire network. Finally, two methods were used to validate model's outcome. The paper also compares model's performance when other clustering methods are used.

In future, we intend to improve on the approach used to validate the Focal Structures Analysis model's outcome by analyzing the sets' growth or changes over time. We also intend apply the model in other fields such as epidemiology to study FSA's viability in containing spread of infection or disinformation.

Acknowledgment. This research is funded in part by the U.S. National Science Foundation (OIA-1946391, OIA-1920920, IIS-1636933, ACI-1429160, and IIS-1110868), U.S. Office of Naval Research (N00014-10-1-0091, N00014-14-1-0489, N00014-15-P-1187, N00014-16-1-2016, N00014-16-1-2412, N00014-17-1-2675, N00014-17-1-2605, N68335-19-C-0359, N00014-19-1-2336, N68335-20-C-0540), U.S. Air Force Research Lab, U.S. Army Research Office (W911NF-17-S-0002, W911NF-16-1-0189), U.S. Defense Advanced Research Projects Agency (W31P4Q-17-C-0059), Arkansas Research Alliance, the Jerry L. Maulden/Entergy Endowment at the University of Arkansas at Little Rock, and the Australian Department of Defense Strategic Policy Grants Program (SPGP) (award number: 2020-106-094). Any opinions, findings, and conclusions or recommendations expressed in this material are those of the authors and do not necessarily reflect the views of the funding organizations. The researchers gratefully acknowledge the support.

Appendix I: Zachary Karate Club Network [6]

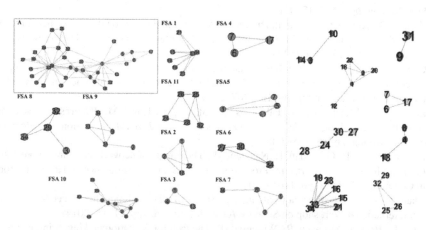

A) Karate club network clustered by modularity method into 4 communities.
B) Results presented from the model proposed by Şen et al. [1].
(F1) – (F11) Focal structure sets identified by the proposed method, overcome the state of the art drawbacks.

References

1. Şen, F., Wigand, R., Agarwal, N., Tokdemir, S., Kasprzyk, R.: Focal structures analysis: identifying influential sets of individuals in a social network. Soc. Netw. Anal. Min. **6**(1), 17 (2016)
2. Hussain, M.N., Tokdemir, S., Agarwal, N. , Al-Khateeb, S.: Analyzing disinformation and crowd manipulation tactics on YouTube. In: 2018 IEEE/ACM International Conference on Advances in Social Networks Analysis and Mining, pp. 1092–1095 (2018)
3. Zafarani, R., Abbasi, M.A., Liu, H.: Social Media Mining: An Introduction. Cambridge University Press, Cambridge (2014)
4. Girvan, M., Newman, M.: Community structure in social and biological networks. PNAS **99**(12), 7821–7826 (2002)
5. Yazdanparast, S., Havens, T.C.: Modularity maximization using completely positive programming. Phys. A Stat. Mech. Appl. **471**, 20–32 (2017)
6. Tsung, C.K., Ho, H., Chou, S., Lin, J., Lee, S.: A spectral clustering approach based on modularity maximization for community detection problem. In: Proceedings of the International Computer Symposium, ICS 2016, pp. 12–17 (2017)
7. Leskovec, J., McGlohon, M., Faloutsos, C., Glance, N., Hurst, M.: Cascading behavior in large blog graphs. In: Proceedings of the 2007 SIAM International Conference on Data Mining, pp. 551–556 (2007)
8. Li, C., Wang, L., Sun, S., Xia, C.: Identification of influential spreaders based on classified neighbors in real-world complex networks. Appl. Math. Comput. **320**(11), 512–523 (2018)
9. Borgatti, S.P.: Centrality and network flow. Soc. Netw. **27**(1), 55–71 (2005)
10. Agarwal, N., Liu, H., Tang, L., Yu, P.S.: Modeling blogger influence in a community. Soc. Netw. Anal. Min. **2**(2), 139–162 (2012)
11. Agarwal, N., Liu, H., Tang, L., Yu, P.S.: Identifying the influential bloggers in a community. In: Proceedings of the 2008 International Conference on Web Search and Data Mining, pp. 207–218 (2008)
12. Richardson, M., Domingos, P.: Mining knowledge-sharing sites for viral marketing. In: Proceedings of Eighth ACM *SIGKDD* International Conference on Knowledge Discovery and Data Mining, pp. 61–70 (2002)
13. Kempe, D., Kleinberg, J.: Maximizing the spread of influence through a social network. In: Proceedings of Ninth ACM SIGKDD International Conference on Knowledge Discovery and Data Mining, pp. 137–146 (2003)
14. Chen, W., Wang, Y.: Efficient influence maximization in social networks categories and subject descriptors. In: Proceedings of 15th ACM SIGKDD International Conference on Knowledge Discovery and Data Mining, pp. 199–207 (2009)
15. Leskovec, J., McGlohon, M., Faloutsos, C., Glance, N., Hurst, M.: Patterns of cascading behavior in large blog graphs. In: Proceedings of the 2007 SIAM International Conference on Data Mining, pp. 551–556 (2007)
16. Kivran-Swaine, F., Govindan, P., Naaman, M.: The impact of network structure on breaking ties in online social networks. In: Proceedings of the SIGCHI Conference on Human Factors in Computing Systems, pp. 1101–1104 (2011)
17. Chua, T.-S.: The Multimedia Challenges in Social Media Analytics. In: Proceedings of the 3rd International Workshop on Socially-Aware Multimedia, pp. 17–18 (2014)
18. Page, L., Brin, S., Motwani, R., Winograd, T.: The PageRank citation ranking: bringing order to the web. World Wide Web Internet Web Inf. Syst. **54** (1999–66) 1–17 (1998)
19. Kleinberg, J.O.N.M.: Authoritative sources in a hyperlinked environment. In: Proceedings of the ACM-SIAM Symposium on Discrete Algorithms, vol. 46, no. 5, pp. 604–632 (1999)

20. Richardson, M., Domingos, P.: Mining knowledge-sharing sites for viral marketing. In: Proceedings of the Eighth ACM SIGKDD International Conference on Knowledge Discovery and Data Mining, pp. 61–70 (2002)
21. Von Luxburg, U.: A tutorial on spectral clustering. Stat. Comput. **17**(4), 395–416 (2007)
22. Hagen, L., Member, S., Kahng, A.B.: New spectral methods for ratio cut partitioning and clustering. IEEE Trans. Comput. Des. Integr. Circ. Syst. **11**(9), 1074–1085 (1992)
23. Blondel, V.D., Guillaume, J., Lefebvre, E.: Fast unfolding of communities in large networks. J. Stat. Mech. Theory Exp. **10**, 10008 (2008)
24. Sato, K., Izunaga, Y.: An enhanced MILP-based branch-and-price approach to modularity density maximization on graphs. Comput. Oper. Res. **106**, 236–245 (2018)
25. Newman, M.E.J.: Detecting community structure in networks. Eur. Phys. J. B **38**(2), 321–330 (2004). https://doi.org/10.1140/epjb/e2004-00124-y
26. Java, A., Joshi, A., Finin, T.: Detecting communities via simultaneous clustering of graphs and folksonomies. In: Proceedings of Tenth Workshop Web Mining. and Web usage Analysis (2008)
27. Newman, M.E.J.: Modularity and community structure in networks. Proc. Natl. Acad. Sci. **103**(23), 8577–8582 (2006)
28. Wang, G., Shen, Y., Luan, E.: Measure of centrality based on modularity matrix. Prog. Nat. Sci. **18**(8), 1043–1047 (2008)
29. Newman, M.E.J., Girvan, M.: Finding and evaluating community structure in networks, pp. 1–16 (2003)
30. Søe, S.O.: Algorithmic detection of misinformation and disinformation: Gricean perspectives. J. Doc. **74**(2), 309–332 (2018)
31. Zhang, X., Ghorbani, A.A.: An overview of online fake news: characterization, detection, and discussion. Inf. Process. Manag. **57**, 102025 (2019)
32. Shao, C., Ciampaglia, G.L., Flammini, A., Menczer, F.: Hoaxy: a platform for tracking online misinformation, pp. 745–750 (2016)
33. Shu, K., Sliva, A., Wang, S., Tand, J., Liu, H.: Fake news detection: network data from social media used to predict fakes. ACM SIGKDD Explor. Newsl. **19**(1), 22–36 (2017)
34. Alassad, M., Agarwal, N., Hussain, M.N.: Examining intensive groups in YouTube commenter networks. In: Proceedings of the 12th International Conference on SBP-BRiMS 2019, no. 12, pp. 224–233 (2019)
35. Alassad, M., Hussain, M.N., Agarwal, N.: Finding fake news key spreaders in complex social networks by using bi-level decomposition optimization method. In: Agarwal, N., Sakalauskas, L., Weber, G.-W. (eds.) MSBC 2019. CCIS, vol. 1079, pp. 41–54. Springer, Cham (2019). https://doi.org/10.1007/978-3-030-29862-3_4
36. Tarjan, R.: Depth-first search and linear graph algorithms. SIAM J. Comput. **1**(2), 146–160 (1972)

Detecting Online Hate Speech: Approaches Using Weak Supervision and Network Embedding Models

Michael Ridenhour[1], Arunkumar Bagavathi[2(✉)], Elaheh Raisi[3], and Siddharth Krishnan[1]

[1] UNC Charlotte, Charlotte, USA
{mridenh7,skrishnan}@uncc.edu
[2] Oklahoma State University, Stillwater, USA
abagava@okstate.edu
[3] Brown University, Providence, USA
elaheh_raisi@brown.edu

Abstract. The ubiquity of social media has transformed online interactions among individuals. Despite positive effects, it has also allowed anti-social elements to unite in alternative social media environments (e.g. Gab.com) like never before. Detecting such hateful speech using automated techniques can allow social media platforms to moderate their content and prevent nefarious activities like hate speech propagation. In this work, we propose a weak supervision deep learning model that - (i) quantitatively uncover hateful users and (ii) present a novel qualitative analysis to uncover *indirect* hateful conversations. This model scores content on the interaction level, rather than the post or user level, and allows for characterization of users who most frequently participate in hateful conversations. We evaluate our model on *19.2M* posts and show that our weak supervision model outperforms the baseline models in identifying indirect hateful interactions. We also analyze a multilayer network, constructed from two types of user interactions in Gab (quote and reply) and interaction scores from the weak supervision model as edge weights, to predict hateful users. We utilize the multilayer network embedding methods to generate features for the prediction task and we show that considering user context from multiple networks help achieving better predictions of hateful users in Gab. We receive upto 7% performance gain compared to single layer or homogeneous network embedding models.

1 Introduction

The widespread adoption of social media has transformed the way in which online interactions among individuals take place. Such interactions, say via tweets and re-tweets, often provide access to real-time news, viral marketing, online recruitment, etc. While the positive effects and applications of social media interactions are prominent, social media has also become a vehicle for degenerative behavior like cyber-bullying and hate speech propagation. Fringe outlets like Gab.com

© Springer Nature Switzerland AG 2020
R. Thomson et al. (Eds.): SBP-BRiMS 2020, LNCS 12268, pp. 202–212, 2020.
https://doi.org/10.1007/978-3-030-61255-9_20

(shortly as Gab), under the guise of 'free speech' have become channels for anti-social viewpoints like anti-Semitism and are able to galvanize supporters for the spread of hateful messages. Therefore, it has become imperative to develop automated methods that can detect such messages and users who spread hateful ideologies to allow policymakers and stakeholders of social media sites to take appropriate measures to the spread of the anti-social content.

For the purposes of this paper we focus on the topic of anti-Semitism in Gab. We choose this topic specifically because our dataset of choice for the modeling, Gab, has been shown to harbor users who are significantly more enthusiastic about posting anti-Semitic content than users on other sites [10]. Furthermore, [5] has shown that religious-based hate speech tends to be targeted at an entire group, meaning we see more anti-Semitic content on the Jewish faith than at a specific person, thereby yielding a more comprehensive view on Gab users' vocabulary and beliefs surrounding the subject.

There have been several advances in developing approaches to study hate speech propagation [23], but most approaches use direct markers that do not incorporate the context of the interaction. We define a weak supervision model, that takes a first step to address a specific gap in the research, by employing only very few lexicon labels to determine hate speech. We exploit a qualitative observation that the foundation of a lot of hate speech is based in content that does not overtly contain hate speech term, such as a slur. Our model is capable of detecting conversations containing nuances of hateful content, such as coded language, or hateful comments that do not contain previously identified hateful speech terms. We use the user interaction scores given by our model on user interaction networks to predict if a hateful or not. To this problem, we utilize multilayer network embedding frameworks [1,4] to extract user features for the classification task.

In this paper we aim to answer following research questions to study hate speech and users in online social media:

- **How to identify hate speech that are hidden in the meaning in social media interactions?** We define a weak supervision model and its corresponding function to qualitatively identify indirect hateful user interactions in Gab forum.
- **How useful are user interaction networks to identify hateful users in the social media?** We define two weighted multilayer network random walk techniques: *metapath* and *multilayer* based methods to collect the node context. With features extracted using a skip-gram model, we define the user classification as a binary classification problem.

2   Related Work

A significant research thrust has been formed to study the characteristics and dynamics of hate speech in Gab [23] in past years. Hate speech encompasses a wide variety of topics and defining what exactly hate speech means can be an arduous task [23]. Anti-Semitism and alt-right topics are specifically proven to have a growing influence in the Gab ecosystem [14]. In an effort to understand how hate speech diffuses through Gab, a lexicon based approach [13] and belief network models [18] are available. Our model is adapted from a cyberbullying detection model that analyzes messages between users and outputs a representative score for the interaction [7,17]. Another major challenge of defining hate speech is determining what language equates to hate speech since the use of a simple lexicon to identify hate speech can be imprecise and the vocabulary is ever changing [2,16]. Our work address this issue by getting the sense of words based on their context. In the light of these limitations on lexicon-based approaches, we use feature representation of posts as a whole [3,12].

Wide range of network embedding ideas have been introduced, including *LINE* [21], *node2vec* [8], *SDNE* [22], and *GraphSAGE* [9], after the success of skip-gram based word embedding model *word2vec* [15]. Parallel to such research works on homogeneous networks, large number of research have been done on complex networks with multiple network layers, node types, and edge types [20]. Based on such complex connectivity patterns there exists network embedding models to extract features of nodes in the network, for example *metapath2vec* [4], *multi-net* [1], and *HIN* [19]. In this work, we utilize such embedding algorithms on a multilayer network of user interactions with interaction scores, and perform node classification task on whether a user is hateful or not.

3   Methodology

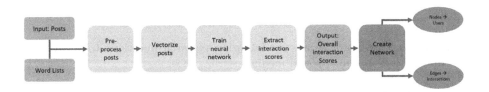

Fig. 1. Methodology overview - User interactions are quantified as interaction scores using the weak supervision model. These scores are given as edge weights to the multilayer network.

The technical aspect of our work can be two-fold: 1) Obtain user interaction scores using our weak supervision model which are capable to capture indirect markers of hate speech, and 2) Predict hateful users based on features extracted from multilayer networks built from multiple interaction types.

3.1   Weak Supervision Model

Weak supervision allows us to use far more data than we could label, providing more insights into such a large dataset. The overview of our methodology is summarized in Fig. 1. We obtain interaction scores via an adaption of the *Co-trained Ensemble model* introduced by [17]. The original work co-train their model based on user interactions and network representations simultaneously, whereas we only use the textual representations from interactions. We employ such weak supervised model to use far more data than we could label, providing more insights into such a large dataset. The input of our model is a message/post M, and the output is a score indicating the level of anti-Semitic hate incident in the message, i.e., $f : M \mapsto \mathbb{R}$. To train the model, we optimize the *weakly supervised* loss function given in Eq. 1.

$$\min_{\Theta} \frac{1}{|M|} \sum_{m \in M} \ell\left(f(m; \Theta)\right) \tag{1}$$

where Θ is a model parameter, l is the loss function, f is the learning function, and $|M|$ is the total number of messages. Along with two set of keywords which are being used in the existing method: 1) anti-Semitic indicator words, 2) positive-sentiment words, we add *context dependent words* also to the model. The anti-Semitic indicators are obvious hateful keywords. The context dependent words are associated with a topic, but are not considered hateful without a hateful context. Example words are "jew", "rabbi", and "zionism". Most of these terms are used in a negative context in Gab, but are not irrefutable hate speech terms on their own.

Messages $m \in M$ is given a general range of bound values for what its ultimate score should be. The weak supervision is based on the fraction of values of aforementioned key-phrases. For a message $m \in M$ with n total key phrases, if we assume $n^+(m)$ be the number of anti-Semitic phrases, $n^-(m)$ be the number of positive-sentiment words, and $n^\oplus(m)$ is the number of context dependent words, then we bound the learning function by fraction of these indicators in the message m as given in Eq. 2.

$$\underbrace{2 \times \frac{n^+(m)}{n(m)} + \frac{n^\oplus(m)}{n(m)}}_{\text{Lower Bound}} < y_m < \underbrace{1 - \frac{n^-(m)}{n(m)}}_{\text{Upper Bound}}, \tag{2}$$

In the lower bound, we emphasize the anti-Semitic phrases with respect to the context dependent words by multiplying the fraction associated with anti-Semitic bound by 2. If the final score by the learner falls outside of the determined bounds, the model is penalized using weak supervision loss given in Eq. 3.

$$\ell(y_m) = -\log\left(\min\left\{1, 1 + (1 - \tfrac{n^-(m)}{n(m)}) - y_m\right\}\right)$$
$$- \log\left(\min\left\{1, 1 + y_m - \left(2 \times \tfrac{n^+(m)}{n(m)} + \tfrac{n^\oplus(m)}{n(m)}\right)\right\}\right) \tag{3}$$

With these bounds, we use a linear neural network for our learner to transform the n-dimensional message representations, given by doc2vec, into a single score.

3.2   Multilayer Network Embedding

Multilayer networks can be formally defined as $G = \left(V_l, E_l\right)_{l=1}^{\mathscr{L}}$, where the network composes $\mathscr{L} > 1$ networks$(G_1, G_2, ..., G_{\mathscr{L}})$ and each network(G_l) holds their own set of nodes(V_l) and edges(E_l). Although the definition of multilayer networks is similar to heterogeneous networks [4], multilayer networks have the property of single node types and multiple($\mathscr{L}$) edge types. Given that condition, each network in multilayer networks has some level of overlap in nodes (i.e) $\{V_1 \cap V_2 \cap ... \cap V_{\mathscr{L}}\} \neq \emptyset$.

Given a multilayer network $G = (V_l, E_l)_{l=1}^{\mathscr{L}}$, where $\mathscr{L} > 1$, we utilize the skip-gram model based network embedding ($node2vec$) [8] for the mutilayer context. Thus, we get n-dimensional vector representation for each node (f_u) based on their multilayered network structural patterns. We use the optimization function, given in Eq. 4, similar to the ones proposed in $Metapath2Vec$ [4] and $Multi$-Net [1] frameworks to maximize observing the neighborhood $N(u)$ across all network layers conditioned on the node u. We give in-depth analysis on how these vector space features are utilized for hateful user classification in Sect. 4.3

$$\max_f \sum_{u \in V} \sum_{l \in \mathscr{L}} \sum_{v \in N(u)_l} log\ Pr(v_l|f_u), \tag{4}$$

where $N(u)_l$ is the neighborhood of node u at the lth network and we model the $Pr(v_l|f_u)$ using a softmax function.

Random Walks. *Random walks* are used to define a node's neighborhood or context for node embedding models. Although, several types of random walks are available, we explore random walks defined specifically for multilayer networks [1, 4] and give the context of edge weights for each walk. In this work, we employ two strategies: 1) metapath based random walk and 2) multilayer random walk.

Metapath Based Random Walks. Metapath based random walks are used in heterogeneous networks [4], where there exists multiple types of nodes and edges. In metapath based random walks, a structural schema($\mathcal{S}$) is designed to bias the random walker to visit all the network layers. We define a metapath schema as: $\mathcal{S} = E_1 \rightarrow E_2 \rightarrow ... \rightarrow E_l \rightarrow E_1$, where E_i is an edge type. Given a multilayer network G and a metapath schema $\mathcal{S}$, we define the transition probability for each edge as given in Eq. 5

$$P(V_{i+1} \mid V_i) = \begin{cases} w_{V_i}^{V_{i+1}} & if\ E(V_i, V_{i+1}) \in E_{t+1} \\ 0 & otherwise \end{cases} \tag{5}$$

where $w_{V_i}^{V_{i+1}}$ is the normalized edge weight and $t \in \mathcal{S}$ denotes the current state in the metapath schema.

Multilayer Random Walks. In multilayer random walks, we relax the idea of metapath schema and the random walker is allowed to choose 2 options at a time step i: 1) stay in the same network with probability p and visit the next node V_{i+1} or 2) shift to a random network layer with probability $1 - p$ and visit V_{i+1}. The transition probability for visiting the next node is given in Eq. 6.

A transition to another network layer(say G_n from G_m) happens if and only if the node V_i is available in G_n.

$$P(V_{i+1} \mid V_i) = \begin{cases} w_{V_i}^{V_{i+1}} & if \ E(V_i, V_{i+1}) \in E_{l=1}^{\mathscr{L}} \\ 0 & otherwise \end{cases} \tag{6}$$

4   Experiments and Results

4.1   Dataset Description

We utilize a dataset sample collected from *Gab.com* containing 19,127,608 posts [6] for our experiments and observations. The distribution of posts is given in Table 1 and a representative sample of our indicator lexicons is given in Table 2. The highest concentration of anti-Semitic indicator terms is in quotes(similar to re-tweet in Twitter), with 0.36% more instances than replies and almost three times more instances than original posts. Interestingly, these types of posts are originally sourced from other users. This coupled with the higher concentration of hateful terms in replies points to the observation that Gab users are more hateful or exposed to more hateful content when interacting with other users than they are when posting original content to their followers. This observation, coupled with the findings that posts from hateful users spread more than posts from non-hateful users [13], lead us to believe that detecting hateful content at the interaction level will provide valuable information when classifying hateful users.

Table 1. Properties of the Gab Dataset - Numbers indicate the quantity of each post type in the total dataset. Percentages indicates the volume of anti-Semitic indicators in each type of post.

Post type	# in Dataset	% with direct indicator(s)
Quote	2,321,744	1.11%
Reply	6,916,904	0.75%
Original	9,888,960	0.38%

Table 2. Example lexicons used to determine the bounds for each post (see Methodology)

Anti-semitic indicators	'k*ke'
	'#hitlerwasright'
	'h*eb'
Context dependent phrases	'jew'
	'talmud'
	'zionism'

4.2 Weak Supervision Model

We examine interactions and interaction scores from the weak supervision model [17] to get useful information from user posts. We first generate doc2vec representations of the posts using both our modified bounds function given in Eq. 2, and we use the original bounds function which excludes the presence of the context dependent term list and weight the indicator list and positive words list equally as a baseline model. Figure 2 gives the distribution of scores for each model variant, indicating that the majority of posts have little anti-Semitic content. To ensure the model will suffice our multilayer network embedding model, we qualitatively look at the distribution of scores and the textual content of the top 100 most hateful interactions produced by each bounds and representation variant.

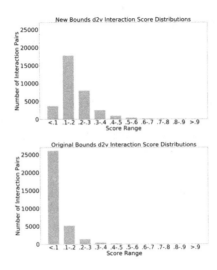

Fig. 2. Distributions of Scores for each variant of the model and embedding options.

Table 3. Example direct and indirect anti-Semitism interactions. Direct interaction contains a hateful key word, while indirect interaction contains hateful content as an insulting language.

Direct hate speech example	Indirect hate speech example
User 1: *because mo****kers like you think israel should die off!!!*	User 2: *i say we expel ((them)) all to israel, and then flood israel with muslims. let them enjoy some forced "diversity"*
User 2: *if jews been kicked out ... f**ing pathetic with your keyboard temper tantrums there, jew b**ch*	User 1: *....they have to be probed for jewish connections. This is a ritual psyop preying on white children*
User 2: *and you do the k*kes work so well !*	
User 2: *because mother f**kers like me are sick of usury , religious bigots,...*	User 1: *.......they control america with #pedo #f*ggots*

By studying 100 interactions we notice two types of anti-Semitic hate speech: *direct* and *indirect*. Direct hate speech contains a word or hashtag from our lexicon of anti-Semitic indicators, while indirect hate speech does not contain any of our anti-Semitic indicators, but often link a word from our context dependent word list to a hateful content. Example direct and indirect hate interactions are given in Table 3. Both of these interactions are sourced from the top 100 posts using the new bounds method and doc2vec representations. The ability of this model to pick up on examples of indirect hate speech further shows this model is useful when detecting hateful users.

4.3   User Classification

We predict hateful users from their structural patterns in reply and quote (re-tweet in Twitter) networks of Gab. We represent these networks as a weighted 2-layer multilayer network, where network vertices are user accounts, network edges are user replied to/quoted another user, and edge weight represent interaction score from the weak supervision model. Summary of our networks is given in Table 4. As the Gab data users are unlabeled, we replicate the methods used by [13] to label a user hateful if they have used words in our anti-Semitic indicators list at a frequency of z. In our experiments, we set $z = 5$.

Table 4. Network statistics

Property	Reply network	Quote network
# nodes	9,813	4,069
# edges	45,728	16,836
Avg. degree	4.66	4.14
# components	174	35

We define the user classification problem as a binary mapping function: $f : f_u \mapsto 0|1$, where f_u is a feature vector of user u obtained from network embedding and labels 0 and 1 defines that the user is not-hateful and hateful respectively.

Baseline Setup. We utilize 2 random-walk based frameworks: *node2vec* [8] and *Line* [21] as baseline models, which support both directed and weighted graphs.

- **node2vec** (*n2v*): This method uses biased random walk to explore the neighborhood. We set the parameters $p = 1$ and $q = 1$ for their random walks
- **LINE**: This method aims to maximize the second order proximity of nodes to collect their neighborhood.

Since the above-mentioned methods are designed for single layer networks, we strategize in following methods to combine feature representations from the multilayer setup.

Table 5. Binary classifier results - average of 10 F1 measures. Green - best model performance and Blue - second best model performance.

Method type	Algorithm	Merge type	Training ratio								
			10%	20%	30%	40%	50%	60%	70%	80%	90%
Flatten networks	node2vec	–	0.48	0.47	0.46	0.46	0.46	0.46	0.46	0.56	0.49
	LINE	–	0.61	0.61	0.63	0.65	0.66	0.66	0.65	0.65	0.66
Merge embeddings	node2vec	Average	0.67	0.67	0.67	0.68	0.68	0.71	0.71	0.68	0.68
		Max-pooling	0.65	0.65	0.65	0.66	0.67	0.71	0.70	0.68	0.69
		Gated reply	0.42	0.43	0.43	0.43	0.43	0.45	0.45	0.53	0.47
		Gated quote	0.66	0.67	0.69	0.70	0.70	0.71	0.72	0.70	0.70
	LINE	Average	0.66	0.64	0.62	0.62	0.62	0.63	0.64	0.64	0.64
		Max-pooling	0.60	0.60	0.61	0.61	0.63	0.65	0.65	0.65	0.63
		Gated reply	0.33	0.32	0.30	0.41	0.47	0.50	0.50	0.50	0.45
		Gated quote	0.63	0.64	0.64	0.66	0.66	0.67	0.68	0.64	0.63
Multilayer embedding	Metapath2vec	–	0.70	0.73	0.72	0.73	0.75	**0.77**	**0.77**	0.75	0.75
	MultiNet	–	0.72	0.73	0.74	0.75	0.77	0.79	0.78	0.76	0.76

- **Flatten networks**: We collapse all network layers into one network. If there exists multiple edges, we take average of their edge weights and normalize the weights.
- **Merge embeddings**: Embedding from two models are merged using the function $f_v = w_1(f_{v_a}) \, o \, w_2(f_{v_b})$, where f_{v_a} and f_{v_b} are feature vectors of the node v from layers a and b respectively, o is one of the component-wise merge operation called *Gated embedding*, where we apply a simple sigmoid function(σ) to combine vectors, and w_1 and w_2 are weighted operations over corresponding vectors [11].

We use both *node2vec* and *LINE* along with all the above mentioned embedding generation methods. User embeddings are passed as inputs to the binary classifier. We give the *F1 measure* of the model for varying training data size in Table 5. Overall, we get significant performance gain (atleast 7%) with the multilayer based network embedding methods (*metapath2vec* and *multi-net*) compared to other two methods (flatten networks and merge embeddings). Out of the two models, we show atleast 2% performance improvement with the multi-net based random walks. We also can evidence that flattening the networks does not yield good results with both *node2vec* and *LINE* models, while they give varied performance with different merge strategies. Even though we have given results based on weighted graphs only, we found atleast 10% performance decrease with embedding using unweighted networks and are not reported due to space limitations. The performance gain with weighted networks is due to collecting better node context based on interaction scores. Figure 3 give models performance in terms of accuracy, precision, and recall. For these results, we fix the training sample size to be 60% and average all results from 10 iterations.

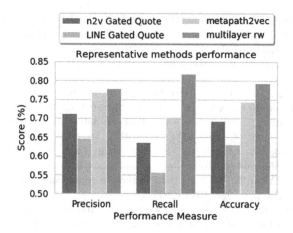

Fig. 3. Performance measure of baseline and proposed methods. Each measure is averaged over 10 times.

5   Conclusion and Discussion

As the language of anti-Semitism, racism, white supremacy, and other forms of hate speech evolves and spreads through social media, it is of the utmost importance that we develop tools to monitor its proponents. Using methodologies defined as weak supervision and multilayer network embedding model, we have provided a qualitative way to identify indirect hate speech and quantitatively classify hateful users in Gab based on their neighborhood patterns. With our experiments, we showed that multilayer based classification performs atleast 7% better than baseline models. This work involve multiple scopes in the future including: 1. Quantitative evaluation of indirect hate speech detection in user conversations 2. Systematic update and maintenance of more precise lexicons to increase the performance of this model, 3. Add a transfer learning aspect, where we model interactions propagate between social media forums, 4. Design a multi-modal classification algorithm to use multiple user features like their network properties, language, information they consume and share to perform the user classification task.

References

1. Bagavathi, A., Krishnan, S.: Multi-Net: a scalable multiplex network embedding framework. In: Aiello, L.M., Cherifi, C., Cherifi, H., Lambiotte, R., Lió, P., Rocha, L.M. (eds.) COMPLEX NETWORKS 2018. SCI, vol. 813, pp. 119–131. Springer, Cham (2019). https://doi.org/10.1007/978-3-030-05414-4_10
2. Davidson, T., Warmsley, D., Macy, M., Weber, I.: Automated hate speech detection and the problem of offensive language. In: AAAI ICWSM (2017)
3. Djuric, N., Zhou, J., Morris, R., Grbovic, M., Radosavljevic, V., Bhamidipati, N.: Hate speech detection with comment embeddings. In: ACM WWW, pp. 29–30 (2015)

4. Dong, Y., Chawla, N.V., Swami, A.: metapath2vec: scalable representation learning for heterogeneous networks. In: ACM SIGKDD, pp. 135–144 (2017)
5. ElSherief, M., Kulkarni, V., Nguyen, D., Wang, W.Y., Belding, E.: Hate lingo: a target-based linguistic analysis of hate speech in social media. In: AAAI ICWSM (2018)
6. Fair, G., Wesslen, R.: Shouting into the void: A database of the alternative social media platform gab. In: AAAI ICWSM, pp. 608–610 (2019)
7. Fortuna, P., Nunes, S.: A survey on automatic detection of hate speech in text. ACM Comput. Surv. (CSUR) **51**(4), 85 (2018)
8. Grover, A., Leskovec, J.: node2vec: scalable feature learning for networks. In: ACM SIGKDD, pp. 855–864 (2016)
9. Hamilton, W., Ying, Z., Leskovec, J.: Inductive representation learning on large graphs. In: NIPS, pp. 1024–1034 (2017)
10. Kalmar, I., Stevens, C., Worby, N.: Twitter, gab, and racism: the case of the Soros myth. In: ACM International Conference on Social Media and Society, pp. 330–334 (2018)
11. Kiela, D., Grave, E., Joulin, A., Mikolov, T.: Efficient large-scale multi-modal classification. In: Thirty-Second AAAI Conference on Artificial Intelligence (2018)
12. Le, Q., Mikolov, T.: Distributed representations of sentences and documents. In: ICML, pp. 1188–1196 (2014)
13. Mathew, B., Dutt, R., Goyal, P., Mukherjee, A.: Spread of hate speech in online social media. In: ACM Web Science, pp. 173–182 (2019)
14. McIlroy-Young, R., Anderson, A.: From "welcome new gabbers" to the Pittsburgh synagogue shooting: the evolution of gab. In: AAAI ICWSM, pp. 651–654 (2019)
15. Mikolov, T., Sutskever, I., Chen, K., Corrado, G.S., Dean, J.: Distributed representations of words and phrases and their compositionality. In: NIPS, pp. 3111–3119 (2013)
16. Nobata, C., Tetreault, J., Thomas, A., Mehdad, Y., Chang, Y.: Abusive language detection in online user content. In: ACM WWW, pp. 145–153 (2016)
17. Raisi, E., Huang, B.: Weakly supervised cyberbullying detection using co-trained ensembles of embedding models. In: IEEE/ACM ASONAM, pp. 479–486 (2018)
18. Ribeiro, M.H., Calais, P.H., Santos, Y.A., Almeida, V.A., Meira Jr, W.: Characterizing and detecting hateful users on twitter. In: AAAI ICWSM (2018)
19. Shi, C., Hu, B., Zhao, W.X., Philip, S.Y.: Heterogeneous information network embedding for recommendation. IEEE Trans. Knowledge Data Eng. **31**(2), 357–370 (2018)
20. Starnini, M., Boguñá, M., Serrano, M.: The interconnected wealth of nations: shock propagation on global trade-investment multiplex networks. Sci. Rep. **9**(1), 13079 (2019)
21. Tang, J., Qu, M., Wang, M., Zhang, M., Yan, J., Mei, Q.: Line: Large-scale information network embedding. In: ACM WWW, pp. 1067–1077 (2015)
22. Wang, D., Cui, P., Zhu, W.: Structural deep network embedding. In: ACM SIGKDD, pp. 1225–1234 (2016)
23. Zannettou, S., Bradlyn, B., De Cristofaro, E., Kwak, H., Sirivianos, M., Stringini, G., Blackburn, J.: What is gab: a bastion of free speech or an alt-right echo chamber. In: ACM WWW, pp. 1007–1014 (2018)

Critical Spatial Clusters for Vaccine Preventable Diseases

Jose Cadena[1]([✉]), Achla Marathe[2,4], and Anil Vullikanti[3,4]

[1] Lawrence Livermore National Laboratory, Livermore, CA, USA
cadenapico1@llnl.gov
[2] Department of Public Health Sciences, University of Virginia, Charlottesville, USA
[3] Department of Computer Science, University of Virginia, Charlottesville, USA
[4] Network Systems Science and Advanced Computing Division, Biocomplexity Institute, University of Virginia, Charlottesville, VA, USA

Abstract. The standard public health intervention for controlling the spread of highly contagious diseases, such as measles, is to vaccinate a large fraction of the population. However, it has been shown that in some parts of the United States, even though the average vaccination rate is high, geographical clusters of undervaccinated populations are emerging. Given that public health resources for response are limited, identifying and rank-ordering *critical* clusters can help prioritize and allocate scarce resources for surveillance and quick intervention.

We quantify the criticality of a cluster as the additional number of infections caused if the immunization rate in a cluster reduces. This notion of criticality has not been studied before, and, based on clusters identified in prior research, we show that the current underimmunization rate in the cluster, and its criticality are not correlated. We apply our methods to a population model for the state of Minnesota, where we find undervaccinated clusters with significantly higher criticality than those obtained by other natural heuristics.

1 Introduction

Many highly contagious childhood diseases, such as measles, can be prevented by vaccination. Thus, it is worrisome that large disease outbreaks have occurred in recent years, such as the measles outbreaks in the Pacific Northwest in 2019, in New York City in 2018, and in Minnesota in 2017—this is despite high vaccination coverage in the US—e.g., ~95% for MMR, the measles vaccine.

One of the reasons for the emergence of underimmunized geographical clusters, such as in California [15] and Minnesota [5], is misperceptions about the side effects of vaccines [2]. The typical response by public health agencies is to monitor clusters where immunization rates are falling, run active information campaigns, and engage community leaders.

Analyzing public school immunization records, Cadena et al. [5] identify six clusters in Minnesota that are statistically significant in terms of lower immunization rates relative to the statewide level. However, implementing public health

© Springer Nature Switzerland AG 2020
R. Thomson et al. (Eds.): SBP-BRiMS 2020, LNCS 12268, pp. 213–223, 2020.
https://doi.org/10.1007/978-3-030-61255-9_21

interventions in all these clusters would be costly and time-consuming for public health agencies, which motivates the following question: *which of these clusters pose the most risk, and should be prioritized for treatment?* A similar question was raised by Metcalf et al. [18], who stated that *"[t]here is also a need to understand under what conditions such clusters become at risk for epidemic spread, and the risk they pose to surrounding groups where vaccine coverage may be high."* It is useful to consider not only clusters in which the rates are presently low, but also the clusters that would pose a risk if fewer people within them were vaccinated. We develop a method to address these important public health policy questions. Our contributions are summarized below.

1. Formalizing Criticality. We formalize the notion of *criticality* of a subset $S \subseteq V$ in a social contact network $G = (V, E)$, as the *expected number of additional infections* that would occur if the immunization rate within S is "low" compared to the statewide rate. Extending this notion, we introduce the MaxCrit problem: find a cluster S, which is (1) contiguous in space and (2) has the maximum criticality. The spatial proximity is moti-

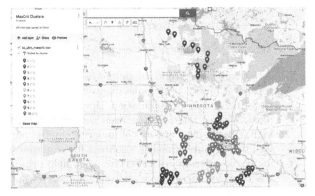

Fig. 1. Critical sets in Minnesota discovered using our methods. These are contiguous regions that lead to large simulated measles outbreaks if left undervaccinated.

vated by the structure of clusters identified in [2,5,15], which are small and connected—this is desirable from a public health response perspective, since interventions involve field work. Spatial clustering can also help identify common risk factors, such as vulnerable communities and neighborhoods [3]. We estimate the criticality of a given cluster using a detailed agent-based simulation of the spread of measles in a population. However, solving the MaxCrit problem turns out to be a computationally challenging, and we design a greedy algorithm APPROXMAXCRIT for this problem.

2. Application. We study the phenomenon of criticality on a detailed population and contact network model for the state of Minnesota. We compute the criticalities of the significant underimmunized clusters reported in [5]. Quite surprisingly, we find that: (1) the cluster with the lowest vaccination rate among these is not the most critical, and (2) the criticality of the cluster computed using our algorithm is more than 10 times that of any of the clusters identified by [5]. We solve the MaxCrit problem and find clusters with very high criticality, compared to heuristics commonly considered for public health interventions. Our algorithm also achieves over 25% higher criticality for the objective compared to all the baselines. Our methods can also combine social and demographic data for these clusters, available from the US Census, so they can be characterized, which may further guide targeted interventions. The critical clusters shown in Fig. 1 involve people with lower than average income and age (Sect. 4).

Finally, due to lack of publicly available high-resolution, geo-located outbreak data, there is no easy way to validate our results, but we note that *one of the clusters we found to be critical lies in the Minneapolis metropolitan area where a large measles outbreak occurred in 2017* [10].

Social Impact. Our method for finding critical sets, applied to detailed population and contact network models, provides an operational tool for public health agencies to prioritize their limited surveillance and public outreach resources towards the most critical clusters. Our results imply that it is important to not only identify the undervaccinated clusters as in [5], but also determine which among them will likely cause an outbreak or an epidemic.

2   Preliminaries

2.1   Disease Spread on a Social Contact Network

Let V denote a population, and let $G = (V, E)$ be a contact graph on which a disease can spread. A person or node $v \in V$ can propagate the disease to its neighbors. There is an edge between two people if they come into close proximity during a typical day. Additionally, each person v is associated with a geographical location— i.e., their place of residence—denoted by $loc(v)$; we will consider such locations at the resolution of census block groups. Let $\mathcal{R}$ denote the geographical area where the nodes V are located—

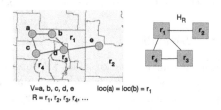

Fig. 2. Notation example. The 5 circle nodes (a–e) form a social contact network. Each node resides in a block group r_i, and these block groups form the block group graph $H_{\mathcal{R}}$, where an edge represents that the block groups are adjacent on the map.

for example, the state of Minnesota—and let $\mathcal{R} = \{r_1, \ldots, r_N\}$ be a decomposition of $\mathcal{R}$ into census block groups. For a block group $r_i \in \mathcal{R}$, we use $V(r_i)$ to denote the set of nodes associated with location r_i; that is, those with $loc(v) \in r_i$. Analogously, for a set of block groups or *region* $R \subset \mathcal{R}$, let $V(R) = \cup_{r_i \in R} V(r_i)$ be the set of nodes located within R. We consider a graph $H_{\mathcal{R}} = (\mathcal{R}, E_{\mathcal{R}})$ on the set of block groups, where two block groups are connected if they are geographically contiguous, i.e., they are adjacent on a map. In particular, we are interested in *connected* subgraphs of $H_{\mathcal{R}}$. We use $\text{Conn}(\mathcal{R})$ to denote all the subsets $R \subset H_{\mathcal{R}}$ that are spatially connected. These definitions are illustrated in Fig. 2.

For $u, v \in \mathcal{R}$, let $\text{dist}_{H_{\mathcal{R}}}(u, v)$ denote the distance between u and v in the graph $H_{\mathcal{R}}$, which is equal to the length of the shortest path between them. The ball centered at v, with radius ℓ is defined as $B_{H_{\mathcal{R}}}(v, \ell) = \{u : \text{dist}(u, v) \leq \ell\}$, which is the set of all nodes within distance ℓ of v. When the graph is clear from the context, we drop it from the subscript in the notation for $B(\cdot)$ and $\text{dist}(\cdot)$.

Disease Model. We use an SEIR model for diseases like measles [1], where a node is in one of four states: Susceptible (S), Exposed (E), Infected (I), and Recovered/Removed (R). Measles is highly contagious; an infected node spreads the disease to each susceptible neighbor with high probability. In our simulations, we assume a transmission probability of 1, but our methods extend to the more general case. If a node is vaccinated, it does not get infected. We assume 100% vaccine efficacy, but this assumption is not crucial for our methodology.

Let γ denote the average region-wide vaccination rate—around 0.97 in Minnesota. Let $\mathbf{x}$ be a *vaccination* or *intervention* vector: $x_i \in [0, 1]$ denotes the probability that node (i.e., person) i is vaccinated (so $x_i = \gamma$, by default). Let Src_A denote the source of the infection or *initial conditions* of the disease process: this could be one or a small number of nodes from a region $A \subset \mathcal{R}$, which initially get infected. We use $\#\text{inf}(\mathbf{x}, \text{Src}_A)$ to denote the expected number of infections given an intervention $\mathbf{x}$ and initial conditions Src_A. When Src_A is clear from the context, we simply use $\#\text{inf}(\mathbf{x})$.

2.2 Criticality

For a vaccination vector $\mathbf{x}$, let $\mathbf{x}^S$ denote the corresponding intervention where a subset $S \subset V$ of nodes is undervaccinated. That is, $\mathbf{x}_i^S = \mathbf{x}_i$ for $i \notin S$ and $\mathbf{x}_i^S = \gamma'$ for $i \in S$, where γ' is much lower than γ, the region-wide vaccination rate. Without loss of generality, we consider $\gamma' = 0$ for mathematical convenience.

We define the **criticality** of a set $S \subset V$ as the *expected number of additional infections that occur if S is not vaccinated*, with respect to some initial condition Src_A. Since we are interested in finding spatial clusters of high criticality, we focus on $S = V(R)$ for a connected region $R \in \text{Conn}(\mathcal{R})$. Then, we define the criticality of a region as

$$\text{crit}(R, \mathbf{x}, \text{Src}_A) = \#\text{inf}(\mathbf{x}^R, \text{Src}_A) - \#\text{inf}(\mathbf{x}, \text{Src}_A),$$

which is the expected number of extra infections if nodes in the region R are undervaccinated. In order to simplify the notation, we will drop $\mathbf{x}$ and Src from the inputs to $\text{crit}(\cdot)$, whenever it is clear from the context.

2.3 Problem Formulation

Modeling Considerations. In practice, public health interventions involve intensive field work, and they are most effective when focused within small, localized geographical regions. Therefore, we aim to find regions that have high criticality *and* are small in size. In modeling terms, this can be accomplished by adding a size parameter k, which can be tuned based on the available public health resources. Given the discussion above, we pose the task of finding spatial clusters of high criticality as the following optimization problem.

Problem 1 (MaxCrit(G, H_R, k)). Given an instance (G, H_R, k), find a connected region $R \in \mathrm{Conn}(\mathcal{R})$ of size at most k that maximizes criticality over all choices of source:

$$R = argmax_{R' \in \mathrm{Conn}(\mathcal{R}), |R'| \leq k} crit(R', \mathbf{x}, \mathrm{Src}_{R'})$$

In words, the MaxCrit problem involves maximizing over *all* possible choices of the sources $\mathrm{Src}_{R'}$ in the cluster R'. From a public health perspective, our problem models the following question: *what is the most critical cluster of size k if the disease starts within the undervaccinated cluster itself?* An obvious question is how should the parameter k be chosen. This can depend on a number of factors, such as availability of medical resources, jurisdiction constraints, social and ethical considerations, location of under-served communities etc. [7].

3   Our Approach

MaxCrit is closely related to the Influence Maximization problem [12]. The influence function is known to be submodular—informally, this means that the function has a diminishing returns property, as a result of which, a greedy algorithm gives a good approximation. We show that the crit function is also submodular by following the approach of Kempe et al. [12]. However, a crucial difference in our case is that the decision space is restricted to sets S that are connected. We design algorithm APPROXMAXCRIT (as discussed in [4]), by adapting the technique of Kuo et al. [13], who give an $\Omega(1/\sqrt{k})$ approximation algorithm to find a connected subset of size k that maximizes a submodular function.

4   Experimental Results

Our experiments focus on the following questions:

1. **Relationship between criticality and underimmunization.** Is the criticality of a cluster directly correlated with its underimmunization rate?
2. **Finding critical clusters.** Can we find highly critical regions with our methods? How do they compare to standard public health heuristics?
3. **Characteristics of critical clusters.** What are the demographic properties of critical clusters? Where are they located?

Dataset and Disease Model. Simulation of an infectious disease epidemic that spreads through physical proximity requires social contact networks in which an edge represents physical contact between two people. Such networks cannot be constructed easily because of the difficulty in tracking contacts for a large set of people throughout the day. This has been recognized as a significant challenge in the public health community, and multiple methods have been developed to construct realistic contact network models by integrating diverse public datasets (e.g., US Census, land use, and activity surveys) and commercial data (e.g., from Dun & Bradstreet on location profiles). We use agent-based models developed by the approach of [8]; see also [9,17] for network models developed by other public health groups. Multiple such network models were evaluated in a study by the Institute of Medicine [11].

Here, we focus on the population of Minnesota (MN) with 5,048,920 individuals in total, aggregated into 4,082 census block groups from the 2010 U.S. census. We consider an SEIR stochastic model for measles, as described in Sect. 2. The criticality of a region R of block groups is assessed by leaving every individual inside R unvaccinated; everybody else in the population is vaccinated with probability 0.97, which is the statewide vaccination rate. We also use the underimmunized clusters in MN computed by [5] in our analysis here.

Baseline Methods. We compare our algorithms with two heuristics used in public health and a naive random baseline.

1. POPULATION. Find a cluster of size k with the largest total population. The motivation behind this heuristic is leaving as many people as possible unvaccinated.
2. VULNERABILITY. The vulnerability of an individual is the probability that this person will get infected when the disease is left to propagate with no intervention—i.e., $x_v = 0$ for all nodes. This baseline finds a cluster of size k with as large total vulnerability as possible, thus prioritizing individuals who are most likely to get infected.
3. RANDOM. Find a connected cluster of size k by doing a random walk on the auxiliary graph H_R.

1. Relationship Between Criticality and Underimmunization. We compute the criticality of the four most significant underimmunized clusters in MN, as identified by authors in [5]. The clusters are numbered 1–4 based on their statistical significance with respect to underimmunization rates, so that cluster 1 is more significant than cluster 4. However, as shown in Fig. 3 (left), it seems clear that *the outbreak size of cluster 4 is much higher than that of cluster 1*— the 95th percentile value for the number of infections in cluster 4 is almost four times that of cluster 1. The results show that criticality is not directly correlated with the level of underimmunization. Instead, network structure plays a more important role in determining the criticality.

2. Optimization Power. In Fig. 3 (right), we show the criticality obtained by APPROXMAXCRIT compared to the three baseline methods as a function of k. As expected, selecting subgraphs at random performs poorly and results in almost no additional infections compared to the initial disease conditions. Surprisingly,

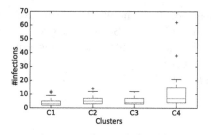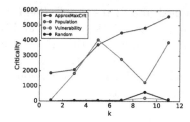

Fig. 3. Left: Distributions of the number of infections resulting from an outbreak starting in each of four underimmunized clusters in MN identified in [5]. Right: Comparison of algorithms for the MaxCrit problem as a function of the solution size k.

VULNERABILITY does not perform much better than RANDOM. It is also interesting that the population-based heuristic does not have monotonic improvement with k. Even though the subgraph of size 9 has 55,800 inhabitants, the smaller subgraph of size 5 with a population of 34,000 leads to a much larger outbreak. Overall, the POPULATION heuristic has better performance among the baselines, and it even surpasses our algorithm for $k = 5$. However, APPROXMAXCRIT exhibits notably better performance in general. The maximum improvement on criticality occurs on the 9-node cluster, where our method finds a cluster that leads to 4 times more infections than the POPULATION baseline.

Another important quantity is the probability of having a large outbreak. In Fig. 4, we show the distribution of criticality values for each method over 100 simulations of the disease model. We observe that even the largest outbreaks caused by VULNERABILITY and RANDOM are much smaller than those of APPROXMAXCRIT and the POPULATION baseline. We also note that the population-based clusters have larger variance in criticality and can result in larger outbreaks than those from our algorithm. This suggests that if the goal for a public health department is to prevent the worst-case scenario, then intervening the most-populated areas is a good heuristic. However, in doing so, one could miss smaller regions that, on average, are likely to infect more people.

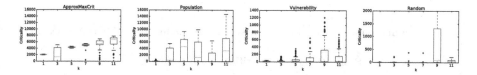

Fig. 4. Criticality scores over 100 runs of the disease model for each method evaluated

3. Critical Clusters and Demographics.
We compare the distribution of age and income in the cluster discovered by APPROXMAXCRIT ($k = 11$) to that of the entire state. We aggregate household income into "Low" (below \$25,000), "Medium" (between \$25,000 and \$75,000), and "High" (above \$75,000). Ages

are binned into "Pre-school" (below 5 years old), "School" (between 5 and 18 years old), "Adult" (between 18 and 70 years old), and "Senior" (above 70 years old). In Fig. 5, we see the critical cluster has significantly more households of low income compared to the entire state—19.6% to 34.9%. Similarly, children are over-represented; 26.6% of the population are children in "School" age compared to the average of 18.7%.

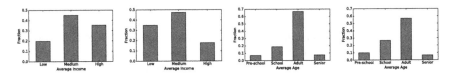

Fig. 5. Average income (top) and age (bottom) in the entire state (left) and in the cluster discovered by APPROXMAXCRIT (right). There are more children in school age and lower income households in the discovered critical cluster.

We find critical clusters in different regions over Minnesota. Figure 1 shows the top 10 non-overlapping clusters discovered using APPROXMAXCRIT. The most critical cluster—with over 5,000 infections—is located on the rural northern part of the state, spanning the Leech Lake and Red Lake reservations. We note that this cluster results in the largest spread despite having a relatively small population of 14,910 people compared to clusters in urban regions. For example, the second most critical cluster—north of Minneapolis—has 48,889 inhabitants.

In addition to analyzing the most critical cluster, we look at the top-5 non-overlapping clusters discovered by APPROXMAXCRIT. These correspond to different choices of root on the k-MAXST algorithm. In Table 1, we report the total population size, criticality, and percentage of infections to the total population of the cluster—i.e., criticality/population. Note that this latter number could be larger than 1, since there are infections outside the cluster. As we discussed before, the top region leads to a large spread (41% of its population size) despite having less inhabitants than the successive clusters. The second cluster has very similar criticality score, but in a more urban region.

Table 1. Population and criticality in the top 5 clusters found by APPROXMAXCRIT

Rank	Population	Criticality	% population
1	14,910	6,138	41.2%
2	48,889	6,093	12.5%
3	23,391	1,388	5.9%
4	15,731	647	4.1%
5	9,936	372	4.7%

Finally, we repeat our experiments for MaxCrit on the Minneapolis area instead of the entire state. The most critical cluster covers Brooklyn Park, where measles outbreaks occurred in 2017 and 2019[1]. However, we emphasize the need for domain-expert analysis to better interpret and make use of these results.

5   Related Work

Mathematical models have played an important role in epidemiology for over a century [1]. Traditionally, epidemiological models have been differential equation models, which assume very simplistic mixing patterns of the underlying population. In the last decade, several research groups have developed agent-based methods using complex networks as a way to model more realistic mixing [8,9,16,17]. Such methods have been used for policy analysis by local and national government agencies [11]. We use this paradigm in our work.

All prior work on undervaccinated clusters has been restricted to identifying these clusters. For instance, [15] analyze health records of children in Northern California to identify significant clusters of underimmunization and vaccine refusal using spatial scan statistics. However, such methods are not directly useful for the question of identifying *critical* clusters, which is our focus. There is a large body of work related to outbreak detection in networks. [6] use the "friend of random people" effect to monitor a subset of people and infer characteristics of the epidemic curve for the entire population. [14] study early detection of different kinds of events—e.g., in social networks. However, these approaches have been focused on either just detecting that some event (e.g., start of an infection) has occurred or the epidemic characteristics for the entire region. Instead, we are interested in finding regions that would lead to a big number of infections if left unvaccinated.

6   Conclusions

Prior research has identified geographical clusters of undervaccinated populations in many states. However, the potential risk of causing large outbreaks from such clusters is not well understood, and actionable response requires a way to prioritize the threat from these undervaccinated clusters. Public health response (e.g., surveillance and field work) is very costly, and therefore, a method to quantify such risk is an important public health contribution.

This research makes several contributions: (i) we formalize the problem MaxCrit for finding critical clusters for highly contagious diseases that can be prevented by vaccination, and that will lead to large outbreaks if left unvaccinated; (ii) we combine a detailed agent-based model of Minnesota and its social contact network with a disease model to compute a realistic measure of clusters' criticality; (iii) we find clusters that have higher criticality than discovered by

---

[1] https://tinyurl.com/y359zapv.

baseline methods; (iv) we characterize the clusters, and (v) we provide a way to prioritize intervention based on the availability of resources.

This research has a broader applicability than just the spread of measles and infectious diseases. Other societal problems that have a component of social connectedness and propagation potential e.g. depression, addiction, suicides etc. can also be studied with this methodology.

Acknowledgements. This study has been partially supported by the NIH grant 1R01GM109718, NSF BIG DATA Grant IIS-1633028, NSF DIBBS Grant ACI-1443054, DTRA subcontract/ARA S-D00189-15-TO-01-UVA. This work was performed under the auspices of the U.S. Department of Energy by Lawrence Livermore National Laboratory under Contract DE-AC52-07NA27344. LLNL-CONF-806042.

References

1. Anderson, R., May, R.: Infectious Diseases of Humans. Oxford University Press, Oxford (1991)
2. Atwell, J.E., et al.: Nonmedical vaccine exemptions and pertussis in California, 2010. Pediatrics **132**, 624–630 (2013)
3. Azman, A.S., Lessler, J.: Reactive vaccination in the presence of disease hotspots. Proc. R. Soc. B Biol. Sci. **282**(1798), 20141341 (2015)
4. Cadena, J., Marathe, A., Vullikanti, A.: Finding spatial clusters susceptible to epidemic outbreaks due to undervaccination (extended abstract). In: Proceedings of AAMAS (2020)
5. Cadena, J., Falcone, D., Marathe, A., Vullikanti, A.: Discovery of under immunized spatial clusters using network scan statistics. BMC Med. Inform. Decis. Making **19**(1), 28 (2019)
6. Christakis, N., Fowler, J.: Social network sensors for early detection of contagious outbreaks. PLoS ONE **5**(9), e12948 (2010)
7. Dummer, T.J.: Health geography: supporting public health policy and planning. CMAJ **178**(9), 1177–1180 (2008)
8. Eubank, S., et al.: Modelling disease outbreaks in realistic urban social networks. Nature **429**, 180–184 (2004)
9. Ferguson, N., Cummings, D., Fraser, C., Cajka, J., Cooley, P., Burke, D.: Strategies for mitigating an influenza pandemic. Nature-London **442**(7101), 448 (2006)
10. Hall, V., Banerjee, E., Kenyon, C., et al.: Measles outbreak–Minnesota April-May 2017. MMWR Morb Mortal Wkly Rep, pp. 713–717 (2017)
11. Halloran, M., et al.: Modeling targeted layered containment of an influenza pandemic in the United States. In: PNAS, pp. 4639–4644, 10 Mar 2008. pMCID: PMC2290797
12. Kempe, D., Kleinberg, J., Tardos, É.: Maximizing the spread of influence through a social network. In: KDD, pp. 137–146 (2003)
13. Kuo, T.W., Lin, K.C.J., Tsai, M.J.: Maximizing submodular set function with connectivity constraint: theory and application to networks. IEEE/ACM Trans. Networking **23**(2), 533–546 (2015)
14. Leskovec, J., Krause, A., Guestrin, C., Faloutsos, C., VanBriesen, J., Glance, N.S.: Cost-effective outbreak detection in networks. In: KDD, pp. 420–429 (2007)
15. Lieu, T.A., Ray, G.T., Klein, N.P., Chung, C., Kulldorff, M.: Geographic clusters in underimmunization and vaccine refusal. Pediatrics **135**(2), 280–289 (2015)

16. Liu, F., et al.: The role of vaccination coverage, individual behaviors, and the public health response in the control of measles epidemics: an agent-based simulation for California. BMC Public Health **15**(1), 447 (2015)

17. Longini, I.M., et al.: Containing pandemic influenza at the source. Science **309**(5737), 1083–1087 (2005)

18. Metcalf, C., et al.: Seven challenges in modeling vaccine preventable diseases. Epidemics **10**(Suppl. C), 11–15 (2015). https://doi.org/10.1016/j.epidem.2014.08. 004. http://www.sciencedirect.com/science/article/pii/S1755436514000395. Challenges in Modelling Infectious DIsease Dynamics

Multi-cause Discrimination Analysis Using Potential Outcomes

Wen Huang[ORCID], Yongkai Wu[ORCID], and Xintao Wu$^{(\boxtimes)}$[ORCID]

University of Arkansas, Fayetteville, AR 72701, USA
{wenhuang,yw009,xintaowu}@uark.edu

Abstract. Discrimination analysis recently aroused wide attention in the fairness-aware learning field. Most existing causal modeling based fair learning research focuses on single cause effect of one protected attribute on decision. In this paper, we focus on discrimination discovery when multiple protected attributes and redlining attributes are present in addition to other covariates. We regard those protected and redlining attributes as multiple causes of the outcome variable. To deal with unobserved variables, especially hidden confounders, we adopt the potential outcome framework and leverage the state-of-the-art *deconfounder* algorithm to do causal inference under multiple causes. The deconfounder algorithm infers a latent variable as a substitute for unobserved confounders and then uses that substitute to perform causal inference. Our approach is more appropriate for discrimination discovery as it is able to relax the Markovian assumption and avoid the unidentifiability issue in structural causal modeling approaches. We conduct empirical evaluation on both synthetic data and real data. Empirical evaluation results demonstrate the effectiveness of our proposed approach.

Keywords: Causal inference · Potential outcome · Fairness

1 Introduction

Discrimination or unfairness has been a paramount concern in many big data applications like employment, credit, and insurance. How to strike a balance between accurate predictions and fairness is receiving increasing attention in the machine learning field. Causal modeling based fair learning models [2–4,8,13–15], which are based on Pearl's (probabilistic) causal model [6], have been developed to capture and quantify different fairness measures (e.g., direct/indirect discrimination, counterfactual fairness) through counterfactual inference along specific paths in causal graphs. However, most existing causal modeling based fair learning research focuses on single cause effect of one protected attribute on decision.

In this paper, we focus on discrimination discovery when multiple protected attributes and redlining attributes are present in addition to other covariates. Protected attributes refer to certain characteristics that are the subject of discrimination analysis, such as race, gender, marital status, whereas redlining

© Springer Nature Switzerland AG 2020
R. Thomson et al. (Eds.): SBP-BRiMS 2020, LNCS 12268, pp. 224–234, 2020.
https://doi.org/10.1007/978-3-030-61255-9_22

attributes (e.g., zipcode in loan application) are a set of attributes that cannot be legally justified if used in decision-making. We are interested in evaluating the causal effects of those protected and redlining attributes on the decision (the outcome variable). We regard those protected and redlining attributes as multiple causes of the outcome variable.

One big challenge for causal modeling is to deal with hidden variables. Most previous works [4,8,15] based on Pearl's structural causal modeling make the Markovian assumption (i.e., there is no hidden variable that affects both protected attribute and decision) to facilitate the causal inference. In open world scenario, the existence of the hidden variable mentioned above (also known as hidden confounder) is an inescapable fact. Simply ignoring the presence of these variables in a causal model can lead to erroneous conclusions about the causal relationship among endogenous variables. Furthermore, causal effects are not computable from observational data in some situations known as the unidentifiable situations. Those methods have to make simplified assumptions to avoid the unidentifiable situations, but the validity issue of the assumptions imposes uncertainty on the performance and reliability of these methods.

To deal with hidden confounders, we adopt the potential outcome framework [7] and leverage the state-of-the-art *deconfounder* algorithm [12] to do causal inference under multiple causes. The potential outcome framework focuses on the causal relationship between a treatment and its effect given other covariates. Potential outcomes are expressed in the form of counterfactual conditional statements of the case conditional on a prior event occurring. For each instance, only one potential outcome can be observed. The *deconfounder* algorithm combines unsupervised machine learning and predictive model checking to perform causal inference in multiple-cause settings. Its main idea is to infer a latent variable as a substitute for unobserved confounders and then use that substitute to perform causal inference. Combining them, we are able to relax the Markovian assumption and avoid the unidentifiability issue in structural causal modeling approaches. We compare our approach with the widely adopted structural casual modeling approach [6] in our empirical evaluation on both synthetic data and real data. Empirical evaluation results demonstrate the effectiveness of the proposed approach.

2   Preliminaries

2.1   Potential Outcome Framework

The potential outcome framework has been widely used in many research areas to perform causal inference. It refers to the outcomes one would see under each treatment option. Given the treatment variable A and the outcome variable Y, the potential outcome $Y_i(A = a)$ is defined as the value of Y for individual i that would be observed if we set $A = a$.

Definition 1 (Average Treatment Effect). *Average Treatment Effect, $ATE = \mathbb{E}[Y_i(a)] - \mathbb{E}[Y_i(a')]$, is the quantity that measures the mean difference of outcome variable under two configurations of treatment A, a and a'.*

One major challenge when estimating ATE is the presence of hidden confounding variables that affect treatment variable and outcome variable simultaneously. The existence of confounders induces dependence between treatment variables and potential outcome and will thus bias the estimator when estimating treatment effects in observational studies. In order to estimate ATE in the presence of confounders, researchers often leverage propensity score techniques that aim to find a unit j (or a weighted set of units) that closely resembles i in its covariates. Identical propensity score ensures the identity of the distribution of observed baseline covariates between the treatment and control group. However, those matching methods may still fail to derive accurate causal effects with the presence of hidden confounding variables.

2.2   Structural Causal Model and Intervention

Definition 2 (Structural Causal Model [6]). *A structural causal model $\mathcal{M}$ is represented by a triple $\langle \mathbf{U}, \mathbf{V}, \mathbf{F}, P(\mathbf{u}) \rangle$ where*

1. *$\mathbf{U}$ is a set of exogenous variables.*
2. *$\mathbf{V}$ is a set of endogenous variables that are determined by variables in $\mathbf{U} \cup \mathbf{V}$.*
3. *$\mathbf{F}$ is a set of arbitrary functions mapping from $\mathbf{U} \cup \mathbf{V}$ to $\mathbf{V}$. Specifically, for each $X \in \mathbf{V}$, there is a function $f_X \in \mathbf{F}$ mapping from $\mathbf{U} \cup (\mathbf{V} \setminus X)$ to X, i.e., $X = f_X(\mathsf{Pa}(X), U_X)$, where $\mathsf{Pa}(X) \subseteq \mathbf{V} \setminus X$ stands for the endogenous variables that directly determine the value of X, and $U_X \subseteq \mathbf{U}$ represents disturbances due to omitted factors.*
4. *$P(\mathbf{u})$ is a distribution over the exogenous variables $\mathbf{U}$.*

A causal model $\mathcal{M}$ is associated with a DAG $\mathcal{G}$ where the exogenous variables $\mathbf{U}$ are discarded. Every node in the causal graph $\mathcal{G}$ corresponds an endogenous variable in $\mathbf{V}$ and each directed edges, denoted by an arrow, points from a node X to another node Y if X is an input of f_Y. In the causal model, the quantitative measure of causal effects is facilitated by interventions [6], which simulates the model manipulations where a variable X is forced to take a certain value x. Formally, the intervention that fixes the value of X to x is denoted by $do(x)$. The mathematical meaning of $do(x)$ in a causal model $\mathcal{M}$ is defined as the substitution of equation $X = f_X(\mathsf{Pa}(X)_{\mathcal{G}}, U_X)$ with $X = x$. For another observed variable Y which is affected by the intervention, its post-intervention distribution under $do(x)$ is denoted by $P(y|do(x))$.

The causal effect measures the effect of the change of A from a to a' on $Y = y$. It is given by $CE(a', a) = \mathbb{E}[Y|do(a')] - \mathbb{E}[Y|do(a)]$ where a and a' are two configurations of treatment A. The causal effects along certain paths are unidentifiable with the existence of the "kite graph" in the causal graph [1] and the causal effects of A on Y conditioned on another set O of variables are unidentifiable with the existence of the "w graph" [10]. The unidentifiable situations are big barriers to causal modeling-based approaches applying to real situations. Much previous research has to make simplified or even unrealistic assumptions to evade the identifiability issue. For example, to evade the unidentifiable situation caused by the "kite graph", [15] chose to cut off all causal paths to remove the "kite graph" from the causal graph. To evade the unidentifiable situation caused by the "w graph", [4] made three different assumptions: 1) only using non-descendants of X to build the classifier, 2) the full knowledge of the underlying causal model, or 3) the causal model is a linear model. However, such simplifications would severely damage the performance.

3   Modeling Multi-cause Discrimination

3.1   Problem Formulation

Assume that there is a population over the space $\mathbf{S} \times \mathbf{X} \times Y$ where $\mathbf{S}$ are the protected attributes, Y is the decision attribute, and $\mathbf{X}$ are the covariates. The underlying mechanism that determines the values of all the attributes is represented by a causal model. In practice the causal model is unknown, but we can observe a training dataset $\mathcal{D} = \{(\mathbf{s}_i, \mathbf{x}_i, y_i); i = 1, \cdots, n\}$ drawn from the population and consider it as in fact generated by the causal model. Among covariates $\mathbf{X}$ there is a set of attributes that cannot be legally justified if used in the decision making process, referred to as the redlining attributes denoted by $\mathbf{R}$. In discrimination discovery, we are interested in the causal effects of protected attributes $\mathbf{S}$ and redlining attributes $\mathbf{R}$ on the decision Y. Traditional causal inference usually uses an upper letter A to represent a single treatment variable. In this paper we generalize the notation A to a bold letter $\mathbf{A} = \{A_1, ..., A_m\} = \mathbf{S} \cup \mathbf{R}$ to represent m possible multiple treatments and aim to estimate their causal effect on Y. In addition to the observed attributes $(\mathbf{S}, \mathbf{X}, Y)$, there may exist a set $\mathbf{U}$ containing unobserved hidden confounders.

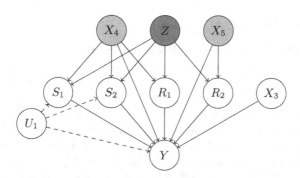

Fig. 1. Graph structure under multiple treatments setting. S_1,S_2,R_1,R_2 are multiple causes, X_3 is a pre-treatment covariate, U_1 is a hidden confounder, X_4 is a multi-cause confounders and X_5 is a single-cause confounder. The shaded node Z denotes the substitute variable from the deconfounder algorithm.

Figure 1 shows an illustrative example under the multiple treatments setting. Y is the outcome variable; $\mathbf{S} = \{S_1, S_2\}$ is the protected attributes set; $\mathbf{X} =$

$\{R_1, R_2, X_3, X_4, X_5\}$ is the covariate set, among which lies the redlining attribute set $\mathbf{R} = \{R_1, R_2\}$; $\mathbf{A} = \{S_1, S_2, R_1, R_2\}$ represents the multiple treatments set. X_4 is a single-cause confounder that affects exactly one cause and the outcome variable. X_5 is a multiple-cause confounder that affects more than two causes and the outcome variable simultaneously. $\mathbf{U} = \{U_1\}$ is hidden variable set and U_1 is also a multi-cause hidden confounder.

The ATE of $\mathbf{A}$ on Y under multiple treatments scenario can then be expressed as $\mathbb{E}[Y_i(\mathbf{a})] - \mathbb{E}[Y_i(\mathbf{a}')]$ where $\mathbf{a}$ and $\mathbf{a}'$ are two treatment configurations. However, the presence of hidden variables (especially hidden confounders such as U_1 in Fig. 1) can make the estimate of ATE inaccurate. In this paper, we develop a Multi-Cause Discrimination Analysis (MCDA) algorithm to derive the ATE of $\mathbf{A}$ on Y with the presence of hidden confounders. Our MCDA involves two phases. In phase 1, we apply the deconfounder algorithm [12] to infer a latent variable as a substitute for unobserved confounders and then use that substitute to perform causal inference. The shaded node Z in Fig. 1 is the substitute variable derived from the deconfounder algorithm. Note that the deconfounder algorithm relaxes the assumption of no hidden confounders to that of no single-cause confounders, which significantly improves the applicability of causal inference. In phase 2, we apply the propensity score approach, in particular, the inverse probability of treatment weighting method, to estimate the causal effect. We emphasize that the deconfounder provides a checkable approach to estimating closer-to-truth causal effects as its weakened assumption is more likely held in practice. The causal inference based on the combination of the deconfounder and the propensity score approach is more appropriate for analyzing the simultaneous effects of multiple protected and redlining attributes on the decision in discrimination discovery and fair learning.

3.2   The Deconfounder Algorithm

In [12], the authors proposed the deconfounder algorithm to conduct causal inference under multiple treatments setting. The algorithm relaxes the strong ignorability assumption to single ignorability assumption. The single ignorability assumes that there are no unobserved single-cause confounders. Roughly speaking, single ignorability implies that we observe all the confounders that affect exactly one of the causes and the outcome variable. The assumption is much weaker than the strong ignorability that requires all confounders are observed. For those application problems which may involve multiple causes in the model, confounders are unlikely to have effect on only one cause. Hence, single ignorability is more likely to be satisfied in practice. The deconfounder algorithm can be divided into two parts: the assignment model and the outcome model.

Assignment Model. The assignment model is basically a factor model of the assigned causes. The main point is that if we can infer a reasonable latent variable Z (shown in Fig. 1) such that each cause is conditionally independent given Z, then Z could be regarded as a substitute confounder. This is because if there exists any other multiple-cause confounder, it will break the conditional independence between treatments. Through the use of substitute confounders, we can get rid of the barrier of unobserved confounders when the single ignorability assumption is satisfied.

To implement the deconfounder algorithm we firstly define and fit a probabilistic factor model to capture the joint distribution of causes $p(a_1, \cdots, a_m)$. The factor model posits per-instance latent variables Z_i and uses them to model the assigned causes. The model can be represented as:

$$
\begin{aligned}
Z_i &\sim p(\cdot|\alpha) & i = 1, \cdots, n \\
A_{ij}|Z_i &\sim p(\cdot|(z_i, \theta_j) & j = 1, \cdots, m
\end{aligned}
\tag{1}
$$

where α parameterizes the distribution of Z_i and θ_j parameterizes the per-cause distribution of A_{ij}. Generally Z_i can be multi-dimensional and factor models include many methods from Bayesian statistics and probabilistic machine learning. In our paper, we use probabilistic principal component analysis proposed by [11] as a factor model. Its structure can be expressed as follows:

$$
\begin{aligned}
Z_{ik} &\sim \mathcal{N}(0, \lambda^2) & k = 1, \cdots, K \\
A_{ij}|Z_i &\sim \mathcal{N}(z_i^T \theta_j, \sigma^2) & j = 1, \cdots, m
\end{aligned}
\tag{2}
$$

In Eq. 2 both z_i and θ_j are real-valued K-dimension vectors, λ and σ are hyper parameters. Since the deconfounder rests on finding a good factor model to capture the dependent relationship of all assigned causes, posterior predictive checks are used to assess the fidelity of the model. We use the fitted factor model to calculate the posterior distribution $p(Z_i|A_i)$ by applying Bayes' theorem and then derive the conditional expectation $\hat{Z}_i = \mathbb{E}[Z_i|A_i]$ as the approximation of Z_i. Since the factor model captures the population distribution of assigned causes, we have essentially discovered a variable (set) that captures all multiple-cause confounders.

Outcome Model. The outcome model aims to estimate causal effects given the information from the augmented dataset $\{A, Z\}$, where Z is the substitute confounder inferred in assignment model. It can be formulated as the function $f(a, z) = \mathbb{E}[Y_i(A_i)|A_i = a, Z_i = z]$. From the equation above, we can see the outcome modal could have various expression form. Any reasonable model can be fitted here if it passes the model checking and has a good performance on approximating the causal effects. For example, we can simply fit a linear regression model. If the outcome variable is binary, we can apply logistic regression and each coefficient of the logistic regression corresponds to the causal odds ratio of a certain covariate.

We emphasize that causal effects can be accurately estimated since strong ignorability is guaranteed with the help of substitute confounder derived from phase 1. In the illustrative example shown in Fig. 1, after we infer a reasonable substitute confounder Z from the assignment model, both observed and unobserved multiple confounders (such as X_4 and U_1) can be well represented by the substitute confounder Z. Hence we can apply classical causal inference methods (e.g., matching and weighting methods) without worrying any biases caused by those hidden confounders. In this paper we focus on inverse probability of treatment weighting method as one legitimate choice of the outcome model.

3.3 Inverse Probability of Treatment Weighting

Definition 3 (Propensity Score). *Propensity score, $e(x) = Pr(A = 1|X = x)$, is the conditional probability of receiving treatment A given the pretreatment variables X.*

With the help of the propensity score, we can divide individuals with the same propensity score into one stratum and treat those strata as randomized controlled trial. Treatment effect is then automatically identified within each stratum and simple methods can be applied to obtain unbiased estimation of the average treatment effect. In statistics, the propensity score is usually estimated using regression models. There are four predominating propensity score methods used for removing the confounding bias when estimating causal effects: propensity score matching (PSM), propensity score stratification, inverse probability of treatment weighting (IPTW) and covariate adjustment using the propensity score.

In this paper, we mainly focus on the IPTW method. The main idea is to use inverse propensity score as the weight for each individual. By multiplying such a weight to all the data points we can create a pseudo-population to synthesize randomized controlled experiments and estimate the average treatment effect unbiasedly. Specifically, the weight for individual i can be defined as

$$\omega_i = \frac{I(A_i)}{e(x_i)} + \frac{1 - I(A_i)}{1 - e(x_i)} \tag{3}$$

where $e(x_i)$ is the propensity score for i-th individual, $I(A_i)$ is an indicator variable denoting whether i-th individual received treatment.

After weighting procedures we generate a balanced dataset such that each individual has the same chance to receive the treatment. The average treatment effect can thus be estimated by a naive estimator shown in Eq. 4 and Eq. 5.

$$\widehat{ATE} = \frac{1}{N_{A=1}} \sum_{i:A_i=1} w_i Y_i - \frac{1}{N_{A=0}} \sum_{i:A_i=0} w_i Y_i \tag{4}$$

$$N_{A_i=1} = \sum \frac{A_i}{e(x_i)} \qquad N_{A_i=0} = \sum \frac{1 - A_i}{1 - e(x_i)} \tag{5}$$

$N_{A_i=1}$ and $N_{A_i=0}$ denote the number of instances under treatment and control. In our paper, we generalize the treatment variable A to multiple treatments set $\mathbf{A}$ and use $\mathbf{A} = \mathbf{a}$ to represent a certain treatments configuration. The selection of covariates to condition on will also influence the estimated propensity scores, and IPTW method may be sensitive to whether the propensity score has been accurately estimated. However, our multi-cause discrimination analysis combines the potential outcome framework and the deconfounder algorithm to deal with the hidden confounders.

4   Empirical Evaluation

We implement our MCDA algorithm and compare with the traditional IPTW method to evaluate how the deconfounder can improve the estimation of causal effects. Furthermore, we compare with the structural casual model [6], denoted as SCM. We use Tetrad [9] to learn the causal graph and then calculate the causal effect using the truncated factorization.

4.1   Synthetic Data

We generate $10,000$ data points following the data generating process:

$$H_1, H_2 \overset{iid}{\sim} \mathcal{U}(0,1)$$
$$A_1, A_2 \overset{iid}{\sim} \mathcal{B}(0, f(H_1, H_2)) \tag{6}$$
$$Y \sim \mathcal{B}(0, g(H_1, H_2, A_1, A_2))$$

Here $\mathcal{U}$ refers to uniform distribution and $\mathcal{B}$ refers to binomial distribution. f and g are functions with linear form. We consider A_1, A_2 as treatment variables, Y as outcome variable, and H_1, H_2 as confounders. As we have the full knowledge and the ground truth here, we can compare the performance of different methods under multiple scenarios (based on whether the confounders are observed or hidden) against the ground truth.

Table 1. Causal effects for synthetic data where the most accurate estimates are highlighted

Causal effect	H_1, H_2 observed	H_1 hidden	H_1, H_2 hidden
Ground truth	0.3982	0.3982	0.3982
SCM	**0.3982**	0.7241	0.7729
IPTW	0.4063	0.7732	0.6978
MCDA	0.5763	**0.5763**	**0.5763**

We observe that the graph structure of the synthetic data satisfies the back-door criterion. Hence we apply the structural equation model and use the truncated factorization to get the true causal effect of X_1 and X_2 on Y. We measure the causal effect between two different treatment configurations: $(X_1, X_2) = (1,1)$ and $(X_1, X_2) = (0,0)$. The ground truth ATE is 0.3982. Our evaluation focuses on the scenario with H_1 and H_2 hidden. We see this scenario has two treatments and no single-cause confounder. As shown in the last column of Table 1, our MCDA algorithm achieves more accurate estimate (0.5763) than the IPTW (0.6978) and SCM (0.7729) compared with the ground truth (0.3982). We also conduct comparisons under the scenario with only H_1 hidden. As shown in the third column of Table 1, MCDA achieves the best estimate. We also show the scenario with both H_1 and H_2 observed. Note that in this scenario, there are no hidden variables. It is not surprising that SCM and IPTW outperform MCDA because of no hidden variables in this scenario.

4.2   Adult Dataset

We also use the adult dataset [5] that contains 65, 123 records with 11 attributes. We assume there are no unknown variables associated with this dataset. Under this assumption, we also have the ground truth. We binarize the categorical variables due to the data sparsity issue. We then apply the PC algorithm in Tetrad to build the causal graph. Since *native country, sex, age, race* are unlikely to be caused by other covariates, we set them in the first tier. The built causal graph is shown in Fig. 2. We take *income* as the outcome variable, *sex* as the protected attribute, *workclass* and *relationship* as two redlining attributes, *education, occupation, hours, marital-status* as observed covariates, and *native country* and *age* as two unobserved covariates. The causal effect can be calculated accurately if we know the whole knowledge of the graph. We may still estimate the causal effects using structural equation model when there exits hidden confounders, which is usually the case in observational study (SCM). From the graph structure we can see that there are no single-cause confounders. Hence our MCDA algorithm is applicable.

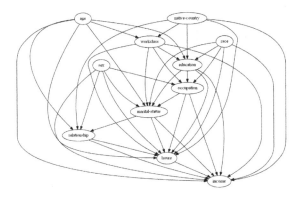

Fig. 2. Causal graph for adult dataset with *sex* as protected attribute, *occupation* and *relationship* as redlining attributes, *native country* and *age* as unmeasured confounders, *income* as the outcome variable.

We focus on estimating the causal effects with two redlining attributes *workclass* and *relationship* and the sensitive attribute *sex*. We emphasize our MCDA algorithm can analyze multi-cause effects simultaneously. Table 2 shows the expected potential outcome value for each treatment configuration of *workclass, relationship,* and *sex.* By applying average treatment effect formula, we can calculate the average treatment effect between any pair of two configurations. For example, the causal effect between two different treatment configurations $(A_1, A_2, A_3) = (1, 0, 1)$ and $(A_1, A_2, A_3) = (0, 0, 0)$ is 0.418 (0.695 − 0.277), which is also close to the ground truth 0.398. The result shows that MCDA significantly outperforms the SCM and is more robust to unmeasured confounding.

Table 2. Comparison result from adult dataset, where A_1, A_2, and A_3 correspond to *workclass*, *relationship*, and *sex*.

Treatment configuration	MCDA	SCM	Ground truth
$(A_1, A_2, A_3) = (0,0,0)$	0.277	0.464	0.275
$(A_1, A_2, A_3) = (0,0,1)$	0.526	0.397	0.610
$(A_1, A_2, A_3) = (0,1,0)$	0.185	0.333	0.201
$(A_1, A_2, A_3) = (0,1,1)$	0.434	0.250	0.288
$(A_1, A_2, A_3) = (1,0,0)$	0.446	0.493	0.400
$(A_1, A_2, A_3) = (1,0,1)$	0.695	0.481	0.673
$(A_1, A_2, A_3) = (1,1,0)$	0.354	0.352	0.250
$(A_1, A_2, A_3) = (1,1,1)$	0.603	0.088	0.362

In other words, we can easily conduct counterfactual analysis and answer "what-if" questions in causal inference, which is imperative for exploration based fair learning.

5   Conclusion

In this paper, we developed one approach based on the potential outcome framework to analyze the discrimination effects of protected and redlining attributes on the decision. The developed approach is based on the potential outcome framework and combines the deconfounder and inverse probability of treatment weighting. It can better handle the presence of hidden confounders and can lead to a more robust estimate of causal effects. We have empirically compared our approach with the structural causal modeling based approach and experimental results demonstrated the advantages of the proposed approach.

Acknowledgments. This work was supported in part by NSF 1646654, 1920920, and 1940093.

References

1. Avin, C., Shpitser, I., Pearl, J.: Identifiability of path-specific effects. In: IJCAI International Joint Conference on Artificial Intelligence, vol. 2, pp. 357–363, August 2005
2. Chiappa, S.: Path-specific counterfactual fairness. In: The Thirty-Third AAAI Conference on Artificial Intelligence, AAAI 2019, Honolulu, Hawaii, USA, 27 January–1 February 2019, pp. 7801–7808. AAAI Press (2019)
3. Huang, W., Wu, Y., Zhang, L., Wu, X.: Fairness through equality of effort. In: Companion of The 2020 Web Conference 2020, Taipei, Taiwan, pp. 743–751 (2020)
4. Kusner, M.J., Loftus, J.R., Russell, C., Silva, R.: Counterfactual fairness. In: Neural Information Processing Systems (2017)

5. Lichman, M.: UCI machine learning repository (2013). http://archive.ics.uci.edu/ml

6. Pearl, J.: Causality: Models, Reasoning and Inference, 2nd edn. Cambridge University Press, New York (2009)

7. Rubin, D.B.: Causal inference using potential outcomes. J. Am. Stat. Assoc. **100**(469), 322–331 (2005)

8. Russell, C., Kusner, M.J., Loftus, J., Silva, R.: When worlds collide: integrating different counterfactual assumptions in fairness. In: Advances in Neural Information Processing Systems, pp. 6414–6423 (2017)

9. Scheines, R., Spirtes, P., Glymour, C., Meek, C., Richardson, T.: The tetrad project: constraint based aids to causal model specification. Multivar. Behav. Res **33**(1), 65–117 (1998)

10. Shpitser, I., Pearl, J.: What counterfactuals can be tested. In: Proceedings of the Twenty-Third Conference on Uncertainty in Artificial Intelligence, pp. 352–359. AUAI Press (2007)

11. Tipping, M.E., Bishop, C.M.: Probabilistic principal component analysis. J. Roy. Stat. Soc. Ser. B (Stat. Methodol.) **61**(3), 611–622 (1999)

12. Wang, Y., Blei, D.M.: The blessings of multiple causes. arXiv preprint arXiv:1805.06826 (2018)

13. Wu, Y., Zhang, L., Wu, X.: Counterfactual fairness: unidentification, bound and algorithm. In: Proceedings of the Twenty-Eighth International Joint Conference on Artificial Intelligence, IJCAI 2019, Macao, China, 10–16 August 2019, pp. 1438–1444 (2019). ijcai.org

14. Wu, Y., Zhang, L., Wu, X., Tong, H.: PC-fairness: a unified framework for measuring causality-based fairness. In: Advances in Neural Information Processing Systems NeurIPS 2019, Vancouver, BC, Canada, 8–14 December 2019, pp. 3399–3409 (2019)

15. Zhang, L., Wu, Y., Wu, X.: A causal framework for discovering and removing direct and indirect discrimination. In: Proceedings of the Twenty-Sixth International Joint Conference on Artificial Intelligence, pp. 3929–3935 (2017)

Twitter Is the Megaphone
of Cross-platform Messaging
on the White Helmets

Sameera Horawalavithana$^{(\boxtimes)}$ ⓘ, Kin Wai Ng ⓘ, and Adriana Iamnitchi ⓘ

University of South Florida, Tampa, USA
{sameera1,kinwaing,aii}@usf.edu

Abstract. This work provides a quantitative analysis of the cross-platform disinformation campaign on Twitter against the Syrian Civil Defence group known as the White Helmets. Based on four months of Twitter messages, this article analyzes the promotion of URLs from different websites, such as alternative media, YouTube, and other social media platforms. Our study shows that alternative media URLs and YouTube videos are heavily promoted together; fact-checkers and official government sites are rarely mentioned; and there are clear signs of a coordinated campaign manifested through repeated messaging from the same user accounts.

Keywords: Cross-platform information diffusion · Disinformation campaigns

1 Introduction

Online disinformation is of critical concern for both academic research and industry. Facebook and Twitter recently detected coordinated users who were spreading rumors as part of a large network referencing a "significant state-backed information operation" [1]. Previous research in disinformation campaigns focused on single social media channels, more specifically Twitter [9]. However, several studies have shown that the interdependence between digital sources (e.g., news media outlets) and other social media platforms play a significant role in the diffusion and amplification of information [6]. For example, a coordinated group built its social presence in Google+, YouTube, Facebook, Twitter, Tumblr, Soundcloud, and Instagram around *Black Lives Matters* topics [2].

In disinformation campaigns, Twitter has played a significant role along with YouTube [12] and alternative media sites [10]. In addition to the sources of disinformation, which tend to be YouTube and alternative media sites, other parties that engage in response to disinformation campaigns are main stream media, which are typically providing factual information; government websites, which post the official positions of their countries; and fact-checking organizations that aim to reduce the spread of disinformation. Starbird et al. [12] emphasized the

© Springer Nature Switzerland AG 2020
R. Thomson et al. (Eds.): SBP-BRiMS 2020, LNCS 12268, pp. 235–244, 2020.
https://doi.org/10.1007/978-3-030-61255-9_23

importance of multiple platforms in promoting the disinformation campaign against the White Helmets.

This work studies how different categories of digital platforms are represented in Twitter conversations related to the White Helmets. The White Helmets are a search-and-rescue Syrian volunteer organization that threatened the Assad regime by its reporting and documenting of chemical attacks on civilians by the government and its allied forces. A disinformation campaign was coordinated [9] in order to discredit the White Helmets and thus delay the intervention of international organizations against the regime in power [2]. In this campaign, White Helmets are often framed as criminals and terrorists, and are responsible for staging chemical weapons attacks [9]. Based on four months of data that records two important events in the White Helmets campaign, we characterize Twitter activity in promoting content from eight categories of digital platforms: YouTube, alternative media, main stream media, social media, fact checking, government, official White Helmets websites, and others which consist of digital sources that could not be mapped to the previously mentioned categories. We capture the promotion of this content by analysing URLs shared on Twitter.

Our study shows the following. First, we confirm a recent study [12] surrounding the White Helmets that shows that YouTube is at the center of this campaign. Second, we discover that alternative media URLs are promoted via exploiting the accessibility of video content: these URLs are often co-appearing with YouTube URLs in the same tweets. Third, unlike previously believed, other social media platforms in addition to Twitter and YouTube have a significant role in this campaign. Specifically, Facebook, Gab and Steemit URLs are present along with YouTube videos on Twitter. Fourth, our data-driven investigation shows signs of coordination for promoting URLs for particular domains.

2   Data Collection and Processing

We focus on cross-platform information diffusion data specific to the White Helmets (WH) disinformation campaigns during four months starting from April 2018. The dataset was provided privately as part of DARPA SocialSim program. The data was collected from April 1, 2018 to July 31, 2018 using terms related to the WH in Twitter (listed in Table 1). This data collection period covers two critical offline events, a chemical attack in April 2018 and the intervention of the Israeli forces to save the White Helmets in July 2018. While the keywords used for the data collection were general, the resulting Twitter dataset captures a significant portion of the anti-White Helmets discussions as also seen in previous studies [12]. To understand the patterns of sharing other platforms' information in Twitter conversations, we only consider the Twitter messages that contain at least a URL, which consist of 25% from the total messages. We filtered out URLs to Twitter itself (that typically refer to other tweets) and URLs to web domains that are mentioned only once in our dataset (3,025 such URLs had no effect on information diffusion).

The main characteristics of the dataset are listed in Table 2. The resulting dataset consists of 53,297 seed messages including tweets, replies and quotes

Table 1. Keywords used for data collection.

'#cascosblancos', '#casquesblancs', '#weissehelme', '#weisshelme', '#whitehelmet', '#whitehelmets', 'caschi bianchi', 'capacetes brancos', 'cascos blancos', 'cascosblancos', 'casques blancs', 'elmetti bianchi', 'weisshelme' , , 'syria civil defence', 'syria civil defense', 'syrian civil defence', 'syrian civil defense', 'weiß helme', 'weiße helme', 'white helmet', 'WH', 'whitehelmet', 'whitehelmets'

(78% in English, 4% in Arabic, 3% in German, 2% in French, 1% in Russian, 12% other) and 42,230 retweets that are in response to the original tweets. While we do not analyze content other than URL mentions, including tweets in different languages captures a better picture of URL dissemination across languages.

Table 2. Dataset size. Seeds are tweets (42,087), replies (9,824) and quotes (1,386) that introduce at least one URL. Retweets (42,230) are in response to seeds. Replies are comments to tweets, quotes are comments to retweets.

	Seed messages	Retweets
# Distinct URLs	14,307	12,865
# Distinct Domains	983	957
# Users	18,162	16,578
# Records	53,297	42,230

Each message (tweet, retweet, quote, reply) in our dataset contains the following information: an assigned unique identifier, the anonymized ID of the user who posted it, the timestamp of when it was posted, and its type (whether tweet, retweet, quote, or reply). If the message is a retweet, quote, or reply, the unique identifier of the post that this message is referring to is also included. In addition, the external links (e.g., a tweet mentioning a YouTube video, or an external website domain) mentioned in the messages are pre-processed as following. The shortened URLs are expanded, and HTML parameters are removed from the URLs. The YouTube URLs are resolved to the base URL if they include a parameter referencing a specific time in the video. This pre-processing code of resolving URLs is publicly available [7].

3   Mentions of Digital Platforms in Twitter Messages

We classify the URLs mentioned in Twitter messages into eight classes: i) YouTube; ii) social media platforms (SM) (excluding YouTube); iii) mainstream media domains (MSM), iv) alternative media domains (ALT), v) government (GOV), vi) fact-checking (FACT_CHECK), vii) WH official media outlets, and viii) other web domains (OTHER) that are not mapped to any other classes.

We used an existing classification of the mainstream and alternative media outlets as identified and publicly available [8]. The first two authors manually performed the classification for the majority of the web domains (94%) appearing in our dataset but outside of the existing identification. This approach followed an iterative and collaborative decision process to finalize the identification. However, we have to stress that the classification of alternative news media domains is considered pejorative to the classification of mainstream news media domains [10]. There are only four fact-checking web-domains (i.e., snopes.com, mediabiasfactcheck.com, factuel.afp.com, and stopfake.org) that appeared in our dataset. We identify government media outlets mainly using the regex expression *.gov.* The other popular government websites that have not been mapped to this regex pattern include the UK parliament (parliament.uk), European parliament (europa.eu), Ministry of Foreign Affairs France (diplomatie.gouv.fr), United Nations (un.org), and the government of Canada (canada.ca). We also include an intergovernmental organisation opcw.org (i.e., the Organisation for the Prohibition of Chemical Weapons) as a government web domain. OPCW was an official voice on the issue of chemical weapon usage in Syria during our observation period. We also identified three official websites thesyriacampaign.org, syriacivildefense.org, and whitehelmets.org that are directly owned or handled by WH and their subsidiaries. There are 171 (17%) web domains that are not mapped to the seven categories discussed above. This list includes web search, entertainment, university, petition web domains, etc. In the end, we identified 620 alternative media domains, 112 mainstream media domains, 50 social-media domains, and 18 government media outlets. We made this complete list of web domains and the associated media categories available online [3].

Table 3. Top-10 domains by URLs.

Domain	# URLs
facebook.com	1880
youtube.com	1811
paper.li	291
rt.com	255
mintpressnews.com	232
sputniknews.com	209
globalresearch.ca	178
southfront.org	175
theguardian.com	146
gab.ai	140

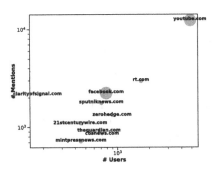

Fig. 1. Top-10 domains by mentions.

Table 3 shows the top 10 domains by the number of URLs in our dataset. Facebook and YouTube are the most popular social media platforms that were referenced by URLs. The third most shared domain is paper.li, a "content curation platform that enables individuals to create newspapers based on topics they choose". The next five domains (rt.com, mintpressnews.com, sputniknews.com, globalresearch.ca, southfront.org) are alternative media domains that spread master narratives in the Russia's disinformation campaign. Guardian.com is the only mainstream media that breaks in to the top 10 most shared domains. This is mostly due to an active journalist, Olivia Solon, who is documenting the disinformation campaign against the WH. We also notice the URLs referenced to gab.ai, the notorious hate-speech platform.

Figure 1 shows the number of mentions and users involved in these URL-sharing activities. The size of the markers in this plot are proportional to the number of URLs associated with the domain. One would expect that the volume of mentions of a web domain and the number of users who share URLs from that domain are correlated with the number of distinct URLs from that domain, thus the domains that appear in Table 3 appear in Fig. 1. However, clarityofsignal.com, zerohedge.com, and 21stcenturywire.com are the alternative media sites that have unexpected popularity for the relatively small content shared (number of URLs). Moreover, we notice that clarityofsignal.com acquires its many mentions from very few users: 177 users made 2,146 mentions during our observation period. Similarly, with few URLs shared (255), rt.com has high popularity in both users (1,670) and number of mentions (2,958). rt.com is directly handled by the Russian state media, while clarityofsignal.com promotes conspiracy theories criticizing Western governments.

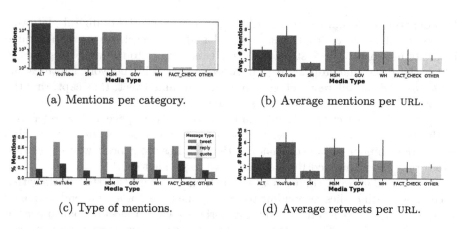

(a) Mentions per category.

(b) Average mentions per URL.

(c) Type of mentions.

(d) Average retweets per URL.

Fig. 2. URL sharing activities per media category.

Figure 2 shows the characteristics of URL mentions, the rate of mentions, and the rate of retweets received for the URL messages. The results are presented according to the eight media categories of the shared URLs. First, the majority of URL mentions are referencing alternative media domains (Fig. 2a). This is mainly due to the number of alternative media domains (63%) that participate in this disinformation campaign. However, a YouTube URL has higher rate of mentions relative to any other media category (Fig. 2b). Mainstream media URLs also receives more mentions than alternative media. Notably, the official WH web sites received similar number of mentions compared to alternative media URLs on average (Fig. 2b). This is despite the fact that WH and alternative web domains promote opposing views on related events. The URLs referencing articles hosted at government media outlets and the fact checking websites are relatively low compared to other media domains, but such URLs have higher rate of mentions compared to social-media URLs.

Second, 25% of URLs are injected via quotes and replies, suggesting a concerted effort to promote those URLs, as shown in Fig. 2c. We note that less than 1% URLs are mentioned via quotes and replies in another Twitter dataset collected outside the topic of this study [4]. We also notice that URLs referencing government and fact-checking websites are mentioned proportionally more in replies compared to any other URLs. Unlike previously observed [11], the diffusion of URLs in this particular dataset is very limited: on average, less than one retweet is posted for every mention of a URL. A YouTube video URL and a mainstream media URL are mentioned in relatively higher number of retweets than any other URL (as shown in Fig. 2d). Compared to other media categories, YouTube videos provide audio and visuals to attract users, and the mainstream media are often used for validation and credibility.

4   Media Co-sharing Patterns

In order to understand the relationships between categories of digital platforms as expressed at tweet level, cascade level and user level, we construct three bipartite networks. The first network connects a tweet to the web categories to which the URLs that appear in that tweet belong. This network captures the co-occurrences of different web categories in the same tweet, thus capturing the potential similarity of the views expressed in the content published in those categories. We project this network in the web category space and we refer to it as the *tweet-sharing network*, where nodes are web categories and edge weights record the number of tweets that mentioned URLs from both web categories. (Note that the mentioned URLs do not have to be identical.)

The second network connects a cascade (i.e., a conversation that starts with a tweet along with replies responding to the original tweet, or a set of endorsements via quotes and retweets) to the web categories to which the URLs that appear in that cascade belong. This network captures the co-occurrences of different web categories in the same cascade which might consist of a set of users who hold similar or opposite views. We project this network in the web category space and call it the *cascade-sharing network*; nodes are web categories and edge weights record the number of cascades that mentioned URLs from both categories.

The third network connects users with the web categories to which the URLs they share belong. This network captures the co-occurrence of different web categories in the content posted by a user and reflects the user interest over multiple

types of digital platforms. We project this network again in the category space
and obtain a network that we call *user-sharing network* in which nodes are web
categories and edge weights represent the number of users who posted on Twitter content that includes URLs from both categories. Figure 3a and b present the
tweet-sharing and cascade-sharing networks, respectively. User-sharing network
is shown in Fig. 3c.

4.1   Tweet/Cascade-Sharing Network

The tweet-sharing network (Fig. 3a) is missing five edges in total. There are no
tweets that contain references to government sites along with references to social
media pages, fact-checkers, WH official websites or other websites. On one hand,
mentioning fact-checking and government URLs could serve the same purpose of
verifying facts: government sites publish the official information, fact checkers
verify the information. This assumption is confirmed by the fact that the two
types of information sources do not appear in the same cascade either (Fig. 3b).
While mentioning fact-checking and government sites in the same tweet may be
redundant or cumbersome, the lack of tweets that refer to both social media and
government sites is less intuitive. However, social media URLs are mentioned in
the replies of the three cascades originated from a government website, as shown
in Fig. 3b. We also noticed the lack of tweets (or cascades) that mention a WH
official website along with a fact-checking or a government website. We believe
this fact is due to the content promoted by the WH official websites. A majority
of these URLs redirects to WH donation campaign websites, mostly shared by
WH sympathizers.

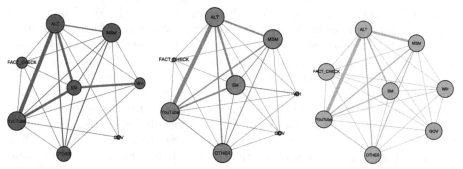

(a) Tweet-sharing network (b) Cascade-sharing network   (c) User-sharing network

Fig. 3. Visualization of entity-sharing networks, Entity is a tweet (a, c), cascade (b),
and user (d). The thickness of an edge is proportional to the number of entities that
mention at least two URLs referencing both media categories.

The strongest edge connects YouTube with alternative media (via 250
tweets), while the weakest edge connects mainstream media and fact-checking

sites via one tweet. A strong relationship is also seen in the tweet-sharing network between social media and YouTube (164 tweets) and between social media and alternative media (154 tweets). We also noticed social media and WH official websites are mentioned together in 131 tweets. 98% such tweets are in Korean, and promote the WH donation campaign via posts from multiple social media platforms. Similar patterns are seen in the cascade sharing networks: YouTube and alternative media sites appear together in the largest number of conversations (577), while alternative and social media co-appear 313 times.

Because YouTube is the largest player in this ecosystem, we zoom in on the web domains that co-appear with a YouTube URL in the same tweet. The top-5 web domains are `rt.com` (78), `clarityofsignal.com` (60), `russia-insider.com` (59), `steemit.com` (56) and `facebook.com` (48) according to the number of tweets in which the website and a YouTube URL were mentioned together. For calibration, the median number of tweets is 3 (between YouTube and `21wire.tv`) and the mean is 9. Apart from `facebook.com` and `steemit.com` social-media domains, the other three domains are known to promote alternative narratives that denigrate the WH [2]. On the other hand, URLs from these three domains often co-occur in the same tweet: `russia-insider.com` and `clarityofsignal.com` co-occured with `rt.com` in 59 and 46 tweets, respectively, while `russia-insider.com` co-occured with `clarityofsignal.com` in 47 tweets. These sites are known to post the same content occasionally [10]. Moreover, `rt.com` and `clarityofsignal.com` are the two domains from the top-10 most popular in mentions that have relatively few URLs in our dataset, as previously discussed on Fig. 1.

Another observation is related to the 7th most popular web domain `21stcenturywire.com` that co-occured with a YouTube URL in 19 tweets. Videos from two YouTube channels are co-tweeted with `21stcenturywire.com` URLs: i) the official Russian Television YouTube channel, and ii) the YouTube channel of UK blogger Vanessa Beeley, a well-known anti-WH voice. Along with other user accounts, she repeatedly includes both URLs to these channels and her own articles posted on `21stcenturywire.com` in a typical card-stacking propaganda device manner [5]. This proves the cross-platform disinformation practice where a message is pushed on multiple digital platforms in their respective formats.

The top three social media sites that co-occured with a YouTube URL are `steemit.com`, `facebook.com` and `gab.ai`. We manually inspect the corresponding tweets and the content of these URLs and observe the following. First, 95% of the Twitter messages (51 out of 56) that contain both a `steemit.com` URL and a YouTube video URL have exactly the same content and are authored by the same user. The majority of such duplicated messages are in the form of replies or quotes. These messages are not available in Twitter anymore as of February 2020, which might be due to account suspension.

Second, Facebook connects to YouTube in two ways. On one hand, a pro-WH voice disseminates videos published by the official WH YouTube and Facebook accounts in the same tweet in Arabic. There are 22 tweets authored by this user with this similar pattern. On the other hand, two anti-WH users also tweet

Facebook and YouTube videos in Arabic, but this time the Facebook URLs point to the Facebook page of each user, where the same YouTube videos already shared in their tweets are also found.

Finally, `gab.ai` and YouTube are connected via 32 tweets in which they co-occur (all the articles referenced by Gab URLs in this set are not available as of February 2020). 60% of these messages are promoted by the same usernames in both Twitter and Gab. This is another example of promoting content from one platform to Twitter via exploiting the appeal of YouTube videos.

4.2 User-Sharing Network

Figure 3c that visualizes the user-sharing network suggests the following four observations. First, the network has no missing edges (full clique). But the missing edges in the tweet-sharing network appeared in the user-sharing network with very small edge weights. The weakest edges connect government and fact-checking (3), WH official web domains with fact-checking (5) or government (6) web domains. Second, the majority (1,242) of users who share alternative media URLs also share YouTube video URLs. Many alternative websites and YouTube channels that appeared in our dataset promote anti-WH content. This shows the existence of users who promote anti-WH content from different digital platforms. Third, the next largest population (859) disseminates both alternative and mainstream media. Notably, the majority of mainstream media sites that appeared in our dataset produce more pro-WH content than anti-WH content, which is analogous to the findings in [10]. Anti-WH users in Twitter often shared mainstream media and alternative media URLs in the same tweet. The alternative media articles were used as evidence to strengthen their arguments in order to debunk the narratives presented in the mainstream media articles. Fourth, very few users who tweet an alternative media or a YouTube video URL share a fact-checking URL. Out of 7,377 users who shared an alternative URL, only 32 (0.004%) users shared a fact-checking URL. One possible explanation is the disregard of fact-checking sites by anti-WH users. For example, a popular narrative among users who shared anti-WH content framed WH as a terrorist organization. `Snopes.com` verified this claim as false in an article published in December 2016, yet the alternative media articles and YouTube videos promoted the same claim even two years later.

5 Summary

This study investigates how Twitter is used to disseminate White Helmets-related information hosted on other platforms, and especially YouTube. From four months of data we identified the following patterns of URL promotion on Twitter. First, YouTube videos and alternative media URLs are often bundled in the same message. Second, main stream media and alternative media URLs are also bundled together in the same message or in messages posted by the same user. From manual inspections, the majority of such messages use alternative media content to attack the narratives and the interpretations published by mainstream media. Third, we discovered a small number of websites with unusual popularity despite the small number of related URLs in our dataset. In some cases, these websites are aggressively and repeatedly promoted by a small group of users via mentions. And finally, very few messages include official government websites or fact-checking websites in the Twitter conversations on White Helmets, despite the active disinformation campaign going on during our observation period.

Our study demonstrates the need to develop intervention techniques to limit disinformation spread across a broader media ecology than a single platform in isolation.

Acknowlegements. This work is supported by the DARPA SocialSim Program and the Air Force Research Laboratory under contract FA8650-18-C-7825. The authors would like to thank Leidos for providing data.

References

1. Baca, M., Romm, T.: Twitter and Facebook take first actions against china for using fake accounts to sow discord in Hong Kong (2019). https://www.washingtonpost.com/technology/2019/08/19/twitter-suspends-accounts-it-accuses-china-coordinating-against-hong-kong-protesters/
2. DiResta, R., et al.: The Tactics & Tropes of the Internet Research Agency. New Knowledge. (2018). https://disinformationreport.blob.core.windows.net/disinformation-report/NewKnowledge-Disinformation-Report-Whitepaper.pdf. Accessed 28 Sept 2020
3. Horawalavithana, S.: Wh_twitter_megaphone (2018). https://github.com/SamTube405/WH_Twitter_Megaphone
4. Horawalavithana, S., Bhattacharjee, A., Liu, R., Choudhury, N.O., Hall, L., Iamnitchi, A.: Mentions of security vulnerabilities on Reddit, Twitter and GitHub. In: IEEE/WIC/ACM International Conference on Web Intelligence, pp. 200–207 (2019)
5. Lee, A., Lee, E.B.: The Fine Art of Propaganda. Harcourt, San Diego (1939)
6. Myers, S.A., Zhu, C., Leskovec, J.: Information diffusion and external influence in networks. In: 18th ACM KDD (2012)
7. PNNL, P.N.N.L.: Socialsim (2018). https://github.com/pnnl/socialsim
8. Starbird, K.: Examining the alternative media ecosystem through the production of alternative narratives of mass shooting events on Twitter. In: AAAI ICWSM (2017)
9. Starbird, K., Arif, A., Wilson, T.: Disinformation as collaborative work: surfacing the participatory nature of strategic information operations. Proc. ACM Hum.-Comput. Interact. **3**(CSCW), 127:1–127:26 (2019)
10. Starbird, K., Arif, A., Wilson, T., Van Koevering, K., Yefimova, K., Scarnecchia, D.: Ecosystem or echo-system? Exploring content sharing across alternative media domains. In: AAAI ICWSM (2018)
11. Suh, B., Hong, L., Pirolli, P., Chi, E.H.: Want to be retweeted? Large scale analytics on factors impacting retweet in Twitter network. In: 2010 IEEE Second International Conference on Social Computing, pp. 177–184. IEEE (2010)
12. Wilson, T., Starbird, K.: Cross-platform disinformation campaigns: lessons learned and next steps. The Harvard Kennedy School (HKS) Misinformation Review (2020)

Learning Behavioral Representations
from Wearable Sensors

Nazgol Tavabi[(✉)], Homa Hosseinmardi, Jennifer L. Villatte, Andrés Abeliuk,
Shrikanth Narayanan, Emilio Ferrara, and Kristina Lerman

USC Information Sciences Institute, University of Washington, Seattle, USA
nazgolta@isi.edu

Abstract. Continuous collection of physiological data from wearable
sensors enables temporal characterization of individual behaviors. Understanding the relation between an individual's behavioral patterns and
psychological states can help identify strategies to improve quality of life.
One challenge in analyzing physiological data is extracting the underlying behavioral states from the temporal sensor signals and interpreting
them. Here, we use a non-parametric Bayesian approach to model sensor data from multiple people and discover the dynamic behaviors they
share. We apply this method to data collected from sensors worn by a
population of hospital workers and show that the learned states can cluster participants into meaningful groups and better predict their cognitive
and psychological states. This method offers a way to learn interpretable
compact behavioral representations from multivariate sensor signals.

1 Introduction

Advances in sensing technologies have made wearable sensors more accurate and
widely available, enabling continuous and unobtrusive acquisition of physiological data. This data potentially allows quantitative characterization of human
behavior, which provides a basis to assess an individual's health [1] and psychological well-being [30]. To make sense of physiological data, a number of
challenges have to be met. Sensor data is dynamic and covers different time
periods. Another challenge is the heterogeneity of data collected from a population of differently-behaving individuals. These issues make aggregating and
modeling sensor data challenging. Researchers have used Hidden Markov Models
(HMMs) to address some of these challenges and effectively capture temporal
trends within physiological data [21,22]. HMMs are a family of generative probabilistic models for sequential data, which can be represented as a Markov process
with latent, or "hidden," states. These hidden states capture common patterns
that determine the dynamics of the data. One weakness of traditional HMMs is
that they constrain the model to a predefined number of states. When learning
dynamic behaviors from multiple physiological signals, it may be difficult to enu-
merate the states best representing the data without making strong assumptions.
To address this challenge, we propose to use a non-parametric Markov Switching

© Springer Nature Switzerland AG 2020
R. Thomson et al. (Eds.): SBP-BRiMS 2020, LNCS 12268, pp. 245–254, 2020.
https://doi.org/10.1007/978-3-030-61255-9_24

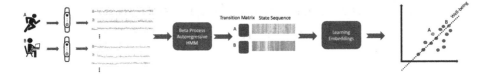

Fig. 1. Overview of the modeling framework. Sensor data collected from participants A and B is fed into BP-AR-HMM model which outputs an HMM per participant, where states are shared among participants. Output from BP-AR-HMM model is used to learn embeddings, which are later used to predict personal attributes.

Autoregressive model [9]—the *Beta Process Autoregressive HMM*. The number of states in this model is learned from the data: if an unusual new pattern appears, another state is added to model that segment. This is beneficial in cases where there is a malfunction or noise in the sensors. By assigning a separate state to that segment, we can identify and disregard that state. We apply the model to physiological data collected from about 200 workers at a hospital and show that the proposed model learns states that correspond to shared behaviors of the workers. We use these behavioral representations to better understand and analyze the data, group similar individuals together, and as features to predict their personality traits. Figure 1 shows an overview of our framework.

2   Related Work

Learning compact representations becomes especially important when dealing with physiological data. In these types of problems we usually don't have a large number of participants; however, for each participant we have rich longitudinal data. Since we have one label per data stream–participant–our training data is limited to the number of participants in the study, in this case 180 data points. Complex models, such as those learned by deep neural networks, tend to overfit on small training data, and thus are not applicable for these problems.

Hidden Markov Models (HMMs) represent temporal trends and dynamics of time series using states and transition probabilities. In prior research, HMM models are learned on each time series independently. Consequently, the learned states cannot be compared across different representations. In addition to HMM models, other recent methods for temporal modeling suffer from the same shortcoming; for example, the approach by Hallac et al. [11], which offers a new perspective on clustering subsequences of multivariate time series, cannot be used in learning representations across multiple signals. Another shortcoming of standard HMM models is that the number of states must be fixed a priori. Recent Bayesian approaches overcome these constraints by allowing infinitely many potential states using Beta process, which are shared among all time series [9]. This approach has successfully been applied to different applications [15,27]. Another line of work allows infinite potential states in a Hidden Markov Model [2] by using the Dirichlet process as prior over the hidden states, but the model is again designed to capture each time series independently. Tensor decomposition is another approach in finding shared latent features among multiple time series. Tensor-based methods have been used in different fields including behavioral modeling [13,14]. A popular tensor decomposition method is Parafac2 [12], which offers multilinear higher-order decomposition that can handle missing values and different length time series. Parafac2 itself is considered a traditional method, however there are multiple works published in recent years on improving its inference, imposing constraints, etc. [5,16]. Similarly, a recent work [33] proposes Random Warping Series (RWS), a model based on Dynamic Time Warping, to embed different length, multivariate time series in a multi-dimensional space.

3 Methods

One of the most popular tools for studying multivariate time series is vector autoregressive (VAR) model [19]. In a VAR model of lag r, each variable is a linear function of itself and the other variable's r previous values. However, such models cannot describe time series with changing behaviors. In order to model such cases, Markov switching autoregressive models, which are a generalization of autoregressive and Hidden Markov Models, are used. In this paper, we use a generative model proposed by [9], called *Beta Process Autoregressive HMM* (BP-AR-HMM), to discover states or behaviors shared by different time series. Based on the proposed model, the entire set of time series can be described by the globally-shared states, or behaviors, where each time series is associated with a subset of the states. Behaviors associated with different time series can be represented by a binary matrix F, where $F_{ij} = 1$ means time series i is associated with behavior j. Given matrix F, each time series is modeled as a separate hidden Markov model with the states that it exhibits. Also, each state is modeled using a different autoregressive process. Since the number of such states in the data is not known in advance, the Beta process is used [28]. A Beta process allows infinite number of behaviors but encourages sparse representations. This process is also known as the *Indian Buffet Process* which can be best understood with the following metaphor involving a sequence of customers (time series) selecting dishes (features) from an infinitely large buffet. The n-th customer selects dish k with probability m_k/n, where m_k is the popularity of the dish. S/He then selects $Poisson(\alpha/n)$ new dishes. With this approach, the feature space increases if the data cannot be faithfully represented with the already defined states. However, the probability of adding new states decreases according to $Poisson(\alpha/n)$. For posterior computations the original work is referenced [9].

3.1 Measuring Distance

When applied to physiological signals, the generative model described above learns a hidden Markov model for each participant. In this section we propose two different methods for measuring the distance between HMMs, participants.

Likelihood Distance: To define a similarity measure between two HMMs, one could measure the probability of their state sequences having been generated by the same process. Since each signal is associated with its distinct generative process, we measure state sequences' similarity as the likelihood that sequence (S_λ) was generated by λ', the process that gave rise to $(S_{\lambda'})$ denoted by $p_{\lambda'}(S_\lambda)$, and the likelihood that $S_{\lambda'}$ was generated by λ. We average the two likelihoods to symmetrize the similarity measure. The likelihood $p_\lambda(S_\lambda)$ is computed using the learned transition matrix of λ' and Markov process assumption $z_t|z_{t-1} \sim \pi_{z_{t-1},\lambda'}$, where $\pi_{z_{t-1},\lambda'}$ is a row of the transition matrix corresponding to state z_{t-1}. Because a longer time series would automatically have a smaller likelihood with this approach, we normalize them by dividing $p_{\lambda'}(S_\lambda)$ to $\frac{1}{K}^L$, K being the number of states and L being the length of the time series.

Viterbi Distance: Distance between different HMMs could be also computed with Viterbi distance proposed in [8], which is estimated as follows:

$$d_{\widetilde{Vit}}(\lambda, \lambda') = \sum_{i,j} a_{ij}\phi_\lambda(i)(\log a'_{ij} - \log a_{ij}) \tag{1}$$

a_{ij} represent the probabilities in transition matrix of λ; $\phi_\lambda(i)$ is the probability of state i in the stationary distribution of λ (The stationary distribution will be further explained in Sect. 3.2). The *Likelihood Distance* computes the distance based on both the state sequences and HMMs, where state sequence is a sample of the HMM (generative) model. The other method, *Viterbi Distance*, computes the values by only comparing the HMMs. This makes Viterbi distance less susceptible to noises observed in state sequences, or in other words, less sensitive to small changes. This trade-off causes one method to perform better than the other depending on the targeted ground truth construct.

3.2   Learning Representations

We describe two methods for learning representations from the HMMs. The first method is interpretable and could be used for analyzing the data. The second method however gives better performance in predicting most of the constructs.

Stationary Representation: Each HMM is defined by a transition matrix. The transition matrix gives the probability of transitioning from one state to another, so $z_t T_i$ is the probability distribution for z_{t+1}, and $\lim_{x\to\infty} z_t T_i^x$ is the probability distribution for $\lim_{t\to\infty} z_t$, which is the stationary distribution. Regardless of the starting state, the relative amount of time spent in each state is given by the stationary distribution, which is the eigenvector corresponding to the largest eigenvalue of the transition matrix. We treat these stationary distributions as representations for time series, i.e., participants.

Spectral Representation: A drawback of using stationary representation to represent participants is that it does not capture the relation between behavioral states, hence it might not be able to distinguish between participants with similar behaviors but that are ordered differently. In order to capture these differences we use the spectral representation, which is similar to spectral clustering [29]. Specifically, we perform these steps: **1)** Calculate the distance matrix between

Table 1. Extracted Features from OMsignal.

Signal	Feature
Biometrics: 6 features	Avg. Breathing Depth, Avg. Breathing Rate, Heart Rate
	Std. Breathing Depth, Std. Breathing Rate, R-R Peak Coverage
Movement: 15 features	Intensity, Cadence, Steps, Sitting, Supine, Low G Coverage
	Avg. G Force, Std. G Force, Angle From Vertical
	Avg. X-Acceleration, Std. X-Acceleration, Avg. Y-Acceleration
	Std. Y-Acceleration, Avg. Z-Acceleration, Std. Z-Acceleration

participants using either the likelihood distance or the Viterbi distance described in Sect. 3.1 **2)** Compute the normalized Laplacian of the distance matrix **3)** Use K largest eigenvectors (i.e., eigenvectors corresponding to largest eigenvalues) as representations of participants (K is a hyperparameter).

4   Data

Data used in this work comes from a study of workplace well-being that measures physical activity and physiological states of hospital workers [20]. The study recruited over 200 volunteers for ten weeks. Participants were 31.1% male and 68.9% female and ranged in age from 21 to 65 years. Participants held a variety of job titles: 54.3% were registered nurses, 12% were certified nursing assistants, and the rest with some other job title, such as respiratory therapist, technician, etc. Participants wore the sensors for different number of days, depending on the number of workdays during the study. Furthermore, participants exhibited varying compliance rates. Hence, the length of the collected data varies across participants. For this paper, we focused on 180 participants from whom at least 6 days of data was collected. In addition to wearing sensors, participants were also asked to complete surveys prior to the study. These pre-study surveys measured cognitive ability, personality and health states, which serve as ground truth constructs for our study. Constructs are shown in Table 2. Data used in this paper was collected from a suite of wearable sensors produced by *OMSignal Biometric Smartwear*. These OMSignal garments include sensors embedded in the fabric that measure physiological data in real-time and can relay this information to participant's smartphone. Table 1 shows the sensor signals used in this work.

5   Results

We used BP-AR-HMM with autoregressive lag 1 to model the temporal data collected from sensors worn by the 180 high-compliance participants. For each participant, we used Z-score to normalize signals for data analysis, however since some statistical features such as mean and variance are useful for predicting constructs like age, both normalized and unnormalized signals were used in the prediction tasks in Table 2. The model, trained on normalized signals, identified

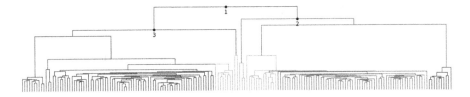

Fig. 2. Dendrogram showing the similarity of participants based on their learned states. (Color figure online)

23 shared latent states describing participants' behavior. Some of the states were only exhibited by a few participants. These rare states could convey useful information that helps identify noise or anomalies in the data; however, their sparseness is not beneficial to the prediction and clustering tasks. Therefore, we ignore states observed in fewer than 5% of the participants.

5.1   Clustering

For validating the states learned by the model, we apply hierarchical agglomerative clustering on the distance matrix generated with likelihood distance. The resulting dendrogram is shown in Fig. 2. We used pre-study surveys to perform statistical tests and evaluate differences between the clusters. We partitioned the dendrogram into clusters with more than five members by cutting the dendrogram horizontally on different depths. Based on the P-values obtained, the most important features differentiating the clusters were job type, age and gender in that order. This was aligned with our expectations, since different job types require different activities, also age and gender affect physiological signals.

The first cut point (marked 1 in Fig. 2) separates registered nurses from other jobs types. The main difference between the two clusters (red and blue) is the frequency of three latent states, which we call **A**, **B**, and **C**. Variables related to acceleration and movement are almost zero for state **A**, which has a higher frequency for participants in cluster 3–non-nurse (blue). State **B** is more representative of higher activity levels and is more frequent for participants in cluster 2–nurses (red). This also is aligned with our expectations, since the nurse occupation requires more activity compared to other job types in the study. State **C** mostly captures flexibility of work hours for non-nurses (non-nurse participants are more likely to finish their shifts earlier and have less than 12 h worth of data in one shift). This clustering also separates participants based on their work shifts, day or night shifts. Work shifts are distinguished by state **D**. In this state, binary supine signal, which is activated when the participants is lying down, is on. It appears that state **D** captures quick naps in the workplace and has a higher frequency for night shift participants. Participants who exhibit state **D** are shown by color yellow in Fig. 2.

5.2   Prediction

We use the learned representations for each participant as features to predict the ground truth constructs. The objective is two-fold: not only do we want to

Table 2. Evaluation of the model. The best performing model's results are highlighted in bold.

Construct	Description/ Instrument	ρ	RMSE	ρ	RMSE	ρ	RMSE	ρ	RMSE	ρ	RMSE
		HMM-S		HMM-SL		HMM-SV		RWS		Parafac2	
NEU	Personality: neuroticism [10]	0.066	0.726	0.159	0.718	**0.174**	**0.722**	0.048	0.728	0.116	0.724
CON	Personality: conscient. [10]	−0.165	0.62	**0.245**	**0.591**	0.181	0.6	−0.033	0.613	0.093	0.612
EXT	Personality: Extraversion [10]	0.154	0.655	0.152	0.659	**0.264**	**0.642**	0.178	0.65	0.038	0.66
AGR	Personality: agreeableness [10]	−0.428	0.491	0.122	0.485	**0.191**	**0.479**	0.079	0.488	0.099	0.488
OPE	Personality: openness [10]	0.224	0.586	0.217	0.581	**0.28**	**0.571**	0.216	0.585	−0.386	0.598
POS-AF	Positive affect [32]	0.37	6.547	**0.254**	**6.614**	0.231	6.686	0.139	6.821	0.112	6.822
NEG-AF	Negative affect [32]	−0.278	5.293	**0.235**	**5.139**	0.206	5.195	0.045	5.286	0.139	5.238
STAI	Anxiety [26]	0.016	8.975	**0.196**	**8.817**	0.112	8.919	0.128	8.912	0.095	8.966
AUDIT	Alcohol use disorders test [25]	0.1	2.159	**0.362**	**2.017**	0.153	2.142	0.053	2.169	0.244	2.113
IPAQ	Physical activity [18]	−0.57	15352	0.094	15191	**0.115**	**15316**	0.033	15311	0.097	15246
PSQI	Sleep quality [4]	−0.682	2.366	0.178	2.318	0.142	2.33	0.193	2.322	**0.194**	**2.311**
Age	–	**0.461**	**8.613**	0.091	9.662	0.084	9.667	0.243	9.406	0.363	9.035
Health limit	Limitations due to health [31]	−0.75	23.284	0.196	22.704	**0.333**	**21.986**	0.222	23.325	0.118	23.264
Emotional limit	Limitations due to emotion [31]	−0.704	22.71	**0.211**	**22.102**	0.164	22.504	0.042	22.652	0.091	22.553
Well being	Psychological well-being [31]	0.077	18.458	0.152	18.302	**0.276**	**17.904**	0.011	18.682	0.167	18.277
Social functioning	Social interaction ability [31]	0.057	21.94	0.109	21.684	0.191	21.547	0.085	21.857	**0.218**	**21.541**
Pain	Index of physical pain [31]	0.167	18.613	0.134	18.448	**0.239**	**18.164**	0.023	18.658	0.102	18.571
General health	Index of general health [31]	0.211	17.062	**0.27**	**16.792**	0.171	17.28	0.151	17.311	0.2	17.105
Life satisfaction	Global life satisfaction [7]	−0.655	1.354	0.106	1.338	**0.22**	**1.317**	−0.125	1.362	0.207	1.317
Perceived Stress	Perceived stress indicator [6]	0.196	0.511	0.201	0.51	**0.209**	**0.511**	0.195	0.513	−0.728	0.524
PSY flexibility	Ability to adapt [24]	−0.793	0.821	0.187	0.806	**0.233**	**0.795**	−0.077	0.823	0.103	0.813
PSY inflexibility	Inability to adapt [24]	−0.66	0.803	**0.182**	**0.785**	0.152	0.79	−0.013	0.803	0.006	0.8
WAAQ	Work acceptance [3]	**0.31**	**5.65**	0.284	5.705	0.205	5.833	0.153	5.878	0.163	5.866
Psych-capital	Psychological capital [17]	**0.188**	**0.656**	0.129	0.661	0.17	0.662	0.12	0.662	0.08	0.664
Challenge stress	Challenge stress indicator [23]	−0.639	0.622	**0.171**	**0.615**	0.078	0.62	−0.097	0.623	−0.789	0.621
Hindrance stress	Hindrance stress indicator [23]	0.132	0.644	0.005	0.646	**0.206**	**0.633**	0.035	0.647	0.143	0.637

predict, but also to gain understanding about what the latent states represent. A possible way to understand latent behaviors is to quantify their importance in explaining constructs. The stationary representation described in Sect. 3.2 has a clear interpretation, with each dimension representing the percentage of time spent in the corresponding state. We explain the behavioral states using the stationary representation with the following process: **1)** Get the stationary representations of participants **2)** Run classification/regression on the representations to predict construct. **3)** Retrieve the learned coefficients. **4)** Select the states with highest absolute coefficients and interpret these states based on their relation with the targeted construct. Based on this approach, we recognized state **D**, described in the Sect. 5.1, as the most relevant state for differentiating between day and night shift employees. State **D** also has a high positive coefficient in predicting POS-AF and Well-being, whereas for hindrance stress it has a high negative coefficient. Hindrance stress is generally perceived as a type of stress that prevents progress toward personal accomplishments. Thus a plausible interpretation of this result is: Quick breaks during work hours could increase positive affect and well-being and decrease hindrance stress.

Quantitative Results: For predicting constructs, we obtained stationary representations and spectral representations using both distance measures (likelihood and Viterbi distance). Spectral representation requires a hyperparameter K, the number of eigenvectors to include in the representation. We set the K to 10, 20, ..., 100 and use it to train the regression model. Since there are many ground truth constructs, one model can not be chosen for all the regression tasks. We use the ridge, kernel ridge and random forest regression on proposed representations and baselines and report the best model. The results are reported in correlation to the target construct (ρ) and Root Mean Squared Error (RMSE) using Leave-one-out cross validation. We compare our results against *Random Warping Series (RWS)* [33] and *Parafac2* [12]. RWS generates time series embeddings by measuring the similarity between a number of randomly generated sequences and the original sequence. This method has three hyper-parameters. Based on authors suggestion, we fixed the dimension of the embedding space to 512, and experimented with different values for the other two parameters. The second baseline we use is *Parafac2* [12]. This approach views the data as a tensor (3 dimensional array) of participants-sensors-time and decomposes it into hidden components. For Parafac2 the number of hidden components is a hyper-parameter. We varied the number of hidden components from one to ten and report the best results. Overall, the results of the predictions based on the HMM's latent states were systematically better, outperforming the baseline method in 25 of the 27 constructs predicted. It's worth mentioning that, except for HMM-S, which is non-parametric, all other four models in Table 2 have hyperparameters that need to be set. We tune the hyperparameters by running 10 different settings and selecting the setting with best results. Between our own representations HMM-Stationary, HMM-Spectral-Likelihood and HMM-Spectral-Viterbi (HMM-S, HMM-SL and HMM-SV respectively), HMM-SV performs better for some construct while HMM-SL gives better results for others. This could be because of differences between Viterbi and likelihood distance's sensitivity to small variations in the data (discussed in Sect. 3.1). Also, HMM-S is not a good representation for prediction and is better suited for analysis of the data.

6   Conclusion

We described a method for learning behavioral representations from physiological data captured by wearable sensors. We used this framework to model data collected from workers in a hospital. The latent states learned by the model can be used to predict their self-reported health and psychological well-being. In comparison to alternative models, our framework improves performance with compact representations of the multivariate time-series, leading to less overfitting and easier interpretation of the states learned. Concluding, we show that this framework can also cluster study participants into meaningful groups. This work can be extended in a number of ways. One possible direction is making this framework supervised. Using our current framework helps in analyzing data, but making this framework supervised could be more suited for a prediction task.

Acknowledgements. The research was supported by the Office of the Director of National Intelligence (ODNI), Intelligence Advanced Research Projects Activity (IARPA), via IARPA Contract No 2017-17042800005.

References

1. Aral, S., Nicolaides, C.: Exercise contagion in a global social network. Nat. Commun. **8**, 14753 (2017)
2. Beal, M.J., Ghahramani, Z., Rasmussen, C.E.: The infinite hidden Markov model. In: Advances in Neural Information Processing Systems, pp. 577–584 (2002)
3. Bond, F.W., Lloyd, J., Guenole, N.: The work-related acceptance and action questionnaire: initial psychometric findings and their implications for measuring psychological flexibility in specific contexts. J. Occup. Organ. Psychol. **86**(3), 331–347 (2013)
4. Buysse, D.J., Reynolds III, C.F., Monk, T.H., Berman, S.R., Kupfer, D.J.: The Pittsburgh sleep quality index: a new instrument for psychiatric practice and research. Psychiatry Res. **28**(2), 193–213 (1989)
5. Cohen, J.E., Bro, R.: Nonnegative PARAFAC2: a flexible coupling approach. In: Deville, Y., Gannot, S., Mason, R., Plumbley, M.D., Ward, D. (eds.) LVA/ICA 2018. LNCS, vol. 10891, pp. 89–98. Springer, Cham (2018). https://doi.org/10.1007/978-3-319-93764-9_9
6. Cohen, S., Kamarck, T., Mermelstein, R., et al.: Perceived stress scale. In: Measuring Stress: A Guide For Health and Social Scientists, pp. 235–283 (1994)
7. Diener, E., Emmons, R.A., Larsen, R.J., Griffin, S.: The satisfaction with life scale. J. Pers. Assess. **49**(1), 71–75 (1985)
8. Falkhausen, M., Reininger, H., Wolf, D.: Calculation of distance measures between hidden Markov models. In: Fourth European Conference on Speech Communication and Technology (1995)
9. Fox, E.B., Hughes, M.C., Sudderth, E.B., Jordan, M.I., et al.: Joint modeling of multiple time series via the beta process with application to motion capture segmentation. Ann. Appl. Stat. **8**(3), 1281–1313 (2014)
10. Gosling, S.D., Rentfrow, P.J., Swann Jr., W.B.: A very brief measure of the big-five personality domains. J. Res. Pers. **37**(6), 504–528 (2003)
11. Hallac, D., Vare, S., Boyd, S., Leskovec, J.: Toeplitz inverse covariance-based clustering of multivariate time series data. In: Proceedings of the 23rd ACM SIGKDD, pp. 215–223. ACM (2017)
12. Harshman, R.A.: Foundations of the PARAFAC procedure: models and conditions for an "explanatory" multimodal factor analysis (1970)
13. Hosseinmardi, H., Ghasemian, A., Narayanan, S., Lerman, K., Ferrara, E.: Tensor embedding: a supervised framework for human behavioral data mining and prediction. arXiv preprint arXiv:1808.10867 (2018)
14. Hosseinmardi, H., Kao, H.T., Lerman, K., Ferrara, E.: Discovering hidden structure in high dimensional human behavioral data via tensor factorization. In: WSDM Heteronam Workshop (2018)
15. Houpt, J.W., Frame, M.E., Blaha, L.M.: Unsupervised parsing of gaze data with a beta-process vector auto-regressive hidden Markov model. Behav. Res. Methods **50**(5), 2074–2096 (2018)
16. Jørgensen, P.J., Nielsen, S.F., Hinrich, J.L., Schmidt, M.N., Madsen, K.H., Mørup, M.: Probabilistic parafac2. arXiv preprint arXiv:1806.08195 (2018)
17. Luthans, F., Avolio, B.J., Avey, J.B., Norman, S.M.: Positive psychological capital: measurement and relationship with performance and satisfaction. Pers. Psychol. **60**(3), 541–572 (2007)
18. Maddison, R., et al.: International physical activity questionnaire (IPAQ) and new Zealand physical activity questionnaire (NZPAQ): a doubly labelled water validation. Int. J. Behav. Nutr. Phys. Act. **4**(1), 62 (2007)

19. Monbet, V., Ailliot, P.: Sparse vector Markov switching autoregressive models. Application to multivariate time series of temperature. Comput. Stat. Data Anal. **108**, 40–51 (2017)

20. Mundnich, K., et al.: Tiles-2018: a longitudinal physiologic and behavioral data set of hospital workers. arXiv preprint arXiv:2003.08474 (2020)

21. Novak, D., et al.: Morphology analysis of physiological signals using hidden Markov models. In: Proceedings of the 17th International Conference on Pattern Recognition, ICPR 2004, vol. 3, pp. 754–757. IEEE (2004)

22. Pierson, E., Althoff, T., Leskovec, J.: Modeling individual cyclic variation in human behavior. In: 2018 World Wide Web Conference, pp. 107–116 (2018)

23. Rodell, J.B., Judge, T.A.: Can "good" stressors spark "bad" behaviors? the mediating role of emotions in links of challenge and hindrance stressors with citizenship and counterproductive behaviors. J. Appl. Psychol. **94**(6), 1438 (2009)

24. Rogge, R.: The multidimensional psychological flexibility inventory (MPFI), May 2016. https://doi.org/10.13140/RG.2.1.1645.9129

25. Saunders, J.B., Asaland, O.G., Babor, T.F., la Fuente, J.R.D., Grant, M.: Development of the alcohol use disorders identification test (AUDIT): WHO collaborative project on early detection of persons with harmful alcohol consumption-II. Addiction **89**(6), 791–804 (1993)

26. Spielberger, C.D., Jacobs, G.A., Russell, S., Crane, R.S.: Assessment of anger: the state-trait anger scale. In: Advances in Personality Assessment. Erlbaum, Hillsdale, New Jersey (1983)

27. Tavabi, N., Bartley, N., Abeliuk, A., Soni, S., Ferrara, E., Lerman, K.: Characterizing activity on the deep and dark web. arXiv preprint arXiv:1903.00156 (2019)

28. Thibaux, R., Jordan, M.I.: Hierarchical beta processes and the Indian buffet process. In: Artificial Intelligence and Statistics, pp. 564–571 (2007)

29. Von Luxburg, U.: A tutorial on spectral clustering. Stat. Comput. **17**(4), 395–416 (2007)

30. Wang, R., et al.: Studentlife: assessing mental health, academic performance and behavioral trends of college students using smartphones. In: 2014 ACM International Joint Conference on Pervasive and Ubiquitous Computing, pp. 3–14 (2014)

31. Ware Jr., J.E., Sherbourne, C.D.: The MOS 36-item short-form health survey (SF-36): I. Conceptual framework and item selection. Med. Care, 473–483 (1992)

32. Watson, D., Clark, L.A., Tellegen, A.: Development and validation of brief measures of positive and negative affect: the PANAS scales. J. Pers. Soc. Psychol. **54**(6), 1063 (1988)

33. Wu, L., Yen, I.E.H., Yi, J., Xu, F., Lei, Q., Witbrock, M.: Random warping series: a random features method for time-series embedding. arXiv preprint arXiv:1809.05259 (2018)

The Rise and Fall of Humanitarian Citizen Initiatives: A Simulation-Based Approach

Erika Frydenlund[1](✉) ⓘ, Jose Padilla[1], Hanne Haaland[2], and Hege Wallevik[2]

[1] Old Dominion University – VMASC, Suffolk, VA 23435, USA
efryden1@odu.edu
[2] University of Agder, Kristiansand, Norway

Abstract. Citizen Initiatives for Global Solidarity (CIGS) are small, ad hoc, volunteer organizations that arise in certain humanitarian and development contexts. They operate outside of traditional aid structures and may or may not cooperate with traditional government and nongovernmental organizations. Using agent-based modeling, we derive narrative-based, qualitative scenarios from simulation data to extend the theoretical discussions of CIGS as a phenomenon. The scenarios allow further discussion of the role that CIGS may play as development and humanitarian response actors outside of the traditional context-specific descriptions of CIGS that permeate the development literature. We find that scenarios generated from the simulation data align somewhat with the qualitative researchers' field observations, specifically in describing conditions under which some types of CIGS thrived while others failed. The points of departure from the model scenarios generated a dialogue that promises to further the theoretical and conceptual development of a generalizable framework for understanding CIGS as a phenomenon, which has been lacking in the field where most insights have been generated from country-specific, small sample case studies.

Keywords: Citizen initiatives · Humanitarianism · Agent-based modeling · Ethnography

1 Introduction

Citizens mobilizing volunteer efforts to address social justice and humanitarian issues is not new, yet globalization forces and the impacts of crowdfunding platforms that allow more people to travel the world and mobilize resources has led to an uptick in the number of these individual-level efforts. What we call Citizen Initiatives for Global Solidarity (CIGS) are small-scale, agile, adaptive, resource-mobilizing projects which may consist of anywhere from one individual to a few dozen organized volunteers [1]. While this can have positive impacts on the humanitarian and development landscapes as the initiatives rapidly adapt and respond to emergent needs, they may also impede stable, longer-term aid environments as they operate outside and out of sync with larger, traditional nongovernmental organizations (NGOs) such as the United Nations [2–5]. We observe these initiatives quickly arise in a variety of ways, including tourists who

© Springer Nature Switzerland AG 2020
R. Thomson et al. (Eds.): SBP-BRiMS 2020, LNCS 12268, pp. 255–265, 2020.
https://doi.org/10.1007/978-3-030-61255-9_25

stumble accidentally into a humanitarian volunteer career [2]. Just as quickly as they arise, however, many simply disappear due to lack of funding, experience, and/or stamina for the intense pressures of providing humanitarian aid.

Our research centers on understanding the role that these citizen initiatives play in the context of humanitarian crisis and development. In this paper, we focus on our efforts to explicitly define the context in which CIGS emerge and either thrive or fail. Most studies of CIGS are country-specific case studies that have not undergone a rigorous metanalysis to resolve disparate perspectives and competing explanations for the phenomenon [2, 6–8]. As a multidisciplinary team—two development ethnographers (the Subject Matter Experts (SMEs)), a computational social science and refugee studies researcher, and an engineering and simulation expert—we are attempting to develop a generalizable theory of the emergence, rise, and fall of CIGS in humanitarian and development contexts. This requires a step outside the traditionally means of researching CIGS, their relationships, and impacts and finding a structure that can accommodate and explore the many competing ideas about CIGS in one framework. For this, we turn to simulation models that we have iteratively designed from conceptual and theoretical development to qualitative data collection and field observations. This paper presents the next step in our multidisciplinary journey: the use of co-designed simulation models to generate scenarios that inform new research questions and deeper exploration of the existing characterizations and theories about CIGS and their environments.

2 Methodology

Inspired by the iterative Modeling and Simulation System Development Framework (MS-SDF) [9], our team has conducted a number of multidisciplinary meetings—three in Greece, two in Norway, two in the US, and many others virtually—to build trust and understanding and to advance from the initial field observations to the simulation scenarios presented in this paper (Fig. 1). This simulation approach breaks down the modeling process into steps starting with reference modeling to establish all assumptions and relationships, then conceptual modeling to formalize the factors, actors, and mechanisms of the phenomenon, to then produce a simulation; each step is revisited to further refine the model and incorporate subject matter expertise. The first iterative phase—from fieldwork to reference model to questions and back—was summarized in an earlier paper [10]. The current paper presents the work highlighted in the dashed-border box in Fig. 1, where we move from questions to scenarios. These scenarios, as presented later, give rise to more questions and plans for future qualitative data collection in the field.

To facilitate these multidisciplinary team meetings, the modelers elicited from ethnographers narratives to describe, from their vantage point, the actors and dynamics of CIGS in humanitarian crisis and development. As ethnographers, much of their data was recorded in physical notebooks by hand of the observations they made in-country over several years and the notes from semi-structured interviews and fieldwork observations in Lesvos. They relied on these data to drive this conversation, which ultimately led to the model specification presented here. This model was implemented as an agent-based model and simulated to generate quantitative values for team-identified factors. A quantitative analysis of these results was then translated into qualitative, narrative-based scenarios for the qualitative team members to review and use to reflect on their field observations. These reflections have in turn generated new modeling, theoretical, and empirical questions for which researchers will return to the data collection and reference modeling phases. The following sections describe the model and process for generating insights from these qualitative, narrative-based scenarios.

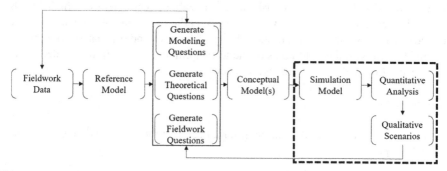

Fig. 1. Transdisciplinary process for iterative simulation model development involving qualitative fieldwork based on MS-SDF

3   Model Specification

The origins of this model lie in the authors' mutual connection and efforts to conduct qualitative fieldwork in Lesvos, Greece since 2016 on different aspects of the European Refugee Crisis. Looking at the specific phenomenon of CIGS across the island in response to the humanitarian crisis, the team generated the following model characterization:

- Model:

  - Input: variables that allow for adjustment of the regeneration of each of CIGS, needs, and NGOs in the system.
  - Output: how many needs go *unfulfilled*; how many needs are *in-progress*; how many *fulfilled-needs* have been completed; and how many *failed-CIGS* have "died" out of the system.

- Agent types: CIGS, needs, funding (derived from the SMEs)
- Agent attributes: (derived from conversations with the SMEs)

  - CIGS: have *expertise* available to address a need; *time-available* before resources/funding run out; *risk-profile* strategy that explains how they determine the need/cause to pursue; *unemployed* to capture how long they will go before they "die" from the system; *cause* that they are currently addressing (if any).

- Needs: have a *need-size* which helps potential organizations assess whether they can tackle that need based on the funding they have; a random, heterogeneous value for the *time-required-to-complete* to show how difficult the need is to address.
- Funding: has a random, heterogeneous *funding-amount* that they can give to CIGS that ask them for funds.

This is a very simple model to describe a generalizable environment in which "needs" are not differentiated by specific type or for a specific environment. The simplicity of the model was preserved to ensure traceability of features and translation to narratives that might align with the field notes of the team's ethnographers. In the model, agents behave according to the following pseudocode:

● CIGS:

- Move around the "world" searching for a need that they can tackle based on their *risk-profile* strategy.

  ● There are two risk profiles in the current model. Type (1) CIGS will only pursue a need that they find if it requires less than the funding *and* the experience possessed by that CIGS. Type (2) CIGS will pursue a need if it requires less than its funding *and* experience *or* has other CIGS already working on it from which the inexperienced CIGS can gain additional experience.
  ● If their funding is insufficient to find a need to tackle, pursue funding

- Co-locate with the chosen need/*cause* and begin to "fulfill" this need by expending resources.

● Needs:

- Decrement *time-required-to-complete* variable until zero based on the number of organizations working on the need.
- When the *time-required-to-complete* = 0, give *expertise* to participating CIGS and then die.

● Funding:

- Give CIGS a certain amount of money when they ask for it and decrement bank accordingly.
- Regenerate funds at a certain rate
- If funds = 0, die.

The user is able to input the starting and replacement values for CIGS, Needs, and Funding. Needs are created regularly, but new funding and CIGS only occur when there are outstanding unfulfilled needs. All agent types in the model are heterogeneous across all variables in the specification of attributes above.

4 Scenario Development and Evaluation

The Citizen Initiatives for Global Solidarity (CIGS) model was developed to facilitate concept development rather than predict the outcome of a particular grassroots movement. Inspired by the teams' qualitative observations in Lesvos, Greece during the humanitarian crisis, the model is the product of efforts between ethnographers and simulation modelers. The quantitative analysis of simulation runs, however, has very little value for the ethnographers, who want to see the model in terms that they can relate to their field notes from various contexts in which they have observed CIGS emerge, perform, and thrive or fail. To that end, we used statistical analysis of the simulation runs to construct narrative-based scenarios which we then shared with each of the ethnographers. This involved extracting statistically significant relationships between the six variables and translating these into statements about the environment, outcomes in terms of humanitarian needs being addressed, and the emergence and failure of CIGS.

Given the six variables at three levels, of course the simulation generated 729 possible "scenarios," many of which were qualitatively indistinguishable. We used exploratory statistical analyses to determine which factors at which levels were significant in order to narrow down the field of possible scenarios for the ethnographers to assess. We further used genetic algorithms to search the parameter space for particular outcomes in the measured model variables [11], such as maximizing the number of needs in-progress, which additionally helped to generate scenarios. For the current study, we focused on five scenarios, three reflecting "high-need" and two "low-need" scenarios. Table 1 summarizes some of the regression models used to predict the number of unfulfilled needs in the model at various starting need levels.

Table 1. Regression with dependent variable: unfulfilled needs.

Needs	Low	Medium	High
Funder start	−0.983	1.112	−0.696
CIGS start	5.897***	4.627***	5.258***
Funder replacement	−8.265*	−8.224*	−12.055***
Needs replacement	98.799***	101.971***	101.062***
CIGS replacement	−74.800***	−81.280***	−80.596***
Adj R-sq	0.742	0.783	0.778

Significance: *<0.05; **<0.01; ***<0.001

These lead to some obvious connections that align with our respective field experiences, namely that the more CIGS there are, the fewer unfulfilled needs and the higher needs are generated in the system, the more that go unfulfilled. Interestingly, the higher the number of CIGS at the start of the simulation, the higher the unfulfilled needs. It is not clear at this time why this would be and is an area for further investigation. After discussion with the research team, one possible reason for the phenomenon may result from the lack of coordination and experience of CIGS at the start, leading to a high number of unmet needs. The ethnographers suggested this reflects some of the initial stages of humanitarian response in Lesvos, where many volunteers/CIGS founders who had taken holidays in Greece had a proximity and familiarity with the context and thus were able to emerge very early. These initiatives lacked coordination where CIGS were operating in parallel and catering to the same needs, but with different approaches, and not necessarily with a holistic view of migrants' needs outside of their vantage points.

Table 2 summarizes a regression of factors to predict the number of in-progress needs in the system. We also tracked the types of CIGS based on the particular strategy they employ. Of interest here is the finding that an increase in Strategy 1 type CIGS leads to a decline of in-progress needs, while an increase in Strategy 2 leads to an increase. In other words, those who adopt a strategy of partnering with others when they do not have experience increases the number of ongoing projects by CIGS across the whole system. This finding is another that we plan to explore more deeply in future iterations, since the team has not discussed in detail the strategies of organizations addressing needs in humanitarian or development contexts in the real-world. The two findings we cannot explain serve as a good example of how simulation feeds back into new questions for future fieldwork or theory development.

Table 2. Regression with dependent variable: in-progress needs.

Needs	Low	Medium	High
Average time required of unfulfilled	-0.756^{***}	-0.902^{***}	-0.993^{***}
Average need size of unfulfilled	2.810^{***}	4.037^{***}	5.326^{***}
Fulfilled needs	0.182^{***}	0.178^{***}	0.184^{***}
CIGS Strategy 1 working	-0.218^{***}	-0.181^{***}	-0.197^{***}
CIGS Strategy 1 failed	0.024	-0.020	0.106^{**}
CIGS Strategy 2 working	0.152^{***}	0.133^{***}	0.122^{***}
CIGS Strategy 2 failed	0.028	0.087^{*}	-0.025
Adj R-sq	0.901	0.783	0.778

Significance: *<0.05; **<0.01; ***<0.001

It should be noted here that the simulation generated conditions that we characterized as "humanitarian"—meaning large numbers of urgent needs with low funding and experience requirements to initially address and "development"—by which we meant a low but steady volume of needs that had more funding and experience requirements. For the purposes of this paper, though the ethnographers have observed CIGS in both humanitarian and development contexts, we restrict our reporting to just the humanitarian context for which the modelers and ethnographers share field experience. Below are two scenarios (simplified for brevity) and the ethnographers' mapping of these scenarios to their own field observations. For this preliminary attempt to characterize models with ethnographers, we worked only with two—who are co-authors of this paper— using individual email interactions. The long-term goal of the team is to further develop this method of modeling and share it with the broader CIGS scholarly, and possibly practitioner, community for more feedback to establish consensus about the findings. Each ethnographer was presented with the "simulation-based conditions" below, and the characterization is a summary of their responses.

4.1 Humanitarian Crisis Onset Scenario

Simulation-Based Conditions: The population has a high number of needs that are going unfulfilled and needs are increasing quickly. These needs do not require much time or expertise to fulfill. The funding environment is moderately favorable. Organizations have difficulty thriving (few start; high failure rate) and rarely work together to accomplish their goals.

Ethnographer Characterization: This scenario seems to correspond with the first phase of the Lesvos crisis, as seen in 2015 when thousands of refugees arrived every day by boat to Lesvos, using the island as an entry point to Europe. Volunteers came in high numbers to help refugees and local and international CIGS rapidly emerged. They helped with basic needs such as food, water, and shelter; some also helped with transporting refugees from the shores to central transit points. CIGS/volunteers worked side by side with the local population which also formed CIGS. Some of these local initiatives were, after some time, very good at coordinating their efforts; we aren't so sure whether the foreign CIGS coordinated to the same extent. The UN refugee agency (UNHCR) came late to the island as did the large humanitarian NGOs often assisting in crisis. Thus the funding and action from within the established humanitarian apparatus was a bit slow. The CIGS, however, got funding from everyday citizens for their work towards immediate needs. Not all contributions were equally valuable; in the early stage of the crisis, CIGS uncritically distributed clothes unfit to culture and context.

4.2 Humanitarian Crisis Stabilization Phase Scenario

Simulation-Based Conditions: The population has a high number of needs, but the vast majority are being fulfilled, albeit at a very slow pace. Thus, needs are high but sustaining without rapidly increasing. Most ongoing needs require a large time and funding investment and significant expertise to tackle. Many CIGS are tackling the same issues, gaining expertise from each other. A large number of needs have gone unfulfilled, but there is high turnover: there are many active CIGS, but also many have failed.

Ethnographer Characterization: Based on our own field work and knowledge of the situation from 2016 onwards, this scenario fits with late 2015, early 2016, when the UNHCR is in place, camps are established, and needs beyond food and shelter are met through larger organizations. CIGS team up with the establishment (i.e. government) as they are not yet acknowledged by larger NGOs. Some of them are, however, acknowledged by the local government which is forming partnerships with the ones focusing on service provision. In this scenario the local government is rather reluctant towards those CIGS advocating for systemic and political change as part of their work. In fact, they think they should go elsewhere with their activities. The "banana girl initiatives"[1] die out and many volunteers go to the larger CIGS established early on in the crisis and which have gained experience and continuously develop their activities to the situation. Organizations that focus on helping refugees on their way to the mainland either change their activity or stop operating/become dormant. For CIGS that responded during the onset of crisis, that scenario became a training ground for volunteers who gained skills and insights in order to identify emerging needs. Those CIGS become important in the next phase of the crisis in setting up the new initiatives for activities (sports, training, legal help, education, etc.) rather than basic needs. These organizations generally keep the refugees active and engaged in a situation where waiting for asylum adjudications has become a new dimension of their stay in the host country.

4.3 Scenario Development as Evaluation

In this particular stage of our model development, we generated very general scenarios—two of which were provided above as examples—that the two ethnographers were asked to look at only with the prompt "give some thoughts on what you see and/or what comes to mind." They noted that the scenarios are very general, but being so general, they are also fairly applicable to a number of instances from the field they recall. This serves as a trigger for thoughts and discussion about what is really perceived as "needs" by whom and what types of approaches to addressing needs occurs in different contexts (e.g. humanitarian vs. development).

The ethnographers noted that it was easier to translate the humanitarian-based scenarios than the development ones (not included in this article) with regards to their field notes and experiences. This may be because the definition of "needs" is clearer in a humanitarian crisis situation, which is also very context specific. After seeing the simulation scenarios, they pondered how needs are really perceived in the development context, noting (personal communication, 27 February 2020),

From the CIGS donors' point of view, I would argue, needs are initially identified from the context of a particular individual. That is, the emotional first encounter with a particular person makes the donor identify needs among certain individuals, which forms the basis of their initial projects. This is different from the crisis situation. With so many people arriving, the individual disappears, and needs are seen and acted upon in terms of groups.

Working through the simulation-generated scenarios, the ethnographers began to discuss how needs differ in different situations, and what kinds of organizations grew out of these conditions. Of importance for the next phase of development is a question that arose about "CIGS failure" versus CIGS "becoming dormant." These organizations

---

[1] "banana girls" is a term local to the ad-hoc NGO environment in Lesvos, Greece used to describe the influx of tourists-turned-volunteers who generated donation money online, usually through crowdfunding, and only wanted to be the ones who pull refugees from the water or give them their first meals or other highly visible activities. Other needs that were less visible, such as preparing food in the kitchen or washing dirty clothes, did not attract as many of these accidental volunteers.

are observed in the real-world, later activating to answer particular needs, but cannot emerge in the model after they "die." The qualitative researchers are currently reflecting on when and how organizations reactivate after dormancy and to what extent this changes the nature of their involvement in aid. These are questions that require the collection of more empirical data.

The exercise of developing scenarios from the simulation offers several insights. First, the ethnographers' description of their interpretation of the scenario and its relevance to field observations and qualitative assessments of real-world organizations provides some recognition that, without directly coding scenarios into the model, the simulation produces recognizable outcomes. This could, on a larger scale where we engage more CIGS researchers and stakeholders who were not involved in the model design, be one form of validation that we plan to pursue in the future.

Second, the ethnographers drew their own insights simply from seeing their research presented in these very general terms. We have shared methodological insights on this phenomenon of transdisciplinary research efforts previously, illustrating how modeling-thinking and design aid qualitative researchers in exploring their data in new ways to ask new questions and inspire future data collection and analysis efforts [10]. The ethnographers on our team have described the usefulness of seeing their data through the eyes of simulation modelers to allow them to see where data exists and where it does not, which stimulates further questions, inspires new fieldwork, and sometimes even seeds doubts about their findings (in a productive way). The types of questions modelers ask about factors and their relationships while designing the model help the ethnographers make new connections and see patterns they may not have noticed before. Continued engagement through the use of models as a *lingua franca* across disciplines has already generated new research questions, such as those about CIGS dormancy and differentiation of needs in different environments, that will further enhance the model's ability to capture a generalizable conceptualization of CIGS.

5 Discussion and Future Research

The authors of this paper have been engaged in a multi-year, multidisciplinary effort to use simulation in order to advance social science theory. This relationship has evolved into an effort to let simulation results lead the next phase of critical analysis of field observations and other qualitative and quantitative data on CIGS. The feedback provided by the ethnographers serves not only as insight into potential means to validate this type of social science model, but also to generate new questions that will improve the model and further investigations into CIGS. We see these questions as two-fold.

First, methodologically, how can we better distill and present simulation findings in ways that engage social science researchers to reflect on their own observations without providing so much detail that the scenario descriptions bias their interpretations? How might these advances help us to qualitatively evaluate the validity of simulations for which there are only small-sample, qualitative data available? Of course, there is ongoing dialogue in the literature about the ways qualitative research and simulation can be more effectively joined [12–14]. We plan to pursue research to determine how a small social science community like that studying CIGS would be able to engage in simulation development in ways that will enrich the theoretical development of the topic. For our team, this also means increasing the type and mechanisms for collaboration as we move into the next iterative development loop in Fig. 1, which is a return to questions and data to generate further model development and theoretical insights.

Second, the exercise of seeing the ethnographers' interpretations of the simulation scenarios in terms of their own field observations and theoretical understanding has revealed specification issues in our original reference model where we defined our assumptions, terminology, and the environment surrounding CIGS. We need to move forward by further characterizing what "needs" are in this environment, how different needs change CIGS behaviors, and what other strategies CIGS might employ to "survive" in a humanitarian or development context (including dormancy). Additionally, while this paper has focused on the humanitarian scenarios for the sake of brevity, the development scenarios generated several questions about how these environments are actually different and what that means for the rise and fall of CIGS.

Further, we see the application of CIGS in new ways after evaluating the simple algorithms that lead to relatively realistic simulations of the rise and fall of CIGS. Specifically, the model has helped us to think more about what purpose CIGS serve (or could serve) in responding to crisis when governments and larger NGOs cannot be agile or adaptive enough. In this way, CIGS may fit within a larger conversation on resilience. If we consider adaptability as one of the "three critical features of resilience" [15], CIGS are the first manifestation of adaptive resilience in a humanitarian situation. When people mobilize to attend to others during crises and form associations that later evolve into organized and semi-permanent groups, this showcases an organic, decentralized effort of self-organization which potentially speaks to the capacity of a region to adjust without pre-planning. As such, the rise of CIGS becomes an indicator of a society's capacity to adapt through citizen self-organization.

In the context of this research, this adaptation seems triggered when, in the right environment, a large demand for humanitarian needs are left unfulfilled by traditional government and nongovernmental agencies. Citizens respond by volunteering and/or raising funds to meet what they perceive to be unmet needs of the community. The citizen initiatives can act in concert with the larger community needs and within the community's norms of charity and humanitarianism, or they can be in discord with traditional actors such as the government, NGOs, or even the public sentiment. By further exploring the role that CIGS play in enhancing response, as well as determining how the environment becomes intolerant of CIGS, we expect to gain insight into how self-organizing citizens fit within the larger humanitarian governance architecture to bolster community resilience and contribute to social stability.

Acknowledgements. This material, in part, was funded by project seed funds from the University of Agder in Norway.

This material, in part, was funded by a grant through the Office of Naval Research under the Minerva Research Initiative under agreement number N00014-19-1-2624. The U.S. Government is authorized to reproduce and distribute reprints for Governmental purposes notwithstanding any copyright notation thereon. The views and conclusions contained herein are those of the authors and should not be interpreted as necessarily representing the official policies or endorsements, either expressed or implied, of the Office of Naval Research.

References

1. Schulpen, L., Huyse, H.: Citizen initiatives for global solidarity. The new face of European solidarity. Forum Dev. Stud. **44**(2), 163–169 (2017)
2. Haaland, H., Wallevik, H.: Citizens as actors in the development field: the case of an accidental aid-agent's activities in aid-land. Forum Dev. Stud. **44**(2), 203–222 (2017)
3. Haaland, H., Wallevik, H.: Beyond crisis management? The role of Citizen Initiatives for Global Solidarity in humanitarian aid: the case of Lesvos. Third World Q. **40**(10), 1869–1883 (2019)
4. Kinsbergen, S., Schulpen, L., Ruben, R.: Understanding the sustainability of private development initiatives: what kind of difference do they make? Forum Dev. Stud. **44**(2), 223–248 (2017)
5. Schnable, A.: New American relief and development organizations: voluntarizing global aid. Soc. Probl. **62**(2), 309–329 (2015)
6. Kinsbergen, S.: Behind the pictures: understanding private development initiatives. Radboud University Nijmegen (2014)
7. Pollet, I., Van Ongevalle, J.: The Drive to Global Citizenship.: Motivating people, Mapping public support, Measuring effects of global education. Maklu (2013)
8. Oikonomakis, L.: Solidarity in transition: the case of Greece. In: della Porta, D. (ed.) Solidarity Mobilizations in the 'Refugee Crisis'. PSEPS, pp. 65–98. Springer, Cham (2018). https://doi.org/10.1007/978-3-319-71752-4_3
9. Tolk, A., et al.: Reference modelling in support of M&S: foundations and application. J. Simul. **7**(2), 69–82 (2013)
10. Padilla, J.J., Frydenlund, E., Wallewik, H., Haaland, H.: Model co-creation from a modeler's perspective: lessons learned from the collaboration between ethnographers and modelers. In: Thomson, R., Dancy, C., Hyder, A., Bisgin, H. (eds.) SBP-BRiMS 2018. LNCS, vol. 10899, pp. 70–75. Springer, Cham (2018). https://doi.org/10.1007/978-3-319-93372-6_8
11. Lambrecht, M.R., et al.: Active nonlinear tests (ants) of complex simulation models. Manage. Sci. **44**(6), 820–830 (1998)
12. Edmonds, B.: A context- and scope-sensitive analysis of narrative data to aid the specification of agent behaviour. J. Artif. Soc. Soc. Simul. **18**(1), 17 (2015)
13. Poile, C., Safayeni, F.: Using computational modeling for building theory: a double edged sword. J. Artif. Soc. Soc. Simul. **19**(3), 8 (2016)
14. Yang, L., Gilbert, N.: Getting away from numbers: using qualitative observation for agent-based modeling. Adv. Complex Syst. **11**(2), 175–185 (2008)
15. Béné, C., et al.: Resilience, poverty and development. J. Int. Dev. **26**(5), 598–623 (2014)

Developing an Epidemiological Model to Study Spread of Toxicity on YouTube

Adewale Obadimu[✉][iD], Esther Mead[iD], Maryam Maleki[iD],
and Nitin Agarwal[iD]

University of Arkansas at Little Rock, Little Rock, AR 72204, USA
{amobadimu,elmead,mmaleki,nxagarwal}@ualr.edu

Abstract. The increased global salience of social media has fueled the propagation of various forms of toxicity. As digital technologies and interactive websites proliferate, cyberspace has become a venue through which toxic users torment their victims. Numerous platforms are trying to combat this phenomenon by training computational methods that are capable of automatically recognizing these toxic contents and removing them from the user-generated text on their platforms. However, given the immensity and speed of content posted on online platforms, identifying and deterring these behaviors at scale remains challenging. Aiming to address this challenge, in this paper, we describe a novel approach to understand and explain the spread of toxicity on YouTube by using well-known epidemic models. Our underlying hypothesis is that the spread of toxicity on YouTube is comparable to the spread of disease. Since mathematical epidemiology has been widely studied, being able to express the spread of toxicity as an epidemic model will enable us to use a wide range of tools and techniques that have been proven to be analytically rich and operationally useful. We leveraged the YouTubeTracker application to extract comments on YouTube. We then employed Google's Perspective API to assign a toxicity score to each comment. The results of our analysis show that our approach can be fruitfully combined with other strategies to moderate the spread of toxicity on online platforms.

Keywords: Social network analysis · Toxicity analysis · Social contagion

This research is funded in part by the U.S. National Science Foundation (OIA-1946391, OIA-1920920, IIS-1636933, ACI-1429160, and IIS-1110868), U.S. Office of Naval Research (N00014-10-1-0091, N00014-14-1-0489, N00014-15-P-1187, N00014-16-1-2016, N00014-16-1-2412, N00014-17-1-2605, N68335-19-C-0359, N00014-17-1-2675, N00014-19-1-2336, N68335-20-C-0540), U.S. Air Force Research Lab, U.S. Army Research Office (W911NF-16-1-0189), U.S. Defense Advanced Research Projects Agency (W31P4Q-17-C-0059), Arkansas Research Alliance, the Jerry L. Maulden/Entergy Endowment at the University of Arkansas at Little Rock, and the Australian Department of Defense Strategic Policy Grants Program (SPGP) (award number: 2020-106-094). Any opinions, findings, and conclusions or recommendations expressed in this material are those of the authors and do not necessarily reflect the views of the funding organizations. The researchers gratefully acknowledge the support.

ⓒ Springer Nature Switzerland AG 2020
R. Thomson et al. (Eds.): SBP-BRiMS 2020, LNCS 12268, pp. 266–276, 2020.
https://doi.org/10.1007/978-3-030-61255-9_26

1   Introduction

Technological advancements in recent years have transformed the traditional constructs of human communication. The proliferation of smart devices and mobile applications, which provide unprecedented access to digital information, have necessitated additional theoretical consideration to encompass our modern information-centric society [1]. Enhanced by multimedia and hyperlinks that help convey a personal message, cyberspace has created an optimal opportunity for communicators to share intimate and sensitive issues in a typical pattern that is intensified by reciprocity [2]. Although, online social interactions are now becoming a familiar part of modern society due to their numerous benefits [3], malicious actors (hereafter referred to as toxic users) often hide under the auspices of anonymity to perpetuate their pernicious acts [4]. In this study, similar to extant literature, we give an operational definition of toxicity as "the usage of rude, disrespectful, or unreasonable language that will likely provoke or make another user leave a discussion" [4–6]. Therefore, in this regard, toxicity analysis is different from sentiment analysis, which is the attempt to assign sentiment scores of positive, neutral, and negative to text data.

Toxicity is an important problem that is seriously affecting the dynamics and usefulness of online social interactions [4]. The *online disinhibition effect*[1] [7] and the relative anonymity that social media provides makes it a fertile ground for the propagation of various forms of toxicity. According to a report by the Pew Research Center, 41% of Americans have been the target of online harassment, a modest increase from the 35% of adults who were targets of online harassment in the Center's 2014 report on the topic [8]. In another journalistic account by The Guardian in 2013, a 12-year-old girl committed suicide after being targeted by cyberbullying [9]. In 2012, Charlotte Dawson, who at one time hosted the "Next Top Model" TV program in Australia, committed suicide after being targeted with malicious online comments [10]. Due to the growing concerns about the impact of online toxicity, many platforms are now taking several steps to curb this phenomenon [11]. For instance, on YouTube, a user can choose to activate the safety mode to filter out offensive language [4,11].

Despite the Internet's theoretical relevance to understanding the dynamics of the spread of toxicity on social media, scholarly research into its effects is scarce. Although a few studies have attested to the widespread manifestation of toxicity within comments on YouTube [4,11,12], there is still a dearth of systematic research concerning toxicity within the user-generated content on YouTube. With over 300 h of videos uploaded every minute, and 5 billion videos watched every single day, YouTube has become one of the most relevant platforms in the age of digital mass communication [13]. YouTube also allows the consumer of this digital content to interact with the content that resonates with them by utilizing the comments section. This capability has turned passive consumers into active actors of the content they enjoy - a major shift in online behavior.

---

[1] Online disinhibition is the lack of restraint one feels when communicating online in comparison to communicating in-person.

While the burden of access to such a large dataset has made a permanent extraction of toxic users challenging, understanding the dynamics of the spread of toxicity can enable us to systematically develop a richer and more robust model for understanding and preventing "toxic behaviors" on various online social media networks.

Some of the existing literature has already demonstrated that our emotional state depends not just on the actions and choices that we make, but also on the actions and choices of other people around us [14–16]. For instance, Fig. 1 depicts the contagion process of toxicity whereby a comment with an average toxicity instigated a more toxic reply. Emotions as diverse as happiness [14], loneliness [17], and depression [18] have already been shown to be contagious. However, despite the significant advances made within the past few decades on this topic, to the best of our knowledge, no research has been able to model the spread of toxicity from one individual to another. To address this gap, in this paper, we describe a mathematical model to explain how the commenting activity on YouTube can be described by using well-known epidemic models for infectious diseases. The epidemic model described in this paper is simple enough to be operationally useful and can also help us identify the factors that leads to the persistence and stability of toxicity on a specific YouTube video. Furthermore, the results obtained from this study will help us gain an understanding of the propagation of toxicity on YouTube.

Fig. 1. Contagion of toxic behavior on YouTube.

The remainder of this paper is set out as follows. In Sect. 2, we give a brief review of extant literature that are germane to our discussion. We then describe our methodology in Sect. 3. Finally, Sect. 4 provides the conclusions including the limitations of our work, and ideas for future work.

2   Literature Review

This section briefly describes the literature that is germane to our discussion. First, we discuss the literature concerning the identification of toxicity on social media. And, second, we discuss the literature concerning the use of epidemiological models.

2.1 Identifying Toxicity on Social Media

Zampieri et al. used SemEval-2019 to identify and categorize toxicity in social media using over 14,000 English tweets [19]. In another study, Aroyo et al. evaluated toxicity in online conversations using metrics such as "subjectivity", "bias", and "ambiguity" [20]. Hosseini et al. proposed an attack to a toxicity detection system using various adversarial examples [21]. The finding demonstrated that an adversary could influence the toxicity score of a highly toxic phrase such that it would ultimately be scored as being very low in toxicity. They showed that these adversarial examples can consistently decrease the toxicity score and can be harmful for toxicity detection systems. Another study analyzed the toxicity and sentiments presented by political parties of two countries in south Asia and their pattern in using Twitter [22]. They showed that there was toxicity in the political discussion of these two countries. Another study proposed and utilized a detector that could identify different types of toxicity in text content [23]. They used a dataset of Bulgarian news articles and classified them into different toxicity groups. They designed a separate model for each aspect type and then combined all models into a "meta-classifier".

2.2 Epidemiological Models

An epidemiological or epidemic model is a compartment model that divides a population into different groups. This division is the base and mathematical framework for the dynamics of epidemics. The simplest epidemic model is the SI model which divides the population into two different susceptible (S) and infected (I) compartments [24]. Moreover, the SI model can be considered as an SIS model that means that there is a possibility that when an individual is in the infected compartment, they can become susceptible again [25]. The SIR model, also known as the Kermack-McKendrick model [27], is the archetype and one of the most frequently used epidemic models [26]. This model typically tracks the flows of people between three compartments: susceptible (S), infected (I), and recovered (R). Epidemiological models are used in many subjects, such as news dissemination [28], and information diffusion, including rumors [30]. In one study, the SEIR model is used for information diffusion introducing an Exposed (E) state where individuals have a period of incubation before getting infected by others [31]. The SEIZ (susceptible, exposed, infected, skeptic) model was also used for modeling the spread of news and rumors on twitter [32]. In another study, an epidemiological model was used for fact-checking and misinformation in social media [33].

3   Methodology

Here we briefly describe the methodology employed in this work. First, we discuss our data collection process. Second, we describe the spread of toxicity on YouTube. And, third, we describe our model validation technique.

3.1   Data Collection

To build the dataset for illustrating our proposed method, we utilized the Google's perspective API [34] to compute the toxicity scores for comments in the YouTubeTracker [13] application. This API uses a Convolutional Neural Network (CNN) trained with word vector inputs to determine whether a comment could be perceived as "toxic" to a discussion. Table 1 is an excerpt of the resultant toxicity dataset where toxicity scores have been assigned to each comment by using Algorithm 1.

Table 1. Convenience sampling of five (5) toxic comments in our dataset.

S/N	Comment	Likes	Total replies	Overall toxicity
1	Tell the banksters to go f*ck themselves	62	133	0.97
2	Flat earth idiots unite!	235	134	0.95
3	What kind of c*nt do this to a child?	58	117	0.91
4	The EU must die	1539	135	0.93
5	F*cking Zionist government must be stopped!	131	105	0.94

Algorithm 1 Research methodology

Input: V : Video id
Output: R_0 : Spread of toxicity
    for each $v \in V$ **do**
        comments ←getAllComments(v)
        for each $c \in$ *comments* **do**
            data ← PerspectiveAPIRequest(c)
        end for
        Susceptible, Infected, Recovered ← STRS(v)
    end for
    function STRS(v)
        $\frac{dS}{dt} = -\beta S(t)T(t) + \mu R(t)$
        $\frac{dT}{dt} = \beta S(t)T(t) - \gamma T(t)$
        $\frac{dR}{dt} = \gamma T(t) - \mu R(t)$
        $R_0 = \beta N/\gamma$
    end function

3.2   Spread of Toxicity

To develop an epidemiology model for the spread of toxicity on YouTube, it is imperative to pick the right model and the corresponding parameters that paint a complete and realistic picture of the problem at hand. In our approach, we see a basic similarity between the spread of toxicity in YouTube comment threads and the spread of a "contagious disease". For instance, we can identify the following sets of individuals in the comments thread of a YouTube video at a steady state[2]:

---

[2] A steady state is a state in which dynamics no longer grow nor decline.

1. *Susceptible*: These are commenters that have replied with a non-toxic comment on a specific YouTube video.
2. *Toxic*: These are commenters that have posted toxic comments on a specific YouTube video.
3. *Recovered*: These are commenters that have posted non-toxic comments after some time of being exposed to a toxic comment.

Inspired by the work of Hethcote [29], we present the Susceptible-Toxic-Recovered-Susceptible (STRS) compartment model as shown in Fig. 2 where $S(t)$, $T(t)$, and $R(t)$ represent the number of individuals that are susceptible, toxic, and recovered at time t. The parameters λ, γ, and μ control how fast people move between each of the compartments. For instance, λ controls the rate of toxicity contagion per unit time. Similarly, γ governs the recovery rate per unit time and μ determines the rate at which a recovered individual becomes susceptible per unit time. The rate of change of susceptible, toxic and recovered

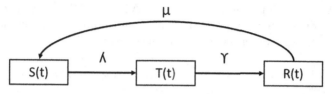

Fig. 2. The STRS model.

compartments over a certain period can be expressed with the following system of quadratic Ordinary Differential Equations (ODEs);

$$\frac{dS}{dt} = -\lambda S(t) + \mu R(t) \tag{1}$$

$$\frac{dT}{dt} = \lambda S(t) - \gamma T(t) \tag{2}$$

$$\frac{dR}{dt} = \gamma T(t) - \mu R(t) \tag{3}$$

In the equation above, $\frac{dS}{dt}$ implies that the susceptible compartment diminishes at the rate of $\lambda S(t)$. However, after some time, individuals in the recovered compartments can also become susceptible to toxicity once again, thereby joining the susceptible compartment. Similarly, for $\frac{dT}{dt}$, the $\lambda S(t)$ individuals that are exiting from the susceptible compartment are entering into the toxic compartment, and $\gamma I(t)$ individuals are exiting the toxic compartment into the recovered compartment. Since the toxicity rate is dependent on the likelihood of a susceptible commenter coming into contact with a toxic commenter (e.g., by reading and replying to a toxic comment on a specific YouTube video), then the rate of contagion of toxicity λ can be effectively expressed as;

$$\lambda = \beta T(t) \tag{4}$$

where β is the probability of an effective contact, i.e., the likelihood of a susceptible commenter replying to a toxic commenter. We can therefore rewrite Eq. (1), (2) and (3) as follows:

$$\frac{dS}{dt} = -\beta S(t)T(t) + \mu R(t) \tag{5}$$

$$\frac{dT}{dt} = \beta S(t)T(t) - \gamma T(t) \tag{6}$$

$$\frac{dR}{dt} = \gamma T(t) - \mu R(t) \tag{7}$$

Will the Spread of Toxicity Become an Epidemic on a Specific YouTube Video? Suppose S $\approx$ N, where $N(t) = S(t) + T(t) + R(t)$ and a small number of commenters start posting toxic comments on the video. Then toxicity will start spreading on that video whenever

$$\frac{dT}{dt} > 0 \iff \beta S(t)T(t) - \gamma T(t) > 0 \iff \beta N/\gamma > 1 \tag{8}$$

The value $\beta N/\gamma$ is the basic reproduction number, R_0, which is used to represent the expected number of toxic comments that will be directly generated by one toxic commenter on a video when that commenter first posted a toxic comment on the video. If the value of R_o is greater than 1, then toxicity will begin to spread on the video. Similarly, if the value of R_0 is less than 1, toxicity will start to shrink on the video. More intuitively, equation (8) implies that if the likelihood of interacting with a toxic commenter is very high or the recovery rate of a toxic commenter is very low, then toxicity will begin to spread.

3.3   Model Validation

To implement the STRS model, the values for the initial conditions, T_0, S_0 and R_0, along with the transition rate parameters between the compartments, β, γ, and μ need to be known. The steady states for our STRS model occurs when:

$$S = N, T = 0, R = 0 \tag{9}$$

$$T(t) = \frac{N - \frac{\gamma}{\beta}}{1 + \frac{\gamma}{\mu}} \tag{10}$$

As a proof of concept, we demonstrate the spread of toxicity by varying these transition rate parameters on one of the videos in the YouTubeTracker application. This particular video has 16,831 susceptible, 845 toxic, and 7 recovered commenters at steady state. Figure 3 illustrates the graph of a solved STRS model by showing the impact of β, γ, and μ on the video. The x-axis shows the duration

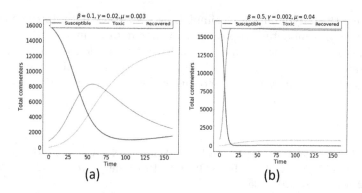

Fig. 3. Solutions of STRS system of ODEs. (a) shows the dynamics of toxicity when the toxicity rate is low. (b) shows an epidemic of toxicity when the toxicity rate is high (Color figure online)

of toxicity and the y-axis depicts the total commenters. In Fig. 3a, we reduced the rate of contact between a toxic and a susceptible commenter. Initially, the number of susceptible (blue) decreases as the number of toxic (red) increases. Gradually, the number of recovered (green) also increases. After a while, the recovered individuals start becoming susceptible again. Thereby increasing the number of susceptible commenters. In Fig. 3b we increased the effective rate of contact between a toxic and a susceptible commenter. As such, the rate of toxicity increases, thereby causing an epidemic of toxicity on this video. The epidemic of toxicity is evident by the number of recovered (green) remaining relatively low and stagnant.

4   Conclusions and Future Work

In this paper, we have demonstrated how toxicity can spread like an infectious disease on YouTube. We also presented the STRS model which can be used to model the spread of toxicity on YouTube. The observation from our analysis suggests that under certain circumstances, toxicity can spread from one individual to another. We are only beginning to scratch the surface and uncover some of the specific mechanisms of how toxicity can spread in online communities; however, this study is an important first step in this line of research. Although the description of several real-world problems often includes stochastic fluctuations, from a practical perspective, the proposed model could be used to understand the dynamics of toxicity among user comments on a YouTube video. For instance, if $R_0 > 1$ on a specific video, we can decrease the values of β by filtering out some toxic comments on the YouTube video, thereby reducing the rate at which susceptible commenters come into contact with toxic commenters. Another contribution of our work is that we describe the threshold that determines whether a toxicity epidemic will occur or fail on a YouTube video. This work will serve as a good step to open up a richer line of research on this topic. As of now, we are modeling these dynamics with simulations over static data. In the future, we plan to adapt this model for capturing real-time data by fitting other YouTube data to this model. Since the number of likes (in addition to comments) play an important role in bringing the comment to spotlight, we also plan to include this variable and conduct a more rigorous evaluation of our model.

References

1. Obadimu, A., Mead, E., Al-Khateeb, S., Agarwal, N.: A comparative analysis of Facebook and Twitter bots. In: SAIS 2019 Proceedings, vol. 25 (2019). https://aisel.aisnet.org/sais2019/25
2. Lapidot-Lefler, N., Barak, A.: The benign online disinhibition effect: could situational factors induce self-disclosure and prosocial behaviors? Cyberpsychol. J. Psychosoc. Res. Cyberspace 9(2) (2015)
3. O'Keeffe, G.S., Clarke-Pearson, K.: The impact of social media on children, adolescents, and families. Pediatrics 127(4), 800–804 (2011)
4. Obadimu, A., Mead, E., Hussain, M.N., Agarwal, N.: Identifying toxicity within YouTube video comment. In: Thomson, R., Bisgin, H., Dancy, C., Hyder, A. (eds.) SBP-BRiMS 2019. LNCS, vol. 11549, pp. 214–223. Springer, Cham (2019). https://doi.org/10.1007/978-3-030-21741-9_22
5. Martens, M., Shen, S., Iosup, A., Kuipers, F.: Toxicity detection in multiplayer online games. In: International Workshop on Network and Systems Support for Games (NetGames 2015) IEEE/ACM, December 2015, pp. 1–6 (2015). ISBN 978-1-5090-0068-5
6. Cheng, J., Bernstein, M., Danescu-Niculescu-Mizil, C., Leskovec, J.: Anyone can become a troll: causes of trolling behavior in online discussions. In: Proceedings of ACM Conference on Computer Supported Cooperative Work and Social Computing (CSCW17), ACM Press, February 2017, pp. 1217–1230. https://doi.org/10.1145/2998181.2998213
7. Suler, J.: The online disinhibition effect. Cyberpsychol. Behav. 7(3), 321–326 (2004)
8. https://www.pewresearch.org/internet/2017/07/11/experiencing-online-harassment/ . Accessed 8 Feb 2020
9. The Guardian. Florida cyberbullying: Girls arrested after suicide of Rebecca Sedwick, 12. The Guardian, 15 October 2013. http://www.theguardian.com/world/2013/oct/15/florida-cyberbullying-rebecca-sedwick-two-girls-arrested
10. Lee, S.H., Kim, H.W.: Why people post benevolent and malicious comments online. Commun. ACM 58(11), 74–79 (2015)
11. Obadimu, A., Mead, E., Agarwal, N.: Identifying latent toxic features on YouTube using non-negative matrix factorization. In: The Ninth International Conference on Social Media Technologies, Communication, and Informatics, IEEE (2019)
12. Chen, Y., Zhou, Y., Zhu, S., Xu, H.: Detecting offensive language in social media to protect adolescent online safety. In: 2012 International Conference on Privacy. Security, Risk and Trust and 2012 International Conference on Social Computing, Amsterdam, Netherlands, pp. 71–80. IEEE (2012)
13. Marcoux, T., Agarwal, N., Adewale, O., Hussain, M.N., Galeano, K.K., Khateeb, S.: Understanding information operations using YouTubeTracker. In: IEEE/WIC/ACM International Conference on Web Intelligence-Companion Volume, pp. 309–313, October 2019. https://doi.org/10.1145/3358695.3360917

14. Fowler, J.H., Christakis, N.A.: Dynamic spread of happiness in a large social network: longitudinal analysis over 20 years in the Framingham Heart Study. BMJ **337**, a2338 (2008)
15. Rosenquist, J.N., Murabito, J., Fowler, J.H., Christakis, N.A.: The spread of alcohol consumption behavior in a large social network. Ann. Internal Med. **152**(7), 426–433 (2010)
16. Christakis, N.A., Fowler, J.H.: The spread of obesity in a large social network over 32 years. N. Engl. J. Med. **357**(4), 370–379 (2007)
17. Cacioppo, J.T., Fowler, J.H., Christakis, N.A.: Alone in the crowd: the structure and spread of loneliness in a large social network. J. Pers. Soc. Psychol. **97**(6), 977 (2009)
18. Rosenquist, J.N., Fowler, J.H., Christakis, N.A.: Social network determinants of depression. Mol. Psychiatry **16**(3), 273–281 (2011)
19. Zampieri, M., Malmasi, S., Nakov, P., Rosenthal, S., Farra, N., Kumar, R.: SemEval-2019 Task 6: identifying and categorizing offensive language in social media (OffensEval). In: Proceedings of the 13th International Workshop on Semantic Evaluation, pp. 75–86, June 2019
20. Aroyo, L., Dixon, L., Thain, N., Redfield, O., Rosen, R.: Crowdsourcing subjective tasks: the case study of understanding toxicity in online discussions. In: Companion Proceedings of The 2019 World Wide Web Conference, pp. 1100–1105, May 2019
21. Hosseini, H., Kannan, S., Zhang, B., Poovendran, R.: Deceiving Google's perspective API built for detecting toxic comments (2017)
22. Qayyum, A., Gilani, Z., Latif, S., Qadir, J.: Exploring media bias and toxicity in South Asian political discourse. In: 2018 12th international conference on open source systems and technologies (ICOSST), pp. 01–08. IEEE, December 2018
23. Dinkov, Y., Koychev, I., Nakov, P.: Detecting toxicity in news articles: application to Bulgarian (2019)
24. Kabir, K.A., Kuga, K., Tanimoto, J.: Analysis of SIR epidemic model with information spreading of awareness. Chaos Solitons Fractals **119**, 118–125 (2019)
25. Liu, T., Li, P., Chen, Y., Zhang, J.: Community size effects on epidemic spreading in multiplex social networks. PLoS ONE **11**(3) (2016)
26. Nika, M.M.: Synthedemic modelling and prediction of internet-based phenomena (2014)
27. Kermack, W.O., McKendrick, A.G.: A contribution to the mathematical theory of epidemics. Proc. Roy. Soc. London Ser. A Containing Papers Math. Phys. Charact. **115**(772), 700–721 (1927)
28. Abdullah, S., Wu, X.: An epidemic model for news spreading on Twitter. In: 2011 IEEE 23rd International Conference on Tools with Artificial Intelligence, pp. 163–169. IEEE, November 2011
29. Hethcote, H.W.: Qualitative analyses of communicable disease models. Math. Biosci. **28**(3–4), 335–356 (1976)
30. Zhao, L., Cui, H., Qiu, X., Wang, X., Wang, J.: SIR rumor spreading model in the new media age. Physica A Stat. Mech. Appl. **392**(4), 995–1003 (2013)
31. Bettencourt, L.M., Cintrón-Arias, A., Kaiser, D.I., Castillo-Chávez, C.: The power of a good idea: quantitative modeling of the spread of ideas from epidemiological models. Physica A Stat. Mech. Appl. **364**, 513–536 (2006)
32. Jin, F., Dougherty, E., Saraf, P., Cao, Y., Ramakrishnan, N.: Epidemiological modeling of news and rumors on Twitter. In: Proceedings of the 7th Workshop on Social Network Mining and Analysis, pp. 1–9, August 2013

33. Tambuscio, M., Ruffo, G., Flammini, A., Menczer, F.: Fact-checking effect on viral hoaxes: a model of misinformation spread in social networks. In: Proceedings of the 24th International Conference on World Wide Web, pp. 977–982, May 2015
34. Perspective. http://perspectiveapi.com/

Predicting Student Flight Performance with Multimodal Features

Zerong Xi[1](✉) , Olivia Newton[1] , Greg McGowin[1] ,
Gita Sukthankar[1](✉) , Steve Fiore[1] , and Kevin Oden[2]

[1] University of Central Florida, Orlando, FL, USA
zxi@knights.ucf.edu, gitars@eecs.ucf.edu
[2] Lockheed Martin, Orlando, FL, USA

Abstract. This paper investigates the problem of predicting student flight performance in a training simulation from multimodal features, including flight controls, visual attention, and knowledge acquisition tests. This is a key component of developing next generation training simulations that can optimize the usage of student training time. Two types of supervised machine learning classifiers (random forest and support vector machines) were trained to predict the performance of twenty-three students performing simple flight tasks in virtual reality. Our experiments reveal the following: 1) features derived from gaze tracking and knowledge acquisition tests can serve as an adequate substitute for flight control features; 2) data from the initial portion of the flight task is sufficient to predict the final outcome; 3) our classifiers perform slightly better at predicting student failure than success. These results indicate the feasibility of using machine learning for early prediction of student failures during flight training.

Keywords: Intelligent training simulations · Supervised learning · Gaze tracking · Multimodal features · Pilot training

1 Introduction

The aim of our research is to monitor and track complex knowledge and skill acquisition by applying machine learning algorithms to a mixture of physiological and performance-based indicators extracted from pilot training sessions. As the complexity of aircraft cockpit operations increases, so does the risk of human error. With training this risk can be reduced immensely. Automating the delivery of instruction through the use of intelligent training simulations and commercially available virtual reality headsets may offer a scalable and cost effective solution for increasing the amount of training pilots receive. If the data collected during training can be leveraged to predict task performance using machine learning, both student and instructor training time can be allocated wisely.

Research supported by Lockheed Martin Co.

R. Thomson et al. (Eds.): SBP-BRiMS 2020, LNCS 12268, pp. 277–287, 2020.
https://doi.org/10.1007/978-3-030-61255-9_27

This paper describes a set of experiments conducted to evaluate the suitability of different machine learning paradigms for predicting student performance on simple flight tasks executed in virtual reality. Supervised machine learning has achieved notable successes across multiple domains including image and speech recognition. However these successes were achieved through the use of complex deep learning models which can only be effectively trained with huge training sets, due to the large number of parameters. For instance, one of most popular computer vision systems, ResNet-50 has over 23 million parameters that need to be fit from training data. Hence our study only considers machine learning models that can be trained on data from a relatively small number of students. To compensate for the limited number of training examples, we assume that it is possible to capture data from multiple modalities, including knowledge tests, user interface controls, and visual attention, to create a small but rich dataset of student interactions.

Experiments were conducted in the Prepar3D flight simulator, which was designed to deliver immersive, experiential learning for both professional and academic pilot skills training. Subjects wore an HTC Vive Pro VR headset, and visual attention data was collected from a built-in Tobii eye tracker. During a two hour period, novice subjects were trained to perform simple flight tasks in Prepar3D. Each flight task tested their ability to achieve a target direction, airspeed, and altitude while monitoring the correct instruments. Students were graded as successful if they were able to achieve and maintain the target direction, airspeed, and/or altitude.

We evaluated the accuracy and F_1 score of two supervised learning classifiers, random forest (RFC) and support vector machines (SVM), at predicting student success using different multimodal feature sets. This paper examines the following research questions:

- **RQ1**: are features derived from gaze tracking and knowledge tests an acceptable substitute for flight control features?
- **RQ2**: can data from the initial portion of the task be used to predict the final outcome?
- **RQ3**: is it possible to accurately predict student failure?

2   Related Work

There is a rich body of related work on predicting student performance [2,8], pilot monitoring [3,6], and leveraging visual attention features [4,5]. Much of the research on predicting student performance has been conducted over the time horizon of a semester long course, using assignment grades as features [8]. These student coursework features can be supplemented with Learning Management System (LMS) data collected from platforms such as Moodle. An LMS system can collect detailed data about student engagement, including clicks, edits, page views, and total time spent online. Disappointingly, a sizable study conducted by Conijn et al. [2] revealed little benefit was gained by adding LMS features to in-between knowledge assessment tests for creating early intervention systems to detect students at risk for course failure. Our research aims to predict performance over a significantly shorter time horizon (minutes rather than months). Rather than using click data, student attention is measured using a gaze tracking system.

Visual attention features have been employed to track many aspects of student cognition, including workload, mind wandering [5], and problem solving progress [7]. Peysakhovich et al. [6] endorsed eye tracking integration as a general tool for enhancing cockpit safety and highlighted both pilot training and performance analysis as fruitful application areas. Here we include features to represent both the visual attention distribution and gaze entropy [4] across cockpit instruments.

Within the machine learning community, there has been previous work on training classifiers on small datasets. Commonly used strategies include transfer learning and supplementing the dataset with synthetic training examples. Our classifiers were trained using the SMOTE [1] technique to create synthetic minority class examples to supplement our small, unbalanced dataset. The next section describes our data collection procedure.

3 Experiments

Experiments were conducted on 23 subjects recruited from the University of Central Florida. The participant pool consisted of 15 male (64%) and 8 female aged 18–29 (M = 19.5, SD = 2.4). The subjects are considered novice pilots as none of them has received any prior flight training. Most (87%) of the subjects report little or no familiarity with flight simulators, and most (78%) of them rate fair or less on their video expertise and report an average weekly video game playing of 7.5 h (SD = 8.4).

3.1 Procedure

The full timeline of the study is as follows:

- Informed consent process (5 min)
- Video game experience survey (5 min)
- Cognitive tasks (10 min)
- Training (15–20 min)
- Card sort I (5–10 min)
- Knowledge acquisition assessment (10–15 min)
- Flight simulator practice tasks (15 min)
- Card sort II (15–20 min)
- Flight simulator experimental tasks (15 min)
- Demographics survey (5 min)
- Study wrapup (5 min)

The training consisted of both text and images, and is organized into five sections: aircraft model; aircraft controls; flight maneuvers; flight instruments; simulator tasks. Participants are able to review the training materials at their own pace, and are free to move forward and backward through the materials but are instructed that they would not be able to return to any portion of the training once they began the testing session. Within the training, they receive conceptual information about the physics of flight, practical information for successful flight maneuver execution in the VR environment, and specific information about the flight simulator tasks used in the experiment.

During the testing session, subjects are tested on the concepts they learnt using a questionnaire consisting of 10 recall questions, 10 descriptive questions and 10 conceptual questions. An example question is "Attempting to ascend too quickly can result in the aircraft __". Data from the subject responses is encoded into knowledge mastery features to be used by the machine learning classifiers. Vectors $Q_i \in \{correct, incorrect\}^M, i = 1, 2, 3, ...$ are reported where i is the subject's ID and M is the number of questions. The time the subjects spend on each question and their confidence are reported as well.

During the simulation session, subjects perform nine practice tasks and then nine experimental tasks in virtual reality using the Prepar3D flight simulator. Each task consists of flying the aircraft to a target direction, altitude, airspeed, or combination of two, within a limited time. Table 1 presents a summary of the experimental tasks. To keep the task easier, the aircraft is initialized in the air, and subjects are not asked to perform takeoff or landings. During task execution, customized programs harvest aircraft status and gaze data as a time series.

Table 1. Scenario descriptions

Task ID	Time (seconds)	Difficulty	Initial direction (degrees)	Target direction (degrees)	Initial airspeed (mph)	Target airspeed (mph)	Initial altitude (feet)	Target altitude (feet)
1	60	Easy	180	270	130	NA	3000	NA
2	60	Easy	180	NA	130	80	3000	NA
3	60	Easy	180	NA	130	NA	3000	3500
4	80	Medium	180	90	130	NA	3000	3000
5	80	Medium	180	NA	130	80	3000	3000
6	80	Medium	180	NA	130	NA	3000	4000
7	100	Hard	180	270	130	NA	3000	1000
8	100	Hard	180	90	130	80	3000	NA
9	100	Hard	180	NA	130	80	3000	4000

3.2   Equipment

The following software and hardware are used in our experimental setup:

Qualtrics is a multimedia survey software platform that is used to administer experimental materials and collect participant responses in addition to interaction information (e.g.., time to submit a response or time spent viewing materials). We use the platform to administer training, our experimental measures of knowledge acquisition and mental models, and demographics and video game experience surveys.

Prepar3D is a 3-D flight simulator developed by Lockheed Martin Co. to deliver immersive, experiential learning for professional and academic pilot training programs. Subjects interact with Prepar3D using a Logitech G X56 H.O.T.A.S. RGB Throttle and Stick Simulation Controller. Using the customized tools developed with the SDK, we are able to extract both the aircraft status data and controller data directly from Prepar3D.

HTC Vive Pro is a virtual reality headset with a built-in Tobii eye tracker. It has a resolution of 1440 × 1600 per eye, a refresh rate 90 Hz, and a field of view of 110°. The built-in Tobii eye tracker has a gaze data output frequency 120 Hz, an accuracy of 0.5–1.1°, and a trackable field of view of 110°.

Qualtrics is used during the training and testing sessions, while the other tools are used during the flight simulation sessions.

3.3 Data Collection

While the subjects perform the flight simulator experimental tasks, time series data is collected from three sources:

1. aircraft status data including the aircraft's *geodesic coordinates* (degree), *altitude* (feet), *3-D orientation* (degrees) and *3-D velocity* (feet per second);
2. flight control data including the *aileron* (percentage), *elevator* (percentage) and *throttle* (percentage);
3. subject gaze data (Fig. 1), including *3-D gaze direction, pupil diameters* (mm), *eye openness* (percentage) and *area of interest*.

Additionally, we infer *outcome* ∈ {success, fail} for each subject and task from aircraft status data by determining if the aircraft achieves the target status (within predefined error bounds) for a continuous period of greater than five seconds.

Data for training the machine learning classifiers is created by synchronizing the three sources and then only retaining the data from the time periods during which the subject is attempting to complete the task. The initial instruction phase during which the subject is still receiving verbal directions from the experimenter and the final success period (if any) are both removed from the time series. Obviously the aircraft status and flight control data captured during task success would be highly informative; however, our aim is to determine whether it is possible to predict task success before it occurs. All subsequent data processing and feature extraction procedures are performed on the truncated data.

Then we create a subset of the data from the first half of the time series to train the machine learning classifiers. Classifiers are either trained with data from the first half (*half*) or the entire time series minus the success period (*full*). By comparing the performance of these classifiers, we can explore the role of early student behaviors on overall flight performance. This is a key element of being able to create an early intervention system for preemptively detecting student failures.

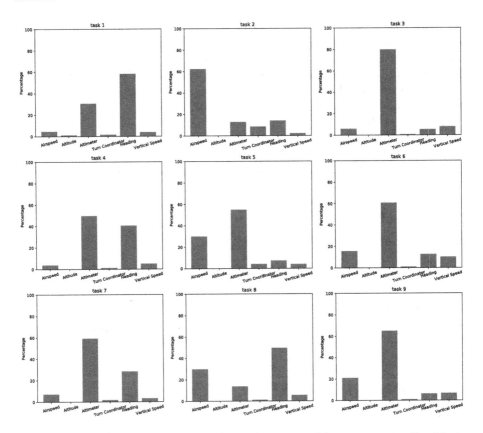

Fig. 1. Average visual attention distribution on areas of interest across all subjects. We observe that 1) within the same task, the subjects tend to have similar visual focus resulting in a sharp skewness in the average distribution; 2) the focus varies drastically among different types of tasks; 3) visual attention is highly related to tasks in an expected way, e.g. the subjects pay significant attention to the *heading indicator* in turning-related tasks {1, 4, 7, 8}, to the *airspeed indicator* in airspeed-related tasks {2, 5, 8, 9}, to the *altimeter* in all altitude-related tasks excluding {1, 2, 8}.

4   Multimodal Features

We evaluate the performance of different combinations of multimodal features (gaze, flight control, and knowledge mastery) at predicting student flight performance.

4.1   Gaze Data

Since the tasks require the subjects to use the instrument panel to verify that the aircraft has achieved target status, the distribution of visual attention across the instruments is likely to be an informative feature. Six areas of interest (AOI) are designated as follows: *airspeed indicator, attitude, altimeter, turn coordinator, heading indicator* and *vertical speed indicator*. Figure 2 shows the instrument panel marked with the AOIs. The gaze feature vector includes the proportional time distribution and stationary/transition entropy for the AOIs, both of which are explained below. How the subjects allocate their attention between the indicators reveals what information they consider most relevant to the ongoing task. Since our flight tasks require combinations of climbing, descending, slowing down and turning, each task is likely to be associated with a subset of the indicators. Therefore, we expect that a reasonable visual attention distribution is crucial to success. Hence the proportional time distribution of visual attention over the AOIs is used as a feature vector. The averages of these distributions across all the subjects are shown in Fig. 1.

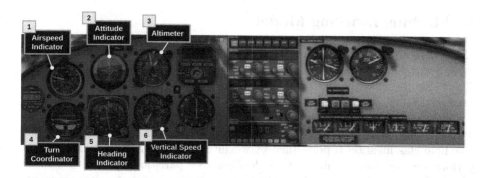

Fig. 2. The instrument panel of the aircraft (Maule Orion) marked with our six AOIs.

According to [6], there exists an optimal visual scan path for a given visual problem. We propose that the theory is true for a given operational problem as well, since attention and operation are generally consistent. Instead of searching the visual scan path, we apply gaze transition entropy [4] here, which reflects the degree of the path's randomness.

Given a set $\mathcal{S}$ of AOIs and a gaze switching sequence across $\mathcal{S}$, the procedure of computing gaze transition entropy is as follows: firstly, a gaze transition matrix $C \in \mathbf{N}^{\|\mathcal{S}\| \times \|\mathcal{S}\|}$ is obtained by counting gaze transition from $i \in \mathcal{S}$ to $j \in \mathcal{S}$ as entry C_{ij}; secondly, stationary probabilities $\pi_i = \sum_{k \in \mathcal{S}} C_{ik} / \sum_{l,m \in \mathcal{S}} C_{lm}$ and transition probabilities $p_{ij} = C_{ij} / \sum_{k \in \mathcal{S}} C_{ik}$, where $i, j \in \mathcal{S}$, are calculated; finally, we obtain the entropy of transition distribution $Ht = -\sum_{i \in \mathcal{S}} \pi_i \sum_{j \in \mathcal{S}} p_{ij} \log_2 p_{ij}$ and the entropy of stationary distribution $Hs = -\sum_{i \in \mathcal{S}} \pi_i \log_2 \pi_i$.

4.2   Flight Control Data

All control data collected from Prepar3D, including *aileron* (percentage), *elevator* (percentage) and *throttle* (percentage), are utilized. Similar to [5], the features are the descriptive statistics of their distributions, including mean, median, standard deviation, skew and kurtosis. Range, maximum and minimum are excluded here because the time series automatically have a fixed range.

4.3   Knowledge Mastery

This feature vector is collected from the knowledge acquisition assessment test given in Qualtrics. Subjects are tested on the concepts they learnt using a questionnaire consisting of thirty questions, divided equally between recall, descriptive, and conceptual questions. Knowledge mastery is represented by a matrix $Q \in \{correct, incorrect\}^{N \times M}$, where N is the number of subjects and M is the number of questions. Many of the questions relate to the instruments required to complete the flight task and are thus likely to be a good indicator of performance.

5   Machine Learning Models

Since there are equal magnitudes of samples and features in our data collection, we only considered machine learning techniques that are resistant to overfitting. This paper presents an evaluation of the random forest (RFC) vs. support vector machine (SVM) classifiers.

The random forest classifier is an ensemble method consisting of multiple decision trees, each of which is independently grown with a subset of features. The final classification is performed by weighting the voting based on the trees' performance on the training set. A decision tree partitions the feature space progressively to achieve an information gain in regions based on a measurement, such as Gini index or entropy, and assigns a class to each of them. Our RFC was constructed with 300 trees; a grid search was performed to select the best parameters for the maximum number of tree features and the best information measurement.

A support vector machine (SVM) is a discriminative classifier which employs a hyperplane to segregate the samples belonging to different classes. A kernel is generally applied to map the original feature space to a more separable space in which the hyperplane is placed. In our experiments, a grid search is performed to determine the best parameters for kernel, kernel coefficient, and misclassification penalty.

Similar to [5], a chance model is included as a baseline. It works by stochastically selecting the class for each testing sample with respect to the probability of the corresponding class in training set.

Due to the limited number of samples, models were evaluated with leave-one-out cross validation, which iteratively reserves one sample exclusively for testing purposes and includes all the other samples in the training set. Additionally, the high variance on the task success rate unbalances the dataset. Thus, for each individual experiment in cross validation, the training set is resampled with the oversampling method SMOTE [1] while leaving the testing sample unchanged.

6 Results and Discussion

Table 2 shows the accuracy and F_1 scores for predicting student flight task success and failure. Both RFC and SVM perform comparably well. The best performing model generally yields an improvement of more than 0.25 in all metrics over the chance model. Results are reported only for the best models based on the parameter grid search. Identifying where and how trainees fail is a key step towards engendering deliberate practice. Therefore, the F_1 score on predicting failure is of more importance than the other metrics listed in the table.

Table 2. Performance metrics for the models using the best parameters.

Feature	RFC accuracy	RFC F_1 success	RFC F_1 failure	SVM accuracy	SVM F_1 success	SVM F_1 failure
(Chance)	.55	.35	.48	.55	.35	.48
Knowledge mastery	.78	.47	.70	.73	.52	.67
Control (full)	.79	.59	.72	.77	.59	.73
Control (half)	.80	.55	.71	.81	.62	.77
Gaze (full)	.70	.46	.64	.75	.54	.69
Gaze (half)	.70	.48	.65	.71	.52	.68
Control + Gaze (full)	.78	.55	.71	.78	.60	.74
Control + Gaze (half)	.82	.62	.73	.79	.61	.77
Knowledge + Gaze (full)	.80	.48	.70	.79	.53	.74
Knowledge + Gaze (half)	.81	.47	.74	.79	.53	.74
All sources (full)	.80	.57	.70	.79	.56	.74
All sources (half)	.81	.58	.73	.82	.54	.78

Among the models learned from a single data source, those learned on the control data achieve the best performance. This is unsurprising since the control data relates fairly directly to aircraft status, which in turn is used to judge task performance. Note that these results do not include features that relate to target achievement such as *airspeed, altitude* and *heading*. The models trained on gaze data are more predictive on failure cases than success. Improper allocation of visual attention can unilaterally result in task failure; however other factors such as proficiency of manipulation affect success. Combining control and gaze features results in an observable improvement. Like visual attention, the knowledge mastery features are more valuable for predicting failure. Theoretical knowledge appears to be a necessary but not sufficient condition to guarantee successful flight execution. Combining gaze and knowledge mastery features performs equivalently well to the control data alone at predicting task failure.

Finally, classifiers trained on the first half of the data yield similar performance to classifiers trained on the full dataset. It is possible that 1) behavioral observation over a short time window is sufficient to determine student performance or 2) manipulations during early flight stages are crucial to the final outcome.

7   Conclusion and Future Work

Our experiments show that it is feasible to accurately predict student failure on simple flight tasks from visual attention features gathered from the initial flight phase, combined with knowledge mastery features; these results affirmatively answer all our research questions. We also demonstrate that it is possible to train the machine learning classifiers on a very small dataset using a combination of techniques. These are important stepping stones towards the long-term vision of scalable, automated delivery of flight instruction using off the shelf virtual reality headsets. In future work, we will investigate the usage of failure predictions to modify the order of practice tasks as well as conducting a deeper exploration of the data collected outside the flight tests.

References

1. Chawla, N.V., Bowyer, K.W., Hall, L.O., Kegelmeyer, W.P.: SMOTE: synthetic minority over-sampling technique. J. Artif. Intell. Res. **16**(1), 321–357 (2002)
2. Conijn, R., Snijders, C., Kleingeld, A., Matzat, U.: Predicting student performance from LMS data: a comparison of 17 blended courses using Moodle LMS. IEEE Trans. Learn. Technol. **10**(1), 17–29 (2017)
3. Dehais, F., Behrend, J., Peysakhovich, V., Causse, M., Wickens, C.D.: Pilot flying and pilot monitoring's aircraft state awareness during go-around execution in aviation: a behavioral and eye tracking study. Int. J. Aerosp. Psychol. **27**(1–2), 15–28 (2017)
4. Krejtz, K., et al.: Gaze transition entropy. ACM Trans. Appl. Percept. **13**(1), 1–20 (2015)
5. Millsa, C., Bixlera, R., Wang, X., D'Mello, S.K.: Automatic gaze-based detection of mind wandering during narrative film comprehension. In: International Conference on Multimodal Interaction (2015)
6. Peysakhovich, V., Lefrançois, O., Dehais, F., Causse, M.: The neuroergonomics of aircraft cockpits: the four stages of eye-tracking integration to enhance flight safety. Safety **4**, 8 (2018)

7. Susac, A., Bubic, A., Kaponja, J., Planinic, M., Palmovic, M.: Eye movements reveal students' strategies in simple equation solving. Int. J. Sci. Math. Educ. **12**(3), 555–577 (2014)
8. Thai-Nghe, N., Drumond, L., Krohn-Grimberghe, A., Schmidt-Thieme, L.: Recommender system for predicting student performance. Procedia Comput. Sci. **1**(2), 2811–2819 (2010). Proceedings of the Workshop on Recommender Systems for Technology Enhanced Learning (RecSysTEL 2010)

A Game-Transformation-Based Framework to Understand Initial Conditions and Outcomes in the Context of Cyber-Enabled Influence Operations (CIOs)

Girish Sreevatsan Nandakumar[(✉)] [iD] and Jose Padilla [iD]

Virginia Modeling Analysis and Simulation Center, Suffolk, USA
{gnand002,jpadilla}@odu.edu

Abstract. A hybrid methodology that combines qualitative and quantitative analytical techniques is discussed in the context of Cyber-enabled Influence Operations (CIOs). Beginning with primary inputs from detailed qualitative analyses of political, economic, social, technological, and legal ground realities, our Game-Transformation-based Framework uses 2×2 games - with ordinal rankings of preferences as payoffs - to attain a macro-level perspective. Using the periodic table of 2×2 games, we show how payoff swaps, which represent shifts in ground realities, can change the nature of the game and therefore the resulting equilibrium. Our framework's exploration of various permutations, that hypothetical changes in input might lead to, can be used by analysts and policymakers to reverse-engineer favorable scenarios. The framework is useful for scenario planning as it allows for both detailed micro-level analyses and strategic macro-level analyses.

Keywords: Game theory · CIO · Scenario planning

1 Introduction

Cyberwarfare is living up to Clausewitz's characterization of war as 'continuation of politics by other means.' Cyberattacks have been increasing in numbers and magnitude by the day [1]. In the blink of an eye, cyberattacks can affect the entire global economy, cripple major global companies, and disrupt critical infrastructures across borders. One form of cyberwarfare is cyber-enabled influence operations (CIOs). CIOs can be defined as "the deliberate use of information by one party on an adversary to confuse, mislead, and ultimately to influence the choices and decisions that the adversary makes [2]." Liberal democracies are the prime victims of CIOs simply because they are open societies where openness is manifested in every realm. Freedom of expression, frequent elections, and a free press - some of the hallmarks of democracies - are often easily exploited by foreign actors through CIOs. Cyberwarfare efforts, especially CIOs, take advantage of vulnerabilities and successfully impact policies, economies, and societies. Russia's

© Springer Nature Switzerland AG 2020
R. Thomson et al. (Eds.): SBP-BRiMS 2020, LNCS 12268, pp. 288–297, 2020.
https://doi.org/10.1007/978-3-030-61255-9_28

campaign to influence the 2016 presidential election in the US is considered a CIO with the objectives to sow social unrest and a preferred political outcome.

Prompted by this ever-increasing threat, countries and coalitions, such as NATO, have looked for ways to improve the identification and deterrence of these operations. The Secretary-General of the North Atlantic Treaty Organization (NATO) recently penned an article asserting that NATO will defend its cyber domain and "invoke collective defense if required [3]". This strong posture of the largest military alliance prompts the challenge on how NATO can achieve deterrence, considering enemy dismissals such as "cheap signals," against CIOs within a complex decision- and policy-making process. Such an approach would require establishing a context under which parameters of decision/policymaking are agreed upon and the means of assessing their evolution towards a desired outcome.

This paper aims to establish an approach that can explore such challenges with the use of game theory. Such effort would provide means for assessment and training to arrive at a parameter combination that achieves a particular objective. Inspired by DeCanio and Fremstad's paper on 'game theory and climate diplomacy [4],' we use highly simplified representations of strategic interactions between players to deduce such insights. To demonstrate the usage of our methodology, we discuss Cyber-enabled Influence Operations (CIOs) along with various factors that influence the decision to carry out cyber-warfare for norm-diffusion purposes through CIOs. Lastly, we provide an example of how an organization, such as NATO, can use this approach for training and assessment. We use NATO, as an example, to provide context for the flexibility of the approach.

The paper is organized as follows: Sect. 2 provides a brief background on NATO, Sect. 3 elaborates on the proposed approach, Sect. 4 provides a theoretical application of the approach, and Sect. 5 provides a discussion on the insights and future work.

2 Background

NATO has been able to achieve deterrence in the context of nuclear warfare and most forms of kinetic aggression. This is attributed to Article 5 - the clause that commits its members to collective defense. Game theory has been used to explain why deterrence through such alliances is effective [4]. The fear of 'mutually assured destruction' prevents rational actors from prompting large-scale retaliation. But cyberwarfare is difficult to model with such methods because it is much more complicated than kinetic warfare. Take, for instance, the ability of non-state actors - individuals and organizations - to effectively carry out attacks that many nation-states in the world are not capable of. There is also the problem of establishing the point of origin (attribution) [5]. It is sometimes difficult to take legal action even when attribution is known because enforcement provisions in international law are nonexistent [6]. This problem gets worse in the area of CIOs. Cyber-Warfare is, however, widely recognized as a breach of the UN Charter's principles of sovereign equality and territorial integrity [7]. However, unlike events involving kinetic attacks, cyberattacks and CIOs usually do not lead to substantial responses [8]. This further encourages bad actors to continue cyberattacks and CIOs.

Given the complexities of cyberwarfare, especially CIOs, it is difficult to quantify and structure its factors and effects. One way to analyze such scenarios at a strategic level is through simplified methods such as 2×2 order games that allow us to forego such calculations yet help understand the nature of the game. In order games, outcomes stemming from policy choices are ranked ordinally. Ordinal rankings have been used in literature to model international relations [9, 10]. However, to our knowledge, there has been no application of this game theoretic approach to analyze CIOs. A similar approach in extant literature is the methodology used by Ouenniche et al. [11] to model selection of partners in public-private partnerships using ordinal games. In addition to an ordinal game theory-based framework similar to ours, they also include an algorithm for ranking proposals that take stock of the various perspectives of all players. The proposed algorithm is designed to find an optimal generalized Nash equilibrium. The same can be done for our study. Our approach extends the ordinal ranking method by combining it with political, economic, social, technological, and legal (PESTL) factors in order to capture more explanatory power in cyberwarfare [12] with simplified 2×2 order games. The PESTL framework provides a qualitative component to capture the perspective of subject matter experts. The game theory component provides a deductive framework towards a formal assessment.

3   Methodology

Game-theoretic models have been used to provide formalizations of the strategic inter-actions that form the basis of international negotiations [4, 9, 10]. We agree with scholars such as Barrett [8] that the essence of many international relations situations can be cap-tured by the simple 2×2 framework. Game theory is well suited to this practice because the two main schools of thought in international relations - realism and liberalism – were already essential components of game theory's development from its inception [9]. The game-theoretic approach used in this paper - ranked order preferences - is in line with agent rationality. The rankings are transitive. The biggest advantage of this approach is that inferences based only on ordinal rankings are more generalizable. The "New Periodic Table" (NPT) of 2×2 order games introduced by Robinson and Goforth [13] has been used to provide an exhaustive treatment of the possible game-theoretic charac-terizations of strategic interactions between States (Fig. 1). Briefly, the NPT shows the different types of games and how they are positioned relative to each other. This helps in understanding what types of swaps are required to change a game from one type to another, which highlights the extent of the framework's applications. The table will be discussed further in Sect. 4.2.

The methodology includes two levels of analysis. Level one implements four steps and level 2 reverses those steps.

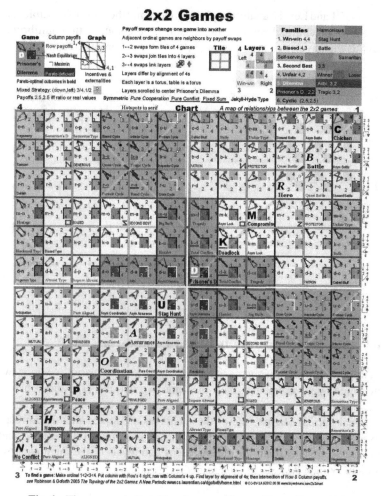

Fig. 1. The new periodic table of games (Source: Bryan Bruns [16])

Step 1 involves a detailed qualitative analysis of ground realities in the political, economic, social, technological, and legal realms. In Step 2, information gathered in Step 1 is synthesized and converted into scenarios identified by ordinal values, which serve as aggregates representing those derived scenarios. Step 3 involves choosing the best strategy given the ground realities on both sides – since each player evaluates both sides before making their choice. By Step 4, the macro-level perspective of the overall game once both players have each made their move becomes evident.

A Level 2 process entails a 'reverse engineering' approach wherein we understand how the outcomes would vary if the players' choices of strategies were different and under what conditions the aggregate value, i.e. the estimated payoff, from choosing a particular strategy would change. A change in the payoff is required to justify a change to the originally chosen strategy. To this end, a more detailed 'what if' analysis in Step 1 is necessary. Level 1 and Level 2 analyses help us understand the array of possible scenarios. Level 2 also involves comprehending how the game's outcome, i.e. the equilibrium, shifts accordingly as the payoffs change. Figure 2 illustrates the proposed approach.

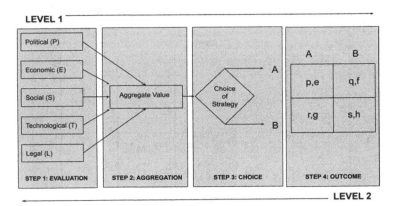

Fig. 2. The game-transformation-based framework

4   The Game Transformation-Based Framework

We use a simplified 2 × 2 order game to model macro-level scenarios in which two players - represented by governments - have the same two options: (1) Abide - not carrying out CIOs, abiding by international norms, or (2) Breach - carrying out CIOs in breach of international norms. The payoffs of these choices are represented in corresponding quadrants as shown in Fig. 3. We assume the player (government) to be a rational actor. The following sections explain the various steps and levels of the methodology in the context of analyzing CIOs.

		Nation 2	
	Strategies → ↓	Abide (A)	Breach (B)
Nation 1	Abide (A)	p, e	q, f
	Breach (B)	r, g	s, h

Fig. 3. Game structure

We will rely on an example to highlight the approach. The Disruptive Technology Assessment Game (DTAG) – a wargame by NATO's Innovation Hub - is used to understand the impacts of new and emerging technologies on NATO operations in the future.

The wargame involves teams of military officers and students from various backgrounds working together to understand various perspectives. We wanted to design an approach that is versatile enough to be applied during DTAG exercises on different technologies. In this paper, we essentially approach CIOs as an impact of a ubiquitous technology - the internet - on society and nations. In the future, we intend to build automated systems that constantly scan for political, social, economic, technological, and legal advancements within the context of a wargame. It is noted that while the game theory proposition can be extended at length, in actual settings, achieving desired equilibriums in CIOs may require 'backchannels' that are not discussed in open settings, or enforcement mechanisms outside the game frameworks discussed. Yet, these models can be used to illustrate pathways to even reach agreements.

4.1 Level One

Step 1: Evaluation

In our model, the political, social, technological, legal, and economic conditions in a nation form the basis of cost-benefit analysis for the other side. Each nation's decision to carry out CIOs i.e. the choice of strategy is based on this analysis. These factors indicate how favorable the situation is for CIO activity. The *political* landscape would be assessed based on an analysis of the current government's stance on CIOs. While some governments have aggressive stances such as immediate retaliation, some do not take any action. In our DTAG example, if NATO amended its by-laws to include CIOs to the list of provocations that would trigger collective action by all NATO allies against the actor responsible for the attack, the chances of Russian CIOs on NATO nations would reduce significantly. *Social* factors include the effectiveness of civil societies, distribution of population, and how polarized the population is. If civic societies are active and effective, the fabric of the society will be strongly woven. This will decrease the effectiveness of CIOs, which rely on dividing societies. *Technological* factors include both offensive and defensive capabilities each nation has at its disposal. This includes but is not limited to surveillance and tracking the origins of online activities. If a nation is strong in cybersecurity, there is less incentive for the other nation to carry out CIOs. *Legal* aspects matter because if there are no legal provisions to carry out CIOs or retaliate to CIOs, it does not matter how powerful a nation is in terms of its abilities to carry out these attacks. While political will is necessary to execute such attacks, legal provisions are necessary in order to allow such political will to be carried out. For example, after 9/11, the US Congress gave the Executive branch much more powers to carry out special operations and other strikes [14]. This drastically changed the nature of military options the President had because congressional approval was no longer necessary. The *economic* landscape indirectly affects the cost-benefit calculus because economic anxiety makes the population much more vulnerable to CIOs [15]. In Step 2, these conditions are synthesized and aggregated.

Step 2: Aggregation

Step 2 involves calculating payoffs for both sides given the conditions analyzed in Step 1. These payoffs also get represented in the game quadrant represented in Step 4. The payoffs (see Fig. 3) to each player are measured in ordinal terms, so the terms {p, q, r, s} and {e, f, g, h} can take on values {4, 3, 2, 1}, where 4 represents the most favorable outcome and 1 represents the least favorable outcome (Fig. 4).

		Nation 2	
	Strategies → ↓	Abide (A)	Breach (B)
Nation 1	**Abide (A)**	4, 4	3, 3
	Breach (B)	2, 2	1, 1

Fig. 4. A sample game with payoffs

Payoffs will be calculated based on how favorable the political, social, technological, legal, and economic conditions are. This is a proxy for how successful CIOs will be. In our DTAG example, if Nation 1 assesses the situation in Nation 2 - based on the political, social, technological, legal, and economic conditions in Nation 2 - to be highly conducive for successful cyber-enabled influence operations (CIO), the payoff for Nation 1 in breaching international laws and executing CIOs in Nation 2 would be 4. All 2 × 2 games discussed in this paper use the exact same strategy choices and payoff methods as discussed above.

Step 3: Choice of Strategy
Based on ground realities reflected by the aggregated payoffs, each player chooses one of two strategies - "Abide" or "Breach" (Fig. 4). By choosing to 'abide', the nation decides to not carry out CIOs, thereby abiding by the international rules that recognize and respect sovereignty. When a nation chooses to 'breach', it is disregarding international rules and norms by interfering in another nation's internal matters through CIOs. In line with game theory's assumptions, we assume that the choice of strategy will be based on the players' calculations of payoffs resulting from choosing each strategy.

Step 4: Outcome
Step 4 involves assessment of dominant strategies. In game theory, a dominant strategy is the course of action that results in the highest payoff for a player regardless of what the other player does. A 'Nash Equilibrium' is where neither Nation 1 nor Nation 2 can improve their payoff by deviating unilaterally from the outcome if the other continues to play the equilibrium strategy. While the Nash equilibrium is the most common equilibrium concept, there are other equilibriums that also help us understand most likely outcomes. In our methodology, we also look at the Maxi-min strategy, which ensures the highest payoff that a player can guarantee themselves [13]. When maxi-min strategy is used, the worst possible payoff is at least as good as the worst payoff from any other

strategy. For Example, in the hypothetical game shown in Fig. 3, given the payoffs represented, the dominant strategy for both Nation 1 and Nation 2 is to Abide. The Nash equilibrium and the Maxi-min equilibrium are the same - (Abide, Abide).

4.2 Level 2

A Level 2 analysis is the inverse process i.e. after identifying a desired change or swap in payoffs in the game structure, we move back to reevaluate whether there needs to be a change in strategy choice. We also go back to step 1 and step 2 to understand what needs to change in order to realize the desired change in the game structure. Level 2 analysis starts with a big-picture perspective on game transformations (from the NPT of Fig. 1) as shown in Fig. 5. In this hypothetical case, the game changes from an unstable 'chicken' to a stable 'no conflict'. In our DTAG example, analysis involves changes in payoffs stemming from political, economic, social, technological, and legal changes that affect one or both players. For example - a change in political leadership, which leads to drastic changes in legislation, might make technological strengths irrelevant if there is no political will or legal provision to carry out CIO attacks. Such changes will correspond to a change in the ordinal number that represents a scenario. Such analyses can help policymakers perform experiments to explore various pathways.

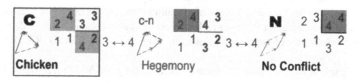

Fig. 5. Game transformation from 'Chicken' to 'No Conflict' (Source: Bryan Bruns [16])

5 Discussion and Conclusion

Consider, for instance, a NATO effort to understand how it can deter Russia from carrying out CIOs against NATO members. Our framework would use Step 1 to analyze existing conditions across the PESTL landscape for Russia and every NATO nation in order to understand which countries are not well equipped. In this step, narrative analysis can be used to model the spread of false information using an adapted version of the SIR epidemiological model by coding PESTL conditions that prevent or promote the spread. In Step 2, the confluence of PESTL factors will be aggregated to understand the overall condition in each nation. A similar analysis for the entire alliance will involve more synthesis because of the differences between a supranational institution and individual nations. In Step 3, we decide which strategy is best suited given the conditions on the ground. In Step 4, we realize what the game looks like and what the equilibriums are. This Level 1 analysis is followed by a Level 2 analysis where we explore what needs to change in order to change the game into a cooperative game, and what changes – i.e. payoff swaps - are necessary in order to achieve this change. The payoffs i.e. the aggregate values from Step 2 reflect changes in ground realities that may be political, economic, social, technological, or legal. Some hypothetical examples that can change the game could be – a coup, an election, an economic crisis, a revolution, a radical invention, a radical legislation, etc. Changes that are not as radical as the ones listed above can also often lead to significant changes in the game. For instance, the exercise can also generate permutations on stronger smaller coalitions within NATO members that can deter Russia from carrying out CIOs. The outcomes of such an exercise could be recommendations for legal provisions that enable retaliation, increased governmental efforts to prevent the populace from falling prey to CIOs, agendas for research labs to improve technical capabilities, etc. Similar exercises could give a better understanding of the conditions under which Russia is likely to 'abide.'

While the approach is reductionist, we believe it works as support for brainstorming during exercises such as DTAG. The framework can be used in settings beyond military wargames thanks to the versatility of 2×2 order games. This versatility also becomes useful as it would provide the basis for developing game-theory-driven agent-based models with the different steps providing the underlying behavioral rules.

Acknowledgments. This material, in part, is based on research sponsored by the Office of the Assistant Secretary of Defense for Research and Engineering (OASD (R&E)) under agreement number FAB750-15-2-0120. The U.S. Government is authorized to reproduce and distribute reprints for Governmental purposes notwithstanding any copyright notation thereon. The views and conclusions contained herein are those of the authors and should not be interpreted as necessarily representing the official policies or endorsements, either expressed or implied, of the Office of the Assistant Secretary of Defense for Research and Engineering (OASD (R&E)) or the U.S. Government.

This material, in part, is based on research sponsored by the NATO Innovation Hub under ODURF Project Number 600225-01. The views and conclusions contained herein are those of the authors and should not be interpreted as necessarily representing the official policies or endorsements, either expressed or implied, of the NATO Innovation Hub or of any other NATO entity.

References

1. Holt, T.J., Stonhouse, M., Freilich, J., Chermak, S.M.: Examining ideologically motivated cyberattacks performed by far-left groups. Terrorism Polit. Violence 1–22 (2019)
2. Lin, H.S., Kerr, J.: On cyber-enabled information/influence warfare and manipulation. SSRN, August 2017
3. NATO News. https://www.nato.int/cps/en/natohq/news_168435.htm?selectedLocale=en. Accessed 28 Feb 2020
4. DeCanio, S.J., Fremstad, A.: Game theory and climate diplomacy. Ecol. Econ. **85**, 177–187 (2013)
5. Rowe, N.C.: The attribution of cyber warfare. In: Cyber Warfare, pp. 75–86. Routledge (2015)
6. Shackelford, S.: From nuclear war to net war: analogizing cyber attacks in international law. Berkley J. Int. Law (BJIL) **25**(3), 198 (2009)
7. Green, J.A.: The regulation of cyber warfare under the jus ad bellum. In: Cyber Warfare: A Multidisciplinary Analysis, pp. 96–124 (2015)

8. Sklerov, M.J.: Solving the dilemma of sate responses to cyberattacks: a justification for the use of active defenses against states who neglect their duty to prevent. Mil. L. Rev. **201**, 6–8 (2009)
9. Barrett, S.: Environment & Statecraft: The Strategy of Environmental Treaty-Making. Oxford University Press, Oxford (2003)
10. Stein, A.A.: Why Nations Cooperate: Circumstance and Choice in International Relations. Cornell University Press, Ithaca (1990)
11. Ouenniche, J., Boukouras, A., Rajabi, M.: An ordinal game theory approach to the analysis and selection of partners in public–private partnership projects. J. Optim. Theory Appl. **169**(1), 314–343 (2016)
12. Whyte, C., Mazanec, B.: Understanding Cyber Warfare: Politics, Policy and Strategy. Routledge, Abingdon (2018)
13. Robinson, D., Goforth, D.: The Topology of the 2 × 2 Games: A New Periodic Table. Routledge, New York (2005)
14. Fisher, L.: Presidential War Power. University Press of Kansas, Lawrence (2013). https://muse.jhu.edu/book/39876
15. Bechtel, G.G.: The societal impact of economic anxiety. J. Data Sci. **10**, 693–710 (2012)
16. Bruns, B.: Escaping prisoner's dilemmas: from discord to harmony in the landscape of 2x2 games. arXiv preprint arXiv:1206.1880 (2012)

The Human Resource Management Parameter Experimentation Tool

Carmen Iasiello[1]([⊠]) [iD], Andrew Crooks[1,2] [iD], and Sarah Wittman[1] [iD]

[1] George Mason University, 4400 University Dr, Fairfax, VA 22030, USA
{ciasiell,swittman}@gmu.edu
[2] University at Buffalo, Buffalo, NY, USA
atcrooks@buffalo.edu

Abstract. Human resource management (HRM) draws on the field of organizational theory (OT) to identify, quantify, and manage people-based phenomena that impact organizational operations and outcomes. OT research has long used computational methods and agent-based modeling to understand complex adaptive systems. Agent-based modeling methodologies within HRM, however, are still rare. Within the HRM and management science literature, Herzberg's et al. (1959) Two-Factor Theory (TFT) is a framework that has been tested and used for decades. Its ability to capture the interaction between a work force's motivation and their environment's hygiene lends itself well to agent-based modeling as a method of study. Here, we present the development of the Human Resources Management-Parameter Experimentation Tool (HRM-PET) as the first explicit ABM instantiation of TFT, filling the gap between the study of HRM and computational OT tools like agent-based modeling.

Keywords: Human resources management · Management science · Workforce dynamics · Agent-based modeling

1 Introduction

Human resource management (HRM) involves "the acquisition, motivation, development and management of the organization's human resources (Armstrong 1999)." Thus, the study and practice of HRM aims to identify, quantify, and manage people-related issues that have the potential to impact organizational functioning and performance. In doing so, HRM engages heavily with organizational theory (OT), a field that has largely embraced computational methods and agent-based modeling to illuminate complex adaptive systems and the processes by which microlevel organizational interactions engender macrolevel phenomena emergence (Prietula et al. 1998; Miller and Page 2007). But while HRM—for its relevant topic area, its roots in industrial-organizational psychology, and its reliance on laboratory methods—lends itself to using agent-based models (ABMs), it has yet to embrace simulation methodology. To address this issue, we have developed an ABM to explore HRM, specifically, one that simulates heterogenous work unit constraints on heterogeneous agents.

© Springer Nature Switzerland AG 2020
R. Thomson et al. (Eds.): SBP-BRiMS 2020, LNCS 12268, pp. 298–307, 2020.
https://doi.org/10.1007/978-3-030-61255-9_29

Because the questions the HRM field aims to address are inherently multi-level, scholars have sought and leveraged methodologies to capture and predict cross-level effects. For example, data-based algorithms have been used to explore stakeholder concerns and workforce issues (Cheng and Hackett 2019; Lafuente and Barcellos 2010). Similarly, industrial-organizational psychology data studies using multilevel structural equation modeling have demonstrated links between such diverse phenomena as positive organizational climate and increased worker commitment (Woznyj et al. 2019); so-called high-performance human resource (HR) practices and organizational citizenship behavior (Wei et al. 2010); and abusive supervision and employee creativity (Liu et al. 2012). However, recent work has argued that these existing methods do not sufficiently capture or measure either the complexity of HR issues (e.g., what a "good employee" is), or rare, but significant HR events (e.g., firings) (Tambe et al. 2019). Because simulation methods can identify the mechanisms that translate local behaviors into global phenomena, they are ideal for analyzing HRM issue complexity—simulating both commonplace and rare, emergent events.

Among simulation methodologies, agent-based modeling is particularly well suited to managerial science questions pertaining to decision making trade-offs (such as those dealing with resource allocation); indeed, ABMs have been used in surveys of organizational behavior and performance (Wall 2014). Thus, an agent-based model capturing heterogeneity across individual-level actors and organizational work units to simulate organizational outcomes could improve the precision of HRM experiment design and real-world organization interventions. This is what the Human Resource Management-Parameter Experimentation Tool (HRM-PET) we present here purports to do. Leveraging the theoretical underpinnings of Herzberg's et al. (1959) Two-Factor Theory (TFT), the HRM-PET is built in the highly user-accessible open source software NetLogo (Wilensky 1999), which allows users to explore parameter variations that not only test the theory as Herzberg et al. (1959) developed it but also the theory's critiques in silica.

As the first agent-based model (ABM) to apply and test Herzberg's et al. (1959) full TFT, the HRM-PET model we present in this paper provides a bridge for agent based modeling methods into the HRM literature and, thus, provides a unique contribution to both the HRM and simulation fields. HRM-PET captures each of the heterogenous motivation factors and heterogenous hygiene factors as outlined by Herzberg et al. (1959), thus allowing for local agent-environment, and agent-agent interaction that leads to emergent organizational-level traits. In the remainder of this paper, Sect. 2 presents the background of TFT and its use in HRM. Next, we turn to methodology which describes the process of translating TFT into an abstract ABM (Sect. 3). This is followed by some initial results emerging from the ABM (Sect. 4), and a summary of the paper and areas of further work in Sect. 5.

2 Background

Since Herzberg et al. (1959) introduced the TFT, it has been applied in HRM and industrial-organizational psychology studies. Although scholars testing its parameters have found mixed results, its primary contribution to the field has been distinguishing those personal and organizational factors that can affect job satisfaction versus job dissatisfaction. According to the theory employees' job satisfaction grows or diminishes based on job-related "motivation" factors: achievement, recognition, the work itself, responsibility, advancement or growth. In contrast, job dissatisfaction emerges in function of context-related "hygiene" factors, which include policies & administration, supervision-technical, relationship-superior, working conditions, and salary. Research suggests that job (dis)satisfaction and the macrolevel organizational outcomes of these (e.g., turnover) are functions both of the presence/absence of such factors *and* of heterogeneity in employee need and preference characteristics (e.g., Hom and Kinicki 2001; Kilbridge 1961; Lundberg et al. 2009). To set up the HRM-PET we present in Sect. 3, we first lay out the motivation and hygiene factors TFT comprises and summarize the mixed support the theory has received.

We turn first to the motivation factors that moderate job satisfaction. *Achievement* is related to successful work task completion, seeing one's own work-related results, solutions to problems, etc. This is different from *recognition*, the positive notice or praise people receive for their work. *The work itself* reflects personal positive sentiment for concrete job task requirements. *Responsibility* is having accountability for one's own or others' work. Finally, *advancement* involves upward status or position change. Herzberg et al.'s (1959) work showed *achievement* and *recognition* to contribute to short-term job satisfaction, and *the work itself, responsibility,* and *advancement* to contribute to more enduring satisfaction levels. Herzberg et al.'s (1959) early-stage theory formulations tested additional factors, but found that these empirically added little to job satisfaction beyond the key five factors above; we, thus, exclude them from our model, as well.

TFT similarly outlines five hygiene factors that moderate job dissatisfaction. *Policies and administration* is the organization's rules for work task- and personnel management, and was, in Herzberg et al.'s (1959) model tests, the most significant job dissatisfaction moderator. Supervision, too, is considered a hygiene factor, and mainly impacts dissatisfaction through *supervision-technical*—supervisor competence and fairness, although it also is reflected in *interrelationships*, the quality of one's interactions with supervisors, peers, and subordinates. *Salary* is defined as the quality of compensation, and *working conditions* reflect work physical, facility-based, and quantity elements of work. TFT's main argument is that changes in the five motivation factors will move individuals between satisfied and not satisfied (neutral, but not dissatisfied); changes in the five hygiene factors, in contrast, move people between not dissatisfied (neutral, but not satisfied) and dissatisfied.

TFT has successfully predicted myriad job (dis)satisfaction-driven behaviors, and has been tested across many industries and cultural contexts (see Bassett-Jones and Lloyd 2005; Hasin and Omar 2007; Dobre et al. 2017). However, studies where TFT has failed (e.g., in explaining nurse retention *vis-à-vis* motivation factors; Hunt et al. 2012); where a non-linear relationship between factors and (dis)satisfaction exists (e.g., among white collar Turkish workers; Ozsoy 2019); and where worker responses display heterogeneity (e.g., seasonal workers' lower responsiveness to wage levels and higher responsiveness to interpersonal motivation factors versus resident workers; Lundberg et al. 2009) suggest a need for better TFT model specification and testing. And while agent-based modeling's potential relevance to TFT has engendered some interest within the scholarly simulation community (e.g., Iammartino's (2016) leveraging of agents with heterogenous satisfaction levels to model TFT's measures of organizational satisfaction), the full TFT has yet to be modeled and tested. Doing so will allow future research to examine variations in TFT's application, enabling researchers to both to explain where and why the theory fails, and—based on these findings—better define the theory's boundary conditions and/or provide recommendations for theory changes. Where the time requirements, costs, and particularities of multiple real-world experimental test pools would inhibit such testing and analysis, agent-based modeling provides an efficient and effective solution for such complex analytical tasks.

3   Methodology

Within this section we introduce our HRM-PET model and highlight how it leverages the benefits of agent-based modeling to study HRM. Agent-based modeling allows us to study a system (i.e., the workplace, in this application), emerging from individual agents (i.e., workers) interacting with an environment (i.e., work units). Important aspects relating to this system, its agents, and their environment will be introduced below. A description of the graphical user interface is in Fig. 1. For the interested reader, the model (created in NetLogo 6.1 (Wilensky 1999)) and a detailed Overview, Design concepts, and Details plus Decision making (ODD + D), Müller et al. (2013) which extends Grimm et al. (2006)) document can be found at http://bit.ly/HMR-PET. The rationale for utilizing the ODD + D and for sharing the model is that it allows broader dissemination of the model and its methodology. Furthermore, it provides greater information than the page constraints of this paper allow with respect to model logic, variables, and agents decision-making. Providing this information and model will aid future scholars in replicating the results presented here, and in extending the model if they so desire.

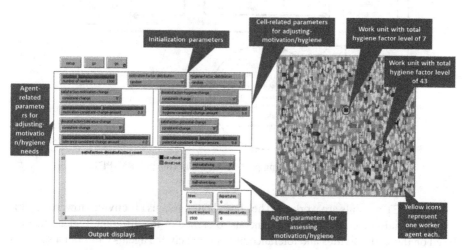

Fig. 1. HRM-PET graphical user interface

Agent-based modeling focuses on individuals—in this case, workers—making decisions; however, capturing such decision making is a major challenge (Crooks et al. 2019). To avoid creating a random (and, thus, unrealistic) model of heterogeneous human behavior- and decision making, we integrate cognitive science (Kennedy 2012). In the HRM-PET, the agents, for example, make sequential determinations about their state, vis-à-vis the hygiene and motivation factors. This method of sequential decision-tree design within agent-based modeling maintains computational parsimony and cognitive-plausibility and has been termed the "fast and frugal" decision making modeling method (Gigerenzer and Goldstein 1996). The fast and frugal method allows us to capture agents' bounded rationality (Simon 1997) and has been successfully used in simulating agents' decision making in a variety of contexts, such as from agriculture, conflict, and evacuations (see Crooks et al. 2019 for a review). Figure 2 provides an overview of the decision making process HRM-PET models.

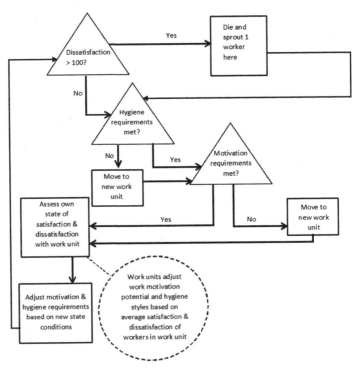

Fig. 2. Decision making process for the agents in HRM-PET.

HRM-PET's agents are workers. They have heterogenous proclivities toward the different motivation factors and heterogeneous tolerance of the different hygiene factors. Based on these proclivities and tolerance levels for each, the agents carry out a series of assessments about their (dis)satisfaction with their work unit. Work units possess corresponding hygiene styles and potentials to enable motivation. Furthermore, the agents have a maximum of two work unit moves in a time-step before they assess their satisfaction and dissatisfaction. The time-steps in the simulation are notional, but abstractly correspond to the time period between received job offer and a job acceptance/refusal from candidate.

The initial factor level distribution is set by the model's experimenter, who may choose a uniform (0 > 10), normal ($\mu = 5$, $\sigma_x = 2.5$), or Poisson ($\mu = 0.5$) distribution. These allow the user to account for industries that are relatively uniform in their distribution of quality work environments, those that have a meaningful average quality, and those that have only very few high quality work environments and a large number of low quality work environments. Each agent begins with 0 level satisfaction and dissatisfaction. Once the agents' needs are satisfied (i.e., their hygiene or motivation needs are at least minimally met), or their two possible moves are exhausted, they assess their satisfaction and dissatisfaction.

As in the TFT, the motivation factors contribute to satisfaction while the hygiene factors contribute to dissatisfaction. If a given agent's motivation factor need is less than the potential for that motivation factor within their work unit, the agent's satisfaction increases. Similarly, if an agent's hygiene factor tolerance is less than the corresponding hygiene factor within the work unit, the agent's dissatisfaction increases. The contribution to increases are pegged to the empirical results Herzberg et al. (1959) originally reported and shown in Table 1. So, too, the HRM-PET preserves the TFT's ratio between factors (e.g., in the HRM-PET, the achievement motivation factor has twice the contribution to job satisfaction as advancement, consistent with Herzberg et al.'s (1959) empirical results).

Table 1. Agent and cell attributes and their ratio of contribution to satisfaction and dissatisfaction based on whether the agent's attributes are higher than that of the work unit.

Factor	Worker attribute	Work unit attribute	Increase in satisfaction	Increase in dissatisfaction
Achievement	Achievement-style	Achievement-potential	0.2	–
Recognition	Recognition-style	Recognition-potential	0.17	–
The work itself	Work-itself-style	Work-itself-potential	0.13	–
Responsibility	Responsibility-style	Responsibility-potential	0.12	–
Advancement	Advancement-style	Advancement-potential	0.10	–
Policy & Administration	Policy-tolerance	Policy-style	–	0.28
Supervision-technical	Supervision-tolerance	Supervision-style	–	0.18
Salary	Salary-tolerance	Salary-style	–	0.15
Interrelationships	Relationship-tolerance	Relationship-style	–	0.14
Work conditions	Conditions-tolerance	Conditions-style	–	0.10

Experimenters may allow the agents to end their activity after their first (dis)satisfaction assessment, or they may set the parameters such that the worker agents either homogeneously or heterogeneously (within a uniform distribution) adjust their motivation factor needs or hygiene factor tolerance.

4 Results

Before presenting the HRM-PET model's results, we lay out how we have verified the model, meaning the process we have used to ensure the model matches its design. We achieved verification of the HRM-PET model using iterative design review (i.e., code walk throughs) and parameter testing sensitivity analysis (for further discussion of sensitivity analysis, see Ligmann-Zielinska et al. 2020). For example, sensitivity testing was carried out using NetLogo's Behavior Space tool, in which we tested the various parameter settings in combination. To determine the initial operability of the model, we performed ten runs in combination for a total of 3490 simulations. Based on the original results of these 3490 simulations, the remaining sensitivity analysis focused on the specific condition of a consistent level of cross-agent change (30 runs each at varying change levels among the factors). This condition allows the experimenter to focus within a smaller set of stochastic elements during validation. This process ensured both that we had made no logical errors in the model's translation into code, and that there were no programming errors in this code. After carrying out these tests, we feel confident that the model behaves as it is intended and matches its design (as outlined in Sect. 3). For model validation, we focused on the purpose of model, that is, as a tool for theory application. To this end, we hypothesized that in cases where work unit quality strongly skews toward low hygiene factor levels, workers would congregate toward fewer select work units.

We tested this hypothesis under work unit distribution conditions of random (uniform distribution), normal, and Poisson. In addition to this, we tested workers in two different conditions. One is where workers exhibit moderately satisficing behavior for their hygiene tolerance and one where the workers exhibit highly selective behavior. In other words, in the former condition, workers remain with their assigned work unit if two hygiene factors are met. In contrast, in the highly selective behavior condition all hygiene factors must be met or the worker leaves the work unit. In all tested cases, the worker population's motivation needs were split between half focusing on their short term needs being met and half focusing on their more enduring needs being met. For the purposes of validating the model in its base state, rather than exploring work unit reactions to workers' (dis)satisfaction levels, we turned off work unit changes to those levels.

The results demonstrated that workers congregated to fewer work units in the Poisson condition. The average of ten validation runs of the simulation in each of the six conditions is displayed in Fig. 3. The validation tests exhibited a qualitative goodness-of-fit, which is a reasonable test for a model meant to exhibit theoretical exploration (Axtell and Epstein 1994).

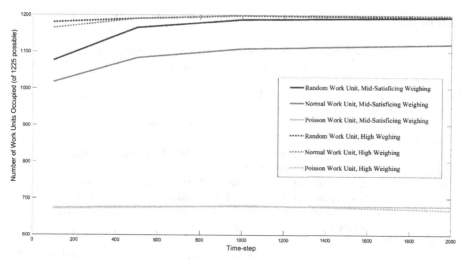

Fig. 3. Worker congregation to work units under three variations of work unit hygiene factor distributions and two variations of weighing worker satisfaction and dissatisfaction.

5 Summary and Further Work

The field of HRM draws on OT research but has not yet extensively leveraged OT's computational tools. We begin to address this gap by developing and presenting a reasonably simple agent-based model to explore the application of a widely used theory in HRM. Agent-based modeling provides an efficient and cost-effective solution for addressing complex HRM tasks. The Two-Factor Theory provides a well-tested theory with which to model agent-work environment interaction. The HRM-PET currently explicitly models agent-environment interaction as the primary mechanism for deriving job (dis)satisfaction and implicitly models agent-agent interaction. This presents a computationally parsimonious approach for those interested in exploring work environments with agent-based modeling. Based on a qualitative validation test of how different distributions of factors among work units affect aggregate behavior of workers, the model generates expected work unit selection patterns.

Using the HRM-PET as a methodological starting point, we see multiple potential paths for future application to examining the TFT and other HRM issues. For example, within the HRM-PET TFT model, agents could engage in strategic exploration versus exploitation action vis-à-vis their work environment interactions (March 1991). Additionally, agent-agent interaction could be extended to model psychological theories of motivation development. For example, McClelland's Motivation Theory for achievement, power, and affiliation seeking (1961, 1975) or Adam's Equity Theory (1975). Allowing the charting of myriad plausible effects of field experiments or workplace interventions, the HRM-PET provides both value to HRM researchers and practitioners, and a foray for ABM simulations into HRM.

References

Adams, J.S.: Toward an Understanding of Inequity. J. Abnorm. Soc. Psychol. **67**, 422–436 (1963)

Armstrong, M.: A Handbook of Human Resource Management Practice. Kogan Page Limited (1999)

Axtell, R., Epstein, J.: Agent-based modeling: understanding our creations. Bull. the Santa Fe Inst. **1994**, 28–32 (1994)

Bassett-Jones, N., Lloyd, G.: Does Herzberg's motivation theory have staying power? J. Manage. Dev. **24**(10), 929–943 (2005)

Cheng, M., Hackett, R.: A critical review of algorithms in HRM: definition, theory, and practice. Hum. Resour. Manage. Rev. 100698 (2019)

Crooks, A., Malleson, N., Manley, E., Heppenstall, A.: Agent-based Modelling and Geographical Information Systems: A Practical Primer. SAGE Publications, Los Angeles (2019)

Dobre, I., Davidescu, A., Eid, M.: Key factors of health employee motivation in jordan: evidence from dual-factor theory based on structural equation models. Econ. Comput. Econ. Cybern. Stud. Res. **51**(2), 39–54 (2017)

Gigerenzer, G., Goldstein, D.G.: Reasoning the fast and frugal way: models of bounded rationality. Psychol. Rev. **104**, 650–669 (1996)

Grimm, V., et al.: A standard protocol for describing individual-based and agent-based models. Ecol. Model. **198**(1), 115–126 (2006)

Hasin, H.H., Omar, N.H.: An empirical study on job satisfaction, job-related stress and intention to leave among audit staff in public accounting firms in Melaka. J. Financ. Reporting Acc. **5**(1), 21–39 (2007)

Herzberg, F.I., Mausner, B., Snyderman, B.: The Motivation to Work, 2nd edn. Wiley, New York (1959)

Hom, P.W., Kinicki, A.J.: Toward a greater understanding of how dissatisfaction drives employee turnover. Acad. Manag. J. **44**(5), 975–987 (2001)

Hunt, S., et al.: Registered nurse retention strategies in nursing homes: a two-factor perspective. Health Care Manage. Rev. **37**(3), 246–256 (2012)

Iammartino, R.: An agent-based model for predicting turnover in the science, technology, engineering, and mathematics (STEM) workforce. Ph.D. dissertation. The George Washington University (2016)

Kennedy, W.G.: Modelling human behaviour in agent-based models. In: Heppenstall, A.J., Crooks, A.T., See, L.M., Batty, M. (eds.) Agent-Based Models of Geographical Systems, pp. 167–179. Springer, Dordrecht (2012). https://doi.org/10.1007/978-90-481-8927-4_9

Kilbridge, M.D.: Turnover, absence, and transfer rates as indicators of employee dissatisfaction with repetitive work. ILR Rev. **15**(1), 21–32 (1961)

Lafuente, A.M.G., Barcellos Paula, L.: Algorithms applied in the sustainable management of human resources. Fuzzy Econ. Rev. **15**(1), 39–51 (2010)

Ligmann-Zielinska, A., et al.: 'One size does not fit all': a roadmap of purpose-driven mixed-method pathways for sensitivity analysis of agent-based models. J. Artif. Soc. Soc. Simul. **23**(1), 6 (2020)

Liu, D., Liao, H., Loi, R.: The dark side of leadership: a three-level investigation of the cascading effect of abusive supervision on employee creativity. Acad. Manag. J. **55**(5), 1187–1212 (2012)

Lundberg, C., Gudmundson, A., Andersson, T.: Herzberg's two-factor theory of work motivation tested empirically on seasonal workers in hospitality and tourism. Tour. Manag. **30**(6), 890–899 (2009)

March, J.G.: Exploration and exploitation in organizational learning. Organ. Sci. **2**, 71–87 (1991)

McClelland, D.C.: The Achieving Society. Van Nostrand, Princeton (1961)

McClelland, D.C.: Power: The Inner Experience. Irvington, New York (1975)

McClelland, D.C.: Motives, Personality, and Society: Selected Papers. Praeger, New York (1984)

Miller, J., Page, S.: Complex Adaptive Systems: An Introduction to Computational Models of Social Life. Princeton University Press, Princeton (2007)

Müller, B., et al.: Describing human decisions in agent-based models – ODD + D, an extension of the ODD protocol. Environ. Model. Softw. **48,** 37–48 (2013)

Ozsoy, E.: An empirical test of Herzberg's two-factor motivation theory. Market. Innov. **1,** 11–20 (2019)

Prietula, M., Carley, K., Gasser, L.: Simulating Organizations: Computational Models of Institutions and Groups. AAAI Press/The MIT Press, Cambridge (1998)

Simon, H.A.: Models of Bounded Rationality: Empirically Grounded Economic Reason. MIT Press, Cambridge (1997)

Tambe, P., Cappelli, P., Yakubovich, V.: Artificial intelligence in human resources management: challenges and a path forward. Calif. Manag. Rev. **61**(4), 15–42 (2019)

Wall, F.: Agent-based modeling in managerial science: an illustrative survey and study. RMS **10**(1), 135–193 (2014). https://doi.org/10.1007/s11846-014-0139-3

Wei, Y.C., Han, T.S., Hsu, I.C.: High-performance HR practices and OCB: a cross-level investigation of a causal path. Int. J. Hum. Resour. Manage. **21**(10), 1631–1648 (2010)

Wilensky, U.: NetLogo. Center for Connected Learning and Computer-Based Modeling, Northwestern University, Evanston, IL (1999). http://ccl.northwestern.edu/netlogo/

Woznyj, H., Heggestad, E., Kennerly, S., Yap, T.: Climate and organizational performance in long-term care facilities: the role of affective commitment. J. Occup. Organ. Psychol. **92**(1), 122–143 (2019)

Utilizing Python for Agent-Based Modeling: The Mesa Framework

Jackie Kazil[1,2]([⊠]) [ID], David Masad[1], and Andrew Crooks[1] [ID]

[1] George Mason University, Fairfax, VA 22020, USA
{jkazil,dmasad,acrooks2}@gmu.edu
[2] Rebellion Defense, Washington DC 20001, USA

Abstract. Mesa is an agent-based modeling framework written in Python. Originally started in 2013, it was created to be the go-to tool in for researchers wishing to
build agent-based models with Python. Within this paper we present Mesa's design
goals, along with its underlying architecture. This includes its core components:
1) the model (Model, Agent, Schedule, and Space), 2) analysis (Data Collector
and Batch Runner) and the visualization (Visualization Server and Visualization
Browser Page). We then discuss how agent-based models can be created in Mesa.
This is followed by a discussion of applications and extensions by other researchers
to demonstrate how Mesa design is decoupled and extensible and thus creating
the opportunity for a larger decentralized ecosystem of packages that people can
share and reuse for their own needs. Finally, the paper concludes with a summary
and discussion of future development areas for Mesa.

Keywords: Agent-based modeling · Python · Framework · Complex systems

1 Introduction

Agent-based modeling (ABM) is a way to simulate the behaviors and interactions of
many autonomous entities, or agents, over time. Such a methodology has many advantages over other mathematical approaches to studying complex systems including the
ability to capture the temporal paths, the spatial paths, and their end states as well as
the ability to study the dynamics of a system and the impact of individual actions and
reactions (Crooks et al. 2019). One of the most novel aspects of ABM is its ability
to explore "transient, non-equilibrium, non-stationary behavior" of a system and along
with that ability, to computationally trace it (Epstein and Axtell 1996). ABMs have seen
tremendous growth over the last 20 years (Crooks et al. 2019), leading a growth of
ABM frameworks (which we further discuss below). However, there also was a void.
There was no framework for easily building a model in Python, as well as no ability to
serve a model over Hypertext Transfer Protocol (HTTP) which takes advantage of modern browser-based technologies. In response to this, we created Mesa[1], an open source

---

[1] We chose the name Mesa for three weak reasons: (1) It sounded like Mason, (2) It evoked the
mesas around Santa Fe, the location of the Santa Fe Institute and home to much complexity
research, and (3) It was a short and memorable name that was available on the Python Package
Index (PyPI).

© Springer Nature Switzerland AG 2020
R. Thomson et al. (Eds.): SBP-BRiMS 2020, LNCS 12268, pp. 308–317, 2020.
https://doi.org/10.1007/978-3-030-61255-9_30

framework for creating agent-based models in Python. Mesa was released under Apache 2 ("Apache License, Version 2.0" 2004) in order to be flexible both for academia and private sector use. Mesa can be installed directly by "pip install mesa" or by downloading it from Github: https://github.com/projectmesa/mesa.

To create and study complex systems from the bottom up, a number of open source frameworks have been developed (see Crooks et al. 2019 for a review). The most widely used one being NetLogo (Wilensky 1999) which made agent-based models accessible for non-professional programmers. In an analysis of comses.net (formally known as openabm.org) which allows researchers to share their agent-based models McCabe (2016) found that approximately 60% of the models created were NetLogo. However, NetLogo does not scale (i.e., in terms of numbers of agents) (North et al. 2013), nor does it have the same execution speed of Mason (Luke et al. 2005) as noted by Railsback et al. (2006). Despite the plethora of frameworks to build agent-based models until the creation of Mesa there was not one utilizing Python. In the remainder of this paper we discuss Mesa's design goals (Sect. 1.1) before introducing its architecture and usage in Sect. 2. In, Sect. 3 we provide insight into applications and extensions to Mesa from its user community, while Sect. 4 provides a summary of the paper and outlines future development directions.

1.1 Mesa's Design Goals

Mesa's design goals go beyond building agent-based models rapidly in Python, headless or displaying them in the browser. Mesa has a permissive license (i.e., Apache 2) and was built to be accessible to a wide range of users, similar to NetLogo, but extensible, like Mason. Similar to other frameworks, Mesa is focused on the core functionality that is needed when building agent-based models (e.g., reusable objects, scheduling, and graphical user interfaces), thus allowing modelers to focus on the development of models rather than parts of the simulation that are not content specific (e.g., the display of the model). Mesa is intended to be extensible, which allows users to easily develop and share their own components through open source ecosystems such as Gitlab and Github. However, it should be noted that Mesa is not intended to be an all-encompassing toolbox; we believe specialized components should be offered as separate packages, similar to how GeoMason (Sullivan et al. 2010) is an extension of Mason. Lastly, Mesa was built to take advantage of the Python and JavaScript ecosystems. Our rationale for using Python was that it is a rapidly growing programing language used throughout academia and industry (Robinson 2017). Furthermore, it seamlessly integrates with popular data science tools such as Jupyter notebooks and Pandas for ease of analysis of data. For example, the continuous space module in Mesa uses the NumPy arrays in the background to speed up neighborhood lookups.

Generally, the approach for Mesa has followed the well-known programming philosophy: "Make it work. Make it right. Make it fast." Mesa was not intended to be a high-performance tool when it was first designed, although over time, some contributions have been made to improve performance, such as the addition of a multi-processing batch runner, which allows for multiple cores to be used to run multiple simulations at the same time. Moreover, we have prioritized accessibility over performance in the building of Mesa. This decision was a part of exercising core Python principles such as simplicity and reliability. In addition to this, Mesa was written to run on a single core. Multicore processing is was not an initial priority, because of its complexity, but we haven't ruled this out as possible future development. In comparison to other well adopted ABM tools, Mesa has two major advantages. The first is that it is written in Python, which is accessible and integrates well with a many of open data science tools (e.g., Jupyter notebooks and Pandas). The second is the architecture of Mesa, which allows users to easily replace components, which is what we turn to next.

2   Architecture and Usage

Mesa is written in Python and has a front end that takes advantage of front-end browser-based technologies. The underlying structure for how Mesa is laid and designed is influenced by Django (2013), a web framework written in Python. Django's design decouples the models, views, and controller architecture. In a similar fashion, we decoupled the components of Mesa to be easily replaceable and in the case of the model, could be used independent of the other components. There are three major components which make up Mesa from a user perspective. These are the model (Model, Agent, Schedule, and Space), analysis (Data Collector and Batch Runner) and the visualization (Visualization Server and Visualization Browser Page) and the relationship of these components can be seen in Fig. 1.

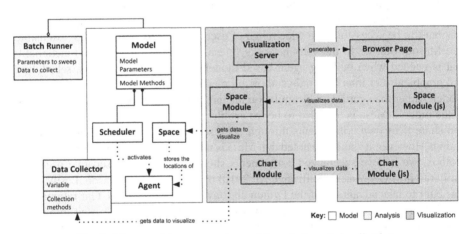

Fig. 1. Mesa model components: model, analysis and visualization.

2.1   The Model

The model is the core of Mesa and the other two components, analysis and visualization would not exist without it. However, the model can stand alone without the other two components. The model as it is referred to here contains the major components of what it means to be an ABM: agents, the space they exist within, and the time and activation controllers. Separately from what is called "the model", there is a Model class, which is the core class for creating a model. In this class, the user defines the initial state of the model, what happens when the model runs, what occurs each step for the environment, and also the space the agents inhabit. In addition to the model class, there is also the Agent class, which is the object that is subclassed when defining the agents. The default Mesa package comes with predefined spaces (which we discuss further below), which are located in the space module. This module provides the following space types: continuous, single grid, multiple grids, hexagonal grid, or a network grid. The default Mesa package also comes with a time module which contains schedules, which handles agent activation. Due to the complexity and nuances of the space and schedule (i.e., time) modules, we will go into depth into those next.

The Scheduler. Special attention was placed into the functionality of Mesa's scheduler. Generally, speaking, most agent-based models are discrete-event simulations and rarely are they continuous (Masad and Kazil 2015). As a result, the activation order of agents can significantly impact the behavior and results of a simulation (Comer 2014). Mesa takes this into account and offers a variety of methods to implement the activation of agents. In comparison to other ABM frameworks, this is a unique feature to Mesa. Each model step, or "a tick", results in the activation of one or more agents. There are many different approaches to scheduling agent activation including synchronous or simultaneous activation, uniform activation, random activation, random interval activation, and more complex activation regimes (Masad and Kazil 2015). It was Comer's (2014) research and impact of different approaches to scheduling that led to the design of the scheduler in Mesa. The simplest scheduler is in BaseScheduler class which is a uniform activation and was created with the intent to replicate the scheduler in Mason. In addition to the BaseScheduler, there is also the RandomActivation class, which behaviors similar to the scheduler in NetLogo, the SimultaneousActivation class, and the StagedActivation class. More details on these activation schedulers are found in Table 1. To understand the impact of various scheduling routines, see Fig. 2, where we show three different activation schemes (i.e., sequential, random, and simultaneous) for the same step even when the initial model configuration was the same.

Table 1. Activation schedules within Mesa

Activation	Agent activation details
BaseScheduler	Agents are activated one at a time, in the order they were added to the scheduler (i.e., sequential activation)
RandomActivation	Agents are activated one at time, once per step, in random order. Reshuffled every time tick
SimultaneousActivation	Each agent's actions are queued based on the state of the model at the end of the previous step. Then all agents advance at the same time
StagedActivation	Allows agent activation to be divided into several stages instead of a single step. All agents execute one stage before moving on to the next. This scheduler tracks steps and time separately

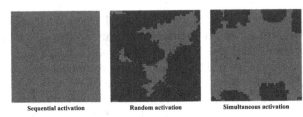

Sequential activation   Random activation   Simultaneous activation

Fig. 2. An illustration of how different activation schemes impact a model, in this case the Prisoner's Dilemma. Defecting agents are in red and cooperating agents are in blue. Each image is from the same step, but different activation schemes are used. (Color figure online)

Space. While the concept of space is not required for all agent-based models (e.g., the Zero Intelligence Traders model (Gode and Sunder 1993)), an ABM framework would be incomplete without a spatial component. Mesa has three general space definitions: continuous, grid, and networks (which are also common in MASON and Repast). Both the continuous and grid spaces have a method, which allows users to designate whether the space is toroidal or not. All the classes have a similar set of methods which allow the user to get information on the agent's position and location, move the agent, and get information on the agent's neighbors.

Neighborhood identification is handled slightly differently in the general space categories. In the continuous space, neighbors are determined by a defined radius. In the grid space, neighborhoods can be defined as Moore neighborhoods (includes diagonal neighbors) or von Neumann neighborhoods (excludes diagonals), except in the case of a hexagonal grid, which provides access to neighbors on each of the six sides of the hexagon. Lastly, neighbors in networks are provided by adjacent nodes.

Each class of spaces works slightly differently. The ContinuousSpace class, agents have an (x, y) position, while all of the grid classes are discrete spaces. The most basic grid class, which all other grid classes are based off of, represents cells as rectangular spaces. The SingleGrid class limits cells to only have one object per cell, while the MultiGrid class allows for a set of objects per cell. The last extension of the Grid class is the HexGrid class. At the time of this paper, agents placed on the HexGrid grid have an (x, y) position, but it is possible for this class to be extended to offer a (x, y, z) position and offer a 3D-like modeling grid (Patel 2019). Finally, the NetworkGrid has nodes that hold zero or more agents. The NetworkGrid requires a graph object as an argument that is created with the Python library NetworkX (Hagberg et al. 2008). By using NetworkX, Mesa is able to take advantage of all the graph metrics and operations that the NetworkX library provides. It is also possible to create multilayer networks by instantiating multiple graphs. Space would be incomplete without mentioning geospatial models. Similar to the early development of other frameworks (e.g., NetLogo and MASON), the current version of Mesa does not have specific support for geospatial data. However, it allows for importation of text files to create artificial landscapes so in a way it does allow for raster data to be added to models like in Sugarscape. Our rationale for not including GIS support into core Mesa is its dependencies on many third-party packages for importing and exporting data etc. However, this is one area we plan on exploring in the future. If readers of this paper want to use geospatial data with Mesa, a core contributor known as Corvince, has created a package which offers this functionality entitled Mesa-Geo (https://github.com/Corvince/mesa-geo).

2.2 Model Analysis

Data Collection. While agent-based models can be interesting to run, it is difficult to gain insights into the model without gathering data and conducting an analysis. To address this issue, Mesa provides the DataCollector class which records, stores, and exports data from the model and agents as well as data that isn't covered in model or agent data abstractions. The DataCollector is initiated with model and agent variables and their respective collection functions. The collector will return the computed value of the model and agent collector at their current state. Data not covered by model or agents can be stored by passing a dictionary object for a table row. One use case might be to log model events or state as the model progresses. These types of data points do not occur at regular intervals. The DataCollector makes data exports easy as well, by using dictionaries and lists to store the data, it makes it easy to export to common data formats such as Pandas DataFrames, JSON, or CSV. By doing this we can take the data out of Mesa and into a popular browser-based workbook-like tool called Jupyter Notebooks, which is used by data scientists for analysis and storytelling with data.

Batch Runner. While it is possible to collect data for individual model runs, this is not the most efficient use of time. Researchers carry out parameter sweeps in order to get a more representative picture of the potential outcomes of a model. To do this, Mesa provides the BatchRunner class. The BatchRunner is instantiated with model and agent-level reporters which are dictionaries with a variable name and function mapping. This class works by generating runs for all possible combinations of values that the user passed to the runner. The iterations argument in the BatchRunner allows user to define how many times they want to run a particular combination of settings in order to account for the stochasticity of their model. Each run terminates after a set number of steps or until the model terminates. At that time, the Batchrunner will collect the reporters. By default, the BatchRunner only collects at the end of a run, but it can be set to collect the whole run by storing the whole DataCollector object.

2.3 Model Visualization

While models can be run headless in Mesa (i.e., no visualization), Mesa also provides a front-end browser-based visualization. We choose a browser-based visualization system over a desktop-based graphical user interface (GUI) for two reasons. First, desktop GUIs lack flexibility in sharing models. By making a model browser based, users can run a model locally on their personal computer or make it accessible to the others to run via the Internet and web browser. Secondly, browser-based front-end technologies develop more rapidly with the changing nature of web application design. Since the creation of Mesa, the front end has been rewritten completely once and changes more rapidly with improvements than the more stable back end. At the time of this publication, the front-end technologies used are HTML5, Bootstrap, D3, JQuery, Sigma.js for displaying networks, and various charting libraries. A screenshot of the front end of two models created with Mesa can be found in Fig. 3.

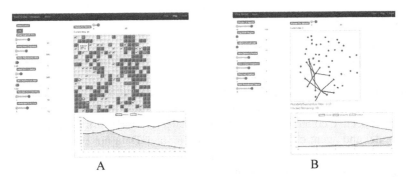

A   B

Fig. 3. Model visualization of two Mesa applications within a web browser: (A) Wolf-sheep predation Model. (B) Virus on a network (Source: https://github.com/projectmesa).

Models built in Mesa are served to the browser using Tornado, a Python based web server. Mesa uses Tornado's coroutines to ensure that the model does not block the front end from being served. In the browser, the user can control the model run with the expected tooling such "start," "stop," and "step" as well as any controls that they have defined. The commands in the browser trigger the back end. The ModularServer class is what handles the passing of the model and visualizations to the front end. At the end of each step, data in JSON form is sent to front end via a WebSocket connection. This data is then displayed to show the current form of the model and to update any charts or counts that the user also defined to be displayed. When launched locally, the front end can be accessed in any browser window at http://127.0.0.1:8521/.

The user defines which data from the DataCollector is passed to the browser and in what form. Mesa will then render the page for them, so the user does not have to think about styling of the page. To do this, Mesa offers a few preset visualization models and controls. Each visualization module in Mesa has a component on the client-side, in JavaScript, and server-side, in Python. The two of these are developed in tandem, because one does not work with other. When a model is being written, the user passes the visualization objects and the model to the ModularServer to pass them to the front end.

Visualizations provided correlate with the offerings in the space module on the back end, which include a CanvasGridVisualization, used to visual the grid objects from the back end, a HexGridVisualization for hexagonal grids, and a NetworkVisualization to display networks. There are also charting modules to render line charts, bar charts, and pie charts. Lastly, there is a TextVisualization, which renders text, such as count values on the front end. All of these modules update when the model is running. By providing these modules, users only have to consider what values they want displayed.

2.4 Creating a Model

While the act of writing code brings a lot of freedom, it can create inconsistencies from one model to another. One example is file organization and layouts. In a framework like NetLogo, there is only one place to write code (i.e., the code tab), but in Mesa, without guidance you can place your code in one file or in twenty files. As a result, we and members of the community converged on standards. To explain the standards, we will use the Wolf-Sheep Predation Model found in the examples folder (http://bit.ly/projec tmesa-examples) in Mesa code repository (see http://bit.ly/WolfSheepMesa). At the top level, a model should be laid out with a Readme.md, a requirements.txt, a run.py, and a folder named after the model using Python naming conventions PEP 8. For the Wolf-Sheep model, the folder is called 'wolf_sheep'. The Readme.md describes the model and is similar to the "Info" tab in NetLogo. The requirements.txt is a Python standard that holds information on the dependencies for a project. Every model will have 'mesa' as one of its dependencies. When building models, it is important to be explicit about which version of Mesa, i.e., 'mesa == 0.8.6', so when core Mesa updates, the model that depends on a certain version of Mesa still continues to function properly. Lastly, the run.py is what launches the server if you are using the front end.

Inside a model folder there should be at least three files: agents.py, model.py, and server.py. In some cases, there may be a schedule.py or other files that are used in the model (e.g., the Wolf-Sheep example). Agents.py house agents, model.py houses the model, and the visualization server details such as charts and grids are in the server.py. When a user launches a model, it looks for the details that define how the server should behave. We tried to make adhering to the standards as easy as possible, so we built a command line tool into Mesa. To start a new project, which lays out all the base files, objects, and text, a user only has to type 'mesa startproject' on the command line in an environment where Mesa is installed. This will prompt a few questions, which after answering will generates the files. In addition to 'mesa startproject' the command line tool will also run the server from inside a model by running 'mesa runserver'.

In addition to the tools and prescriptions we provide, we also encourage users of Mesa to share their models openly so others can learn from them, as well as to isolate development environments by using Virtualenv or something similar in order to make sure dependencies don't come into conflict when building a lot of models, and finally use tools like Flake8 and Black to keep the model code well formatted and clean of extra variables. The purpose of the standards in this section is to make models easy to understand.

3 Applications and Extensions of Mesa

While above, we have introduced Mesa, since its initial release numerous social scientists and researchers have utilized it in a wide range of applications. Over 50 published papers have cited Mesa (Google Scholar 2020) and more than 250 code repositories on GitHub have Mesa as a requirement, which cross many domains such as economics, biology, infrastructure, workplace dynamics etc. (e.g., Pires et al. 2017; Neves et al. 2019). For further applications areas where Mesa has been used see: bit.ly/mesa-publications.

Turning to extensions, as discussed in Sect. 1.1, one of the goals of Mesa is to be extensible and to have interchangeable parts, which allows people to easily integrate specific functionality that might not be a part of the core Mesa package (such as Mesa-Geo). That is not the only geo-spatial modification we found. For example, Heinz (2017) created a modified version which took a simulation server and embedded it into a Django-Channels application and to create a front end with leaflet maps. Another is an open source package called Simulation Occupancy based Agents (SOBA, https://github.com/gsi-upm/soba) which simulates the occupancy of agents in buildings (Delgado 2017). The SOBA project has led to the creation of the simulation tool of building evacuations (Escobar 2017). Lastly, Pike (2018), has created two extensions, Bilateral Shapley and Multi-level Mesa (https://github.com/tpike3/).

4 Conclusion

Motivated by the lack of a Python framework for agent-based modeling, this paper has introduced Mesa. Specially its design goals, the model architecture (along with its key components), how to use it, and some examples of usage and extensions. The success of this framework was highlighted in Sect. 3 with respect to how the Python and agent-based modeling community are utilizing and extending it to meet their modeling needs. However, Mesa is a community effort, and we belief Mesa will continue to evolve to meet the needs of the researchers with the help of the community. For example, as noted in Sect. 1, Mesa only allows for single core processing, however, as multiple cores in machines are becoming the norm, efforts need to be made to explore multithreading and distributed processing. Additional areas of opportunity in core Mesa include the scaling of the data collector by using check pointing, increasing the front-end modules and controls, along with exploring the addition of 3D grids. Beyond Mesa, we look forward to a community of Mesa packages, which extend functionality not offered in core like Mesa-Geo and domain specific extensions that extend the model and agent objects like SOBA.

Acknowledgements. While originally developed by Jackie Kazil and David Masad, Mesa has had over 70 contributors. A special thank you to Corvince, rht, Taylor Mulch, and Tom Pike for their contributions or continuing support to Mesa.

References

Apache License, Version 2.0 (2004). https://www.apache.org/licenses/LICENSE-2.0. Accessed 28 Feb 2020

Comer, K.W.: Who goes first? An examination of the impact of activation on outcome behavior in agent-based models. Ph.D. dissertation, George Mason University, Fairfax, VA (2014)

Crooks, A.T., Malleson, N., Manley, E., Heppenstall, A.J.: Agent-Based Modelling and Geographical Information Systems: A Practical Primer. Sage, London, UK (2019)

Delgado, P.A.: design and development of an agent-based social simulation visualization tool for indoor crowd analytics based on the library Three.Js. Ph.D. dissertation, Universidad Politecnica De Madrid, Madrid, Spain (2017)

Django: Django (version 1.5) (2013). https://www.djangoproject.com/. Accessed 28 Feb 2020

Epstein, J.M., Axtell, R.: Growing Artificial Societies: Social Science from the Bottom Up. MIT Press, Cambridge (1996)

Escobar, G.F.: Design and implementation of an agent-based crowd simulation model for evacuation of university buildings using Python. Ph.D. dissertation, Universidad Politecnica De Madrid, Madrid, Spain (2017)

Gode, D.K., Sunder, S.: Allocative efficiency of markets with zero-intelligence traders: market as a partial substitute for individual rationality. J. Polit. Econ. **101**, 119–137 (1993)

Google Scholar. Papers Citing Mesa (2020). bit.ly/GScholarMesa. Accessed 28 Feb 2020

Hagberg, A., Swart, P., Chult, D.S.: Exploring Network Structure, Dynamics, and Function using NetworkX, Los Alamos National Lab (No. LA-UR-08-05495; LA-UR-08-5495), Los Alamos, NM (2008)

Heinz, T.: Location-based game design pattern exploration through agent-based simulation. In: AGILE 2017 Workshop on Geogames and Geoplay, Wageningen, Netherlands (2017)

Luke, S., Cioffi-Revilla, C., Panait, L., Sullivan, K., Balan, G.: MASON: a multi-agent simulation environment. Simulation **81**(7), 517–527 (2005)

Masad, D., Kazil, J.: Mesa: an agent-based modeling framework. In: Huff, K., Bergstra, J. (eds.) Proceedings of the 14th Python in Science Conference, Austin, TX, pp. 53–60 (2015)

McCabe, S.: Communicating sequential agents: an analysis of concurrent agent scheduling. MA thesis, George Mason University, Fairfax, VA (2016)

Neves, F., Campos, P., Silva, S.: Innovation and employment: an agent-based approach. J. Artif. Soc. Soc. Simul. **22**(1), 8 (2019)

North, M.J., et al.: Complex adaptive systems modeling with repast simphony. Complex Adapt. Syst. Model. **1**(1) (2013). https://doi.org/10.1186/2194-3206-1-3

Patel, A.: Red Blob Games: Hexagonal Grids (2019). https://www.redblobgames.com/grids/hexagons/. Accessed 28 Feb 2020

Pike, T.: Integrating computational tools into foreign policy: introducing mesa packages with a coalition algorithm. J. Policy Complex Syst. **4**(2) (2018). https://doi.org/10.18278/jpcs.4.2.5

Pires, B., Goldstein, J., Molfino, E., Ziemer, K.S.: Knowledge sharing in a dynamic, multi-level organization: exploring cascade and threshold models of diffusion. In: Proceedings of the 2017 International Conference of the Computational Social Science Society of the Americas Santa Fe, NM (2017)

Railsback, S.F., Lytinen, S.L., Jackson, S.K.: Agent-based simulation platforms: review and development recommendations. Simulation **82**(9), 609–623 (2006)

Robinson, D.: Why Is Python Growing So Quickly? (2017). https://stackoverflow.blog/2017/09/14/python-growing-quickly/. Accessed 28 Feb 2020

Sullivan, K., Coletti, M., Luke, S.: GeoMason: GeoSpatial Support for MASON, Department of Computer Science, George Mason University, Technical Report Series, Fairfax, VA (2010)

Wilensky, U.: NetLogo. Center for Connected Learning and Computer-Based Modeling, Northwestern University, Evanston, IL (1999). http://ccl.northwestern.edu/netlogo

Strategic Information Operation in YouTube: The Case of the White Helmets

Nazim Choudhury[✉][iD], Kin Wai Ng[iD], and Adriana Iamnitchi[iD]

University of South Florida, Tampa, USA
{nachoudhury,kinwaing,aii}@usf.edu

Abstract. Strategic information operations (e.g. disinformation, political propaganda, and other forms of online manipulation) are critical concerns for researchers in social cyber security. Two strategies, spoofing and astroturfing, are often employed in disinformation campaigns to discredit truthful narratives, confuse audiences, and manipulate opinions by censoring critics' voices or using one-sided testimonials. This study analyzes patterns of spoofing and astroturfing on YouTube regarding narratives about the White Helmets, a Syrian civil volunteer organization active in the long armed conflict in the country.

Keywords: Information operations · Spoofing · Astroturfing · YouTube

1 Introduction

The Syrian civil war transcended from the battlefield to the digital information space seeking to harness the dissemination of old-fashioned propaganda using various digital information media, including YouTube. The objective of the digital campaign was to manipulate the public perception of the civil war and elicit support from foreign, especially western sympathizers. Since September 2016, pro-Assad supporters and their allies mounted a massive disinformation campaign to discredit a civilian rescue group named 'White Helmets' (WH). The group's humanitarian activities, its efforts to document the targeting of civilians through video evidence, and its refusal to align itself with any other group or military factions engaged in the complex Syrian conflict put the group at odds with the government and their allies, including Russia [12].

Political propaganda, disinformation, influence and information manipulation, also known as Strategic Information Operations [16], denote efforts to manipulate public opinions and perceptions of events via intentional alteration of the information environment. Proliferation of social media platforms and freedom of integrating YouTube videos in tweets, blogs, or social media posts along with YouTube's recommendation algorithms have been exploited to frame public discourse and conduct strategic information operations. Wilson and Starbird [18] presented a tracing of information trajectories across YouTube, Twitter, and non-mainstream news domains to demonstrate how state-sponsored

© Springer Nature Switzerland AG 2020
R. Thomson et al. (Eds.): SBP-BRiMS 2020, LNCS 12268, pp. 318–328, 2020.
https://doi.org/10.1007/978-3-030-61255-9_31

media apparatus shaped the disinformation campaign against the White Helmets. Two conventional techniques for the manipulation of information environments are spoofing and astroturfing. Spoofing involves deception and trickery to misrepresent both source identity and information veracity through falsification, suppression, or amplification [5]. Astroturfing, on the other hand, involves manufactured, deceptive and strategic top-down activities initiated by politically or ideologically-motivated actors to mimic bottom-up activity [11]. This can involve autonomous or non-autonomous individuals who create an illusion of widespread support for a candidate or opinion. Spoofing was found on Twitter [4], while astroturfing was extensively found on Twitter [8,9], Facebook [6], emails [10] and websites [19]. Platform-specific features (such as type of content and type of user interactions) suggest different ways of recognizing astroturfing and spoofing. For example, in Twitter, user attributes and their temporal activities were used to identify spoofed accounts [17], whereas their interactions patterns (e.g., co-tweet and co-retweet) were used to identify astroturfing [9]. Hussain et al. [3] analyzed user engagement on YouTube and applied social network analysis techniques to identify inorganic behaviors.

This article conducts interpretative analyses on four months of YouTube data focusing on the strategic information operations mounted against the WH. Our contributions are twofold: first, we show evidence of inorganic behaviors in user comments on WH-related videos which suggests the possibility of information and identity spoofing. We also highlight unusual correlation between highly visible videos and highly appreciated comments by a small group of users and suspect the existence of astroturfing activities. Second, the methods we present, while inspired by previous work, have been adapted to the particularities of YouTube and can serve for similar studies on this platform.

2   Dataset

For this study, we focus on YouTube data specific to the White Helmets, collected using the YouTube API keyword query tool between April 1, 2018 and July 31, 2018. The dataset was provided privately as part of DARPA SocialSim program. The list of keywords used in the YouTube data collection are 'white helmets', 'cascos blancos', 'capacetes brancos', 'caschi bianchi', 'casques blancs', 'elmetti bianchi', 'weisshelme', 'weiß helme', 'syrian civil defence', and lastly White Helmets in Russian and Arabic. This dataset contains 76 videos from 42 different channels. For each video, we have their corresponding top-comments and replies. Overall, the dataset includes a total of 10,636 comments and 3,633 replies done by 8,071 and 1,892 users, respectively. The total counts of likes (liked by the other commenters) associated with each comment or reply were also collected.

3   Spoofing

As a technique of disinformation, Martin [5] identified two master types of spoofing: identity and information. Identity spoofing involves constructing false digital identities. Information spoofing involves misrepresenting the content of a message through processes of falsification, suppression, amplification or even sometimes blending these techniques together. In order to understand the extent to which identity and information spoofing contributed to the anti-WH campaign on YouTube, we considered the observations in [2] on analyzing the Twitter activities of specialized bot accounts, known as social bots, during the Maidan protest in Ukraine. The authors found that these social bots not only were capable of mimicking humans and thus hide detection via constantly changing the contents of their tweets, but they also promoted certain topics through massive repetition of messages and retweeting of selected tweets.

Instead of focusing on the behavioral characteristics of users accounts, following Schäfer et al. [14], we used a corpus-linguistic approach to detect bots among YouTube commenters. The collected YouTube comments on different videos uploaded by different channels were normalized via cleaning (removing white spaces, punctuation, URLs and emojis), and tokenization. A hash structure via locality sensitive hashing (LSH) [15] with minHash [13] was used to recognize semantic and near-duplicates of the normalized comments. LSH aims to preserve the local relations of the data by significantly reducing the dimensionality of the dataset and ensuring hash collisions for similar items, something that hashing algorithms usually try to avoid. Through the hash structure, we identified near-duplicated comments posted by a small number of users on different videos. In general, near-duplicate comments contained similar texts with small modifications predominantly generated via adding/changing emojis, URLs, or word(s) in the front or end of the comments.

Figure 1 presents network snapshots of videos-comments and videos-commenters constructed by considering the near-duplicate comments posted on different videos. In the left network, the red nodes are videos and the blue nodes denote *top comments* (top-ranked popular comments visible on the first page of all comments) on those videos. The green edges connect a video with its comments and the orange edges represent the near-duplicate relationship between comments. On the right, we present a snapshot of the video-commenters relationships where the purple nodes are the commenters responsible for the near-duplicate comments and the red nodes represent the videos. The thickness of the orange edges is proportional to the number of posts (comments or replies to other users' comments) made by that user on that particular video. Thus, the network on the left presents videos as they are (indirectly) connected by duplicate posts and the network on the right presents the very same videos connected by the user accounts who post the duplicate messages.

Similar to the findings reported in [3], we find inorganic commenting behaviors: First, out of the 76 videos in the initial dataset, 62 appear in Fig. 1 (top) connected by a total of 241 posts with at least one duplicate (out of a total of more than 14K comments and replies), of which only 93 are distinct according to our duplicate evaluations. These messages are posted by 87 users. The most common duplicate message is posted 19 times by the same user on the same video, as depicted by the highly connected cluster in the left network. There are 76 messages that are posted twice in this small dataset. Second, the same

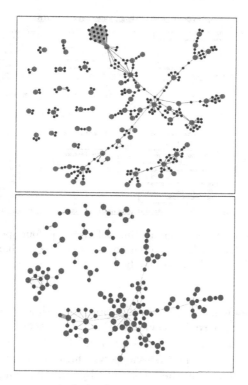

Fig. 1. Videos-comments network (top): red nodes represent videos and blue nodes represent comments; green edges denote a comment on a video and orange edges connect duplicated comments. The corresponding videos-commenters network (bottom): purple nodes represent the user accounts who made the comments in the left network snapshot. The weight of the orange edges is the number of posts made by a user on a video. (Color figure online)

comment is posted repeatedly by the same user on the same video. For example, the 19 duplicate messages posted on the same video are posted by the same user. In another example, one user engages with a video 99 times via comments and replies, as shown by the thick edge in the network on the right. And third, duplicate messages are posted by different user accounts. We found five videos with evidence of identity spoofing. Each such video has pairs of duplicated comments in which duplicate messages are posted by different user accounts. Three of these videos have one such pair of duplicated messages, the fourth has two pairs, and the fifth has three pairs of duplicate messages allegedly authored by different user accounts. Because of the inorganic behavior of the users involved in posting duplicate messages, we will use 'spoofed accounts' and 'social bots' interchangeably to refer to these identified commenters in the rest of the study. A deeper investigation in the behavioral patterns around identity and information spoofing led us to discover the following three types of activity:

Fig. 2. Timeline of coordinated commenting behaviors by four spoofed accounts (B1, B2, B3, B4) on two videos (titled in red and blue colored texts) shared by the channels named 'Lift the Veil' and 'RT', respectively. (Color figure online)

Coordination: We identified the coordination of multiple spoofed accounts who posted comments on two YouTube videos. Figure 2 presents the timeline of comments by four user accounts (shown as B1, B2, B3, B4) on two videos uploaded on two different channels. The first video was hosted by RT, a Russian state-sponsored media channel, and the second one by 'Lift the Veil', a channel mostly dedicated to sharing conspiracy theories. Each commenter, identified in our analysis as spoofed accounts, posted the same message on the two videos at approximately 2-min intervals. Even more unusual is that in both YouTube videos, with different titles on the same topic, these users commented in the same order and with similar inter-arrival time between their postings. This suggests the possibility of a coordinated effort in which spoofed accounts controlled by the same agent promote messages on different videos posted on different channels with the common objective of discrediting WH.

DogPiling: Figure 3 (top) shows two users (green nodes) who posted comments on two videos and who received many reactions (as replies to those comments) from other users. The two videos are hosted by RT and Vesti News channels—a brand used by the Russian broadcaster VGTRK (All-Russia State Television and Radio Broadcasting Company). The arrow directions represent comments to videos or replies to comments. Comments by the green nodes, denouncing/criticizing the Syrian regime and their collaborators, were explicitly challenged and confronted by multiple replies from both spoofed and non-spoofed accounts in a cascade of dissent and insults. This form of attack is a form of "dogpiling" [7] which manifests via hostile efforts to drown out and drive out (through intimidation and harassment) users and content who, in this instance, showed support to the WH.

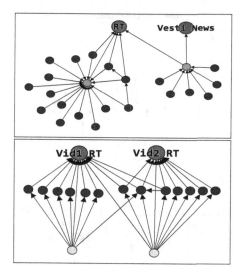

Fig. 3. Dogpiling network (top): Dissenting comments on a video (green nodes) are confronted by multiple users. Replicators network (bottom): Social bots (yellow nodes) replicate and modify the comments by replacing keywords. (Color figure online)

Replication: The third type of attack is portrayed in Fig. 3 (bottom), where two social bots were found replying to multiple commenters. While the commenters were discrediting the Assad regime and its allies as well as the corresponding YouTube channel that hosted the videos, the repliers replicated the same message only by replacing keywords. For example, the comment 'everyone knows Russia is a state of liars' was replied with the text 'everyone knows USA is a state of liars'. The average time spent on bulk replies against 10–12 posts was 4 min in two instances. This may suggest automated behavior or a dedicated human user whose comments are triggered by this type of messaging.

4   Astroturfing?

Online astroturfing creates the illusion of widespread grassroots support by posting or artificially supporting messages that advance a specific opinion or narrative [20]. Astroturfing is a common strategy of disinformation in politics [9] where the goal is to create the impression of popular support.

Due to the anonymity offered by social media platforms, astroturfing is usually covert, sophisticated, and hard to distinguish from genuine grassroots support. To uncover online astroturfing in the campaign against WH, we concentrated on the top commenters with high volume of comments on different YouTube channels. We represent a $n \times r$ matrix with $n = 200$ rows for each commenter who posted comments on different videos uploaded by $r = 27$ channels between April 1st 2018 and July 31st 2018. Figure 4 (top) visualizes this matrix: the red dots represent comments posted by each of the 200 users on

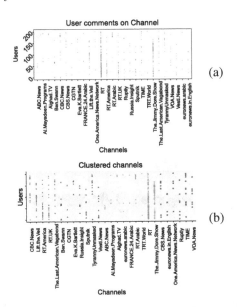

Fig. 4. (a) Commenting patterns by the top-200 active commenters on different YouTube channels (top) and (b) clusters of channels obtained by block clustering. Color codes represent clusters of channels (bottom).

Table 1. Popularity achieved by the videos published in each cluster, identified by the block-clustering approach. Popularity metrics are presented as the average likes of the comments and average likes, and views of the videos.

Cluster	Videos	Spoofed accounts	Views	Likes
C1	11	5	175,971	5,750
C2	8	3	103,197	4,405
C3	10	5	210,819	1,534
C4	10	11	660,383	21,649
C5	9	3	34,208	746

each channel. An entry in m_{xy} is equal to one if commenter x commented on a video uploaded by channel y and zero otherwise. An expectation-maximization algorithm based on a block mixture model [1] was used to cluster the channels by user interactions. Figure 4 (bottom) presents the optimal clustering of the channels according to user interactions. We obtained five such clusters. Clusters C1, C3, and C5 (as per Table 1) contain a mixture of main stream media and questionable sources (conspiracy theories channels or subsidiaries of Russia Today). Thus, C1 contains *CBC News* and four questionable channels: two known for promoting conspiracy theories, *Lift the Veil* and *The Last American Vagabond*, and two subsidiaries of Russia Today, *RT America* and *RT UK*. C3 contains *ABC News, Al Mayadeen Programs, Alghad TV, FRANCE 24 Arabic, RT Arabic, TRT World, euronews arabic.* C5 contains *CBS News, One America News Network, Ruptly, TIME, VOA News,* and *euronews in English.* The other two clusters obtained are more homogeneous, containing channels of well-known anti-WH activists along with news channels classified as heavily biased. C2 contains the YouTube channels *Ben Swann, CGTN, Eva K Bartlett, Russia Insight, Sputnik, TyrannyUnmasked, Vesti News.* C4 contains *RT* and *The Jimmy Dore Show.*

As shown in Table 1, C4 (that consists of the Russia Today channel and a far-left YouTube channel run by the American stand-up comedian and political commentator Jimmy Dore) is the most popular cluster: it attracted the largest number of manipulative accounts as detected by our analysis from the top 200 commenters; and it generated the largest number of likes and views on average per video. Most messages refer to the video titled "Carla Ortiz Shocking Video From Syria Contradicts Corp News Coverage", where Jimmy Dore interviewed Carla Ortiz, a former Hollywood actress and a front-runner anti-WH activist. We will refer to this video as the "Interview" in the rest of the paper.

The "Interview" was posted 2 days after the last video in the RT channel was posted. 110 users commented on videos published by both channels. From these, 60 users commented on RT's videos before they commented on the Jimmy Dore Show's video. We will focus on these 60 users and we will refer to them as *RT-commenters*, as they appear to have engaged earlier with the anti-WH narratives as promoted by the Russian government-sponsored RT channel. 34 users commented on the "Interview" video for the first time in our dataset. The "Interview" video had the highest number of views (205,814) and likes (10,437) in cluster C4, followed by one of the videos from RT with much less popularity: 110,258 views and 3,005 likes. To put things in context, the number of subscribers to the Jimmy Dore's show channel is seven times smaller (567,444 subscribers) compared to the RT channel (3,560,843 subscribers), yet its one video in our dataset received much more attention. Surprisingly, in terms of average number of likes to comments made on the "Interview", the users who commented in both channels received more appreciation (18.8 likes per comment on average) than the users who only commented on the "Interview" (9.19 likes per comment on average). Moreover, the 60 RT-commenters had an even higher average of 24.38 likes per comment for their comments on the "Interview". What makes these dedicated commenters of RT-posted videos be so appreciated on the Jimmy Dore Show's anti-WH video, especially in comparison with the other commenters who never commented on the RT-channel videos?

To better understand the appeal of these RT-commenters, we look at how their comments are appreciated on other channels outside the C4 cluster. In cluster C1 where we observed four questionable channels along with Canadian Broadcasting Corporation (CBC), 34 RT-commenters commented on all 11 videos and achieved an average 2.82 likes against an average of 1.45 likes acquired by the other commenters. Similarly, in cluster C2, where anti-WH self-proclaimed journalists have their own YouTube channels, 16 RT-commenters commented on all eight videos and achieved 8.62 likes on average per comment as opposed to 1.49 likes acquired by the non-RT commenters. In cluster C3, however, we observe a contrasting phenomenon: only one RT-commenter posted a single comment. Most of the channels in this cluster are Assad regime-supporting Arabic language news channels. In cluster C5, we identified 12 RT-commenters who commented on three videos published by the CBS, Euronews in English, and the Time magazine's YouTube channels, respectively. The video published by CBS presented the news of halting US funds to the White Helmets. This was also a chosen narrative by the anti-WH community to defund the humanitarian group. The video published by the Euronews in English and Time had title *Israel Is Evacuating Hundreds of White Helmets Rescue Workers from Syria*, where the Israeli military in coordination with its US and European allies evacuated hundreds of Syrian rescue workers known as the White Helmets from near its volatile frontier with Syria, in a complex and first-of-a-kind operation. Cooperation with the Israeli army and the West is highly denounced in the Middle Eastern political context and was used against WH to portray the group as anti-Muslim. These three videos achieved the highest view counts in that cluster (CBS 6,941, Euronews 4,636, and Time 4,607).

We thus observe that the videos on which the RT-commenters comment have a large number of views independent of the channel in which they are posted (whether mainstream media or conspiracy theory promoters). At the same time, we observe that wherever they comment, the RT-commenters receive on average many more likes than the rest of the commenters in that channel. One possible explanation may be the existence of astroturfing: a concerted effort of promoting some videos by manipulating the YouTube algorithms via comments and likes to comments. There are other possible explanations of this correlation between the high popularity of this group of users and the popularity of the videos with which they interact. We do not claim to distinguish between correlation and causality in this work, thus the question mark in the title of this section. In this work we only highlight this unusual correlation and plan to investigate the causality question in future work.

5   Conclusions

We analyzed four months of YouTube data in an attempt to identify strategic information operations against the White Helmets. We used a corpus linguistic approach and hash structure to uncover patterns of identity and information spoofing. We discovered many instances of the same message (with slight variations in emojis or other embellishments) being repeatedly posted on the same video or on different videos. We also discovered instances where different user accounts post the same message on the same or different videos. We also found three patterns of antagonistic behavior demonstrated by spoofed accounts: coordinated attacks, dogpiling, and automated message replication.

In addition, we used a block clustering approach to cluster the channels that upload WH-related videos based on the user engagement. In the absence of ground truth data, we used three performance metrics (i.e., numbers of video likes, video views and comment likes) to measure the popularity of the videos uploaded to different channels and their associated comments. We found that a small group of users engaged heavily with videos published by channels that support anti-WH narratives promoted by RT channels. Not only that this small group has received higher attention to their comments and replies, but also the popularity of these videos is significantly higher than the videos where these users did not engage. We suspect this unusual behavior can be the effect of astroturfing, in which a small number of user accounts coordinate to exploit the YouTube video promotion algorithm to reach a wider audience and promote specific narratives. We will test this hypothesis in future work.

Acknowlegements. This work is supported by the DARPA SocialSim Program and the Air Force Research Laboratory under contract FA8650-18-C-7825. The authors would like to thank Leidos for providing data.

References

1. Govaert, G., Nadif, M.: An EM algorithm for the block mixture model. IEEE Trans. Pattern Anal. Mach. Intell. **27**(4), 643–647 (2005)
2. Hegelich, S., Janetzko, D.: Are social bots on Twitter political actors? Empirical evidence from a Ukrainian social botnet. In: Tenth International AAAI Conference on Web and Social Media (2016)
3. Hussain, M.N., Tokdemir, S., Agarwal, N., Al-Khateeb, S.: Analyzing disinformation and crowd manipulation tactics on YouTube. In: 2018 IEEE/ACM International Conference on Advances in Social Networks Analysis and Mining (ASONAM), pp. 1092–1095. IEEE (2018)
4. Innes, M.: Techniques of disinformation: constructing and communicating "soft facts" after terrorism. British J. Sociol. **71**, 284–299 (2020)
5. Innes, M., Dobreva, D., Innes, H.: Disinformation and digital influencing after terrorism: spoofing, truthing and social proofing. Contemp. Soc. Sci. 1–15 (2019)
6. Isaac, M.: Facebook finds new disinformation campaigns and braces for 2020 torrent, October 2019. https://www.nytimes.com/2019/10/21/technology/facebook-disinformation-russia-iran.html
7. Jhaver, S., Ghoshal, S., Bruckman, A., Gilbert, E.: Online harassment and content moderation: the case of blocklists. ACM Trans. Comput.-Hum. Interact. (TOCHI) **25**(2), 1–33 (2018)
8. Keller, F.B., Schoch, D., Stier, S., Yang, J.: How to manipulate social media: analyzing political astroturfing using ground truth data from South Korea. In: Eleventh International AAAI Conference on Web and Social Media (2017)
9. Keller, F.B., Schoch, D., Stier, S., Yang, J.: Political astroturfing on Twitter: how to coordinate a disinformation campaign. Polit. Commun. **37**(2), 256–280 (2019)
10. King, G., Pan, J., Roberts, M.E.: How the Chinese government fabricates social media posts for strategic distraction, not engaged argument. American Polit. Sci. Rev. **111**(3), 484–501 (2017)
11. Kovic, M., Rauchfleisch, A., Sele, M., Caspar, C.: Digital astroturfing in politics: definition, typology, and countermeasures. Stud. Commun. Sci. **18**(1), 69–85 (2018)

12. Levinger, M.: Master narratives of disinformation campaigns. J. Int. Aff. **71**(1.5), 125–134 (2018)
13. Rajaraman, A., Ullman, J.D.: Mining of Massive Datasets. Cambridge University Press, Cambridge (2011)
14. Schäfer, F., Evert, S., Heinrich, P.: Japan's 2014 general election: political bots, right-wing internet activism, and prime minister shinzō abe's hidden nationalist agenda. Big Data **5**(4), 294–309 (2017)
15. Slaney, M., Casey, M.: Locality-sensitive hashing for finding nearest neighbors [lecture notes]. IEEE Signal Process. Mag. **25**(2), 128–131 (2008)
16. Starbird, K., Arif, A., Wilson, T.: Disinformation as collaborative work: surfacing the participatory nature of strategic information operations. Proc. ACM Hum. Comput. Interact. **3**(CSCW), 127 (2019)
17. Varol, O., Ferrara, E., Davis, C.A., Menczer, F., Flammini, A.: Online human-bot interactions: detection, estimation, and characterization. In: Eleventh International AAAI Conference on Web and Social Media (2017)
18. Wilson, T., Starbird, K.: Cross-platform disinformation campaigns: lessons learned and next steps. Harvard Kennedy School Misinformation Review **1**(1) (2020)
19. Zerback, T., Töpfl, F., Knöpfle, M.: The disconcerting potential of online disinformation: persuasive effects of astroturfing comments and three strategies for inoculation against them. New Media Soc. (2020). https://doi.org/10.1177/1461444820908530
20. Zhang, J., Carpenter, D., Ko, M.: Online astroturfing: a theoretical perspective (2013)

Artifacts of Crisis: Textual Analysis of Euromaidan

Thomas Magelinski[1]([✉]), Zachary K. Stine[2], Thomas Marcoux[2],
Nitin Agarwal[2], and Kathleen M. Carley[1]

[1] Carnegie Mellon University, Pittsburgh, PA 125213, USA
{tmagelin,kathleen.carley}@cs.cmu.edu
[2] University of Arkansas at Little Rock, Little Rock, AR 72204, USA
{zkstine,txmarcoux,nxagarwal}@ualr.edu

Abstract. We analyze three textual data streams to characterize the
change that occurred during the Ukrainian revolution of 2014. These
data streams include legislative bill text, posts on Ukrainian political
blogs, and Twitter data. Each stream provides a different perspective:
politicians, local citizens, and global citizens. It is apparent that bill
production stalled early on in the demonstrations, and that the post-
revolution government quickly began voting on bills. Topic analysis of
blogs and tweets revealed growing interest in Ukraine following the march
on the legislature. Interest in Ukraine eventually overtook that of the
conflict in the Middle East, before dying back down in the following
month. Our results suggest that a stall in bill production may be an
early indicator of dysfunction in the government, while spikes in Twitter
activity can be seen almost immediately after the event. This effect is
true for blogs as well, although for a prolonged period, implying a more
detailed discourse about the event.

Keywords: Verkhovna Rada · Factions · Social media · Euromaidan

1 Introduction

In November of 2013, a wave of protests overtook Ukraine. These protests are
now called The Euromaidan. The Euromaidan culminated in the Ukrainian
revolution of February 2014, when violence reached the Ukrainian legislator's
doorstep, and the president fled to Russia. At the heart of the movement were
negotiations on the EU association agreement. Due to its placement between the
EU and Russia geographically, Ukrainian politics are of great significance to the

This material is based upon work supported by the Office of Naval Research Multidisciplinary University Research Initiative (MURI) under award number N00014-17-1-2675.
Any opinion, findings, and conclusions or recommendations expressed in this material
are those of the authors and do not necessarily reflect the views of the Office of Naval
Research. Additionally, Thomas Magelinski was supported by an ARCS foundation
scholarship.

© Springer Nature Switzerland AG 2020
R. Thomson et al. (Eds.): SBP-BRiMS 2020, LNCS 12268, pp. 329–339, 2020.
https://doi.org/10.1007/978-3-030-61255-9_32

rest of the world. Methods for characterizing and understanding transformative events such as The Euromaidan play an important role for national security.

More generally, groups of aligned politicians, or "factions" are of great interest in political science. While politicians may technically be aligned with their party, faction analysis can uncover their true political allies. This gives a more data-driven picture of a country's political landscape. Due to Ukraine's geopolitical importance and complex party structure, it is a powerful case-study for developing methods to understand factions.

Much of the prior work on Ukrainian factions has been focused on detection of disruptive events in faction structure or beliefs. The prior work uses roll call voting data from the Verkhovna Rada, Ukraine's legislature, to analyze both how parliamentarian's political positions change, as well as how their political alliances change. This analysis combined with change detection leads to known dates where the Rada has undergone change.

Knowing that a change has occurred is a good first step, but it opens the door to many more questions: What sparked it? Are there early indicators that a change is coming? Did the public react to the change? These and other questions arising cannot be answered using roll call votes alone, but are key to understanding what factors affect change in factions. In this work, we look to answer some of these questions. To do so, we use three sources of media collected around the revolution of 2014: legislative bill text, Ukranian blog posts, and Twitter data. These forms of media were selected in order to take a deeper dive into the inner workings of the parliament, the thoughts of the Ukrainian people, and a more global perspective of the situation. We show that topic analysis on each of these data streams sheds light on different aspects of changes in factions.

2   Prior Work

Various models have been developed to explain the occurrence of nonviolent uprisings (including grievance approaches, resource mobilization theory, modernization theory, and political opportunity approaches), which have been shown to have varied explanatory power when comparatively analyzed [4]. In the case of Ukraine, legislative change points have been studied in Ukraine through two main mechanisms in prior literature [9,14]. First, through changes in relationships between the politicians. Relationships between MPs can be quantitatively studied using a network science perspective by creating a co-voting network. This network uses link weights to encode the frequency that a pair of MPs co-vote, or cast the same vote on a bill. Then, community detection algorithms uncover groups of MPs, or unofficial "factions." Faction detection uncovers many relationships that cut across party lines, and give a sense of the true political landscape [8].

The MP relationship network in the Verkhovna Rada, is inherently dynamic, as alliances are constantly changing. Thus *dynamic* community detection must be used to discover when factions are disrupted. [12]. One such method is time segmentation, which involves segmenting a dynamic network into a series of static networks such that the community structure within time segments is relatively static, and the change between segments is maximized [7]. Applying this methodology to the 8th convocation of the Verkhovna Rada showed a massive shift in faction structure following the revolution in February of 2014 [9].

The second mechanism for analyzing political change in Ukraine is considering the bills themselves [9, 14]. A traditional way of analyzing roll-call bill data is through ideal-points, wherein both bills and politicians are placed on a political spectrum from conservative to liberal [5, 6]. Dynamic ideal points models, then, can uncover changes in political ideology [3, 10]. When applied to the Verkhovna Rada, it was seen that ideological shifts occurred on February 2014, during the revolution that also saw change in faction structure [9].

Beyond just votes, bills themselves contain quite valuable data. Each bill is tied to a committee, and the bill text can be analyzed to understand which issues it addresses. Topic modeling, through Latent Dirchlet Allocation (LDA), provides an automated way of analyzing bill text [1]. From the uncovered topics, bill *novelty* can be calculated, which measures uniqueness of a bills topic mixture, given those that have come before it [14]. Changes in novelty, then, can provide a different type of change occurring in the legislature.

While all of the previously described methods are important for understanding when change occurs, different techniques must be used to understand the implications of each change. To this end, we turn to topic analysis. Topic analysis of bills already informed some of the change-points though bill novelty, but the topics themselves have not yet been deeply studied. Additionally, to understand the implications of major political events, one must look beyond just the legislature and into public discourse, which can be found on blogs and Twitter. Through these three mediums, bills, blogs, and tweets, we can see changes in actual political action, how it is received locally, and how it is discussed globally.

3   Methodology and Data

3.1   Legislation

The legislation produced by the Ukrainian parliament, the Verkhovna Rada, serves as an important record of the political goals and priorities of the parliament over time. The Verkhovna Rada makes the text of registered bills publicly available through their website[1]. We download the text of each available bill from the Verkhovna Rada website for convocations 5–8, resulting in 35,112 total Ukrainian documents, which will serve as training data for topic modeling.

We preprocess bill text by first lowercasing and tokenizing each document. We reduce the vocabulary size by excluding word types based on three criteria: the 100 most frequent word types, word types that occur in more than 25% of the collection of documents, and word types that occur in fewer than ten documents are stopped. This results in a vocabulary size of 36,566 word types. We then train topic models via LDA [1], as implemented in [11], with 30, 50, and

---

[1] https://rada.gov.ua.

100 topics. We find that many of the key topics exist across the three models, but report our results using the 50-topic model due to its interpretable topics which are well-balanced in terms of specificity and generality. Our topic labels are qualitatively determined by examining both high probability words in each topic, as well as exemplar documents that feature the topic.

We next examine bills that were voted on in the parliament before, during, and after the 2014 revolution that began in mid-February of that year. Only eight bills are available in January, with another nine available in December. Therefore, we include November 2013 through January 2014 to represent the period before the revolution. Giving 82 bills in the period before the revolution, 73 bills in February 2014, and 80 bills in March 2014.

To compare differences in bill topics between the three time periods, we assign each document to the dominant topic with the highest probability in the document's topic distribution after ignoring two purely stylistic topics. By organizing the bills in each time period by their topic assignments, we can interpret the changing legislative priorities across each period.

3.2 Blogs

In order to gain insight on social media activity related to the Ukrainian revolution, we collect blog posts discussing political topics relevant to Ukraine. Blog sites were collected identified from various sources such as Twitter, geofencing, Google, etc., using relevant keywords and hashtags. We perform manual relevancy checks on identified blogs to ensure they are relevant, active, and public. Finally, we collect data using the Web Content Extractor (WCE) tool[2].

The range of collected blog posts spans from February 2004 to December 2018 for a total of 168,121 English blog posts. We perform a rigorous data-cleaning routine to remove noise and standardize all publication dates. All text is lowercased, tokenized, and words are removed using a standard list of English-language stopwords. The processed blog posts are used to train a topic model with 50 topics via LDA [1] using the implementation in [11].

With the topic model, we analyze blog posts published before, during, and after the Ukrainian revolution from January 1st to March 31st, 2014, which comprises 2,438 blog posts from 19 unique blog sites. We examine the 20 most frequent dominant topics from these posts and focus our analysis on six highly relevant topics. In order to analyze the change in narratives during this time period, we calculate the average topic proportions for the relevant topics across all blog posts published on a given day and visualize the resulting topic streams.

3.3 Twitter

Twitter data comes in the form of tweets, or short user posts, capped at 280 characters. This data could be analyzed in a similar way to blogs, but one feature opens the door for a more interpretable analysis: hashtags. Hashtags allow users

---

[2] http://www.newprosoft.com/.

to self-label the content of their tweet. Since hashtags are searchable, and are advertised by the platform through the "trending" category, users who use them have potential to reach more users [13]. Thus, the use of hashtags is pervasive throughout twitter, and can be leveraged to understand topics [15].

Here, we use a simple method to uncover twitter topics through the hashtag co-occurrence network. First, a network is created with hashtags represented as nodes. Then, connections between a pair of hashtags are drawn as a link in the graph when both hashtags occur in the same tweet. Link weights are used to reflect the total number of tweets that a pair of hashtags occurred in. Given the short nature of tweets, this is a strong notion of association.

Since individual hashtags are a specific label that a user gives their tweet, large groups of closely related hashtags can be understood as a topic. For example, if a group of hashtags is #rada, #ukrainepolitics, #legislature, the overall topic is Ukrainian politics. At scale, we can uncover these groups through community detection algorithms. Perhaps the most popular community detection algorithm is Louvain grouping, which attempts to maximize modularity [2]. It has gained popularity due to its success in finding empirically validated groups, and its ability to scale to large datasets. Thus, we proceed using Louvain grouping of the hashtag co-occurrence network as topics in our Twitter data.

Table 1. Data summary for Twitter data surrounding the revolution of 2014.

Month	Tweets	Users	Hashtags	Links	Topics
January	38105	17810	2994	22753	6
February	71763	40877	6669	38941	4
March	40945	25784	2811	14714	3

Twitter Data was collected from January to March 2014, using its API. The dataset was broken up into 3 periods, each 1-month long: before, during, and after. Only topics appearing in more than 5% of the tweets were considered in analysis. A summary of the dataset is provided as Table 1.

4   Results

4.1   Legislation

From examining the most frequent topics in the bills from each of the three time periods, we find stark changes between the frequent topics from the period before the revolution and both February and March of 2014. Notably, the most frequent dominant topics from the period before the revolution do not appear to reflect the sociopolitical shifts underway. These bills concern the commemoration of certain anniversaries (topic 30), budgets (topic 18), pensions (topic 31), and crime (topic 3) (see Table 2).

Table 2. Most frequent dominant topics from bills voted on before the revolution.

Dominant topic	Bills	Proportion of bills in period
Topic 30, Commemorations	19	0.2317
Topic 18, Budgets and funds	5	0.0610
Topic 31, Pensions	5	0.0610
Topic 02, Releases and Dismissals	4	0.0488
Topic 03, Offenses	4	0.0488

As stated in Sect. 3.1, votes were only taken on 9 and 8 bills during December 2013 and January 2014 respectively. Careful readings of these bills reveal potential antecedents for the drastic changes observed later in February 2014. These bills include a resolution of no confidence in the Cabinet of Ministers of Ukraine (bill 3692), the formation of an investigative commission on the actions of law enforcement agencies against protesters (bill 3832), and the legal protection of protesters (bill 3787) among other protest-related bills.

Table 3. Most frequent dominant topics from bills voted on during February 2014.

Dominant topic	Bills	Proportion of bills in period
Topic 47, Executive services and agencies	14	0.1918
Topic 11, Administrative–executive	7	0.0959
Topic 01, Administrative–parliamentary	6	0.0822
Topic 02, Releases and dismissals	6	0.0822
Topic 41, Constitutional and human rights	6	0.0822
Topic 33, Conflict, violence, security	5	0.0685
Topic 22, Early terminations	4	0.0548

During February 2014, we find that topic 47 accounts for almost 20% of the bills voted on during this time period, which reflect the remaking of the Ukrainian government including various appointments of new ministers and commissioners, the appointment of Arseniy Yatsenyuk as the new Prime Minister, the formation of a new Cabinet of Ministers, and others (see Table 3).

Each of the topics shown in Table 3 reflect different aspects of the establishment of a new government in response to the revolution. Notably, the topic 2 bills in February are about the dismissal of various government officials while the topic 22 bills concern the early terminations of MPs taking up new positions outside of parliament. Also notable is that three of the five bills dealing with topic 33 address violence carried out against protesters. The two remaining bills concern state security with one referencing Russia.

The most frequent dominant topics in bills voted on after the revolution in March 2014 share several similarities with bills voted on in the month prior. Bills with dominant topics 22, 2, and 47 all continue similar actions seen in February to remake the Ukrainian government. However, several changes are clear. Notably, each of the four bills with dominant topic 33 now concern security threats stemming from Russia, highlighting a shift in priorities from conflict involving protests (as seen in February). Additionally, two of the bills with dominant topic 36 reference Crimea. A summary of the most frequent dominant topics from bills during March 2014 is provided in Table 4.

Table 4. Most frequent dominant topics from bills voted on during March 2014.

Dominant topic	Bills	Proportion of bills in period
Topic 22, Early terminations	10	0.1250
Topic 02, Releases and dismissals	9	0.1125
Topic 47, Executive services and agencies	6	0.0750
Topic 33, Conflict, violence, security	4	0.0500
Topic 34, Parliamentary hearings	4	0.0500
Topic 36, Territorial and local issues	4	0.0500

4.2   Blogs

In Table 5, we present the six topics that are both highly frequent and relevant. These topics have been manually selected because of their high proportion within the corpus and because they are specific political topics. The table gives the number of blog posts in which each topic is dominant in addition to the proportion of documents, and some of the most frequent and relevant words to justify the topic's label.

Table 5. Most frequent dominant topics from blog posts January-March 2014.

Dominant topic	Word 1	Word 2	Word 3	Word 4	Word 5	Count	Proportion
Topic 6: Iran	Iran	Iranian	Political	Regime	Deal	118	0.0484
Topic 46: War	War	Military	Nato	States	United	47	0.0193
Topic 43: Elections	Party	Political	Election	President	Elections	41	0.0168
Topic 17: America	America	Americans	American	Clinton	Trump	109	0.0447
Topic 9: Ukraine	Ukraine	Ukrainian	Poroshenko	Crimea	Kyiv	125	0.0513
Topic 36: Syria	Syria	Islamic	Turkey	Terrorist	Damascus	164	0.0673

In Fig. 1, we show the average topic proportions of the six topics of interest for each day along with the number of blog posts published on that day. From this, we find that the blog discourse in January 2014 is dominated by discussions about the Middle East, specifically Iran (topic 6) and Syria (topic 36). War-related discourse (topic 46) is present throughout.

We see this pattern continue until mid-February, when Ukraine-related discussions (topic 9) begin to dominate and continue to do so throughout much of early March. Several peaks of war-related discourse (topic 46) occur in early March as well. Notably, the daily number of blog posts is elevated throughout much of late February and early March, with posting frequency gradually declining in late March. By late March, the six topics appear more evenly mixed ending with a rise in Syria-related discussions (topic 36).

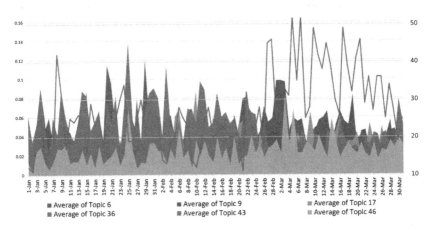

Fig. 1. Average daily topic distribution of Blog posts between January and March 2014 with daily blog count. The left vertical axis shows each topic's average proportion, while the right vertical axis gives the number of posts on each day represented by the line not corresponding to a topic.

4.3 Twitter

The benefit of analyzing Twitter is its wide audience. Given Twitter's global user base, it is expected that conversations span many geo-political issues. This is seen in the topics obtained in our three time periods. Other than Ukrainian unrest, one of the largest developing stories of 2014 was the Syrian civil war. Specifically, there was increase in conflict with Islamist groups in the region.

Both discussion of Ukraine and the Middle East are highly prevalent in the topic groups. In January and March, there is a topic dedicated to Middle Eastern political discussion. This topic had top hashtags "syria", "iran", "iraq", and was present in 20.7% and 16.6%, of tweets in the respective months. In February, the discussion was split. First into a small topic containing hashtags like "iran" and "iraq", occupying 7.7% of tweets. Other hashtags like "syria" entered the main topic, which was focused on Ukraine, and was present in 56.3% of tweets.

While the Middle Eastern topics were a large part of the conversation, topics relating to Ukraine were a larger fraction and increased significantly during the protests. We could expect this given the increase in total tweets when the first protests broke out on February 18th, as shown in Fig. 2. Ukrainian topics were present in 35.1%, 56.3%, and 34.1% of the tweets in each month, with top hashtags: "ukraine", "kiev", "euromaidan" (English and Ukrainian), and "russia".

This analysis demonstrates the power of Twitter analysis in understanding geo-political events in real time. The activity plot in Fig. 2, show that Twitter user's activity can respond almost immediately to a significant event. At the same time, topic analysis shows that not only does the volume of tweets change, but the relative amount of discussion of different events does as well.

4.4 Data Stream Timing

After completing analyses on the different data streams, a key question remains: how do the streams fit together? One way of answering this is by seeing when exactly changes occurred across modalities. To visualize this, Fig. 2 shows the cumulative fraction of media produced at a given time. Thus, the slope of each line is the rate at which new bills, blogs, or tweets are being voted on or created.

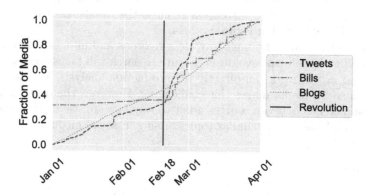

Fig. 2. Cumulative fraction of the data streams over time. As previously noted, data collection for bills goes back further than January.

First, we see that bill production has stalled months before the protests met the Rada. Prolonged inactivity in the legislature, then, may be in early indicator that tensions are rising. Posting frequencies from blogs and Twitter data do not seem to have a recognizable "early indicator" property in the same way.

After the event, Twitter reacts first, with an immediate jump in activity. This combined with the topic analysis shows that this is an increase in tweets specifically about the revolution. So, while it might be difficult to use Twitter to *predict* events such as this, the platform seems very appropriate for detecting and analyzing event once it has taken place.

Next, bill activity is kick-started, breaking the stalemate where no laws could be voted on. There is a slight but prolonged uptick in blog activity, showing it is less sensitive to external events than Twitter but provides a detailed discourse about the event. Since the protests had started in November, Ukrainian citizens were likely invested in the situation from the beginning.

5   Conclusions and Future Work

Through a multi-modal topic analysis of the 2014 Ukrainian revolution, we have constructed a multifaceted view into language characterizing the event, both from within the Ukrainian government itself and from English-language discourse about the event through Twitter and blogs. Within Ukrainian legislation, we find that the vast majority of bills voted on during February and March of 2014 directly concern the formation of a new post-revolution government following a conspicuous drop in the number of bills voted on during December 2013 and January 2014. From English-language discourse on Twitter and various blogs, we find that attention to Ukraine breaks through prevailing concerns about the Middle East and the war taking place in Syria. Among the blogs analyzed, posts about Syria dominate until late February when posts concerning Ukraine become dominant throughout early March 2014. We find that a similar pattern occurs in hashtag usage on Twitter—attention given to the Middle East is replaced by attention to Ukraine during February 2014.

Taken together, these findings provide a rigorous and in-depth characterization of the 2014 Ukrainian revolution. Future research will focus on how tools of analysis used in this work can directly tie into faction analysis. The lack of MP presence on social media makes this challenging. However, the overlap in topic meaning and trends between sources point to way forward: tie factions to topics in bill text, and then study similar topics arising in social media.

References

1. Blei, D.M., Ng, A.Y., Jordan, M.I.: Latent Dirichlet allocation. J. Mach. Learn. Res. **3**(Jan), 993–1022 (2003)
2. Blondel, V.D., Guillaume, J.L., Lambiotte, R., Lefebvre, E.: Fast unfolding of communities in large networks. J. Stat. Mech. Theory Exp. **2008**(10), P10008 (2008)
3. Caughey, D., Warshaw, C.: Dynamic estimation of latent opinion using a hierarchical group-level IRT model. Polit. Anal. **23**(2), 197–211 (2015)
4. Chenoweth, E., Ulfelder, J.: Can structural conditions explain the onset of nonviolent uprisings? J. Conflict Resolut. **61**(2), 298–324 (2017). https://doi.org/10.1177/0022002715576574
5. Clinton, J., Jackman, S., Rivers, D.: The statistical analysis of roll call data. Am. Polit. Sci. Rev. **98**(2), 355–370 (2004)
6. MacRae, D., Jr.: Dimensions of Congressional Voting: A Statistical Study of the House of Representatives in the Eighty-First Congress. University of California Press, Berkeley (1958)

7. Magelinski, T., Carley, K.M.: Community-based time segmentation from network snapshots. Appl. Netw. Sci. **4**(1), 1–19 (2019). https://doi.org/10.1007/s41109-019-0136-1
8. Magelinski, T., Cruickshank, I., Carley, K.M.: Comparison of faction detection methods in application to Ukrainian parliamentary data. In: 2018 International Conference on Social Computing, Behavioral-Cultural Modeling, and Prediction and Behavior Representation in Modeling and Simulation, Washington DC (2018)
9. Magelinski, T., Hou, J., Mylovanov, T., Carley, K.M.: Detecting disruption: identifying structural changes in the Verkhovna rada. In: Thomson, R., Bisgin, H., Dancy, C., Hyder, A. (eds.) SBP-BRiMS 2019. LNCS, vol. 11549, pp. 194–203. Springer, Cham (2019). https://doi.org/10.1007/978-3-030-21741-9_20
10. Martin, A.D., Quinn, K.M.: Dynamic ideal point estimation via Markov chain Monte Carlo for the US Supreme Court, 1953–1999. Polit. Anal. **10**(2), 134–153 (2002)
11. Řehůřek, R., Sojka, P.: Software framework for topic modelling with large corpora. In: Proceedings of the LREC 2010 Workshop on New Challenges for NLP Frameworks, ELRA, Valletta, Malta, pp. 45–5, May 2010. http://is.muni.cz/publication/884893/en
12. Rossetti, G., Cazabet, R.: Community discovery in dynamic networks: a survey. ACM Comput. Surv. (CSUR) **51**(2), 1–37 (2018)
13. Small, T.A.: What the hashtag? A content analysis of Canadian politics on Twitter. Inf. Commun. Soc. **14**(6), 872–895 (2011)
14. Stine, Z.K., Agarwal, N.: A quantitative portrait of legislative change in Ukraine. In: Thomson, R., Bisgin, H., Dancy, C., Hyder, A. (eds.) SBP-BRiMS 2019. LNCS, vol. 11549, pp. 50–59. Springer, Cham (2019). https://doi.org/10.1007/978-3-030-21741-9_6
15. Wang, X., Wei, F., Liu, X., Zhou, M., Zhang, M.: Topic sentiment analysis in Twitter: a graph-based hashtag sentiment classification approach. In: Proceedings of the 20th ACM International Conference on Information and Knowledge Management, pp. 1031–1040 (2011)

Modeling Decisions from Experience Among Frequent and Infrequent Switchers via Strategy-Based and Instance-Based Models

Neha Sharma[1]([✉]) [iD] and Varun Dutt[2] [iD]

[1] School of Computing, Indian Institute of Information Technology Una, Una 177220, Himachal Pradesh, India
neha724@gmail.com
[2] Applied Cognitive Sciences Laboratory, Indian Institute of Technology Mandi, Kamand 175005, Himachal Pradesh, India
varun@iitmandi.ac.in

Abstract. In Decisions from Experience (DFE) research decision-makers search for information before making a final consequential choice in the sampling paradigm. Although DFE research involving the sampling paradigm has focused on accounting for information search and final choices using computational cognitive models. However, it remains to be seen how models implementing strategies (strategy-based models) and models relying upon memory retrievals (instance-based models) perform for final choices of participants with different switching behaviors. In this paper, we perform an individual-differences analysis and test the ability of strategy-based and instance-based models to explain final choices of participants with different switching behavior in the sampling paradigm. An instance-based model, which relies on recency and frequency memory processes, is calibrated to final choices of participants exhibiting frequent switching or infrequent switching between options. Also, we develop two strategy models: a summary strategy model and a round-wise strategy model. Both these models rely upon different switching behaviors and subsequent decision rules to derive choices. Results revealed that at the aggregate level, both the strategy-based and instance-based models explained consequential choices similarly when participants exhibited frequent switching. However, the instance-based model performed better than the strategy-based models when participants exhibited infrequent switching. Furthermore, at the individual level, the instance-based model was among the best models to fit to both frequent and infrequent groups. We highlight the implications of modeling experiential decisions using strategy-based and Instance-based models.

Keywords: Information search · Experience · Strategy-based models · Instance-based models · Frequent switching · Infrequent switching · Sampling paradigm · Gambles

R. Thomson et al. (Eds.): SBP-BRiMS 2020, LNCS 12268, pp. 340–349, 2020.
https://doi.org/10.1007/978-3-030-61255-9_33

1   Introduction

People in different aspects of their daily life make choices that are based on information gathered through searching (e.g., choosing the best institute for higher education) [1]. Here, the key to making consequential decisions is to obtain knowledge by searching the environment [1]. For example, a person could choose to study in a specific educational institute out of all the institutes in the city. For this purpose, one may look for the different courses run by different institutes before making a consequential choice for the preferred institute. This information search before a choice is an essential part of Decisions from Experience (DFE) research [2]. In DFE research the focus is on explaining human choices based upon one's experience with sampled information [2].

DFE research has proposed a "sampling paradigm" [2, 3] to study people's search and choice behaviors in the laboratory. In the sampling paradigm, people can choose between two or more options that are presented to them as blank buttons on computer screen. People are first asked to perform information search (sample outcomes) as they wish and in any order they desire from different button options. Here, the sampling from different options is costless. People sample till they are satisfied with their sampling of options and then they make a single final (consequential) choice for real.

Previous research [4] has analyzed the search strategies of people asked to make choices in the sampling paradigm. Literature [4] reports two types of switchers: frequent and infrequent. The infrequent switchers search one option repeatedly for a long time before switching to the other option. In contrast, the frequent switchers search between options in a zigzag manner, switching back and forth between options.

A number of computational cognitive models have been proposed to account for human choices from information search in the sampling paradigm [5, 6]. Some of these models are based upon retrievals from memory and recency and frequency processes (instance-based models [7, 8]); whereas, some other models are based upon switching behaviors and decision rules (strategy-based models [4, 9]).

For example, the instance-based models are based upon the Instance-based Learning Theory [7, 8, 10, 11] and these models are a popular DFE algorithm for explaining consequential choices from information search [6, 7]. These models consist of experiences (called instances) stored in memory. Each instance's activation is used to calculate the blended values for each option, thereby helping the model make a final choice. The instance-based models rely on ACT-R framework for their functioning [12].

In contrast to the instance-based models, there are also strategy-based models proposed in literature to account for human choices from information search [4, 9, 13]. Two particular strategy-based models in the sampling paradigm include the summary model and the round-wise model [4]. The summary and round-wise models have been shown to account for final choices of both infrequent and frequent switchers, respectively [4]; however, recent evidence has also shown otherwise [9].

Motivated from limited existing research that compares instance-based and strategy-based models [14] in the sampling paradigm, the primary objective of this research is to compare these modeling approaches in capturing consequential decisions from experience. For this purpose, we use gambles involving two options and binary outcomes with different probabilities (small and large). We calibrate an instance-based model and two strategy-based models (summary and round-wise) to final choices of participants showing different switching during information search. We test the ability of these models in accounting for human consequential choices after information search.

2 Problem Dataset

The study was conducted at the Indian Institute of Technology Mandi where eighty students participated. The objective of the study was to make consequential choices after information search in the sampling paradigm. Participants searched for information and then decided an option they preferred across two between-subjects problem conditions: Rare-Event (RE; N = 40) and Common-Event (CE; N = 40). In the RE problem, the variable option had a low probability (0.1) associated with the H outcome (3.28 return on the allocated amount). In the CE problem, a variable option had a high probability (0.8) value associated with a high (H) outcome (1.18 return on the allocated amount). The low (L) outcome (0.88) in the variable option always occurred with a complementary chance across both problems (CE and RE). In both RE and CE conditions, a second option, an alternative with a fixed return on investment (1.1 return on the invested amount with certainty) was present. Thus, in each problem, participants were presented with two options: an option with a fixed return on allocation (non-maximizing option); and, an option with a variable return on allocation (maximizing option). The maximization was defined based upon the expected value of options in problems. The nature of outcomes and probabilities in different CE and RE problems were like those described in previous literature [15].

In each problem, participants were first asked to sample options (presented as blank buttons; sampling phase). During the sampling phase, every time an option was chosen in a problem, participants could see an outcome based upon the associated probability in the option. Sampling of options was costless in the sampling phase and participants were free to sample options in any order and as many times as they desired. At any time during the sampling phase, participants could click the "Make a Final Decision" button. Clicking this button terminated the sampling phase and moved participants to the final-decision phase. In the final-decision phase, participants were asked to make a final choice for one of the options for real.

To understand the effect of different sampling strategies, we calculated the switch ratio, which was defined as the total number of switches made by a participant between options divided by the total number of switches possible (=number of samples − 1) in a problem. Like done in previous literature [4], we calculated the median value of switch ratio by pooling participants across both CE and RE problems. Participants possessing switch-ratios less than median were classified as infrequent switchers and participants possessing switch-ratios greater than or equal to median were classified as frequent switchers. By pooling the CE and RE problems, there were 40 participants in the infrequent group and 40 participants in the frequent group.

3 The Models

In this section, we detail the working of summary, round-wise [4, 9] and instance-based models [7, 8], which were calibrated to infrequent and frequent groups separately.

3.1 The Round-Wise and Summary Models

In round-wise model [4, 9], the sampling oscillates between options, each time drawing the smallest possible sample (see Fig. 1A). Following the sampling phase, model participants make a decision about which option they prefer. The round-wise model compares outcomes over repeated rounds and lead strategists to choose options that win the most rounds (see Fig. 1A).

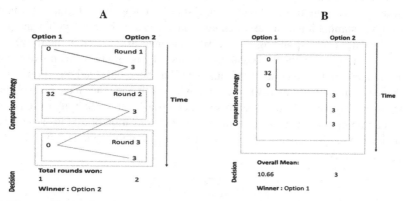

Fig. 1 The sampling and decision-rule in the round-wise model (A) and the summary model (B).

The summary model [4, 9] samples extensively from one option and then samples extensively from the other option (see Fig. 1B). Following the sampling phase, model participants make a decision about which option they prefer. The summary model compares the final mean values (here, the overall expected value) and lead strategists to choose options with the higher final value (see Fig. 1B).

As per literature [4], individuals who sample using frequent switching will be more likely to make decisions consistent with a round-wise decision strategy: determining which option is better in each round of sampling and ultimately choosing the one that wins the most rounds. In comparison, individuals who use infrequent sampling strategy will be more likely to make decisions consistent with a summary decision strategy: evaluating average outcomes and then choosing the option with the larger average outcomes.

3.2 The Instance-Based Model

The instance-based model [6–8, 11] is based upon the ACT-R cognitive framework [12]. The model stores every occurrence of an outcome of an option in the form of an instance in memory. An instance is made up of the following structure: SDU, here S is the current situation (two blank option buttons on a computer screen), D is the decision made in the current situation (choice for one of the option buttons), and U is the goodness (utility) of the decision made (the outcome obtained upon making a choice for an option). All instances of an option are retrieved from memory and blended together when a decision choice needs to be made. A function of activation of instances corresponding to outcomes observed on the option is called blended value. The instance is activated as a function of the frequency and recency of observed outcomes that occur on choosing options during sampling. The blended value of option j at any trial t is defined as [18]:

$$V_{j,t} = \sum_{i=1}^{n} p_{i,j,t} x_{i,j,t} \tag{1}$$

where $x_{i,j,t}$ is the value of the U (outcome) part of an instance i on option j at trial t. The $p_{i,j,t}$ is the probability of retrieval of instance i on option j from memory at trial t. Because $x_{i,j,t}$ is value of the U part of an instance i on option j at trial t, the number of terms in the summation changes when new outcomes are observed within an option j (and new instances corresponding to observed outcomes are created in memory). Thus, $n = 1$ if j is an option with one possible outcome. If j is an option with two possible outcomes, then $n = 1$ when one of the outcomes has been observed on an option (i.e., one instance is created in memory) and $n = 2$ when both outcomes have been observed (i.e., two instances are created in memory). At any trial t, the probability of retrieval of an instance i on option j at trial t is a function of the activation of that instance relative to the activation of all instances $(1, 2, \ldots n)$ created within the option j, given by

$$p_{i,j,t} = \frac{e^{(A_{i,j,t})/\tau}}{\sum_{i=1}^{n} e^{(A_{i,j,t})/\tau}} \tag{2}$$

where τ, is random noise defined as $\sigma.\sqrt{2}$ and σ is a free noise parameter. Noise captures the imprecision of recalling past experiences from memory. The activation of an instance i corresponding to an observed outcome on an option j in each trial t is a function of the frequency of the outcome's past occurrences and the recency of the outcome's past occurrences (as done in ACT-R). At each trial t, activation $A_{i,j,t}$ of an instance i on option j is

$$A_{i,j,t} = \sigma * \ln\left(\frac{1 - \gamma_{i,j,t}}{\gamma_{i,j,t}}\right) + \ln \sum_{t_p \varepsilon\{1..,t-1\}} \left(t - t_p\right)^{-d} \tag{3}$$

where d is a free decay parameter; $\gamma_{i,j,t}$ is a random draw from a uniform distribution bounded between 0 and 1 for instance i on option j in trial t; and, t_p is each of the previous trials in which the outcome corresponding to instance i was observed in the binary-choice task. There are two free parameters that need to be calibrated for the instance-based model: d and σ. The d parameter accounts for the reliance on recent or distant sampled information. Thus, when d is large (>1.0), then the model gives more weight to recently observed outcomes in computing instance activations compared to when d is small (<1.0). The σ parameter helps to account for the sample-to-sample variability in an instance's activation. In the instance-based model, we feed the sampling of individual human participants to generate instance activations and blended values. When the choice is made and outcome is observed, the instance associated with it is activated and blended values are computed for options faced by an individual participant.

In the instance-based model, we calibrated the d and σ parameters to final choices from human participants separately in the two strategy groups. For this calibration, we determine the model's likelihood for making the same choice as made by each human participant given a set of model parameters. For each model participant, the model applied the following softmax function across both options in a problem [16, 17]:

$$Prob(Option\ X) = \frac{e^{S_{Mean}X}}{e^{S_{Mean}X} + e^{S_{Mean}Y}} \tag{4}$$

where, $S_{Mean}X$ and $S_{Mean}Y$ are the blended values calculated for the two options and *Prob (Option X)* is the probability of choosing Option X given a set of model parameters. If *Option X* was chosen by a human participant in a problem, then the *Prob (Option X)* is used to calculate the likelihood value of making the same choice from the instance-based model given its set of parameters. The log-likelihood L is defined as:

$$L = \sum_{i=1}^{i=N} \log(Prob(Option\ X_i)) \tag{5}$$

where, i refers to the ith model participant playing a problem and N is the total number of human participants in the infrequent and frequent groups (the model was calibrated separately to each of the two switching groups). The log in Eq. 5 is the natural logarithm and we calibrated the instance-based model by minimizing the negative of the log-likelihood value $(-L)$.

Furthermore, to derive a choice from the instance-based model, we use the following rule: If the human chose Option X and the value of *Prob (Option X)* is greater than or equal to 0.5, then the model makes a choice like the human choice; else, the model chooses the option that is opposite of what human participant chose. We calculated the error proportion by comparing the model participant's choice to the human participant's choice. The model is expected to predict choices in the infrequent group better than the choices in frequent group.

4 Method

4.1 Dependent Variables

In this paper, we account for the final choices of participants with different search strategies. The choice made by a model participant is compared with a choice made by a corresponding human participant in the infrequent and frequent groups, separately. A maximizing choice is one where the selected option's expected value is greater than the expected value of the non-selected option. A non-maximizing choice was one where this criterion failed. The expected value of an option was calculated as a product of the probability of occurrence of outcomes and the outcomes and summing the products together. For a model, the error proportion was calculated in a problem as:

$$Error\ Proportion = (M_H N_M + N_H M_M)/(M_H N_M + N_H M_M + N_H N_M + M_H M_M) \tag{6}$$

where, $M_H N_M$ was the number of cases where the human participant made a maximizing choice but the model predicted a non-maximizing choice. $N_H M_M$ was the number of cases where the human participant made a non-maximizing choice but the model predicted a maximizing choice. Similarly, the $M_H M_M$ and $N_H N_M$ were the number of cases, where the human participant made the same choice (maximizing or non-maximizing) as predicted by the model. Smaller the value of the error proportion, the more accurate the model is in accounting for maximizing individual choices of human participants.

4.2 Model Calibration

A genetic algorithm was used to calibrate the final choices for both frequent and infrequent groups of the instance-based model (having two free parameters d and σ). The model was calibrated using a single set of parameters by minimizing the negative of log-likelihood value. The genetic algorithm is capable of preventing itself from getting trapped in a local minima. The population size used here was a set of 20 randomly-selected parameter tuples in a generation (each parameter tuple was a value of d and σ parameters). The crossover fractions and mutation were set at 0.8 and 0.1, respectively, for an optimization over 150 generations. The model was calibrated separately in the infrequent and frequent groups. The summary and round-wise models did not possess any parameters.

5 Human Results

Figure 2 shows proportion of final choices for the variable (maximizing) option by human and model participants in the frequent and infrequent conditions. As seen in the Figure, among human participants, a larger proportion chose the variable option among the frequent group (0.48) compared to the infrequent group (0.40). Next, we evaluated whether the round-wise, summary, and instance-based models could account for human choices via their cognitive mechanisms.

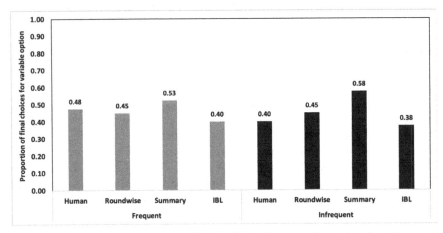

Fig. 2. Proportion of final choices for variable option by human and models in both frequent and infrequent groups.

6 Model Results

The round-wise, summary, and instance-based models were calibrated against human data in both frequent and infrequent groups (see Fig. 3 for model results). For the frequent group, the MSDs between human choices and the round-wise, summary, and instance-based models were 0.0004, 0.0049, and 0.0064, respectively. Thus, all three models fitted the human choices well. For the infrequent group, the MSDs between human choices and the round-wise, summary, and instance-based models were 0.2500, 0.2500 and 0.0006, respectively. Thus, the instance-based model was able to explain human choices in the infrequent group better than the strategy models.

The best calibrated values of d and σ parameters in the instance-based model were found to be 3.19 (d) and 0.01 (σ) (frequent group) and 7.81 (d) and 0.62 (σ) (infrequent group) (see Table 1). The large d value exhibited extreme reliance on recency during sampling (larger among the infrequent group compared to the frequent group). Also, the smaller σ value exhibited lower sample-to-sample variability in instance activations (smaller among the frequent group compared to the infrequent group).

Table 1. Parameters and likelihood values for the instance-based model

Condition	Parameters	Log-Likelihood
Frequent	$d = 3.19$	-25.31
	$\sigma = 0.01$	
Infrequent	$d = 7.81$	-28.11
	$\sigma = 0.62$	

Overall, the calibrated likelihood value was -28.11 in the infrequent group, which was slightly lesser than that in the frequent group. The model parameters fitted using log-likelihoods by us in this paper are for individual participant choices in the two groups, infrequent and frequent. However, the model parameters fitted earlier [6] were for choices aggregated across several participants. Given the high values of d parameter in our results, it seems that the recency and frequency processes are stronger among individual participants compared to the average across several participants.

Lastly, we analyzed the instance-based model's performance in accounting for individual human decisions. According to the error proportion criterion (Eq. 6), more number of $N_H N_M$ and $M_H M_M$ combinations help minimize the error proportion (which is desirable), while higher number of $M_H N_M$ and $N_H M_M$ combinations increase the error proportion. Table 2 shows the individual-level results from different models in the infrequent and frequent groups.

As seen in Table 2, the calibrated instance-based model for frequent group produced 48% of $N_H N_M$ combinations and 35% of $M_H M_M$ combinations, respectively. In contrast, the erroneous $N_H M_M$ and $M_H N_M$ combinations were 05% and 03%, respectively, from the model. Due to comparatively higher values for the $N_H N_M$ and $M_H M_M$ combinations in the frequent group compared to the infrequent group, the instance-based model possessed a smaller error proportion in the frequent group compared to the infrequent group. Overall, the instance-based model showed superior performance for frequent group compared to the infrequent group (18% error proportion <32% error proportion). Also, this model was among the best models to fit to both frequent and infrequent groups.

Table 2. The error proportions from different models in the infrequent and frequent groups

Human and model data combination	Instance based freq	Instance-based infrequent	Round-wise freq	Round-wise infreq	Summary freq	Summary infreq
$N_H N_M$	48	45	45	40	38	28
$M_H M_M$	35	22	28	30	20	30
$N_H M_M$	05	15	08	20	15	32
$M_H N_M$	13	18	20	10	27	10
Error proportion	0.18	0.32	0.27	0.30	0.42	0.42

Finally, the error proportions from the summary model was higher than those from the round-wise model across both frequent and infrequent groups.

7   Discussion and Conclusions

In this research, we compared models based upon memory retrieval processes (instance-based models) with those based upon strategies (strategy-based models) in decisions from experience (DFE) problems involving the sampling paradigm. Results revealed that at the aggregate level, both the strategy-based and instance-based models explained consequential choices similarly when participants exhibited frequent switching. However, the instance-based model performed better than the strategy-based models when participants exhibited infrequent switching. Furthermore, at the individual level, the instance-based model was among the best models to fit to both frequent and infrequent groups.

Mostly, models in DFE problems have been evaluated to aggregate human choices [7, 8] where the average choice from the model is compared to the average choice from human data (average is taken over several participants and problems). However, in this paper, we compared different strategy-based and instance-based models both at the aggregate level and at the individual level. The model comparison at the aggregate level did not clearly reveal the benefits of the instance-based approach. However, the comparison at the individual level showed the superiority of the instance-based approach over the strategy-based models.

Furthermore, the high value of decay parameter in instance-based model across both the frequent and infrequent groups showed stronger reliance on recency effect among both participants who switched more and participants who switched less. The decay parameter was higher among infrequent groups compared to frequent groups. Thus, recency reliance was higher among those who switched less. One likely reason for this differing recency effect is that when participants switch less, they tend to pay attention to the recently sampled outcomes on an option for computing the expected values.

In fact, the observation about high d parameter value for the infrequent switchers also helps us explain why the error proportion from the instance-based model was much less for the infrequent group compared to that from other strategy models.

In this paper, we took three models of experiential choice. In future, the investigation can be extended to include more models. Also, whether recency effects can be seen in environments where the outcomes and probabilities vary over time remains to be investigated. Some of these ideas and others form the immediate next steps for us to pursue in the near future.

References

1. Julian, W.: The 7 things students think about when choosing a college. https://www.chronicle.com/article/The-7-Things-Students-Think/242544. Accessed 27 Feb 2020
2. Hertwig, R., Erev, I.: The description-experience gap in risky choice. Trends Cogn. Sci. **13**, 517–523 (2009)
3. Sharma, N., Debnath, S., Dutt, V.: Influence of an intermediate option on the description experience gap and information search. Front. Psychol. **9**, 364 (2018)
4. Hills, T., Hertwig, R.: Information search in decisions from experience: do our patterns of sampling foreshadow our decisions? Psychol. Sci. **21**(12), 1787–1792 (2010)
5. Erev, I., Ert, E., Roth, A.E., Haruvy, E., Herzog, S.M., Hau, R.: A choice prediction competition: choices from experience and from description. J. Behav. Decis. Making **23**(1), 15–47 (2010)
6. Lejarraga, T., Dutt, V., Gonzalez, C.: Instance-based learning: a general model of repeated binary choice. J. Behav. Decis. Making **25**(2), 143–153 (2012)
7. Gonzalez, C., Dutt, V.: Instance-based learning: integrating sampling and repeated decisions from experience. Psychol. Rev. **118**(4), 523 (2011)
8. Gonzalez, C., Dutt, V.: Refuting data aggregation arguments and how the instance-based learning model stands criticism: a reply to Hills and Hertwig (2012). Psychol. Rev. **119**(4), 893–898 (2012)
9. Hills, T.T., Hertwig, R.: Information search in decisions from experience: Do our patterns of sampling foreshadow our decisions? Psychol. Sci. **21**(12), 1787–1792 (2017)
10. Gonzalez, C., Lerch, J.F., Lebiere, C.: Instance-based learning in dynamic decision making. Cogn. Sci. **27**(4), 591–635 (2003)
11. Sharma, N., Dutt, V.: Modeling decisions from experience: how models with a single set of parameters for aggregate choices explain individual choices? J. Dyn. Decis. Making **3**(3), 1–20 (2017)
12. Anderson, J.R., Lebiere, C.: The Atomic Components of Thought Lawrence Erlbaum. Mathway, New Jersey (1998)
13. Hertwig, R.: The psychology and rationality of decisions from experience. Synthese **187**(1), 269–292 (2012). https://doi.org/10.1007/s11229-011-0024-4
14. Gonzalez, C., Dutt, V., Healy, A.F., Young, M.D., Bourne, L.E., Jr.: Comparison of instance and strategy models in ACT-R. In: Proceedings of the 9th International Conference of Cognitive Modeling (paper 150), Manchester, United Kingdom (2009)
15. Hertwig, R., Barron, G., Weber, E.U., Erev, I.: Decisions from experience and the effect of rare events in risky choice. Psychol. Sci. **15**(8), 534–539 (2004)
16. Bishop, C.M.: Pattern Recognition and Machine Learning. Springer, New York (2006)
17. Sutton, R.S., Barto, A.G.: Reinforcement Learning: An Introduction. MIT press, Cambridge (1998)
18. Lebiere, C.: Blending: an ACT-R mechanism for aggregate retrievals. In: Proceedings of the Sixth Annual ACTR Workshop, George Mason University, Fairfax, VA, USA (1999)

Author Index

Printed in the United States
By Bookmasters